Political Ideologies

Political Ideologies

An Introduction

Andrew Heywood

with a foreword by
Andrew Gamble

MACMILLAN

First published 1992 by
THE MACMILLAN PRESS LTD
Houndmills, Basingstoke, Hampshire RG21 2XS
and London
Companies and representatives
throughout the world

ISBN 0–333–54935–X hardcover
ISBN 0–333–54936–8 paperback

A catalogue record for this book is available
from the British Library.

Printed in Hong Kong

Reprinted 1992, 1993 (twice)

For Jean

Contents

Foreword

Ideology has had a strange history. It is inseparable from the political experience of the modern world, yet few major theorists of politics have a good word for it. Figures as diverse as Karl Marx, Michael Oakeshott and Talcott Parsons all condemned it, for different reasons. To its opponents ideology is the opposite of such wholesome things as truth, science, rationality, objectivity and philosophy. It signifies beliefs and doctrines which are either dogmas beyond the reach of criticism or cloaks for individual and group interests.

It is hardly surprising given the influence of this negative conception that it should at times have been fashionable to bury ideology and declare it at an end. But like similar efforts to bury history and politics, ideology has a habit of coming back. The politics of the modern world have been shaped by the key ideological traditions. Ideologies are a crucial resource for ordering, defining and evaluating political reality and establishing political identities.

The great merit of Andrew Heywood's book is that he takes ideology seriously, and explores patiently and with admirable clarity the different characteristics of the classic western ideologies, as well as the new themes and directions of recent ideological thought. He has produced one of the best available introductions to the subject anywhere in print.

The western ideological tradition which originated in the French and American revolutions of the eighteenth century does not exhaust ways of understanding politics, nor does it eclipse many non-western traditions of political thought. But it is an indispensable tradition none the less, and an ability to understand its key terms and internal development is a basic requirement for citizenship in the modern world. Andrew Heywood is the ideal guide.

University of Sheffield

ANDREW GAMBLE

Preface

The aim of this book is to provide a comprehensive and up-to-date introduction to the political creeds and doctrines that have shaped world politics in the last 200 years. I hope that it will serve both as a useful text for students and a clear and accessible guide for the general reader.

The book is organised around the major political ideologies. I am aware that controversies about the meaning and application of 'ideology' could have imposed constraints upon the book's coverage and have therefore adopted the broadest possible definition of the concept. This has enabled me to include chapters on topics like nationalism, environmentalism and democracy whose ideological credentials may be questionable. The concept of ideology and controversies surrounding it are discussed at some length in the Introduction.

Full glossaries of key terms used in the text and of political thinkers appear at the end, together with suggestions for further reading. In the case of works referred to in the text, they appear in full title and with the date of their first publication. A bibliography listing all works discussed appears after suggestions for further reading and provides current publication details. Where page references occur these refer to the current edition of the work quoted, as listed in the bibliography.

I would like to express my gratitude to Andrew Gamble, Lynton Robins and Bill Coxall for the constructive comments and advice they offered at various points in the production of the text, and to my publisher Steven Kennedy for his encouragement and support throughout. Particular thanks should go to my wife, Jean, who was entirely responsible for producing the typescript and bore my constant revisions with exemplary stoicism. Without her help, the book could not have been delivered so quickly and would have been significantly less intelligible for the reader. Finally, my sons, Mark and Robin, deserve mention for indulging me with patience and good humour while I fed my obsession with writing this book.

ANDREW HEYWOOD

1
Introduction

All people are political thinkers. Whether they know it or not, people use political ideas and concepts whenever they express their opinions or speak their mind. Everyday language is littered with terms like 'freedom', 'fairness', 'equality', 'justice' and 'rights'. In the same way, words like 'conservative', 'liberal', 'socialist', 'communist' and 'fascist' are regularly employed by people either to describe their own views, or those of others. However, even though such terms are familiar, even commonplace, they are seldom used with any precision or a clear grasp of their meaning. What, for instance, is 'equality'? What does it mean to say that all people are equal? Are people born equal, should they be treated by society as if they are equal? Should people have equal rights, equal opportunities, equal political influence, equal wages? Similarly, words like 'communist' or 'fascist' are commonly misused. What does it mean to call someone a 'communist'? What values or beliefs do communists hold, and why do they hold them? How do communist views differ from those of liberals, conservatives or socialists?

In a tradition which goes back to Plato and Aristotle in Ancient Greece and has been revived by modern writers like John Rawls and Robert Nozick, political theorists have attempted to conduct a disciplined investigation of political questions. They have analysed political terms and concepts and tried to uncover the often un-examined assumption upon which they are based. As such, political theory is a way of thinking more critically, and perhaps more clearly, about politics. However, political theory is not a way of uncovering 'the truth' about politics, or of deciding who is 'right' and who is 'wrong'. Political theory is normative, it seeks to analyse and explain the world in terms of moral values and philosophical beliefs. For instance, political theorists have traditionally attempted to

1

describe the nature of the 'Good Society', a society that is 'moral', 'fair', 'just', or 'orderly'. They have been concerned not only to understand the society they live in, to describe what *is*, but also to portray the kind of society they believe *ought*, *should* and even *must* be brought about.

Political ideology, the particular subject of this book, did not emerge until much later, the early nineteenth century. Ideologies are belief systems which help to structure how the world is understood and explained. Political ideologies are sets of ideas which provide the basis for some kind of political action. Political ideology is therefore not the same thing as political theory. Political theorists may, for example, investigate political questions and refine the meaning of concepts and ideas, without subscribing to a particular ideology or endorsing the interests of a specific group, party, movement or government. However, political ideology is so deeply rooted in modern culture that it is difficult, and maybe impossible, for anyone to escape its impact. Modern political theorists, for instance, often operate within ideological traditions and, in some cases, consciously seek to advance these traditions. Earlier genera-tions of political thinkers have even been recruited as supporters of ideologies which did not develop until years, sometimes centuries, after their deaths. These belief systems or ideologies are essentially different ways of understanding the world. They may be more or less coherent, more or less attractive, more or less inspiring, but, like normative political theory, they can never be proved in any scientific sense to be either 'true' or 'false'. Rival conceptions of human nature cannot, for example, be tested by any kind of surgical operation to 'prove' that human beings possess rights, are entitled to freedom, or are naturally selfish or naturally sociable.

1 The role of ideas

Not all political thinkers have accepted that ideas and ideologies are of much importance. Politics has sometimes been thought to be little more than a naked struggle for power. If this is true, political ideas are mere propaganda, a form of words or slogans designed to win votes or attract popular support. Ideas and ideologies are therefore simply 'window dressing', used to conceal the deeper realities of political life. Orthodox Marxists, for example, believe that political ideas can only be understood in the light of the economic or class interests of those who express them. Ideas have a 'material basis', they have little meaning or significance on their own. Marxists therefore analyse politics in terms of social class and some Marxists have held political ideologies to be no more than an expression of the interests of particular classes. Conservatives have also been unwilling to give too much weight to political ideas, though for very different reasons. Although modern conservatism has paid increasingly serious attention to economic doctrines and political principles, conservatives have traditionally believed the world to be simply too complex for human beings to grasp fully. No reliable or systematic analysis of social life is therefore possible. All 'systems of thought' should be regarded with suspicion, and all political principles be viewed with distrust. For a traditional conservative, wise political judgements are based upon experience and tradition, rather than ideological conviction.

The opposite argument has also been put. John Maynard Keynes, for example, asserted that the world is ruled by little other than the ideas of economists and political philosophers. 'Practical men', he argued, 'who believe themselves to be quite exempt from any intellectual influence are usually the slaves of some defunct economist.' All political leaders, parties and governments simply carry out, whether they know it or not, theories and ideas which have been dreamed up by intellectuals or academics. The world is ultimately ruled by 'academic scribblers'. Such a view suggests, for instance, that modern capitalism developed out of the classical economics of Adam Smith and David Ricardo, that Soviet communism was modelled upon the writing of Karl Marx and V.I. Lenin, and that the history of Nazi Germany can only be understood by reference to Hitler's *Mein Kampf*.

In reality, both these accounts of political life are one-sided and inadequate. Political ideas are not merely a passive reflection of vested interests or personal ambition, but have the capacity to inspire and guide political action itself and so to influence material life. At the same time, political ideas do not emerge in a vacuum, they do not drop from the sky like rain. All political ideas are moulded by the social and historical circumstances in which they develop and by the political ambitions which they serve. Quite simply, political theory and political practice are inseparable. Any balanced and persuasive account of political life must therefore acknowledge the constant interplay between ideas and ideologies on one hand, and historical and material forces on the other.

Ideas and ideologies influence political life in a number of specific ways. In the first place, they provide a perspective through which the world is understood or explained. People do not see the world as it really is, but only as they expect it to be, in other words, through a veil of ingrained beliefs, opinions and assumptions. Whether consciously or unconsciously, everyone subscribes to a set of political beliefs and values which guide their behaviour and influence their conduct. In effect, political ideas and ideologies set goals which inspire political activity. In this respect, politicians are subject to two very different influences. Without doubt, all politicians want power. This forces them to be pragmatic, to adopt those policies and ideas which are electorally popular or which win favour with powerful groups like business or the army. However, politicians seldom seek power simply for its own sake. They also possess beliefs, values and convictions about what to do with power when it is achieved.

The balance between pragmatic and ideological considerations clearly varies from politician to politician, and also at different stages in a politician's career. Some, like Adolf Hitler, have been fiercely, even fanatically, committed to a clear set of ideological goals. Hitler's writings are shot through with virulent anti-semitism and openly discuss his desire to found a German-dominated, racial empire in Eastern Europe. Marxist revolutionaries like Lenin have been dedicated to the goal of building a classless, communist society. However, no politician can afford to be blinded by ideological conviction; at the very least, strategic compromises have to be made if power is to won and retained. Anti-semitic attacks undoubtedly increased in Germany after Hitler's appointment as Chancellor in 1933, but it was not until the war years that Hitler embarked upon the policy of racial extermination that some have believed was always his goal. In Lenin's case, despite a distaste for capitalism, in 1921 he introduced the New Economic Policy which permitted the re-emergence of limited private enterprise in Russia. Other politicians, notably those in the United States, have been regarded as little more than political commodities, being willing to sell themselves on the basis of image and personality, while paying no attention to ideas or policies. Nevertheless, American politicians are not simply power-seeking pragmatists. The importance of ideas and values in American politics is concealed by the fact that the two major parties, the Republicans and the Democrats, share the same broad ideological goals. Most American politicians subscribe to what has been called 'the American ideology', a set of liberal-capitalist values about the virtues of a free market economy and respect for the principles embodied in the United States Constitution.

Political ideas also help to shape the nature of political systems. Systems of government vary considerably throughout the world and are always associated with particular values or principles. Absolute monarchies were based upon deeply-established religious ideas, notably the Divine Right of Kings. The political systems in most contemporary Western countries are founded upon a set of liberal democratic principles. Western states typically respect the ideas of limited and constitutional government, and also believe that government should be representative, based upon regular and competitive elections. In the same way, traditional Communist political systems conformed to the principles of Marxism–Leninism. Communist states were dominated by a single party, a ruling Communist party, whose authority rested upon Lenin's belief that the Communist party alone represents the interests of the working class. Even the fact that the world is divided into a collection of nation-states and that government power is usually located at a national level, reflects the impact of political ideas, in this case nationalism and, more specifically, the belief that each nation has a right to self-determination.

Finally, political ideas and ideologies can act as a form of social cement, providing social groups, or indeed whole societies, with a set of unifying beliefs and values. Political ideologies have commonly been associated with particular social classes, for example, liberalism with the middle classes, conservatism with the landed aristocracy, socialism with the working class, and so forth. These ideas reflect the life experiences, interests and aspirations of a social class, and therefore help to foster a sense of belonging and solidarity. However, ideas and ideologies can also succeed in binding together divergent groups and classes within a society. For instance, there is a unifying bedrock of liberal democratic values in most Western countries, while in Moslem countries Islam has established a common set of moral principles and beliefs. In providing society with a unified political culture, political ideas help to promote order and social stability.

A unifying set of political ideas and values can develop naturally within a society. However, it can also be enforced from above in an attempt to manufacture obedience and operate therefore as a form of social control. The values of elite groups, like political and military leaders, government officials, landowners or industrialists, may diverge significantly from those of the masses. Ruling elites may use political ideas to contain opposition and restrict debate through a process of ideological manipulation. This was most obvious in regimes which possessed 'official' ideologies such as Nazi Germany and the Soviet Union, at least until the Gorbachev reform process was initiated. In both cases, official or politically 'reliable' beliefs, those of National Socialism and Marxism–Leninism respectively, dominated political life and indeed all social institutions, art, culture, education, the media and so on. Opposing views and beliefs were simply censored or suppressed. Some argue that a more subtle form of ideological manipulation occurs in all societies. Marxists, for example, believe that all ideas reflect class interests and therefore that the ideas of a ruling class of property owners dominate intellectual life in all capitalist societies and are spread by the educational system, the state and also the media.

2 The meaning of ideology

When political ideas are discussed they are commonly grouped together into 'ideologies'. The term was coined during the French Revolution and first used in 1797 by Destutt de Tracy to refer to a new 'science of ideas'. The concept of ideology is, however, highly contentious, and its meaning has been the subject of fierce political debate. On one hand, all sets of political ideas, or '-isms', have been referred to as ideologies, while, on the other hand, the word ideology sometimes has a pejorative meaning, implying 'dogmatic', 'doctrinaire', 'extreme' or simply 'false'.

In *Politics and Ideology* (1976) Martin Seliger defined an ideology as 'a set of ideas by which men posit, explain and justify the ends and means of organised social action, irrespective of whether such action aims to preserve, amend, uproot or rebuild a given social order'(p.14). Ideologies therefore comprise a set of interrelated, and more or less coherent, ideas. Some would say that they constitute 'systems of thought', but in the case of ideologies like conservatism or fascism the ideas may simply 'hang together' rather than have a systematic or coherent shape. Ideologies contain both descriptive and normative elements; they offer an account of how society works and a picture of how it should or ought to work . Ideologies are political in that they are action-orientated, they inspire and guide groups in undertaking some kind of 'organised social action'. This action can take many forms. Ideologies can defend and uphold a particular social order, preventing change from occurring, as in the case of conservatism. In contrast, liberalism and social democracy have proclaimed the need for reform and social change. Other ideologies, such as communism, fascism and anarchism, have advocated revolution, the overthrow and replacement of the social order itself.

Very different concepts of 'ideology' have, however, been employed by Marxists and some liberal thinkers. Within Marxism itself two contrasting definitions can be identified. For Marx, ideas were 'ideological' if they concealed the contradictions upon which all class societies were founded. 'Ideology' therefore had a negative and critical meaning. 'Ideological' ideas were false, they distorted, indeed inverted, reality, whereas those ideas which, like Marx's own theories, uncovered the contradictions of society were 'scientific'. 'Ideology' also serves an important social function because in concealing the realities of class exploitation and oppression it necessarily upholds the interests of a 'ruling class' of property owners. Later Marxists like Lenin and Gramsci developed a positive conception of 'ideology'. For them, 'ideologies' were sets of ideas which served or embodied the interests of particular social classes. Every social class produces its own 'ideology', so it is possible to speak of 'proletarian ideology' as well as 'bourgeois ideology'. These ideologies could be true or false, right or wrong, and therefore the critical edge of Marx's concept, the distinction between 'ideology' and 'science', was lost.

'Ideology' has also been used in a negative sense by liberal writers such as Karl Popper and Daniel Bell. In their case, they regard ideologies as 'closed' systems of political thought. Ideologies claim a monopoly of truth, they seek to explain everything and in so doing refuse to tolerate rival views or opposing theories. An ideology is thus a 'secular religion', which leads to intolerance, censorship and political repression. Liberal thinkers have often identified Marxism and fascism as 'ideologies', and have pointed out that both have generated repressive, even totalitarian, political systems. However, not all sets of political ideas are ideologies according to this definition. Liberalism, for example, is an 'open' system of thought, it does not claim to possess a monopoly of truth, but is committed to freedom of speech and an open competition of political views. Although Marx's concept and this liberal notion are fundamentally different, they both use the term 'ideology' in a strictly pejorative sense: ideologies are 'bad', 'false' or 'repressive'. The term is therefore used selectively to refer to particular sets of political ideas, those being condemned or criticised, rather than all political views.

The value of Seliger's definition of ideology is that it is comprehensive; it can be applied to all sets of political ideas because it is neutral and does not suggest that ideologies are either 'good' or 'bad'. It simply sees ideologies as sets of ideas which provide the basis for some kind of political action. However, problems still remain. Ideologies are seldom monolithic, they address a broad range of themes and commonly contain a number of divergent, even rival, traditions. Liberalism is divided into classical and modern traditions, Marxist socialists have often disagreed fundamentally with social democrats, and the New Right is highly critical of traditional conservatism. It is not uncommon for disputes between supporters of the same ideology to be more passionate and bitter than arguments between supporters of rival ideologies because what is at stake is the 'true' nature of the ideology. What is 'true' liberalism, 'true' socialism, or 'true' conservatism? Such disputes, however, are based upon the misguided belief that ideologies have a definitive essential core of principles and values, which are fixed and can be preserved like religious dogma. Each ideology may possess a characteristic set of ideas and beliefs, but these ideas are constantly being revised and redefined. In reality, all political concepts are 'elastic'; they have no self-evident or unchallengeable meaning. Political ideologies are therefore broad traditions of thought, which have evolved and developed under the pressure of changing historical circumstances and as a result of argument and debate, and continue to do so.

3 The political spectrum

Many attempts have been made to categorise political ideas and to relate them to one another. The most familiar and firmly-established method of doing this is the Left–Right spectrum. This is a linear spectrum which locates political beliefs at some point between two extremes, the far Left and the far Right. Terms like 'left-wing' or 'right-wing' are widely used to sum up a person's political beliefs or position, and groups of people are referred to collectively as 'the Left', 'the Right' and indeed 'the Centre'. There is also broad agreement about where different ideas and ideologies are located along this spectrum. From Left to Right, most people would accept the following spectrum: communism–socialism–liberalism–conservatism-fascism. Although this spectrum is widely recognised, it is far more difficult to establish precisely what it means and how helpful it is in defining and describing political views.

The origin of the terms 'left' and 'right' dates back to the French Revolution and the positions which different groups adopted at the first meeting of the Estates-General in 1789. Aristocrats who supported the King sat to his right, while radicals, members of the Third Estate, sat on his left. A similar seating pattern was followed in the subsequent French Assemblies. The term 'right' was soon understood to mean reactionary or monarchist, and the term 'left' was used of revolutionary deputies or those who held egalitarian views. In contemporary politics, however, the Left–Right divide has become increasingly complex and no longer reflects a simple choice between revolution and reaction. For example, although right-wing views may often be reactionary, and preach a return to an earlier and better time, fascism, on the extreme Right, has also been revolutionary and, in the case of Italian Fascism, positively forward-looking. Similarly, although left-wing views have often been progressive or revolutionary, socialists and communists have at times resisted change; for instance, they have sought to defend the welfare state or prevent a centrally planned economy being reformed or abolished.

The linear spectrum is commonly understood to reflect different political values or contrasting views about economic policy. In terms of values, the spectrum is sometimes said to reflect different attitudes towards equality. Left-wingers are committed to a belief in human equality and the possibility of achieving it. Right-wingers are characterised by their belief that equality is either undesirable or impossible. This is closely related to different attitudes to the economy and, in particular, the ownership of wealth. Communists, on the far Left, believe in a state planned economy, socialists and modern liberals believe in a mixed economy and government regulation, right-wing conservatives believe in free market capitalism and private property. All such interpretations, however, involve inconsistencies. Fascist regimes, for instance, have practised economic management and state control despite being on the far Right of the spectrum. Moreover, it is unclear where anarchism should be placed on the linear spectrum. Anarchists are strongly committed to the idea of equality, which would normally place them on the far Left of the spectrum, but their opposition to all forms of economic management, and in fact to any form of government, may suggest that they should be on the far Right.

The weakness of the linear spectrum is that it tries to reduce politics to a single dimension, and suggests that political views can be classified according to merely one criterion, be it attitude to change, support for equality, or economic philosophy. Political ideologies are in fact highly complex collections of beliefs, values and doctrines which any kind of spectrum is forced to over-simplify. Attempts have nevertheless been made to develop more sophisticated political spectrums which embody two or more dimensions. For example, the linear spectrum has sometimes been criticised because the ideologies at its extremes, communism and fascism, exhibit similarities. In particular, communist and fascist regimes have both developed repressive, authoritarian forms of political rule, which some have described as 'totalitarian'. As a result, an alternative political spectrum might be horseshoe-shaped, indicating that the extreme points on the Left and the Right tend to converge, and distinguishing both from the 'democratic' beliefs of liberalism, socialism and conservatism. This, however, is also contentious because the similarities between communism and fascism may be more apparent than real. Certainly the values for which the two ideologies stand are fundamentally different, but also in some respects Nazi Germany was very different from Stalinist Russia: for example, capitalism thrived under Hitler, at least until the final years of the war, while it was eradicated under Stalin.

Another spectrum was proposed by Hans Eysenck in *Sense and*

Nonsense in Psychology (1957). Eysenck accepted the conventional Left–Right spectrum as the horizontal axis of his spectrum, but added a vertical axis that measured political attitudes that were at one extreme 'tough minded' or authoritarian, and at the other 'tender minded' or democratic. Political ideas can therefore be positioned on both the Left–Right axis as well as the 'tough' and 'tender' axis. In this case the differences between, for instance, Nazism and Stalinism can be made clear by placing these at opposite extremes of the Left–Right axis, while their similarities can be emphasised by placing both firmly at the 'tough minded' extreme of the vertical axis. All such spectrums raise difficulties, however, because they tend to simplify and generalise about highly complex sets of political ideas. They are, at best, a shorthand method of describing political ideas or beliefs, and must always be used with caution.

4 Outline of the book

This book examines the principal ideas and doctrines of modern political thought. It is organised around the major ideologies which have dominated political life during the last two hundred years, and considers each ideology in turn. Every chapter starts with an introduction which looks at the origins and development of the ideology and considers both its historical and contemporary significance. The second section in each case seeks to identify a common core of values and principles which are distinctive to the ideology. In so doing, it attempts to distinguish a liberal from a socialist, a conservative from a fascist, and so on. Subsequent sections analyse the divergent and sometimes conflicting traditions which have emerged within the ideology and explore their political impact. A clear danger of such an approach is the implication that ideologies occupy discrete and isolated compartments, when in practice they have influenced and fertilised one another. Their ideas and values overlap and the boundary between ideologies is all too often blurred. For example, modern liberals and social democrats share a common belief in economic management and the welfare state, while authoritarian conservatives and fascists agree about the need for national unity and strong government. Parallels and similarities between ideologies will therefore be highlighted, as well as the unique and distinctive features of each.

The ideologies considered are, in origin at least, 'Western ideologies', that is, they arose first in Europe and North America as a result of the process of modernisation. They have, however, subsequently become 'world ideologies', largely because of the struggle against colonial rule and the desire for development in the Third World. The process of modernisation in the West, out of which these ideologies emerged, was simultaneously economic, political and cultural. Society had previously been simple and agricultural, based upon a feudal social order in which land was the principal source of wealth. Social positions were fixed and largely determined by birth; at the top was a landed aristocracy and beneath them the mass of 'bonded' serfs or peasants. Political power was vested in the hands of absolute monarchs who ruled in association with powerful landed interests. Life in such societies was understood in terms of unchanging and usually natural relationships. The dominant form of intellectual life in feudal times was religion. The right of the king to rule, for example, was rarely challenged because it was accepted that he had been chosen by God and so ruled with divine authority.

Between the sixteenth and nineteenth centuries, the structures and certainties of feudal life broke down in the face of a series of revolutions. The first of these was a commercial revolution in which food and other goods started to be produced not to satisfy a particular estate or village, but to be sold in the marketplace. This led to the emergence of an increasingly market-orientated, capitalist economy. By the mid eighteenth century, in Britain at first, an industrial revolution had commenced in which traditional craft skills and manual labour were gradually replaced by more efficient and technological methods of machine and factory production. The productive capacity of society was enormously expanded and the social order became progressively more complex and diverse. A rising middle class of businessmen and industrialists developed, as did a new class of industrial workers. These social and economic upheavals were accompanied by a series of political revolutions. As early as the seventeenth century Britain experienced a Civil War in which the king was divested of absolute power and the first ideas of constitutional government emerged. The American Revolution of 1776 overthrew British rule and produced a republican system of government based upon federal and constitutional principles. The most significant revolution of all, the French Revolution of 1789, swept aside monarchical absolutism in the name of the modern ideas of 'Liberty, Equality and Fraternity'.

This process also produced major cultural changes, notably the growth of science and rationalist thought. By the early nineteenth century, most modern political ideologies had made their emergence. The major ideologies considered in the early chapters, liberalism, socialism and conservatism, developed as contrasting responses to the process of modernisation. Liberals, for instance, supported the growth of industrial capitalism, socialists argued that capitalism was merely another class-based society, founded upon injustice, while conservatives sought to defend and uphold the traditional social order. The ideas of nationalism, anarchism, feminism and democracy were also born out of this period of political and social transformation. Although fascism and Soviet communism did not emerge until the First World War, both drew heavily upon nineteenth century ideas and doctrines. Even the most 'modern' ideology here considered, environmentalism, has roots in a nineteenth century backlash against industrialisation.

The expansion of colonial rule between 1870 and 1914 gave these Western ideologies a worldwide significance. Twentieth century politics in much of the Third World has been shaped by the struggle against colonialism and the subsequent tasks of nation-building, which have been conducted in language largely inherited from the West. However, ideologies like socialism and nationalism and ideas such as democracy and revolution have not simply retained their original meanings. Western ideas have been reinterpreted and reapplied in very different circumstances and been linked to very different political ends. The ideas, for instance, of African and Arab socialism owe as much to traditional social and religious values as they do to classical socialist doctrines. In other cases, Third World ideologies have been non-Western and even anti-Western, reflected in the rising importance of political Islam, which now stands as a major rival to both liberalism and socialism in many parts of Africa and Asia. At the same time, Western ideologies have been reinvigorated by the growing impact of developments in the Third World. For example, the New Left in the 1960s was profoundly influenced by national liberation struggles in Asia, Africa and Latin America, and by the theories of guerrilla warfare developed by Mao Tse-tung and Che Guevara. Similarly, modern environmentalism has been inspired by Gandhi's philosophy of non-violence and by the self-sufficiency of traditional Indian village life.

2
Liberalism

1 Introduction

The term 'liberal' has been in use since the fourteenth century but
has had a wide variety of meanings. It has referred to a class of free
men, in other words, men who are neither serfs nor slaves. It has
meant generous as in 'liberal' helpings of food and drink, or, in
reference to social attitudes, it has had the sense of openness or open-
mindedness. It also came to be increasingly associated with ideas of
freedom and choice. The term 'liberalism' made its appearance
much later: it was not used until the early part of the nineteenth
century, being first employed in Spain in 1812. By the 1840s it was
widely recognised throughout much of Europe as a reference to a
distinctive set of political ideas.

As a systematic political creed, liberalism may not have existed
before the nineteenth century, but it was based upon ideas and
theories which had developed during the previous three hundred
years. Liberal ideas resulted from the breakdown of feudalism in
Europe and the growth, in its place, of a market or capitalist society.
In many respects, liberalism reflected the aspirations of a rising
middle class, whose interests conflicted with the established power
of absolute monarchs and the landed aristocracy. Liberal ideas were
radical, they sought fundamental reform and even, at times, revolutionary change. The English Revolution of the seventeenth century
and the American and French Revolutions of the late eighteenth
century all embodied elements that were distinctively liberal, even
though the word 'liberal' was not yet used in a political sense.
Liberals challenged the absolute power of the monarchy, supposedly
based upon the doctrine of the Divine Right of Kings. In place of
absolutism they advocated constitutional and, later, representative

15

government. Liberals criticised the political and economic privileges of the landed aristocracy and the unfairness of a feudal system in which social position was determined by the 'accident of birth'. They also supported the movement towards 'freedom of conscience' in religion and questioned the authority of the established Church.

The nineteenth century was in many ways the Liberal Century. As industrialisation spread throughout Western countries, liberal ideas triumphed. Liberals advocated an industrialised and market economic order 'free' from government interference, in which businessmen would be allowed to pursue profit, and nations encouraged to trade freely with one another. Such a system of industrial capitalism developed first in Britain, from the mid eighteenth century onwards, and was well-established by the early nineteenth century. It subsequently spread to North America and throughout Europe, first into Western Europe and then, more gradually, into Eastern Europe. During the twentieth century, industrial capitalism has exerted a powerful appeal for developing countries in Africa, Asia and Latin America, especially when social and political development has been defined in essentially Western terms. However, Third World countries have sometimes been resistant to the attractions of liberal capitalism because their political cultures have emphasised the community rather than the individual. In such cases they have provided more fertile ground for the growth of socialism or nationalism rather than Western liberalism. Where capitalism has been successfully established, as in Japan, it has tended to assume a corporate rather than individualistic character. Japanese industry, for example, is motivated more by traditional ideas of group loyalty and duty than by the pursuit of individual self-interest.

Western political systems have also been shaped by liberal ideas and values, so much so that they are commonly classified as liberal democracies. These systems are constitutional in that they seek to limit government power and safeguard civil liberties, and representative in the sense that political office is gained through competitive elections. Developing first in Western Europe and North America, liberal democracy has subsequently taken root in parts of the Third World and, after the political revolutions of 1989–90, in Eastern Europe too. In some cases, Western-style liberal regimes were bequeathed to African or Asian countries upon achieving independence, but with varying degrees of success. India remains the world's largest liberal democracy. Elsewhere, however, liberal democratic systems have sometimes collapsed in the absence of industrial capitalism or because of the nature of the indigenous political culture. In contrast, the political culture of most Western countries is built upon a bedrock of liberal–capitalist values. Ideas such as freedom of speech, freedom of religious worship and the right to own property, all drawn from liberalism, are so deeply ingrained in Western societies that they are seldom challenged openly or even questioned.

Liberalism has come, in effect, to be the dominant ideology of the industrialised West. Some political thinkers have even argued that there is a necessary and inevitable link between liberalism and capitalism. This has been suggested by liberalism's critics as well as its supporters. Marxists, for instance, believe that liberal ideas simply reflect the economic interests of a 'ruling class' of property owners within capitalist society; they regard liberalism as 'bourgeois ideology'. On the other hand, liberal writers like Friedrich Hayek believe that economic freedom – the right to own, use and dispose of private property – is an essential guarantee of political liberty. He argues, therefore, that a liberal democratic political system and respect for civil liberties can only develop in the context of a capitalist economic order.

The very success of liberalism has, however, caused problems. Liberal ideas and values are so deeply entrenched in Western political and economic life that it is sometimes difficult to distinguish between liberalism and 'Western civilisation' in general. Liberalism, moreover, cannot always be easily distinguished from rival Western political ideologies, notably conservatism and socialism, which have frequently borrowed liberal ideas. As a result, Liberal parties have sometimes experienced difficulty in maintaining their electoral appeal. This is evident in Britain where the Liberal Party, once a major party of government, first formed an electoral alliance with the newly-created SDP in 1981, before the two parties fused to create the Liberal Democrats in 1988. In the twentieth century the Liberals have lost support to Labour and Conservative parties, whose policies have been profoundly affected by liberalism. For example, the architect of the expanded welfare state, introduced by Labour after 1945, was the liberal, William Beveridge, and the modern Conservative Party's sympathy for 'free market' economics, particularly during the Thatcher period, draws heavily upon the ideas of early liberal economists like Adam Smith.

Historical developments in the nineteenth and twentieth centuries have also clearly influenced liberal ideology itself. The character of liberalism changed as the 'rising middle class' succeeded in establishing its economic and political dominance. The radical, even revolutionary, edge of liberalism faded with each liberal success. Liberalism, therefore, became increasingly conservative, standing less for change and reform, and more for the maintenance of existing – largely liberal – institutions. Liberal ideas also could not stand still. From the late nineteenth century onwards, the progress of industrialisation led liberals to question, and in some ways revise, the ideas of early liberalism. Whereas early liberals had wanted government to interfere as little as possible in the lives of its citizens, modern liberals have come to believe that government should be responsible for delivering welfare services, such as health, housing, pensions and education, as well as for managing the economy. This has led to the development of two traditions of thought within liberalism, commonly called classical liberalism and modern liberalism. Some commentators have, as a result, argued that liberalism is an incoherent ideology, embracing contradictory beliefs, notably about the desirable role of the state. On the other hand, in common with all political ideologies, liberalism has been subject to change as its basic principles have been applied to changing historical circumstances. No political ideology is rigid or monolithic, all encompass a range of views and even rival traditions. There is, nevertheless, an underlying coherence and a unity at the heart of liberal thought in the form of a fundamental commitment to the importance of individual freedom and to the principles of individualism.

2 Individualism

a The individual

Individualism is a belief in the central importance of the individual human being. Liberal thought focuses upon the needs and interests of the 'individual', rather than those of any group or 'collective'. In the modern world, the concept of the individual is so familiar that its political significance is often overlooked. In the feudal period there had been little idea of individuals having their own interests or possessing personal and unique identities. People were seen, rather, as members of the social groups to which they belonged: their family, village, local community or social class. Their lives and identities were largely determined by the character of these groups in a process that changed little from one generation to the next. However, as feudalism broke down, individuals were confronted by a broader range of choices and social possibilities. They were encouraged, maybe for the first time, to think for themselves, and to think of themselves in personal terms. A serf, for example, whose family may always have lived and worked on the same piece of land, became a 'free man' and acquired some ability to choose who to work for, or, perhaps, the opportunity to leave the land altogether and look for work in the growing towns or cities.

As the certainties of feudal life broke down, a new intellectual climate emerged, variously called the Enlightenment or the Age of Reason. Rational and scientific explanations gradually displaced traditional religious theories and society was increasingly understood from the viewpoint of the human individual. Individuals were thought to possess personal and distinctive qualities; each was of special value. This was evident in the growth of natural rights theories in the seventeenth and eighteenth centuries. These suggested that individuals were invested with a set of God-given, natural rights, defined by John Locke as 'life, liberty and property'. The individual alone possessed such rights and was, in that sense, more important than any social group. Natural rights theorists argued therefore that society should be constructed in such a way that the individual's interests and needs could best be protected.

This belief in the primacy of the individual is the characteristic theme of liberal ideology and has had important implications for liberal thought. It has led some liberals to view society as simply a collection of individuals, each seeking to satisfy his or her own needs and interests. Such a view has been called atomism, in that it conceives of individuals as 'isolated atoms' within society; indeed it can lead to the belief that 'society' itself does not exist, but is only, in reality, a collection of self-sufficient individuals. Such extreme individualism is based upon the assumption that the individual is egotistical, essentially self-seeking and largely self-reliant. C.B. MacPherson characterised early liberalism as 'possessive individualism' because, he argued, it regarded the individual as 'the proprietor of his own person or capacities, owing nothing to society for them' (p.199). In contrast, later liberals have held a more optimistic view of human nature, and have believed that individuals possess a social responsibility for one another, especially for those not able to look after themselves. Whether human nature is conceived as being egoistical or altruistic, liberals are united in their desire to create a society in which each individual is capable of developing and flourishing to the fullness of his or her potential.

b Individual freedom

A belief in the supreme importance of the individual leads naturally to a commitment to individual freedom. Individual liberty is for liberals the supreme political value and, in many ways, the unifying principle within liberal ideology. For early liberals, liberty was a 'natural right', an essential requirement for leading a truly human existence. It also gave individuals the opportunity to pursue their own interests by exercising choice, the choice of where to live, who to work for, what to buy, and so forth. Later liberals have seen liberty as the only condition in which people are able to develop their skills and talents and fulfil their potential.

Nevertheless, liberals do not accept that individuals have an absolute entitlement to freedom. If liberty is unlimited it can become 'licence', the right to abuse others. In *On Liberty* (1859) John Stuart Mill argued that 'the only purpose for which power can be rightfully exercised over any member of a civilised community, against his will, is to prevent harm to others' (p.73). Mill's position is libertarian, in that he was prepared to accept only the most minimal restriction of individual freedom, and then in order to prevent 'harm to others'. He distinguished clearly between actions which were 'self-regarding', over which the individual should exercise absolute freedom, and those that were 'other-regarding', which could restrict the freedom of others or do them damage. Mill did not accept any restriction upon the individual which was designed to prevent a person damaging himself or herself, either physically or morally. Such a view suggests, for example, that laws forcing car drivers to put on seat belts or motor cyclists to wear crash helmets are as unacceptable as any form of censorship which limits what an individual may read or listen to. Radical libertarians may defend the right of people to use addictive drugs like heroin and cocaine on the same grounds. Although the individual may be sovereign over his or her body and mind, each must respect the fact that every other individual enjoys an equal right to liberty. This has been expressed by the modern liberal, John Rawls, in the principle that everyone is entitled to the widest possible liberty consistent with a like liberty for all.

Although liberals agree about the value of liberty, they have not always agreed about what it means for an individual to be 'free'. In his 'Two Concepts of Liberty' (1958), Isiah Berlin distinguished between a 'negative' theory of liberty and a 'positive' one. Early or classical liberals have believed that freedom consists in each person being left alone, free from interference and able to act in whatever way they may choose. This conception of liberty is 'negative' in that it is based upon the absence of external restrictions or constraints upon the individual. Modern liberals, on the other hand, have been attracted to a more 'positive' conception of liberty, defined by Berlin as the ability to be one's own master, to become autonomous. Self-mastery requires that the individual is able to develop skills and talents, broaden his or her understanding, and gain fulfilment. For John Stuart Mill, for example, liberty meant much more than simply being free from outside constraints; it involved the capacity of human beings to develop and ultimately achieve self-realisation. These rival conceptions of liberty have not merely stimulated academic debate within liberalism, but have led liberals to hold very different views about the desirable relationship between the individual and the state.

c Social justice

Liberalism also involves a commitment to equality. If human beings are thought of, first and foremost, as individuals, they must be entitled to the same rights and the same respect. Liberals believe in universalism, that individuals everywhere possess common or universal features, that they are all of equal moral worth. For example, liberals believe that all individuals are endowed with equal rights, which they enjoy by virtue of being human; these are 'natural rights' or 'human rights'. Rights should not be reserved for any particular class of person, such as men, whites, Christians or the wealthy. Consequently, liberals fiercely disapprove of social privileges or advantages which are enjoyed by some but denied to others on the basis of factors like gender, race, colour, creed, religion or social background. Individuals should be 'equal before the law'. Thus liberals regard institutions such as apartheid in South Africa, which segregated individuals on grounds of race, or the caste system of traditional India, which assigned social position on the basis of birth, as fundamentally unacceptable.

The equality to which liberals subscribe is equality of opportunity. Each and every individual should have the same chance to rise or fall in society. The game of life, in that sense, must be played on an even playing field. This is not to say, however, that there should be absolute equality, that living conditions and social circumstances should be the same for all. Liberals believe absolute equality to be undesirable because people are not born equal. They possess different talents and skills, and some are prepared to work much harder than others. Liberals believe that it is right to reward merit, ability and the willingness to work – indeed, they think it essential to do so if people are to have an incentive to develop whatever talents they may have been born with. Equality, for a liberal, means that individuals should have an equal opportunity to develop their unequal skills and abilities.

This leads to a belief in meritocracy, literally rule by the talented or able, a society in which inequalities of wealth and social position are based solely upon an unequal distribution of merit or skills amongst human beings, or upon factors beyond human control, like luck or chance. A meritocratic society is thought to be socially just, because individuals are judged not by their gender, the colour of their skin, or their religion, but according to their talents and willingness to work, by what Martin Luther King called 'the content of their character'.

Wealth, therefore, should reflect merit. Property is gained by hard work and the exercise of abilities. Those with more ability or who have worked hard have 'earned' their wealth and deserve to be more prosperous than the lazy or incapable. However, wealth is not only earned by individual hard work but can also be acquired by the accident of birth. Although the idea of inherited wealth does not conform to strict meritocratic principles, most liberals have been prepared to accept it in the belief that its restriction would interfere with an individual's right to dispose of his or her property according to personal choice.

However, liberal thinkers have sometimes disagreed about how this principle of social justice should be applied in practice. In *A*

Theory of Justice (1971), John Rawls accepted the need for people to be rewarded for the work they do because he recognised that some measure of economic inequality is essential to provide an incentive for people to work. Nevertheless, he argued that economic inequality is only justifiable if it works to the benefit of the poorest and the least advantaged in society. He suggested that social justice should be understood to mean 'fairness', which for him meant a presumption in favour of equality. Consequently, Rawls concluded that a just society would be one in which wealth is redistributed through some form of welfare system for the benefit of the less-well-off. A very different conception of social justice was developed by Robert Nozick in *Anarchy, State and Utopia* (1974), whose libertarian views echo those advanced by John Locke in the seventeenth century. Nozick claimed that any distribution of wealth, however unequal, is socially just provided that certain 'justice preserving' rules have been observed. These rules include that the property was 'justly' acquired in the first place, acquired without being stolen or infringing the rights of others, and that it has been transferred 'justly' by one responsible person to another. Nozick clearly believes that the right to property should not be violated in the name of social equality and therefore rejects the very notion of redistributing wealth, and with it all forms of social welfare.

Such different views about the nature of social justice reflect an underlying disagreement within liberalism about the conditions which can best achieve a just society. Classical liberals believe that the growth of a market or capitalist society, in place of feudalism, created social conditions in which each individual could prosper according to his or her merits. Providing individuals are equal in the eyes of the law, they are thought to enjoy equal opportunities to rise or fall in society. Modern liberals, in contrast, have felt that unrestrained capitalism has led to new forms of social injustice, which have privileged some and disadvantaged others. As a result, they have favoured government intervention in social and economic life, designed to promote greater equality of opportunity, and thereby achieve a socially just society.

d Civil society

Although liberals believe in the primacy of the individual over society, they are, of course, aware that individuals do form social bonds and associations. Very few liberals see individuals as entirely self-reliant Robinson Crusoes. Individuals are, in fact, only able to pursue their own interests successfully if they enter into relationships with others. Their economic needs can only be satisfied when they co-operate and work together with others, achieving some measure of specialisation and the benefits of a division of labour. Individuals must also be able to do business or trade with one another in order to acquire those goods which they cannot produce themselves. A liberal society is therefore not a collection of entirely self-sufficient 'atoms', but a society in which individual needs and interests are satisfied through voluntary co-operation and the formation of free associations.

The concept which underlies the liberal notion of society is that of contract. Associations and social groups are thought to be formed by individuals entering into contractual agreements with one another. A contract is an agreement, but one which is only binding on its parties if it is entered into voluntarily and in full knowledge of its 'terms'. If an individual is coerced or tricked into signing a contract, it has no moral authority and cannot be legally enforced. Contractual agreements therefore enable individuals to form associations without in the process sacrificing their liberty. Feudal obligations, typically based upon birth rather than voluntary agreement, were unacceptable to liberals. The practice of serfdom, for instance, 'tied' peasants to a particular piece of land and the obligation to work for and serve their landowner. Liberals preferred instead the growth of market or capitalist practices, in which workers would be able to choose where to work and for whom to work. The relationship between a worker and an employer in a capitalist society is contractual. Each side enters into it by choice and with a view to pursuing his or her own interests. The obligations which such contracts impose upon the two parties have been freely undertaken, which is why contracts *should* be obeyed and, if necessary, be legally enforced.

A society in which each person pursues self-interest could, however, lead to conflict, either between individuals or amongst the groups that they form. Socialists, for example, believe that capitalism inevitably generates social inequality which leads to conflict between social classes. In fact, Marxist socialists believe that class conflict will eventually result in the overthrow of capitalism itself. Liberals, in contrast, refuse to accept the existence of such fundamental conflict, but believe instead in a balanced society. Although individuals and social groups pursue very different interests, liberals hold that there is a deeper harmony or balance amongst these competing interests. For example, the interests of workers and employers differ: workers want better pay, shorter hours and improved working conditions, while employers wish to increase their profits by keeping their production costs – including wages – as low as possible. Nevertheless, these competing interests also complement one another: workers need jobs, and employers need labour. In other words, each group is essential to the achievement of the other group's goals. Individuals and groups may pursue self-interest but a natural equilibrium will tend to assert itself. This principle of balance has influenced liberal thought in a variety of ways. It has, for instance, led some liberals to believe that a natural and unregulated equilibrium will tend to emerge in economic life. It has encouraged liberals to believe in a balance of interests amongst competing groups in the political system, and it has also pursuaded them that international affairs can be characterised by peace and harmony amongst nations.

Far from fearing that the expression of competing interests and views will lead to fundamental conflict, liberals have tended to welcome a healthy diversity of attitudes and opinions in society. A liberal society is a pluralistic society, composed of a diverse collection of groups and, therefore, one in which a broad range of opinions and views are tolerated. Social diversity is natural and can only be removed by political repression or, perhaps, liberals have feared, the spread of dull conformism. In principle, therefore, liberals oppose censorship or any attempt to prevent the free expression of views in society. This is why the Western liberal conscience was so deeply offended by the *fatwa*, or sentence of death, passed by the Ayatollah Khomeini in 1989 upon the British writer, Salman Rushdie, because of the publication of his book, *The Satanic Verses*. The liberal case for a free expression of views within society was put most forcefully by John Stuart Mill, who argued that society had no more right to overturn the opinion of a single individual, than that single individual had to overturn the opinions of the rest of society. A healthy diversity of opinion is the only way in which ideas and arguments can be tested and, therefore, the only way in which 'truth' can be established. Even democratic elections cannot establish the truth because, as Mill warned, the majority may not always be right.

Underlying this liberal preference for a diversity of views and interests in society is the value of tolerance. Tolerance is the willingness to accept views and opinions with which a person may not be in agreement. Liberalism is sometimes criticised for having fostered the permissive social climate which is said to have existed in the 1960s, reflected in the relaxation or abolition of censorship and the legalisation of abortion, homosexuality and, in some countries, prostitution. However, permissiveness is the abandonment of the right to judge the opinions of others altogether, an acceptance that all freely chosen beliefs or life styles are equally correct. A liberal social morality, in contrast, is one in which each person is able to criticise the opinions and behaviour of others, but not prevent them from holding, expressing or acting upon their own views. Liberals have often echoed the famous words of Voltaire, 'I detest what you say but will defend to the death your right to say it'. Some liberals would argue that such tolerance has its limits; in particular, that it should not be extended to views that are, in themselves, intolerant. Thus liberals may be prepared to support laws which prevent the expression, for example, of racialist opinions, or laws which ban undemocratic political parties. Liberals supported the right of Islamic fundamentalists to criticise the contents of *The Satanic Verses* but, at the same time, sometimes advocated the prosecution of those who publicly endorsed the death sentence upon Salman Rushdie.

e The liberal state

Liberals do not believe that a balanced and tolerant society will develop naturally out of the free actions of individuals and voluntary associations. This is where liberals disagree with anarchists, who believe that both law and government are unnecessary. Liberals fear that free individuals may wish to exploit others, steal their property or even turn them into slaves if it is in their interests to do so. They may also break or ignore their contracts when it is to their advantage. The liberty of one person is always therefore in danger of becoming a licence to abuse another; each person can be said to be both a threat to, and under threat from, every other member of society. Our liberty requires that they are restrained from encroaching upon our freedom, and their liberty requires, in turn, that they are safeguarded from us. Liberals have traditionally believed that such protection can only be provided by a sovereign state, capable of restraining all individuals and groups within society. Freedom can therefore only exist 'under the law'; as John Locke argued, 'where there is no law there is no freedom' (p.306).

This argument is the basis of the social contract theory, developed first by seventeenth century writers like Thomas Hobbes and John Locke, which liberals have frequently employed to explain the individual's political obligations towards the state. Hobbes and Locke constructed a picture of what life had been like before government was formed, in a stateless society or what they called a 'state of nature'. As individuals were selfish, greedy and power-seeking, the state of nature led to an unending civil war of each against all, in which, in Hobbes' words, human life would be 'solitary, poor, nasty, brutish and short'. As a result, they argued, rational individuals had entered into an agreement, or 'social contract', to establish a sovereign government, without which orderly and stable life would be impossible. All individuals recognised that it was in their interests to sacrifice a portion of their liberty in order to set up a system of law; otherwise their rights, and indeed their lives, would constantly be under threat. Hobbes and Locke were aware that this 'contract' was an historical fiction. States are, in reality, rarely formed through a formal agreement amongst citizens wishing to escape from the dangers of anarchy. The purpose of the social contract argument is, however, that it illustrates the value of the sovereign state to the individual. Hobbes and Locke, in other words, wished individuals to behave as if the historical fiction were true, to respect and obey government and law, in gratitude for the safety and security which only a sovereign state could provide.

The social contract argument embodies several important liberal attitudes towards the state in particular and political authority in general. In the first place, it suggests that political authority comes, in a sense, 'from below'. The state is created by individuals and for individuals, it exists in order to serve *their* needs and interests. Government arises out of the agreement or consent of the governed. Political authority must therefore be legitimate, it must be rightful or acceptable in the eyes of those who are subject to it. This implies that citizens do not have an absolute obligation to obey all laws or accept any form of government. If government is based upon a contract, made by the governed, government itself may break the terms of this contract. When the legitimacy of government evaporates, the people have the right of rebellion. This principle was developed by Locke in *Two Treaties of Government* (1690), and was used to justify the Glorious Revolution of 1688 which deposed James II and established a constitutional monarchy in Britain under William and Mary. It was also clearly expressed by Thomas Jefferson in the American Declaration of Independence (1776), which declared that when government became an absolute despotism 'it is the right of the people to alter or abolish it'.

Secondly, social contract theory portrays the state as an umpire or neutral referee in society. The state was not created by a privileged elite, wishing to exploit the masses, but out of an agreement amongst all the people. The state therefore embodies the interests of all its citizens and acts as a neutral arbiter when individuals or groups come into conflict with one another. For example, if individuals break contracts made with others the state applies the 'rules of the game' and enforces the terms of the contract, providing, of course, that each party has acted voluntarily and in full knowledge. The essential characteristic of any such umpire is that its actions are, and are seen to be, impartial, taken in the interests of all, not those of a privileged few. Liberals thus regard the state as a neutral arbiter amongst the competing individuals and groups within society. Some liberals, however, have seen the state as rather more than an umpire prepared to intervene in civil society only when strife or injustice threaten. This is particularly evident in the work of the German philosopher Hegel. In *The Philosophy of Right* (1821), Hegel argued that the state was an ethical idea which embodied the collective aspirations of society. The state was a realm of 'universal altruism', which promoted loyalty and commitment to higher national ideals, in contrast to civil society, which was a realm of individualism and self-interested behaviour. Hegel went as far as to identify the progress of humanity with the development of the modern state, which he referred to as the 'march of God on earth'. Such a belief in the state as a positive good, rather than a necessary evil, has been used to support the ideas of both strong government and interventionist government.

f Constitutional government

Although liberals are convinced of the need for government they are also acutely aware of the dangers which government embodies.

Governments exercise sovereign power and therefore pose a constant threat to individual liberty. All government threatens to become a tyranny against the individual. Early liberalism developed very largely out of a critique of the power of absolute monarchs. In the twentieth century, liberals have been re-alerted to the dangers inherent in government power by the growth of totalitarian dictatorships, especially during the inter-war period.

Liberals have traditionally feared arbitrary government. When political power can be exercised according to the personal whim or prejudice of the ruler it is apt to be despotic or dictatorial. Indeed, liberals have typically believed the experience of political power to be corrupting in itself, encouraging those who possess it to subjugate and exploit those who do not. This was expressed in Lord Acton's famous warning, 'Power tends to corrupt and absolute power corrupts absolutely'. As a result, liberals have sought to establish the principle of limited government. This has traditionally taken the form of a call for 'constitutional government'. A constitution is a set of rules which seek to allocate duties, powers and functions amongst the various institutions of government. It therefore constitutes the rules which govern the government itself. As such, it both defines the extent of government power and limits its exercise.

Constitutional constraints upon government have taken two forms. In the first place, the powers of government bodies and politicians can be limited by the introduction of external and usually legal constraints. For example, all liberal democracies, with the exception of Britain, Israel and New Zealand, possess written constitutions, which codify the major powers and responsibilities of government institutions within a single document. The first such document was the United States Constitution, written in 1787. In many cases, Bills of Rights also exist, which entrench individual rights by providing a legal definition of the relationship between the individual and the state. The first ten amendments of the American Constitution, for example, list individual rights and are collectively called the 'Bill of Rights'. A similar 'Declaration of the Rights of Man' (1789) was adopted during the French Revolution. Where neither written constitutions nor Bills of Rights exist, as in Britain, liberals have stressed the importance of statute law in checking government power through the principle of the rule of law. This was most clearly expressed in nineteenth century Germany in the concept of a Rechtsstaat, a state ruled by law.

Secondly, constitutional government can be established by the introduction of internal constraints, which disperse political power among a number of institutions and create a network of 'checks and balances'. As Montesquieu argued in the eighteenth century, 'power should be a check to power' (p.150). All liberal political systems exhibit some measure of internal fragmentation. This can be achieved by applying the doctrine of the separation of powers, proposed by Montesquieu. This is the belief that the legislative, executive and judicial powers of government should be exercised by three independent institutions, thus preventing any individual or small group from gaining dictatorial power. United States government is, for example, based upon a strict separation of powers between Congress, the Presidency and the Supreme Court. Particular emphasis has also been placed upon the principle of judicial independence. The judiciary interprets the meaning of law, both constitutional and statutory, and therefore reviews the powers of government itself. If the judiciary is going to check the power of the legislature and the executive, it must enjoy formal independence and be politically impartial. A similar division of powers also exists between central and local government in most liberal states. This is achieved most radically by federalism, as exists in America, Canada, Australia, India and Germany, in which each level of government is allocated a range of sovereign powers, defined and guaranteed by the constitution.

Liberal constitutionalism was not, however, without its rivals. A radical democratic tradition emerged during the French Revolution, which drew inspiration from the ideas Jean-Jacques Rousseau had developed in *Social Contract* (1762). Rousseau's conception of the social contract departed significantly from the theories of Hobbes and Locke, which had been based upon a highly pessimistic conception of the 'state of nature'. In Rousseau's view, human beings were essentially innocent, possessed of a capacity for goodness and reason, a notion sometimes represented by the image of the 'noble savage'. Sovereignty therefore could not and should not be surrendered to any kind of government or ruler, it belonged to the people themselves. Popular sovereignty dictated that government be based upon what Rousseau called the 'general will', the collective interests of society, what the people would wish if they were to act selflessly. Rousseau believed that freedom required direct democracy, the direct and continuous participation of all citizens in the affairs of government. As a result, he rejected both the principle of constitutional government and that of representative government.

Nevertheless, the dominant liberal tradition has distanced itself from Rousseau and what it has seen as the dangers of unrestrained democracy. An early critic was Benjamin Constant, an admirer of the British constitutional tradition and author of France's 1830 Constitution. Constant argued that Rousseau had advanced an ancient conception of liberty as collective and direct public participation in government. Such liberty, however, had usually been associated with the sacrifice of personal independence, a fact that had been evident during the revolutionary Terror. In contrast, Constant upheld what he called a modern conception of liberty, defined as 'every man's right to be subject to the law alone'. In so doing, Constant upheld the typically liberal preference for civil liberty, the right to freedom from government, rather than autonomy, the right to participate in the affairs of government. Liberals have often seen themselves as defenders of liberty against the encroachments of democracy. This was clearly reflected in Alexis de Tocqueville's *Democracy in America* (1840). Tocqueville's attitude to democracy was ambivalent. Early volumes of his classic work praised the achievement of America in constructing democratic institutions without degenerating into mob rule. However, in later volumes he warned that democracy posed a threat to individuality, in particular, that public opinion tended to promote uniformity and stagnation, a danger Tocqueville referred to as the 'tyranny of the majority'. The relationship between liberalism and democracy is discussed at greater length in Chapter 10.

3 Classical liberalism

Classical liberalism was the earliest liberal tradition. Classical liberal ideas developed during the transition from feudalism to capitalism, and reached their high point during the early industrialisation of the nineteenth century. As a result, classical liberalism has sometimes been called 'nineteenth century liberalism'. The cradle of classical liberalism was Britain, where the capitalist and industrial revolutions were most advanced. Its ideas have always been more deeply rooted in Anglo-Saxon countries, particularly in Britain and America, than in other parts of the world.

Classical liberal ideas have taken a variety of forms but their common characteristic is a belief in negative freedom. The individual is free in so far as he or she is left alone, not interfered with or coerced by others. Freedom is, as said before, the absence of external constraints upon the individual. Such a conception of liberty creates a very clear distinction between the state and the individual. The state is oppressive, it has the power to punish its citizens, it can take away their property by fines, their liberty through imprisonment and even, at times, their lives by capital punishment. The creation of a state, even through a social contract, inevitably involves the sacrifice of individual liberty: the individual is no longer able to act simply as he or she wishes. Classical liberals therefore see civil society as a 'realm of freedom', while the state is a 'realm of coercion'. The state is at best a necessary evil. It is *necessary* in that, at the very least, it establishes order and security and ensures that contracts are enforced; civil society could not exist in a 'state of nature'. The state is *evil* in the sense that it imposes a collective will upon society and limits the freedom and responsibilities of the individual. Classical liberalism is, therefore, characterised by a belief in a minimal state, which would act merely as a 'night-watchman', whose role is limited to the protection of individuals from each other. All other responsibilities should then be placed in the hands of sovereign individuals.

The wish to restrict, as far as possible, the collective power of government and thereby expand the private responsibilities of the individual had a particular appeal during the nineteenth century. It was thought that the arrival of industrial capitalism had created social conditions which allowed individuals to pursue their own interests and to take responsibility for their own lives. If individuals were largely self-reliant they had little need for the state, except to guarantee basic public order. Classical liberalism, however, is not merely a nineteenth century form of liberalism, whose ideas are now only of historical interest. Its principles and theories have, in fact, exerted growing appeal in the second half of the twentieth century and, once again, its influence has been greatest in Britain and America. The contemporary revival of classical liberalism has, to a large extent, occurred as a reaction against growing state involvement in economic and social life, a development which has characterised government in the twentieth century, and especially since 1945.

a Natural rights

The natural rights theorists of the seventeenth and eighteenth centuries, such as John Locke in England and Thomas Jefferson in America, have had considerable influence upon liberal ideology. Modern political debate is littered with references to 'rights' and claims to possess 'rights'. A bewildering range of rights have been claimed by individuals, described variously as 'natural' rights, 'human' rights, 'civil' rights, 'political' rights and so on. The rights claimed range from freedom of speech and religious worship, to the right to work or to receive free medical treatment. In 1948 the United Nations established a Universal Declaration of Human Rights and a European Convention on Human Rights was introduced in 1953. Rights have also been claimed by groups of peoples, as in the idea of 'trade union rights' or 'the right of national self-determination'. Moreover, rights have, more recently, been claimed to exist for non-humans, for example, 'animal rights', and in environmental theory, 'vegetable rights' or 'the rights of the planet'.

A right is a claim that someone or something is entitled to act or be treated in a particular way. For Locke and Jefferson, rights were natural, in that they were invested in human beings by nature, or by God. Natural rights are what are now more commonly called human rights. They are, in Jefferson's words 'inalienable', because human beings are entitled to them by virtue of being human: they cannot, in that sense, be taken away. Natural rights are thus thought to be the essential conditions for leading a truly human existence. For Locke there were three such rights, 'life, liberty and property'. Jefferson did not accept that property was a natural or God-given right, but rather one that had developed for human convenience. In the American Declaration of Independence, he therefore described inalienable rights as those of 'life, liberty and the pursuit of happiness'.

The idea of natural or human rights has had considerable impact upon liberal political thought. The weight given to such rights, for example, distinguishes an authoritarian thinker, like Thomas Hobbes, from an early liberal, like John Locke. As explained earlier, both writers believed that government was formed through a 'social contract'. However, in *Leviathan* (1631), written at the time of the English Civil War, Hobbes argued that only a strong government, preferably a monarchy, would be able to establish order and security in society. He was prepared to invest the king with sovereign or absolute power, rather than risk a descent into a 'state of nature'. The citizen should therefore accept any form of government because even repressive government was better than no government at all. Hobbes, therefore, placed the need for order above the desire for liberty. Locke, on the other hand, argued against arbitrary or unlimited government. Government was established in order to protect the three basic rights of 'life, liberty and property'. When these were protected by the state, citizens should respect government and obey the law. However, if government violated the rights of its citizens, they, in turn, had the right of rebellion. Unlike Hobbes, Locke approved of the English Revolution of the seventeenth century and applauded the establishment of a constitutional monarchy in 1688. In later centuries, liberals have often used the idea of individual rights to justify popular revolt against government tyranny.

For Locke, moreover, the contract between state and citizens was a specific and limited one; its purpose was to protect a set of defined natural rights. As a result, Locke believed in limited government: he conceived the legitimate role of government to be one limited to the protection of 'life, liberty and property'. The functions of governments should not, therefore, extend beyond the 'minimal' functions of preserving public order and protecting property. Other issues and responsibilities were properly the concern of private individuals. Thomas Jefferson expressed the same sentiment a century later in arguing, 'That government is best which governs least'.

b Utilitarianism

Natural rights theories were not the only basis of early liberalism. An alternative and highly influential theory of human nature was put forward in the early nineteenth century by the utilitarians, notably Jeremy Bentham and James Mill. Bentham regarded the idea of rights as 'nonsense' and called natural rights 'nonsense on stilts'. In their place, he proposed what he believed to be the more scientific and objective idea that individuals were motivated by self-interest and that these interests could be defined as the desire for pleasure, or happiness, and the wish to avoid pain. Bentham and Mill argued that individuals calculated the quantities of pleasure and pain which each possible action would generate, and chose whichever course promised the greatest amount of pleasure over the pain. Utilitarian thinkers believed that it was possible to quantify happiness and pain in terms of utility, taking into account their intensity, duration and so forth. Human beings were thought, therefore, to be utility maximisers, seeking the greatest possible pleasure and the least possible pain or unhappiness.

The principle of utility is, furthermore, a moral principle, in that it suggests that the 'rightness' of an action, decision or even government policy can be established by its tendency to promote happiness. Just as each individual could calculate what was morally good by the quantity of pleasure an action produced, so the principle of 'the greatest happiness for the greatest number' could be used to establish which policies would benefit society at large. In the early nineteenth century in Britain, a group of thinkers and writers gathered around Bentham, called the Philosophic Radicals, who proposed a range of social, political and legal reforms on the basis of this notion of general utility.

Utilitarian ideas have had considerable impact upon liberalism. They have, in particular, provided a moral philosophy which explains how and why individuals act as they do. The utilitarian conception of human beings as rationally self-interested creatures has been adopted by later generations of liberal thinkers. Furthermore, each individual was thought to be able to perceive his or her own interests. This could not be done on their behalf by some paternal authority, for instance, the state. Bentham argued that individuals acted so as to gain pleasure or happiness in whatever way they might choose. No one else could judge the quality or degree of their happiness. If each individual was the sole judge of what would give him or her pleasure, then the individual alone could determine what was morally right.

On the other hand, utilitarian ideas could also be illiberal. Bentham held that the principle of utility could be applied to society at large and not merely to individual human behaviour. Institutions and legislation could be judged by the yardstick of 'the greatest happiness'. However, this formula has majoritarian implications because it uses the happiness of 'the greatest number' as a standard of what is morally correct, and therefore allows the interests of the majority to outweigh those of the minority. Liberals, in contrast, believe that each and every individual should be entitled to pursue his or her own interests, not just those who happen to be in the

majority. Typically they have feared that unrestrained majority rule
will become a tyranny against both the minority and the individual.

c Economic liberalism

(i) Free market

The late eighteenth and early nineteenth centuries witnessed the
development of classical economic theory in the work of political
economists, such as Adam Smith and David Ricardo. Smith's *The
Wealth of Nations* (1776) was, in many respects, the first economics
text book. His ideas drew heavily upon liberal and rationalist
assumptions about human nature and made a powerful contribution
to the debate about the desirable role of government within civil
society. As with many other aspects of early liberalism, classical
political economics developed first in Britain, and its ideas have
been embraced with greatest enthusiasm in Britain and in America.

Adam Smith wrote at a time of wide-ranging government restrictions upon economic activity. Mercantilism, the dominant economic
idea of the sixteenth and seventeenth centuries, had encouraged
governments to intervene in economic life in an attempt to encourage
the export of goods and in the hope of restricting imports. Smith's
economic writings were designed to attack mercantilism and to
argue for the principle that the economy worked best when left alone
by government.

Smith thought of the economy as a market, indeed as a series of
inter-related markets. He believed that the market operated according to the wishes and decisions of free individuals. Freedom within
the market meant freedom of choice, the ability of the businessman
to choose what goods to make, the ability of the worker to choose an
employer, and the ability of the consumer to choose what goods or
services to buy. Relationships within such a market, between
employers and employees, between buyers and sellers, were therefore voluntary and contractual. Indeed, classical economists assumed
that individuals were materially self-interested, motivated by the
desire to gain pleasure or happiness by acquiring and consuming
wealth. Economic theory is largely based upon the idea of 'Economic
Man', the notion of human beings as utility maximisers, bent upon
material acquisition.

The attraction of classical economics was that, although each individual was materially self-interested, the economy itself was thought to operate according to a set of impersonal pressures – market forces – which tended naturally to promote economic prosperity and wellbeing. For example, no single producer could set the price of a commodity, prices were set by the market, by the number of goods offered for sale and the number which consumers were willing to buy. These are the forces of supply and demand. The market is a self-regulating mechanism, it needs no guidance from outside. The market should be 'free' from government interference because it is managed by what Adam Smith referred to as 'an invisible hand'. This idea of a self-regulating market reflects a liberal belief in a naturally existing harmony amongst the conflicting interests within society. Employers, workers and consumers all act in their own best interests, but market forces ensure that these interests are compatible: businessmen, for example, can only make profits by producing what the consumer is willing to buy.

The 'invisible hand' has been used by later economists to explain how economic problems like unemployment, inflation or balance of payments deficits can be removed by the mechanisms of the market itself. Unemployment, for instance, occurs when there are more people prepared to work than there are jobs available: in other words, the supply of labour exceeds the demand for it. As a result, market forces will push down the 'price' of labour, wages. As wages fall, employers will be able to recruit more workers and unemployment will drop. Market forces can therefore eradicate unemployment without the need for government interference, providing wage levels, like other prices, are flexible. A free market will also lead to economic efficiency. Each firm is disciplined by the profit motive, which forces producers to keep their costs low. Waste and inefficiency cannot be tolerated. On the other hand, the possibility of excessively high profits is prevented by competition. If profits are unusually high in a particular industry, this will simply encourage other producers to enter the industry, thereby expanding output and bringing down both prices and profit levels. Economic resources will be attracted to their most profitable use, which means that they will be attracted to growing industries and away from declining ones. The market is also responsive because it is constantly driven by the desires of the consumer. The consumer is, in theory, sovereign: to remain profitable firms are forced to identify the consumers' needs and wishes, and to satisfy them. Market forces therefore will naturally tend to promote a vigorous and efficient economy which responds automatically to any change in consumer demand.

Free market ideas became economic orthodoxy in Britain and America during the nineteenth century. The high point of free market beliefs was reached with the doctrine of *laissez-faire*, literally meaning 'to leave to be'. This is the idea that the state should have no economic role, but should simply leave the economy alone and allow businessmen to act however they may please. *Laissez-faire* ideas opposed all forms of factory legislation, including restrictions upon the employment of children, limits to the number of hours worked, and any regulation of working conditions. Such economic individualism was usually based upon a belief that the unrestrained pursuit of profit would ultimately lead to general benefit. *Laissez-faire* ideas remained strong in Britain through much of the nineteenth century and in America were not seriously challenged until the 1930s. In the late twentieth century, faith in the free market was revived by the Reagan administration in the United States and the Thatcher government in Britain. Both governments expected to promote efficiency and growth by releasing the 'dead hand' of government from the economy and allowing the natural vigour of the market mechanism to reassert itself. In Britain, for instance, this meant a radical policy of privatisation, selling off nationalised industries into private hands in the belief that they would thereby become more efficient and more accountable to the consumer. Such ideas are examined at greater length in relation to the New Right in Chapter 3.

(ii) Free trade

The early liberal belief in a free market was applied not only to national economies, but also to the relationship among countries. This led to the idea of free trade, the notion that trade amongst nations should be free from government interference in the form of tariffs upon imported goods, quotas imposed on the number allowed in, or subsidies which might give one country's goods an unfair advantage against another's. This idea also gained early support in Britain. It was advocated by Richard Cobden and John Bright, leaders of the Anti-Corn Law League, who campaigned during the 1840s against tariffs on corn imported into Britain. The League itself was supported by manufacturers in the Manchester area who hoped for a reciprocal reduction in continental tariffs against British manufactured goods. As a result, the ideas of Cobden and Bright are sometimes referred to as 'Manchester liberalism'. Their justification for free trade was both economic and political. The economic argument proposed by Cobden and Bright was founded upon David Ricardo's belief that free trade would promote trade between nations, leading to mutual benefit as the countries involved would be able to specialise in the production of those goods or services which they were best suited to produce in the light of their climate, natural resources, population, skills and so forth. Economists have called this idea the theory of comparative advantage.

From Cobden's point of view, however, more important were the political advantages of free trade. Economic interdependence brought about by trade would make the possibility of international conflict and war increasingly remote. Indeed, it would promote cosmopolitanism, greater understanding and harmony amongst the peoples of the world. Free trade, according to Cobden, was the 'principle of gravitation in the universe', it would draw people of different races, creeds and languages together in 'the bonds of eternal peace'. Once again, this notion of political and economic harmony, this time at the international level, was based upon a belief in a natural balance or equilibrium in human affairs.

With the repeal of the Corn Laws in 1846, the principle of free trade triumphed in Britain and was subsequently adopted in America and throughout much of continental Europe. Its attraction, though, weakened during times of international depression, such as the late nineteenth century and the Great Depression of the 1930s, periods which stimulated the growth of protectionism. In the aftermath of the Second World War, the international economic order was reorganised by the victorious nations according to the principle of free trade. The General Agreement on Tariffs and Trade (GATT) was set up in 1946 to negotiate the removal or reduction of tariff barriers and prevent a return to protectionism. Liberals argue that the resulting growth in international trade since 1945 has been an important factor in securing widespread prosperity and international harmony in the post-war period. In the past, protectionism and the emergence of economic nationalism had led to international tension, conflict and also war. Liberals point out that both the First and the Second World Wars were proceeded by the collapse of international trade and a widespread adoption of protectionist measures. Free trade is not, however, without its critics, who have claimed that in some respects it merely reflects the economic interests of whichever country is dominant in the world economy. It is a policy which encourages weaker countries to open their markets to the goods of stronger countries. This may help to explain why Britain was the principal proponent of free trade in the nineteenth century, while America became its strongest supporter in the twentieth century.

d Social Darwinism

One of the distinctive features of classical liberalism is its attitude to poverty and social equality. An individualistic political creed will tend to explain social circumstances in terms of the talents and hard work of each individual human being. Individuals make what they want, and what they can, of their own lives. The free market, in allowing all individuals to pursue their own interests, is therefore a guarantee of social justice. Those with ability and a willingness to work will prosper, while the incompetent or the lazy will not. This idea was memorably expressed in 1859 in the title of Samuel Smiles' book *Self-Help*, which begins by reiterating the well-tried maxim that 'Heaven helps those who help themselves'. Such ideas of individual responsibility were widely employed by supporters of *laissez-faire* in the nineteenth century. Richard Cobden, for example, advocated an improvement of the conditions of the working classes, but argued that it should come about through 'their own efforts and self-reliance, rather than from law'. He advised them, 'look not to Parliament, look only to yourselves' (p.297).

Ideas of individual self-reliance reached their boldest expression in Herbert Spencer's *The Man Versus The State* (1884). Spencer developed a vigorous defence of the doctrine of *laissez-faire*, which drew upon ideas the British scientist, Charles Darwin, had developed in *On the Origin of Species* (1859). Darwin had tried to explain the diversity of species found on earth according to a theory of evolution. He proposed that each species underwent a series of random physical and mental changes, or mutations. Some of these changes fitted a species to survive and prosper: they were pro-survival. Other mutations were less favourable and made survival more difficult or even impossible. A wide range of living species had therefore developed on earth, while many other species had become extinct. A process of 'natural selection' decided which species were fitted to survive by nature, and which were not. Although Darwin himself applied these ideas only to the natural world, they were soon employed in constructing social and political theories as well. Spencer, for example, argued that a process of natural selection also existed within human society, which was characterised by the principle of 'the survival of the fittest'. Society was portrayed as a struggle for survival amongst individuals. Those who were best suited by nature to survive rose to the top, while those less well fitted fell to the bottom. Inequalities of wealth, social position and political power, therefore, were natural and inevitable, and no attempt should be made by government to interfere with them. Indeed, any attempt to support or help the poor, unemployed or disadvantaged was an affront to nature itself. Spencer's American disciple, William Sumner, stated this principle boldly in 1884 when he asserted that 'the drunkard in the gutter was just where he ought to be' (p.117).

Social Darwinian liberalism stands in stark contrast to the idea of social welfare. If the state provides pensions, benefits, free education and free health care, the individual is encouraged to be lazy and is deprived of self-respect. If, however, people are encouraged to 'stand on their own two feet', they enjoy dignity and become productive members of society. Such ideas have not been restricted to the nineteenth century but have also influenced New Right thinking in the late twentieth century. The Reagan administration sought to promote a 'frontier ideology', which emphasised self-reliance and enterprise, while the Thatcher government in Britain attacked the 'dependency culture' which it believed the welfare state had encouraged, and tried to foster in its place an American-style 'enterprise culture'.

4 Modern liberalism

Modern liberalism is sometimes described as 'twentieth century liberalism'. Just as the development of classical liberalism was closely linked to the emergence of industrial capitalism in the nineteenth century, so modern liberal ideas were related to the further development of industrialisation. Industrialisation had brought about a massive expansion of wealth for some, but was also accompanied by the spread of slums, poverty, ignorance and disease. Moreover, social inequality became more difficult to ignore as a growing industrial working class was seen to be disadvantaged by low pay, unemployment and degrading living and working conditions. These developments had an impact on British liberalism from the late nineteenth century onwards, but in other countries not until much later; for example, American liberalism was not affected until the depression of the 1930s. In these changing historical circumstances, liberals found it progressively more difficult to maintain the belief that the arrival of industrial capitalism had brought with it general prosperity and liberty for all. Consequently, many came to revise the early liberal expectation that the unrestrained pursuit of self-interest produced a socially just society. As the idea of economic individualism came increasingly under attack, liberals re-thought their attitude towards the state. The minimal state of classical theory was quite incapable of rectifying the injustices and inequalities of civil society. Consequently modern liberals have been prepared to advocate the development of an interventionist state.

a John Stuart Mill

The ideas of the British philosopher and politician, John Stuart Mill, have been described as 'the heart of liberalism'. He provided a 'bridge' between classical and modern liberalism: his ideas both look backwards to the early nineteenth century and forward to the twentieth century. Mill's interests ranged from political economy to the campaign for female suffrage, but it was the ideas developed in *On Liberty* which most clearly show Mill as a contributor to modern liberal thought. This work contains some of the boldest liberal statements in favour of individual freedom. Mill suggested that, 'Over himself, over his own body and mind, the individual is sovereign'(p.73), a conception of liberty which is essentially 'negative', for it portrays freedom as the absence of all restrictions upon an individual's 'self-regarding' actions. Mill believed this to be a necessary condition for liberty, but not in itself a sufficient one. He thought that liberty was a positive and constructive force. It gave individuals the ability to take control of their own lives, to gain autonomy or achieve self-realisation.

Mill was strongly influenced by European romanticism and

found the notion of human beings as utility maximisers both shallow and unconvincing. He believed passionately in individuality, the distinctiveness, even uniqueness, of each individual human being. The value of liberty was that it enabled individuals to develop, to gain talents, skills and knowledge and to refine their sensibilities. Mill disagreed with Bentham's utilitarianism in so far as Bentham believed that actions could only be distinguished by the quantity of pleasure or pain they generated. For Mill there were 'higher' and 'lower' pleasures. Mill was concerned to promote those pleasures which developed an individual's intellectual, moral or aesthetic sensibilities. He was clearly not concerned with simple pleasure-seeking, but with personal self-development, and declared that he would rather be 'Socrates dissatisfied than a fool satisfied'. As such, he laid the foundation for a positive theory of liberty. Nevertheless, Mill did not draw the conclusion that the state should step in and guide individuals towards personal growth and 'higher pleasures' because, like Tocqueville, he feared the spread of conformism in society. For example, although he encouraged the spread of education as perhaps the best way in which individuals could gain fulfilment, he feared that state education would simply mean that everyone shared the same views and beliefs.

b Positive freedom

The clearest break with early liberal thought came in the late nineteenth century with the work of T.H. Green. Green believed that the unrestrained pursuit of profit, advocated by classical liberalism, had given rise to new forms of poverty and injustice. The economic liberty of the few had blighted the life chances of the many. Following J.S. Mill, he rejected the early liberal conception of human beings as essentially self-seeking utility maximisers, and suggested a more optimistic view of human nature. Individuals, according to Green, had sympathy for one another; they were capable of being altruistic. The individual possessed social responsibilities and not merely individual responsibilities, and was therefore linked to other individuals by ties of caring and empathy. Such a conception of human nature was clearly influenced by socialist ideas which emphasised the sociable and co-operative nature of humankind. Green's ideas, as a result, have been described as 'socialist liberalism'.

Green also challenged the classical liberal notion of liberty. Negative liberty merely removed external constraints upon the individual, giving the individual freedom of choice. In the case of the businessman who wished to maximise profits, negative freedom would justify his ability to hire the cheapest labour possible, for example, to employ children rather than adults, or women rather than men. Economic freedom could therefore lead to exploitation. Green argued that contracts of work were not made by free or equal individuals. Workers were sometimes coerced into accepting employment because poverty and starvation was the only alternative, while employers usually had the luxury of choosing from amongst a number of workers. Freedom of choice in the market place was, therefore, an inadequate conception of individual freedom.

In the place of negative freedom, Green proposed the idea of positive freedom. Freedom was the ability of the individual to develop and attain individuality, it involved the ability of the individual to realise his or her potential, attain skills and knowledge and achieve fulfilment. Unrestrained capitalism did not give each individual the same opportunities for self-realisation. The working class, for example, were held back by the disadvantages of poverty, sickness, unemployment and ignorance. Negative freedom had merely given individuals 'freedom to' think and act as they pleased, while positive freedom involved gaining 'freedom from' the social evils which crippled people's lives. Such a notion of positive freedom has had an important place in twentieth century liberal thought. When, in the Atlantic Charter of 1941, Franklin Roosevelt and Winston Churchill described the 'four freedoms' for which they fought the Second World War, they included 'freedom from fear' and 'freedom from want'. The Beveridge Report of 1942, the foundation of the welfare state in Britain, also advocated positive freedoms, this time from the 'five giants' of 'want, disease, ignorance, squalor and idleness'.

If market society did not provide individuals with equal opportunities to grow and develop, modern liberals argued that this could only be achieved through collective action, undertaken by government. Influenced by Hegel, Green believed that the state was invested with social responsibility for its citizens; it was seen not merely as a threat to individual liberty, but, in a sense, as its guarantor. Unlike early liberals, modern liberals have been prepared to view the state positively as an enabling state, exercising an increasingly wide range of social and economic responsibilities.

Although this clearly involved a revision of classical liberal ideas, it did not amount to the abandonment of basic liberal thinking. Modern liberalism has drawn closer to socialism, but has not placed society before the individual. For T.H. Green, for example, freedom ultimately consisted in individuals acting morally. The state could not force people to be good, it could only provide conditions in which they could make more responsible moral decisions. The balance between the state and the individual had been altered, but an underlying commitment to the needs and interests of the individual remained. What had changed was the way in which liberals believed individual liberty could best be achieved.

c Welfarism

The twentieth century has witnessed a growth in state intervention in most Western countries and also in some developing ones. Much of this intervention has taken the form of social welfare, attempts by government to provide welfare support for its citizens by overcoming poverty, disease and ignorance. If the minimal state was typical of the nineteenth century, the modern state has become, in the late twentieth century, a welfare state. This has occurred as a consequence of a variety of historical and ideological factors. Governments have, for example, sought to achieve national efficiency, more healthy work forces and stronger armies. They have also come under electoral pressure for social reform from newly enfranchised industrial workers and in some cases the rural peasantry. The political argument for welfarism has not been the prerogative of any single ideology. It has been put, in different ways, by socialists, liberals, conservatives and even, at times, by fascists. Within liberalism the case for social welfare has been made by modern liberals, in marked contrast to classical liberals, who had extolled the virtues of 'self-help' and individual responsibility.

Modern liberals have argued in favour of welfarism on the basis of equality of opportunity. If particular individuals or groups are disadvantaged by their social circumstances, then the state possesses a social responsibility to reduce or remove these disadvantages. This responsibility was reflected in the development of the welfare state. Such an expansion of the responsibilities of government has not, however, diminished individual rights, but rather broadened them. Citizens have acquired welfare rights and social and economic rights such as the right to work, the right to an education, the right to decent housing. Classical liberals believe that the only rights which the citizen is entitled to are negative rights, those that depend upon the restraint of government power. This applies to most of the traditional civil liberties respected by liberals, such as freedom of speech, religious worship and assembly. These rights constitute a 'private sphere', which should be untouched by government. Welfare rights, however, are positive rights because they can only be satisfied by the positive actions of government, through the provision of state pensions, benefits and, perhaps, publicly funded health and education services.

During the twentieth century, liberal parties and liberal governments have usually championed the cause of social welfare. The foundations of the welfare state in Britain were laid before the First World War by the Asquith Liberal government, which introduced old age pensions and a limited system of health and unemployment insurance. The Liberal Party, now the Liberal Democrats, has remained a modern liberal party in its continuing commitment to the principles of social welfare. When the welfare state in Britain was expanded after the Second World War by the Attlee Labour government, it was according to the Beveridge Report (1942), a blueprint provided by a modern liberal, William Beveridge. This promised to create a comprehensive system of social security which would cover all citizens 'from the cradle to the grave'. The Liberal Party of Canada has similarly campaigned for the adoption of universal welfare policies against the Progressive Conservative Party which advocates individual responsibility and free enterprise.

In the United States, liberal welfarism developed in the 1930s during the administration of F.D. Roosevelt. Ideas of economic individualism and self-help remained dominant well into the twentieth century, but under Roosevelt's 'New Deal' systems of public relief were introduced for the unemployed, the old, children, widows and the blind. New Deal liberalism survived the death of

Roosevelt in 1945, and reached its height in the 1960s, with the 'New Frontier' policies of John Kennedy, and Lyndon Johnson's 'Great Society' programme. The latter concentrated on improving the civil rights of American blacks and countering poverty and squalor in American cities. The idea of positive discrimination, called 'affirmative action' in America, in which individuals and groups are entitled to special considerations to compensate for social disadvantage, has also developed out of a liberal commitment to equal opportunities. In America, for example, the principle has been widely employed since the 1960s to broaden social opportunities for blacks in the light of their low income levels, high rates of unemployment and poor housing. Black students are often able to gain access to higher education in America with lower qualifications than their white counterparts. The principle of positive discrimination need not, of course, only apply to racial disadvantage: it could equally well be employed to compensate for social disadvantages that arise as a result of gender, age or physical disability.

d Keynesianism

In addition to providing social welfare, Western governments have also sought in the twentieth century to deliver prosperity by 'managing' their economies. This has, once again, involved a rejection of classical liberal thinking, in particular its belief in a self-regulating free market and the doctrine of *laissez-faire*. The abandonment of *laissez-faire* came about because of the increasing complexity of industrial capitalist economies and their apparent inability to guarantee general prosperity if left to their own devices. The Great Depression of the 1930s, sparked off by the Wall Street Crash of 1929, led to high levels of unemployment throughout the industrialised world and in much of the developing world. This was the most dramatic demonstration of the failure of the free market. After the Second World War, virtually all Western countries adopted policies of economic intervention in an attempt to prevent a return to pre-war levels of unemployment.

To a large extent, these interventionist policies were guided by the work of the British economist and modern liberal, John Maynard Keynes. In *The General Theory of Employment, Interest and Money* (1936), Keynes challenged classical economic thinking and rejected its belief in a self-regulating market. Classical economists had argued that there was a 'market solution' to the problem of unemployment and indeed all other economic problems. Unemployment would fall if wages were allowed to drop, it would only persist if, because of trade union pressure, wage levels became inflexible. Workers, according to this view, had literally 'priced themselves out of jobs'. Keynes argued, however, that the level of economic activity, and therefore employment, was determined by the total amount of demand – aggregate demand – in the economy. He suggested that if wage levels were cut, purchasing power within the economy would fall and with it aggregate demand. If people had less money in their pockets to spend, firms would produce fewer goods, with the result that unemployment would continue to rise. A free market could consequently spiral downwards into depression and be incapable of reviving itself, which is what Keynes believed had occurred in the 1930s. Unlike previous trade cycles, the Great Depression did not end with a 'natural' up-turn in economic fortunes. Although unemployment peaked in the early 1930s, leading in most countries to a gradual recovery, there was no speedy return to the prosperity of the 1920s.

Keynes suggested that governments could 'manage' their economies through influencing the level of aggregate demand. Government spending was, in effect, an 'injection' of demand into the economy. In building a school, government created employment for construction workers and demand for building materials, the effects of which would ripple throughout the economy, as construction workers, for example, had the money to buy more goods. This is what Keynes called the 'multiplier effect'. Taxation, on the other hand, was a 'withdrawal' from the economy, it reduced aggregate demand and dampened down economic activity. At times of high unemployment, Keynes recommended that government should 'reflate' the economy either by increasing public spending or by cutting taxes. Unemployment could therefore be solved, not by the invisible hand of capitalism, but by government intervention, in this case by running a budget deficit, meaning that government literally 'overspends'. Keynesian demand management thus promised to give governments the ability to manipulate employment and growth levels and so to secure general prosperity.

As with the provision of social welfare, modern liberals have seen economic management as constructive in restoring the prosperity and harmony of civil society. Keynes was not opposed to capitalism; indeed, in many ways he was its saviour. He simply argued that *unrestrained* private enterprise was unworkable within complex industrial societies. The first, if limited, attempt to apply Keynes's ideas was undertaken in America during Roosevelt's 'New Deal'. However, Roosevelt's commitment to a balanced budget and his consequent refusal to allow increased government spending on public works projects to exceed taxation revenues, resulted in only a very gradual decline in unemployment. The Great Depression was, in fact, brought to an end by a widespread and substantial expansion of government expenditure in the form of increased military spending in preparation for war, rather than a deliberate attempt to cure unemployment. This was most evident in Germany where unemployment was halved within eighteen months of Hitler's appointment as Chancellor in 1933. The unemployment of the inter-war period was therefore cured by inadvertent Keynesianism. However, by the end of the Second World War, Keynesian ideas were widely established as an economic orthodoxy in the West, displacing the older belief in *laissez-faire*. Virtually all countries employed the idea of economic management in carrying out post-war economic reconstruction and planning for growth in the future. Keynesianism was credited with being the key to the 'long boom', the historically unprecedented economic growth of the 1950s and 1960s, which witnessed the achievement of widespread affluence, at least in Western countries. During this period Keynesian ideas stood triumphant, drawing support from conservative and socialist parties as well as liberal ones. Keynesianism remained largely unchallenged in the industrialised West until the re-emergence of economic difficulties in the 1970s, which generated renewed sympathy for the theories of classical political economy.

5 Liberalism triumphant?

There is little doubt that liberal ideas and values have triumphed in the industrialised West, in the so called 'First World' – Europe, North America, Australasia and so on. During the nineteenth century, these countries accepted the ideas of limited and representative government and developed modern capitalist economies. However, Francis Fukuyama has argued that liberal democracy now stands on the verge of a worldwide triumph, that its values and beliefs are on the point of triumph in both the communist 'Second World' – the Soviet Union, Eastern Europe and China – and the developing 'Third World' – Africa, Asia and South America. Fukuyama has heralded this process as the 'end of history'. Dramatic changes have undoubtedly taken place and nowhere have they been more remarkable than in Eastern Europe, where a wave of popular uprisings led to the collapse of single party Communist rule in country after country in 1989–90. The Soviet Union, the world's first communist regime and in many ways the model for all other communist states, has undergone a process of sweeping reform since the appointment of Mikhail Gorbachev as Soviet leader in 1985. Reforms have also taken place elsewhere, for example, in South Africa where the dismantling of apartheid led to the release of political prisoners, including Nelson Mandela in 1990, the unbanning of the African National Congress, and the removal of much racialist legislation from the statute book.

Many of these reforms have a clear liberal character, encouraging Fukuyama in his belief that liberal democracy is about to become the dominant ideology throughout the world. This is most evident in former-communist countries where political reform has seen the introduction of civil liberties and competitive party systems, and economic reform has meant the replacement of central planning by private enterprise and the market. A belief in liberalism's ultimate triumph is based upon the assumption that as societies mature and develop they will almost naturally undergo a process of 'liberalisation'. In political life, a more sophisticated and better-educated population will demand freedom of expression and the right to participate in a competitive political system. In economic life, an industrialised society is simply too complex for government or any central body to regulate or control, and must therefore be left to the 'invisible hand' of market forces. In many ways, therefore, Fukuyama's thesis is based upon a long-established liberal belief in progress and an optimistic faith in the superiority of liberal values and theories.

However, liberal triumphalism should be tempered by the emergence of very different political forces. In much of the Third World, socialist and nationalist ideas have remained firmly entrenched, supported by political cultures and traditions which emphasise the importance of the social group rather than the self-seeking individual. Where political change has occurred, it has not always involved a process of 'liberalisation'. Religious fundamentalism has become an increasingly potent force in world politics, especially in North Africa and Asia. The Islamic idea of a 'theocratic state' and a return to traditional religious values contrasts starkly with the liberal conception of individual freedom and its view of politics as a secular and rational activity. In the Soviet Union and Eastern Europe, the 'death of communism' has released older and darker political forces, notably national chauvinism and racialism, suggesting that a smooth and peaceful transition to liberal democracy is by no means inevitable. Moreover, even when the ideas of Western liberalism have been adopted in the Second or Third Worlds, it is far from certain what kind of ideas, indeed what kind of liberalism, is being embraced.

It is difficult to proclaim the imminent worldwide triumph of liberalism when the inheritance liberalism offers the world is unclear, if not contradictory. For example, were the revolutions in Eastern Europe in 1989 an expression of the desire for free market capitalism, individual responsibility and self-help, or were they a demand for economic and social security to be delivered through a managed economy and a welfare state? The irony of the claim that liberalism has triumphed is that in the late twentieth century tension between the ideas of classical and modern liberalism has resurfaced with increasing intensity. Until the 1970s, modern liberal ideas such as welfarism and Keynesianism were dominant, while enthusiasm for the free market was thought to be merely 'nineteenth century liberalism'. Indeed, these modern liberal beliefs amounted to a dominant ideology in many Western countries and commanded support from socialists and conservatives as well as liberals. However, in the final quarter of the twentieth century, there has been a significant revival of interest in classical liberalism, sometimes termed neo-liberalism. This was evident first amongst a relatively small group of intellectuals, such as Friedrich Hayek whose *The Road to Serfdom* was published in 1944 and the American economist, Milton Friedman, author of *Capitalism and Freedom* (1962) and *Free To Choose* (1980). These ideas were taken up by political parties of the New Right, notably by the Conservative Party in Britain under the leadership of Margaret Thatcher and the Republican Party in America during the Reagan administration.

The revival of classical liberalism occurred as a reaction against the onset of a world recession in the 1970s. Keynesian and welfare policies had been underwritten in the 1950s and 1960s by the 'long boom' of the post-war period and the rising living standards it delivered. When economic growth faltered, economic and social orthodoxies were questioned and, in Britain and America at least, overthrown in favour of a renewed faith in the free market and the values of individual responsibility. The ideas of the New Right and policies of the Thatcher and Reagan administrations will be examined in more detail in the next chapter. Nevertheless, the contemporary revival of interest in classical liberalism has created the spectre of an ideology divided against itself, whose heirs include both social democrats and right-wing conservatives. The precise inheritance of liberalism is therefore an issue of fierce political controversy.

3
Conservatism

1 Introduction

In ordinary language, the term 'conservative' has a variety of meanings. It can refer to moderate or cautious behaviour, a life style that is conventional, even conformist, or a fear of, or refusal to, change. 'Conservatism' was first used to describe a distinctive political ideology in the early nineteenth century. Its ideas arose in reaction to the growing pace of political and economic change which, in many ways, had commenced with the French Revolution in 1789. One of the earliest, and in many ways the classic, statement of conservative principles is contained in Edmund Burke's *Reflections on the Revolution in France* (1790), which deeply regretted the revolutionary challenge to the *ancien régime* that had occurred the previous year. During the nineteenth century, Western countries were transformed by pressures unleashed by industrialisation and reflected in the growth of liberalism, socialism and nationalism. While these ideologies preached reform and, at times, supported revolution, conservatism stood in defence of an increasingly embattled traditional social order.

Such origins have had deep impact upon the character of conservative ideology. There is, for example, some truth in the belief that conservatives have a clearer understanding of what they oppose than what they favour. In that sense, conservatism has been thought of as a negative philosophy, simply preaching resistance to, or at least wary suspicion of, change. However, if conservatism consists of no more than a knee-jerk defence of the status quo, it would be merely a political attitude rather than an ideology. In fact, many people or groups can be considered 'conservative' in the sense that they resist change, but certainly cannot be said to subscribe to a

53

conservative political creed. For example, Stalinists in the Soviet Union, who opposed Gorbachev's programme of political and economic reform, and the British Labour Party, which has campaigned for the preservation of the welfare state, are both 'conservative' in their actions, but certainly not conservative in terms of their political principles. The desire to resist change may be a recurrent theme within conservatism, but what distinguishes a conservative from those who hold rival political beliefs is the distinctive arguments and values which they employ in upholding this objective.

To describe conservatism as an ideology, however, is also to run the risk of irritating conservatives themselves. They have often preferred to describe their beliefs as an 'attitude of mind' or an 'approach to life', as opposed to an '-ism' or ideology. Lord Hugh Cecil, for example, described conservatism 'a natural disposition of the human mind' (p.8). Conservatives have typically been suspicious of abstract ideas and doctrinaire thought. Their opponents have also lighted upon this feature of conservatism, sometimes portraying it as little more than an unprincipled apology for the interests of a ruling class or elite. Both conservatives and their critics, however, ignore the weight and range of theories which underpin conservative 'common sense'. For example, conservatives may prefer to base their thinking upon experience and reality rather than abstract principles, but this preference itself is based upon specific beliefs, in this case about the limited rational capacities of human beings. Conservatism is neither simple pragmatism, nor mere opportunism. It is based upon a particular set of political beliefs about human beings, the societies they live in, and the importance of a distinctive set of political values. As such, like liberalism and socialism, it can rightfully be described as an ideology.

Conservative thought has varied considerably as it has adapted itself to existing traditions and national cultures. British conservatism, for instance, has drawn heavily upon the ideas of Burke, who advocated not blind resistance to change, but rather a prudent willingness to 'change in order to conserve'. In the nineteenth century, British conservatives defended a political and social order that had already undergone profound change, in particular the overthrow of the absolute monarchy, which had occurred in the English Revolution of the seventeenth century. Such pragmatic principles have also influenced the Conservative parties established in other Commonwealth countries. The Canadian Conservative Party adopted the title Progressive Conservative precisely to distance itself from reactionary ideas.

In continental Europe, where autocratic monarchies persisted, in some cases, well into the nineteenth century, a very different and more authoritarian form of conservatism developed, which defended monarchy and rigid autocratic values against the rising tide of reform. Only with the formation of Christian Democratic parties after the Second World War have continental conservatives, notably in Germany and Italy, fully accepted political democracy and social reform. The United States, on the other hand, has been relatively little influenced by conservative ideas. It was formed as a result of a successful colonial war fought against the British Crown. The American system of government and its political culture reflect deeply-established liberal and progressive values, and politicians of both major parties, the Republicans and the Democrats, have typically resented being labelled 'conservative'. It is only since the 1960s that overtly conservative views have been expressed by elements within both parties, notably by Southern Democrats and the wing of the Republican party associated in the 1960s with Senator Barry Goldwater and which, in the 1970s and 1980s, supported Ronald Reagan, first as Governor of California and then as President, 1981–9.

As conservative ideology arose in reaction against the French Revolution and the process of modernisation in the West, it is less easy to identify political conservatism outside Europe and North America. In Africa, Asia and Latin America political movements have developed which sought to resist change and preserve traditional ways of life, but they have seldom employed specifically conservative arguments and values. An exception to this perhaps exists in the Liberal-Democratic Party, which has dominated Japanese politics since 1955. The Liberal-Democratic Party has close links with business interests and is committed to promoting a healthy private enterprise economy. At the same time, it has attempted to preserve traditional Japanese values and customs and therefore supported distinctively conservative principles such as loyalty, duty and hierarchy. In other countries, conservatism has exhibited a marked authoritarian character. Peron in Argentina and Khomeini in Iran, for instance, both established regimes based upon strong central authority, which also mobilised mass popular support on issues like nationalism, economic progress and the defence of traditional values.

Although conservatism is the most intellectually modest of political ideologies, it has also been remarkably resilient, perhaps precisely because of this fact. Conservatism has prospered because it has been unwilling to be tied down to a fixed system of ideas. A significant revival of conservative fortunes has in fact been evident since the 1970s with the political Right regaining power in a number of countries, including Germany, Canada, Denmark and Britain. Particularly prominent in this respect have been the Thatcher government in Britain and the Reagan administration in the United States. Both governments, however, practised an unusually radical and ideological brand of conservatism, commonly termed New Right. New Right ideas have drawn heavily upon free market economics and in so doing have exposed deep divisions within conservatism. Some commentators have questioned whether 'Reaganism' or 'Thatcherism' even belong within conservative ideology at all. Milton Friedman, for example, described Margaret Thatcher as 'a nineteenth century liberal', rather than a 'Tory'.

Although the New Right has challenged traditional conservative views about economic policy, it nevertheless remains part of conservatism. In the first place, it has not abandoned traditional conservative social principles, such as a belief in order, authority and discipline, and in some respects it has strengthened them. Furthermore, the New Right's enthusiasm for the free market has exposed the extent to which conservatism had already been influenced by liberal ideas. As with all political ideologies, conservatism contains a range of traditions. In the nineteenth century it was closely associated with an authoritarian defence of monarchy and aristocracy, which has survived in the form of authoritarian–populist movements in the Third World. In the twentieth century, Western conservatives have been divided between paternalistic support for state intervention and a libertarian commitment to the free market. The significance of the New Right is that it sought to revive the electoral fortunes of conservatism by readjusting the balance between these traditions in favour of libertarianism.

2 The desire to conserve

Although, in Burke's words, 'the desire to conserve' is the under-lying theme of conservative ideology, it is not an objective which all conservatives believe can be brought about simply by resisting change. Authoritarian conservatism has often been reactionary, and either refused in principle to yield to change, or else attempted to 'turn the clock back' to an earlier and better time. At the other extreme, the desire to regain or re-establish the past can even at times give conservatism a revolutionary character. The Iranian Revolution of 1979, in which the Shah of Iran was overthrown and an Islamic Republic set up under the leadership of Ayatollah Khomeini, was, in a sense, a conservative revolution. Khomeini's goal was to re-establish long-ignored 'Sharia' or Islamic law and customs.

Traditionally, conservatives have adopted a more pragmatic attitude to change: although change is seldom welcomed, it is nevertheless accepted if it is thought to be either inevitable or prudent. This is a position often associated with Burke who, while deeply critical of the French Revolution, argued that the French monarchy's stubborn resistance to change had contributed to the revolutionary upheaval. In contrast, Burke suggested, the British monarchy's acceptance of constitutional limits upon its power secured its continued existence. Some modern conservatives have been accused of abandoning Burke's cautious attitude to change and of being both doctrinaire and radical as in the case of the New Right, sometimes termed the Radical Right. In Britain, a Conservative government under Margaret Thatcher sought to 'roll back the frontiers of the state' and to overthrow a social democratic consensus amongst major political parties. The Reagan administration in the United States also attacked what it saw as 'big government' and attempted to overthrow a 'pro-government' public philosophy, which had dominated American political life since 1932. Although seldom held as a religious dogma, 'the desire to conserve' remains a cornerstone of conservative belief and is supported by a charac-teristic set of political values and theories.

a Tradition

Conservatives have argued against change on a number of grounds. A central and recurrent theme of conservatism is its defence of tradition, its desire to maintain established customs and institutions. Liberals, in contrast, argued that social institutions should not be evaluated on the grounds of how long they have survived, but according to how far they fulfil the needs and interests of individuals. If institutions fail this test, they should be reformed or perhaps abolished. In many countries liberals have, for example, reached the conclusion that the hereditary monarchy is a redundant institution in the modern world and should be abolished. Conservatives, however, fiercely disagree and believe, for a number of reasons, that customs and institutions should be preserved precisely because they have succeeded in enduring through history.

For some conservatives this conclusion reflects their religious faith. If the world is thought to have been fashioned by God the Creator, traditional customs and practices in society will be regarded as 'God given'. Burke, for example, believed that society was shaped by 'the law of our Creators', or what he also called 'natural law'. If human beings tampered with the world they were challenging the will of God, and would be likely as a result to make human affairs worse rather than better. Since the eighteenth century it has become increasingly difficult to maintain that tradition reflects the will of God. It was possible for Burke to believe that the institution of monarchy had been ordained by God because it had been so long-established and was still almost universally accepted. As the pace of historical change accelerated, however, old traditions were replaced by new ones, and these new ones, like free elections and universal suffrage, were clearly seen to be man-made rather than in any sense 'God given'. Nevertheless, the religious objection to change has been kept alive by modern fundamentalists, who believe that God's wishes have been revealed to humankind in the literal truth of their religious texts. The American New Right, for example, has been deeply influenced by the 'Born Again' Christian movement. Its campaigns against abortion and for the re-introduction of prayers into American schools are ultimately based upon its interpretation of the Bible. Islamic fundamentalists in various parts of the Middle East and North Africa similarly base their belief in Sharia law, according to which women may be stoned to death for adultery, upon the word of Allah, revealed in the Koran.

Most conservatives, however, support tradition without needing to argue that it has Divine origins. Burke, for example, described society as a partnership between 'those who are living, those who are dead and those who are to be born'. Tradition is, in G.K. Chesterton's phrase, 'a democracy of the dead', in which those who 'merely happen to be walking around' should respect the contribution, or 'votes', of their ancestors. Tradition, in this sense, reflects the accumulated wisdom of the past. The institutions and practices of the past have been 'tested by time' and should therefore be preserved for the benefit of the living and for generations to come. This notion of tradition reflects an almost Darwinian belief that institutions and customs which have survived have only done so because they have worked and been found to be of value. They have been endorsed by a process of 'natural selection', and demonstrated their fitness to survive. Conservatives in Britain, for instance, argue that the institution of monarchy should be preserved because it embodies historical wisdom and experience. In particular, the Crown has provided Britain with a focus of national loyalty and respect 'above' party politics; quite simply, it has worked.

Conservatives also venerate tradition because it gives the individual a sense of belonging and stability. Established customs and practices are ones that individuals can recognise, they are familiar and reassuring. Tradition thus provides people with an identity and a feeling of 'rootedness'. The institution of monarchy, for example, links people to the past and provides them with a sense of who they are. Change, on the other hand, is a journey into the unknown, it creates uncertainty and insecurity and thus endangers our happiness. Tradition is therefore rather more than simply political institutions which have stood the test of time. It encompasses all customs and social practices which are familiar and which generate security and belonging, from the insistence of the judiciary upon wearing traditional robes and wigs to campaigns to preserve, for example, the traditional colour of letterboxes or telephone boxes.

b Human imperfection

Conservatism is, in many ways, a 'philosophy of human imperfection'. Other ideologies assume that human beings are naturally 'good', or that they can be made 'good' if their social circumstances are improved. In their most extreme form, such beliefs are utopian and envisage the perfectibility of humankind in an ideal society. Conservatives dismiss such ideas as, at best, idealistic dreams, and base their theories instead on the belief that human beings are both imperfect and unperfectable.

Human imperfection is understood in several ways. In the first place, human beings are thought to be psychologically limited and dependent creatures. People, in the view of conservatives, fear isolation and instability. They are drawn psychologically to the safe and the familiar, and seek, above all else, the security of knowing 'their place'. Such a portrait of human nature is very different from the image of the self-reliant, enterprising 'utility maximiser' proposed by early liberals. The belief that individuals desire security and belonging has led conservatives to emphasise the importance of social order, and to be suspicious of the attraction of liberty. Order ensures that human life is stable and predictable; it provides security in an uncertain world. Liberty, on the other hand, presents individuals with choices and can generate change and uncertainty. Conservatives have often agreed with Thomas Hobbes in being prepared to sacrifice liberty in order to achieve social order.

Whereas other political philosophies trace the origins of immoral or criminal behaviour to society, conservatives believe it is rooted in each individual. Human beings are thought to be morally imperfect. Conservatives hold a pessimistic, even Hobbesian, view of human nature. Humankind is thought to be innately selfish and greedy, anything but perfectable. For some conservatives, this is explained by a religious belief in the doctrine of 'original sin'. Crime is not the product of social conditions, such as poverty or inequality, rather it is the consequence of natural instincts and appetites. Human beings can only be persuaded to behave in a civilised fashion if they are deterred from expressing their violent and anti-social impulses. The only effective deterrent is law, backed up by the knowledge that it will be strictly enforced. Law-breaking can only be deterred by a fear of punishment, and conservatives may therefore argue in favour of long prison sentences, the use of corporal or even capital punishment. For conservatives, the role of law is not to uphold liberty, but to preserve order. The concepts of 'law' and 'order' are so closely related in the conservative mind that they have almost become a single, fused concept.

Humankind's intellectual powers are also thought to be limited. Conservatives believe that the world is simply too complicated for human reason fully to grasp. As Michael Oakeshott wrote, 'In political activity men sail a boundless and bottomless sea'. This explains why conservatives are so suspicious of abstract ideas and 'systems of thought', which claim to understand what is, they argue, simply incomprehensible. Conservatives prefer to ground their ideas in experience and reality, they adopt a cautious, moderate and, above all, pragmatic approach to the world, avoiding, if at all possible, doctrinaire or dogmatic beliefs. Rationalist ideologies, like liberalism and socialism, advocate reform or even revolution in the belief that human beings are able to understand their world, and can therefore see how it could be improved. Conservatives believe such rationalism to be both arrogant and misguided. High-sounding political principles, such as 'the Rights of Man', 'equality' or 'social justice', become very dangerous when they are thought to provide a blueprint for the reform or remodelling of the world. This is why, conservatives suggest, reform and revolution often lead to greater suffering rather than less. They have often pointed out, for example, that both the French and the Russian Revolutions resulted in new forms of terror and oppression, very different from the utopian dreams which inspired the revolutionaries themselves. To do nothing may, for a conservative, be preferable to doing something, and a conservative will always wish to ensure, as Michael Oakeshott said, that 'the cure is not worse than the disease'.

c Organic society

The conservative view of society is very different from that of liberalism. Liberals believe that society arises from the actions of individuals, each intent upon pursuing self-interest. Social groups and associations are 'contractual', in that they are voluntarily entered into. Libertarian conservatives, attracted to liberal, free market ideas, have some sympathy with this view. Margaret Thatcher, for instance, suggested that 'there is no such thing as society, only the individuals and their families who compose it'. Traditional conservatives, on the other hand, believe that this is an 'atomistic' picture of society, based upon the pretence that individuals can be, or want to be, self-reliant. Conservatives believe, as explained earlier, that human beings are dependent and security-seeking creatures. They do not and cannot exist outside society, but desperately need to belong, to have 'roots' in society. The individual cannot be separated from society, but is part of the social groups which nurtured him or her: family, friends or peer group, business or work, local community and even nation. These groups provide individual life with security and meaning. As a result, traditional conservatives are reluctant to understand freedom to mean 'negative freedom', in which the individual is 'left alone'. Freedom is rather a willing acceptance of social obligations and ties by individuals who recognise their value. Freedom involves 'doing one's duty'. When, for example, parents instruct children how to behave, they are not constraining their liberty, but providing guidance for their children's benefit. To act as a dutiful son or daughter and conform to parental wishes is to act freely, out of a recognition of one's obligations. Conservatives believe that a society where individuals know only their rights and do not acknowledge their duties would be atomistic and rootless. Indeed, it is the bonds of duty and obligation which hold society together.

Social groups are, further, thought to be formed 'naturally', rather than through any form of conscious or voluntary contract. Society arises out of natural necessity. The most basic and most important social institution, the family, develops out of the simple need to bear and bring up children. In no sense can the children in a family be said to have agreed to a 'contract' when joining the family, they simply grow up within it and are nurtured and guided by it. Society exists before the individual, it helps to form the individual's character and personality. Society is thought of by conservatives as a living thing, an organism, whose parts work together just as the brain, heart, lungs and liver do within a human organism. Each part of this organic society, family, church, work, government, plays a particular role in sustaining the whole, and maintaining the 'health' of society. Society is not, as liberals think it to be, a 'machine', constructed by rational individuals, which can be tampered with and improved. If society is organic, its structure and institutions have been shaped by natural forces and its fabric should therefore be preserved and respected by the individuals who live within it.

The family is both the most basic institution of society and, in many ways, a model for all other social institutions. The family should be protected and, if necessary, strengthened. The family has not been fashioned by any social thinker or political theorist, but is the product of 'natural' social impulses, such as love, caring and responsibility. The family provides all its members, and particularly children, with safety and security, and teaches individuals about the value of duty and the need to respect others. Conservatives have therefore viewed a healthy family life as essential to the stability of society. Indeed, one of the distinctive themes of modern conservative thought is the 'defence of the family' and the need for a return to 'family values', in the light of what are believed to be the twin threats of permissiveness and materialism.

Conservatism also differs from other political ideologies in stressing the social value of religion. Religion may be understood not only as a spiritual phenomenon but also as the essential 'social cement' of society. Conservatives think that all societies need to be held together by a set of shared values and beliefs, and that religion provides society with such a moral fabric. A close relationship, as a result, has developed between conservatism and religion. The Church of England was traditionally described as 'the Conservative Party at prayer', though the relationship between the two was strained by the Thatcher government's adoption of free market principles. Christian Democratic parties throughout continental Europe openly promote the virtues of the Christian faith and the Italian Christian Democratic Party enjoys a particularly close relationship with the Vatican.

Conservatives are reluctant to leave moral questions to the individual, as was suggested, for example, by libertarians like John Stuart Mill. If morality becomes an issue of personal choice, the moral fabric of society is brought into question and with it the cohesion upon which social order is based. Morality is therefore a social issue, not simply a matter of personal preference. Society has, consequently, the right to protect itself by upholding a set of shared beliefs and values. This can be achieved by promoting respect for religion and the Church but, if necessary, may also require the force of law. A conservative believes that law should not only maintain public order, but should also defend and uphold moral principles. Laws which liberals would object to, for example, prohibiting blasphemy or imposing censorship, may be justified by conservatives on precisely these grounds. In their view, what people watch on television or read in books and newspapers should be subject to the guidance of laws because society must be protected against immorality.

Another example of a social institution for which conservatives reserve particular respect is the nation. Nations, like families, are formed naturally, in this case out of a natural affinity which develops amongst people who share the same language, history, culture and traditions. Conservatives argue that people are drawn towards others who are similar to themselves, in a search for security and a sense of belonging. Patriotism, love of one's country, is therefore both a natural and healthy instinct. At the same time, a suspicion of, and even prejudice against, foreigners may also be regarded as natural, as people from alien cultures may be thought to threaten social cohesion. Burke was amongst the first to argue that such irrational sentiments and prejudices are natural and also constructive, in so far as they helped to 'bind society together'. Conservative campaigns against immigration have been motivated by precisely such beliefs, as in the case of Enoch Powell's warnings in the late 1960s, that further black, Commonwealth immigration into Britain would provoke growing hostility amongst the host, white community and the likelihood of racial violence. Whereas liberals welcome the idea of social pluralism, conservatives have doubts about the very idea of either a multi-cultural or a multi-racial society. Clearly, conservatives do not share the internationalist beliefs held by liberals and socialists. Humanity is not thought to be universal, each member sharing a common human identity, but is rather seen as a collection of nations, each one seeking to maintain its distinctive and unique character, and harbouring natural suspicions about the intentions and behaviour of other nations. Elements in the British Conservative Party have therefore been reluctant to support moves towards political and economic union within the European Community for fear that this would undermine British sovereignty.

d Authority

A further distinguishing theme of conservatism is its stress upon the importance of authority. Conservatives do not accept the liberal belief that authority arises out of a contract made by free individuals. In liberal theory, authority is thought to be established by individuals, for their own benefit. According to social contract theory, citizens, in effect, agree to be governed. In contrast, conservatives believe that authority, like society, develops naturally. Parents have authority over children, they control virtually every aspect of their young lives, but without any contract or agreement having been undertaken. Authority develops, once again, from natural necessity, in this case the need to ensure that children are cared for, kept away from danger, have a healthy diet, go to bed at sensible times, and so on. Such authority can only be imposed 'from above', quite simply because children do not know what is good for them. It does not, and cannot, arise 'from below'; in no sense can children be said to have 'agreed to be governed'.

Authority is thought to be rooted in the nature of society and all social institutions. Within schools, authority should be exercised by the teacher, in the work place, by the employer, and in society at large, by government. Conservatives believe that authority is necessary and beneficial as everyone needs the guidance, support and security of knowing 'where they stand' and what is expected of them. This has led conservatism to place special emphasis upon leadership and discipline. Leadership is a vital ingredient in any society because it is the capacity to give direction and provide inspiration for others. Discipline is not just mindless obedience but a willing and healthy respect for authority. Authoritarian conservatives go further and portray authority as absolute and unquestionable. Most conservatives, however, believe that authority should be exercised within limits and that these limits are imposed not by an artificial contract but by the natural responsibilities which authority entails. Parents should have authority over their children, but not the right to treat them in any way they may choose. The authority of a parent reflects an obligation to nurture, guide and, if necessary, punish their children, but does not empower a parent to abuse a child or, for example, sell the child into slavery.

Conservatives believe the natural structure of society to be hierarchic, they therefore reject any commitment to social equality. They think, as liberals do, that people are born unequal in the sense that talents and skills are distributed unequally amongst people. For liberals, however, this leads to a belief in meritocracy, in which individuals rise or fall only according to their merits or talents. Traditionally, conservatives have believed that inequality is more deep-rooted, it is an inevitable feature of an organic society, not merely a consequence of individual differences. Just as the brain, the heart and the liver all carry out very different functions within the body, the various classes and groups which compose society also have their own specific roles. There must be leaders and there must be followers, there must be businessmen and there must be workers; for that matter, there must be those who go out to work and those who stay at home and bring up children. Genuine social equality is therefore a myth; in reality there is a natural inequality of wealth and social position, justified by a corresponding inequality of social responsibilities. The working class may not enjoy the same living standards and life chances as their employers but, at the same time, they do not have the livelihood and security of many other people resting on their shoulders.

The conservative defence of authority also influences its attitude to the state. In some ways, citizens are seen as children within the family; they need guidance and discipline. Citizens must be taught an awareness of their duties and obligations and not merely of their rights. The classical liberal model of a minimal state has usually been rejected by conservatives in favour of the idea of a strong state. Public order and the moral fabric of society must be upheld by a clear and enforceable set of laws. Wrong doing can only be deterred by a system of punishment, administered by government. Furthermore, within conservatism there is a strong paternalistic tradition which portrays government as a father-figure within society. This implies both that the authority of the state, as with that of the father, is a natural necessity, and exercised for the benefit of its citizens. Nevertheless, conservatives have been quick to warn against the improper use of government power. Government should be limited in the sense that it cannot, and should not, try to change human beings. Politics should be restricted to the central task of reconciling conflicts amongst individuals and groups, and should not be concerned with moral right and wrong. Michael Oakeshott expressed the typically conservative view of politics as a limited activity when he pointed out that government was 'not designed to make men good or even better'.

e Property

Property is a value which possesses a deep and, at times, almost mystical significance for conservatives. Liberals believe that property reflects merit: those who work hard and possess talent will gain wealth. Property, therefore, has been 'earned'. This doctrine has an attraction for those conservatives who regard the ability to accumulate wealth as an important economic incentive. Nevertheless, conservatives also hold that property has a range of psychological and social advantages. For example, property provides security. In an uncertain and unpredictable world, property ownership gives people a sense of confidence and assurance, something to 'fall back on'. Property, whether the ownership of a house or savings in the bank, provides individuals with a source of protection. Conservatives believe therefore that thrift, caution in the management of money, is a virtue in itself and have sought to encourage private savings and investment in property.

Property ownership also promotes a range of important social values. Those who possess and enjoy their own property are more likely to respect the property of others. They will also be aware that property must be safeguarded from disorder and lawlessness. Property owners therefore have a 'stake' in society, they have an interest in maintaining law and order. In this sense, property ownership can promote what can be thought of as the 'conservative values' of respect for law, authority and social order. Conservative parties have sought to create 'property owning democracies'. In Britain, the Thatcher government attempted to achieve this objective by legalising the sale of council houses and by its policy of privatisation, through which it hoped to promote 'popular capitalism'.

A deeper and more personal reason why conservatives may support property is that it can be thought of almost as an extension of an individual's personality. People 'realise' themselves, even see themselves, in what they own. Possessions are not merely external objects, valued because they are useful – a house to keep warm and dry, a car to provide transport and so on – but also reflect something of the owner's personality and character. This is why, conservatives point out, burglary is regarded as a particularly unpleasant crime: its victims suffer not only the loss or damage of their possessions, but also the sense that they personally have been violated. A home is the most personal and intimate of possessions, it is decorated and organised according to the tastes and needs of its owner and comes thereby to reflect his or her personality. The proposal of some socialists that property should be 'socialised', owned in common rather than by private individuals, strikes conservatives as particularly appalling because it threatens to create a soulless and de-personalised society.

Conservatives, however, are not prepared to go as far as *laissez-faire* liberals in believing that each individual has an absolute right to use their property however they may choose. While libertarian conservatives may support an essentially liberal view of property, most conservatives have argued that all rights, including property rights, entail obligations. Property is not an issue for the individual alone, but is also of importance to society. The rights of the individual must be balanced against the wellbeing of society or the nation. If, for example, conservatives believe that the national interest is served by government intervention in the economy, then the freedom of the businessman must be curtailed. Furthermore, property is not merely the creation of the present generation. Much of it, land, houses, works of art, is passed down from earlier generations. The present generation is, in that sense, the custodian of the wealth of the nation and possesses a duty to preserve and protect it for the benefit of future generations. Lord Stockton, formerly Harold Macmillan, expressed just such a position when, in the 1980s, he objected to the Thatcher government's policy of privatisation and described it as 'selling off the family silver'.

3 Authoritarian conservatism

Whereas all conservatives would claim to respect the concept of authority, few modern conservatives would accept that their views are authoritarian. These terms have very different meanings. Authority is a form of power: it enables one person to influence the behaviour of another by virtue of who they are or the office they hold. It is the right to influence the behaviour of others, not simply the ability to do so. For example, a parent has authority over a child if the child believes he has a duty to obey the parent. All governments seek authority, or legitimacy, because without it the obedience of its citizens can only be achieved through the use of force or intimidation. An authoritarian government, however, exercises power rather than seeks authority. It demands obedience, instead of trying to build up consent. Authoritarian rule therefore exists when government power is concentrated in the hands of an individual or a small group, and exercised in such a way that it can neither be questioned nor challenged. A wide range of governments can be considered to be authoritarian: absolute monarchies, modern dictatorships and totalitarian regimes. Although contemporary conservatives are committed to democratic government, there is a tradition within conservatism, especially strong in continental Europe, which has supported authoritarian rule.

The authoritarian tradition dates back to Plato, who proposed that government be entrusted to a small class of philosopher-kings, the Guardians, whose authority was absolute and unquestionable because it was based upon their superior wisdom and understanding. At the time of the French Revolution, the principal defender of autocratic rule was the French political thinker, Joseph de Maistre. De Maistre was a fierce critic of the French Revolution but, in contrast to Burke, he wished to restore absolute power to the hereditary monarchy. He was a reactionary, quite unprepared to accept any reform of the *ancien régime* which had been overthrown in 1789. His political philosophy was based upon a willing and complete subordination to 'the master'. In *Du Pape* (1817), de Maistre went further and argued that above the earthly monarchies a supreme spiritual power should rule in the person of the Pope. De Maistre's conservatism was based upon the benefits he claimed would flow from an unquestioning acceptance of traditional authority, even when that authority was cruel and unreasonable. He believed deeply that society was organic, and would fragment or collapse if it were not bound together by the twin principles of 'Throne and Altar'. De Maistre's central concern was therefore the preservation of order, which alone, he believed, could provide people with safety and security. Revolution, and even reform, would weaken the chains that bound people together and would lead to a descent into chaos and oppression. Even the cruel ruler should be obeyed because once the established principle of authority was questioned, infinitely greater suffering would result.

Throughout the nineteenth century, conservatives in continental Europe remained faithful to the rigid and hierarchical values of autocratic rule, and stood unbending in the face of rising liberal, nationalist and socialist protest. Nowhere was authoritarianism more entrenched than in Russia where Tsar Nicholas I, 1825–55, proclaimed the principles of 'Orthodoxy, Autocracy and Nationality', in contrast to the values which had inspired the French Revolution, 'Liberty, Equality and Fraternity'. Nicholas's successors stubbornly refused to allow their power to be constrained by constitutions or the development of parliamentary institutions. In Germany, constitutional government did develop, but Bismarck, the Imperial Chancellor 1871–90, ensured that it remained a sham. The parliament, the Reichstag, exercised little control over legislation, taxation or the

Imperial government, and was dismissed by the socialist, Karl Liebknecht, as a 'fig leaf covering the nakedness of absolutism'. Elsewhere, authoritarianism remained particularly strong in Catholic countries. The Papacy suffered not only the loss of its temporal authority with the achievement of Italian unification, which led Pius IX to declare himself a 'prisoner of the Vatican', but also an assault upon its doctrines with the rise of secular political ideologies. In 1864 the Pope condemned all radical or progressive ideas, including those of nationalism, liberalism and socialism, as 'false doctrines of our most unhappy age', and when confronted with the loss of the Papal States and Rome, proclaimed the edict of Papal Infallibility in 1870. The unwillingness of continental conservatives to come to terms with reform and democratic government extended well into the twentieth century. In the aftermath of the First World War, for example, conservative groups in Italy and Germany helped to overthrow parliamentary democracy and bring Mussolini and Hitler to power by providing support and respectability for rising fascist movements.

In other cases, conservative-authoritarian regimes have looked for political support to the newly-enfranchised masses. This applied in the case of France, where universal manhood suffrage was introduced in 1848. Louis Napoleon succeeded in being elected President and later establishing himself as Emperor Napoleon III by appealing to the the small-holding peasantry, the largest element in the French electorate. The Napoleonic regime fused authoritarianism with the promise of economic prosperity and social reform in the kind of plebiscitary dictatorship more commonly found in the twentieth century. Bonapartism has clear parallels with modern Peronism. Juan Peron was dictator of Argentina from 1946 to 1955 and proclaimed the familiar authoritarian themes of obedience, order and national unity. However, he based his political support not upon the interests of traditional elites, but upon the impoverished masses, the 'shirtless ones' as Peron referred to them. The Peronist regime was populist in that it moulded its policies according to the instincts and wishes of the common people, in this case popular resentment against 'Yankee imperialism', and a widespread desire for economic and social progress. Similar regimes have developed in parts of Africa and the Middle East, notably Khomeini's Islamic Republic in Iran. In contrast to military dictatorships, which typically suppress all forms of political activity, authoritarian-populist regimes have sought to mobilise active public support, usually through elections, plebiscites or mass demonstrations, and typically base their appeal upon a potent blend of nationalism and modernisation.

Authoritarian-populism does not, however, have a clear political character. Although nationalism is a common component of their ideological appeal, some of these regimes, as in the case of Khomeini's Iran, have been conservative or reactionary, while others, especially in Africa, have embraced socialist or even Marxist principles. Populism proclaims that the attitudes or aspirations of the masses, whatever they might be, should be the only legitimate guide for political leaders. However, in mobilising popular support for dictatorial rule, authoritarian-populist regimes such as Peron's perhaps exhibit features more closely associated with fascism than conservatism.

4 Paternalistic conservatism

Although continental conservatives adopted an attitude of uncompromising resistance to change, a more flexible and ultimately more successful Anglo-American tradition can be traced back to Edmund Burke. The lesson that Burke drew from the French Revolution was that change could be natural or inevitable, in which case it should not be resisted. 'A state without the means of some change', he suggested, 'is without the means of its conservation' (p.285). The characteristic style of Burkean conservatism is cautious, modest and pragmatic; it reflects a suspicion of fixed principles, whether revolutionary or reactionary. As Ian Gilmour has recommended 'the wise Conservative travels light'. The values which conservatives hold most dear – tradition, order, authority and property – will be safe only if policy is developed in the light of practical circumstances and experience. Such a position will rarely justify dramatic or radical change but accepts a prudent willingness to 'change in order to conserve'. Pragmatic conservatives support neither the individual nor the state in principle, but are prepared to support either, or, more frequently, recommend a balance between the two, depending upon 'what works'. In practice, the reforming impulse in conservatism has also been closely associated with the survival into the nineteenth and twentieth centuries of neo-feudal paternalistic values.

a One Nation

The paternalistic conservative tradition is often related to Benjamin Disraeli, British Prime Minister in 1868 and again from 1874 to 1880. Disraeli developed his political philosophy in two novels, *Sybil* and *Coningsby*, written before he assumed ministerial responsibilities. These novels emphasised the principle of social obligation, in stark contrast to the extreme individualism then dominant within the Liberal Party. Disraeli wrote against a background of growing industrialisation, economic inequality and, in continental Europe at least, revolutionary upheaval. He tried to draw attention to the danger of Britain being divided into 'two nations: the Rich and the Poor'. In the best conservative tradition, Disraeli's argument was based upon a combination of prudence and principle.

On one hand, growing social inequality contained the seed of revolution. A poor and oppressed working class, Disraeli feared, would not simply accept its misery. The revolutions which had broken out in Europe in 1830 and 1848 seemed to bear out this belief. Reform would therefore be sensible because, in stemming the tide of revolution, it would ultimately be in the interests of the rich. On the other hand, Disraeli also appealed to moral values. He suggested that wealth and privilege brought with them social obligations, in particular, a responsibility for the poor or less-well-off. In so doing, Disraeli emphasised the traditional conservative belief that society is held together by an acceptance of duty and obligations. He believed that society was naturally hierarchic, but also held that inequalities of wealth or social privilege gave rise to an inequality of responsibilities. The wealthy and powerful must shoulder the burden of social responsibility, which was, in effect, the price of privilege. These ideas were based upon the feudal principle of *noblesse oblige*, the obligation of the aristocracy to be honourable and generous. For example, the landed nobility claimed to exercise a paternal responsibility for their peasants, as the king did in relation to the nation. Disraeli recommended that these obligations should not be abandoned, but should be expressed, in an increasingly industrialised world, in social reform. Such ideas came to be represented by the slogan 'One Nation'. In office, Disraeli was responsible for the Second Reform Act of 1867, which extended the right to vote to the working class in Britain for the first time, and was responsible for social reforms which improved housing conditions and hygiene.

Disraeli's ideas had considerable impact upon conservatism and contributed to a radical and reforming tradition which appeals both to the pragmatic instincts of conservatives and to their sense of social duty. In Britain, these ideas provide the basis of what is called 'One Nation conservatism', whose supporters sometimes style themselves as 'Tories' to denote their commitment to pre-industrial, hierarchic and paternal values. Disraeli's ideas were subsequently taken up in the late nineteenth century by Randolph Churchill in the form of 'Tory Democracy'. In an age of widening political democracy, Churchill stressed the need for traditional institutions, such as the Monarchy, the House of Lords and the Church, to enjoy a wider base of social support. This could be achieved by winning working class votes for the Conservative Party through continuing Disraeli's policy of social reform. Such ideas were also supported by Joseph Chamberlain, whose Liberal Unionists split with Gladstone over the issue of Home Rule for Ireland, and were integrated into the Conservative Party during the 1890s. Chamberlain campaigned for 'Tariff Reform', which he believed would bring both international and social benefits. He hoped that the establishment of tariff barriers against trade from outside the Empire – Imperial Preference – would strengthen Britain's links with her Empire and, in so doing, bolster her economic and strategic position. Tariffs would, furthermore, generate revenue for the government, which he recommended should be devoted to social reform. Chamberlain had achieved fame in 1875 when, as Lord Mayor of Birmingham, he had pioneered a radical programme of slum clearance and urban development.

Pragmatic and reforming ideas were also evident in nineteenth century Germany under Bismarck. Bismarck was alarmed, in particular, at the growth of socialism, which he associated with revolution and terrorism. He sought to combat the 'socialist menace' by a combination of repression – banning socialist meetings and newspapers – and social reform. From 1879 onwards he also supported protectionism, partly because he, like Chamberlain, saw it as a way of financing social welfare expenditure. During the 1880s, Germany constructed the first, if limited, welfare state, which featured a system of medical and accident insurance, sick pay and old age pensions. Bismarck's experiment in what has been described as 'state socialism' was designed to wean the working class away from revolution, but also reflected a neo-feudal sense of paternal duty which was deeply ingrained in the Junker landed nobility from which he came.

The fact that both Bismarck and Chamberlain came to champion the cause of protectionism rather than free trade reflects their essentially pragmatic attitude towards economic policy. The liberal case for free trade is based upon a combination of economic theory and political principle. Conservatives, in contrast, typically cautious about systematic theories or abstract principles, have rather preferred to recommend 'what works' in the prevailing circumstances. Neither free trade nor protectionism is preferred in principle; either policy can be advocated by conservatives according to what is thought to serve the national interest at any particular time. A similarly pragmatic attitude has been adopted by conservatives confronted with a choice between government intervention and the free market.

b The middle way

In the post-war period, conservative governments in various parts of the world have been prepared to accept that government should not only provide social welfare, but should also 'manage' the economy. Conservatives, like modern liberals, have embraced Keynesianism, but for rather different reasons. Conservative parties have tried to pursue what they regard as a non-ideological, 'middle way' between the extremes of, on one hand, *laissez-faire* liberalism and, on the other, socialist state planning. Conservatism is, therefore, the way of moderation, and seeks to draw a balance between rampant individualism and overbearing collectivism. In Britain, the depression and high unemployment of the 1930s reinforced the idea that economic policy should not simply be left to the market. In *The Middle Way* (1938), Harold Macmillan, who was to be Prime Minister, 1957–63, advocated what he called 'planned capitalism', which he described as 'a mixed system which combines state ownership, regulation or control of certain aspects of economic activity with the drive and initiative of private enterprise' (p.185). Macmillan was, at the time, MP for Stockton, an area seriously afflicted by unemployment, and he possessed the privileged social background and sense of moral obligation which have often characterised One Nation or paternalistic conservatives.

During the 1950s, paternalistic values became dominant within the British Conservative Party. By the time the Conservatives were returned to government in 1951, they had come to accept the major and radical reforms which had been enacted by the Attlee Labour government, 1945–51. These reforms included the achievement of full employment through the use of Keynesian economics, a mixed economy brought about through nationalising major industries, and a significant expansion of the welfare state, including the creation of a National Health Service. The common feature of these reforms was an expansion of state intervention into social and economic life. Whereas the Labour government believed that intervention was designed to promote social equality and, therefore, build socialism, Conservatives accepted these reforms on grounds of paternalism. State intervention did not seek to abolish hierarchy and authority, but rather promote the values of compassion and obligation which the One Nation tradition stood for. During the 1950s the policies of the Labour and Conservative parties converged to such an extent that the term 'Butskellism' was coined, which underlined the similarity of views between the Conservative Chancellor of the 1950s, R.A. Butler, and his Labour predecessor and leader of the party, 1955–61, Hugh Gaitskell. The Conservatives therefore came to subscribe to a post-war 'social democratic' consensus, whose principal architects had been the modern liberals, Keynes and Beveridge.

After the appointment of Margaret Thatcher as Prime Minister in 1979, British Tory paternalism came under growing pressure from increasingly fashionable free market ideas and values within the party. The few ministers in the Thatcher government who remained faithful to One Nation conservatism were referred to as the 'wets', in contrast to the Thatcherites or 'drys'. In the 1981 Cabinet resuffle Thatcher shifted the ideological balance of her government by sacking a number of leading 'wets', including Sir Ian Gilmour. Together with former Prime Minister Edward Heath and other Heathites such as James Prior, Gilmour continued to uphold One Nation values by voicing dissent from the backbenches. Those 'wets' who remained in the Cabinet, like Peter Walker, were only able to express their criticism in coded speeches. The fall of Thatcher in 1990, however, demonstrated that the One Nation tradition remained alive within the British Conservative Party. Her successor, John Major, was prepared to endorse welfarist principles and a younger generation of 'wets' like Chris Patten gained promotion.

Interventionist policies were also adopted by Christian Democratic parties in continental Europe after 1945. In the aftermath of war, continental conservatives abandoned their authoritarian beliefs. Their new form of conservatism was committed to political democracy and influenced by the paternalistic social traditions of Catholicism. Protestant social theory has often been associated with the rise of capitalism because it extols the value of hard work and individual responsibility. Catholic social theory, in contrast, has traditionally focused upon the social group rather than the individual, and stressed a harmony of interest amongst social classes. During the nineteenth and early twentieth centuries, despite the Papacy's firm commitment to autocracy, Catholic parties, like the Centre Party in Germany, supported constitutional government, political democracy and social reform. After 1945, this Catholic social ethic was reflected in the willingness of Christian Democratic parties to embrace Keynesian-welfarist policies. German and Italian Christian Democratic parties have enjoyed prolonged periods in power since 1945. These parties have developed into broad coalitions of interests: for example, the Christian Democratic Union (CDU) has attracted substantial support from the majority Protestant community in Germany. The ideological stance of these parties is typically pragmatic, which has allowed them to accept a progressive extension of social welfare and government management of the economy. The conservative CDU has, in fact, been in the forefront of the construction of Germany's successful 'social market economy', through which the market economy is managed by government, acting in conjunction with the industrial banks.

The Progressive Conservative Party (PCP) in Canada also contains various shades of opinion. Ideologically, it favours greater orthodoxy in government finance and less government involvement in social affairs than the Liberal Party. However, the difference between Canada's two major parties is a matter of emphasis rather than principle: PCP policies are usually determined by political expediency, local issues and practical needs, rather than by ideology. In Japan, the Liberal-Democratic Party has dominated government since it was founded in 1955. Its name 'Liberal-Democratic' was adopted to highlight the LDP's acceptance of the democratic constitution imposed upon Japan after her defeat in 1945 but, in other respects, the party can be regarded as a paternalistic conservative party. It has attempted to preserve respect for Japanese culture and traditions, despite the rapid economic growth of the post-war period. The Japanese government, and especially its Finance Ministry, has been the architect of the Japanese 'economic miracle'. Japanese government works closely with the country's major corporations in targeting export markets and planning investment policy, and certainly does not leave such economic decisions to the 'invisible hand' of capitalism.

5 Libertarian conservatism

Although conservatism draws heavily upon pre-industrial ideas such as organicism, hierarchy and obligation, the ideology has also been much influenced by liberal, and especially classical liberal, ideas. This is sometimes seen as a late twentieth century development, the New Right having in some way 'hijacked' conservatism in the interests of classical liberalism. Nevertheless, liberal doctrines, especially those about the free market, have been advanced by conservatives since the late eighteenth century and can be said to constitute a rival tradition to conservative paternalism. These ideas are libertarian in that they advocate the greatest possible economic liberty and the least possible government regulation of economic life. Libertarian conservatives have not simply converted to liberalism but have rather believed liberal economics to be compatible with a more traditional, conservative social philosophy, based upon values such as authority and duty. This is evident in the work of Edmund Burke, in many ways the founder of traditional conservatism, but also a keen supporter of the liberal economics of Adam Smith.

The libertarian tradition has been strongest in those countries where classical liberal ideas have had greatest impact, once again, Britain and the United States. As early as the late eighteenth century, Burke expressed a strong preference for free trade in commercial affairs and a competitive, self-regulating market economy in domestic affairs. The free market was efficient and fair, but it was also, Burke believed, natural and necessary. It was 'natural' in that it reflected a desire for wealth, a 'love of lucre', that was part of human nature. The laws of the market were therefore 'natural laws'. He accepted that working conditions dictated by the market were, for many, 'degrading, unseemly, unmanly and often most unwholesome', but insisted that they would suffer further if the 'natural course of things' were disturbed. Burke saw no tension between his support for a market economy and his defence of a traditional social order, because he believed that the traditional order in Britain had ceased, by the late eighteenth century, to be feudal, and had instead become capitalist. The capitalist free market could therefore be defended on grounds of tradition, just like the monarchy and the church.

During the nineteenth century, support for the free market was pushed to the margins within the British Conservative Party by the dominance of Disraelian, paternalistic ideas, but it was never eradicated. Support for libertarian views grew towards the turn of the century, in reaction to growing government intervention in social and economic life. The British Constitutional Association (BCA), 1905–18, supported largely by Conservatives, was portrayed as 'The New Canute', because of its opposition to the programme of social welfare introduced by the Asquith Liberal government. In contrast to the paternalistic ideas spreading within the Conservative Party, the BCA advocated an extreme *laissez-faire* position, strongly influenced by the views of Herbert Spencer. As A.V. Dicey, noted constitutional authority and BCA member, said – paraphrasing Samuel Smiles – 'State help kills self help'.

The further expansion of the state in the post-Second World War period once again stimulated a libertarian backlash within conservatism. One Nation values, which had dominated British conservatism in the 1950s, were already being challenged during the 1960s by conservatives whose economic philosophies were more influenced by the ideas of Friedrich Hayek and Milton Friedman than by what had become Keynesian orthodoxy. In Britain such views were expressed by Enoch Powell. In contrast to the social democratic policies endorsed by both Conservative and Labour parties in the 1950s and 1960s, Powell proclaimed his support for a 'free economy', which he believed to be an essential guarantee of a 'free society'. He argued that economic management unwisely placed planning decisions in the hands of a 'little Whitehall clique', rather than the 'complex nervous system of the market'. After 1974, similar ideas were taken up by Sir Keith Joseph, who campaigned for the establishment of what he called a 'social market economy', in place of the 'command economy' or 'creeping socialism' which resulted from growing government intervention in social and economic life. Encouraged by the appointment of Thatcher as Conservative leader in 1975, free market or libertarian ideas predominated within the party, this time pushing the One Nation tradition to the margins. This, and similar trends elsewhere in the world, are considered in more detail in relation to the New Right.

Libertarian conservatives are not, however, consistent liberals. They believe in economic individualism and 'getting government off the back of the businessman', but are less prepared to extend this principle of individual liberty to other aspects of social life. Enoch Powell has acknowledged that 'the Tory party is not, never has been, never can be, the party of *laissez-faire*'. Early liberals, like Richard Cobden or John Stuart Mill, were prepared to place social and moral responsibility in the hands of the individual, not merely economic responsibility. As Hayek has emphasised in *The Constitution of Liberty* (1976), liberalism can be distinguished from both conservatism and, in his view, socialism by its belief that moral decisions should be left to the individual, unless they lead to conduct which threatens other people. The individual, therefore, needs as little guidance as possible from the state. Conservatives, even libertarian conservatives, have a more pessimistic view of human nature. A strong state is required to maintain public order and to ensure that authority is respected. Indeed, in some respects, libertarian conservatives are attracted to free market theories precisely because they promise to secure social order. Whereas liberals have believed that the market economy preserves individual liberty and freedom of choice, conservatives have, at times, been attracted to the market as an instrument of social discipline. Market forces regulate and control economic and social activity. For example, they may deter workers from pushing for higher wage increases by threatening them with unemployment. As such, the market can be seen as an instrument which maintains social stability, and which works alongside the more evident forces of coercion: the police and the courts. While some conservatives have feared that market capitalism can lead to endless innovation and restless competition, upsetting social cohesion, others have been attracted to it in the belief that it can establish a 'market order', sustained by impersonal 'natural laws' rather than the guiding hand of political authority.

6 The New Right

During the post-war period, pragmatic and paternalistic ideas had dominated conservatism throughout much of the Western world. The remnants of authoritarian conservatism collapsed with the overthrow of the Portugese and Spanish dictatorships in the 1970s. Just as conservatives had come to accept political democracy during the nineteenth century, after 1945 they came to embrace a Keynesian and welfarist form of social democracy. This tendency was confirmed by the rapid and sustained economic growth of the post-war years, the 'long boom', which appeared to bear out the success of a 'managed capitalism'. During the 1970s, however, a set of more radical ideas developed within conservatism, directly challenging the Keynesian-welfarist orthodoxy. These New Right ideas had greatest impact in Britain and the United States, but were also influential in continental Europe, notably in France and Germany.

The 'New Right' is a broad term and has been used to describe ideas which range from the demand for tax cuts to calls for greater censorship of television and films, and even campaigns against immigration or in favour of repatriation. Two principal themes can, nevertheless, be identified within it. The first is revived support for classical liberal economics, in particular, for the free market ideas of Adam Smith. This feature of the New Right can be called the liberal New Right, or neo-liberalism. The second theme also draws upon nineteenth century ideas, but those of traditional conservatism, especially its defence of order, authority and discipline. Such ideas constitute the conservative New Right, or neo-conservatism. Not all thinkers or politicians who subscribe to New Right ideas hold both neo-liberal and neo-conservative views: for example, Roger Scruton, a noted British neo-conservative, argued in *The Meaning of Conservatism* (1980) that a principled commitment to the free market has no place within conservatism. On the other hand, it is clear that neo-liberal and neo-conservative views often coincide. The two governments most clearly influenced by New Right ideas, the Reagan and the Thatcher administrations, supported, if to different degrees, both the liberal and the conservative New Right. 'Thatcherism' in Britain and 'Reaganism' in the United States were the forms which New Right ideas assumed in these countries. The terms themselves can be misleading, however, because they have been used to refer to the very individual political styles associated with

Margaret Thatcher and Ronald Reagan, as well as to the ideas to which they were committed.

New Right ideas were the product of various historical factors. Perhaps most importantly, the long boom of the post-war period ended in recession in the early 1970s, with rising unemployment coinciding with high inflation, a phenomenon termed by economists 'stagflation'. The renewal of economic difficulties had greatest impact in those countries already subject to relative decline. The United States, for example, became increasingly aware of competition from the reconstructed Japanese and German economies, while the British economy had declined markedly, especially in relation to those countries which had joined the European Community at its creation in 1957. In these circumstances, Keynesian ideas of economic management came under considerable pressure on the political Right. New Right thought was also influenced by social factors, especially the spread of a liberal social philosophy. Conservatives feared that this had led to 'permissiveness' which undermined tradition and also authority, and had generated widespread welfare dependency. Conservatism in America gained a considerable boost from the recruitment of a number of former liberal intellectuals, led by Irving Kristol and Norman Podhoretz, who became outspoken critics of 'big' government. Finally, international factors strengthened nationalist sentiments within conservatism and heightened its fear of communism. The American New Right was alarmed at what it believed to be the growing military might of the Soviet Union and loss of national prestige in Vietnam and Iran. In Britain there was concern about the loss of great power status and the threat to sovereignty posed, after 1973, by membership of the European Community.

a The liberal New Right

The liberal aspects of New Right thinking are, most definitely, drawn from classical rather than modern liberalism, and amount to a restatement of the case for a minimal state. This has been summed up as 'private, good; public, bad'. The liberal New Right is anti-statist. The state is regarded as a realm of coercion and unfreedom; collectivism restricts individual initiative and saps self-respect. Government, however well intentioned, invariably has a damaging effect on human affairs. Faith instead is placed in the individual and in the market. Individuals should be encouraged to be self-reliant and to make rational choices in their own interests. The market is respected as a mechanism through which the sum of individual choices can lead to progress and general benefit. As such, the liberal New Right has attempted to establish the dominance of libertarian ideas over paternalistic ones within conservative ideology.

The dominant theme within this anti-statist doctrine is an ideological commitment to the free market. The New Right has resurrected the classical economics of Smith and Ricardo, as it has been presented in the work of modern economists like Friedrich Hayek and Milton Friedman. Free market ideas, which had been abandoned in favour of Keynesianism during the early twentieth century, gained renewed credibility during the 1970s. Governments experienced increasing difficulty in delivering economic stability and sustained growth. Doubts consequently developed about whether it was in the power of government at all to solve economic problems. Hayek and Friedman, for example, challenged the very idea of a 'managed' or 'planned' economy. They pointed to the inefficiency of centrally planned economies in the Soviet Union and Eastern Europe, arguing that the task of allocating resources in a complex, industrialised economy was simply too difficult for any set of state bureaucrats to achieve successfully. The inevitable result of collectivisation was shortages of vital goods and queuing for the bare necessities of life. The virtue of the market, on the other hand, was that it acted as a central nervous system running through the economy, reconciling the supply of goods and services with the demand for them. It allocated resources to their most profitable use and thereby ensured that consumer needs were satisfied. In the light of the re-emergence of unemployment and inflation in the 1970s, Hayek and Friedman argued that government was invariably the cause of economic problems, rather than the cure. Government had progressively ignored market forces in the mistaken, if well-intentioned, belief that state intervention was necessary and desirable.

The ideas of John Maynard Keynes were one of the chief targets of New Right criticism. Keynes had argued that capitalist economies were not self-regulating. He placed particular emphasis upon the 'demand side' of the economy, believing that the level of economic activity and employment were dictated by 'aggregate demand' in the economy. Keynes's solution to the problem of unemployment was that governments should 'manage demand' by running a budget deficit; government should 'inject' more money into the economy through public spending than they 'withdrew' through taxation. Milton Friedman, however, argued that there was a 'natural rate of unemployment', beyond the ability of government to influence, and that the attempts of government to eradicate unemployment by employing Keynesian techniques had merely caused other, more damaging, economic problems.

Whereas Keynesianism was based upon a belief that unemployment was the most serious of economic problems, free market economists have been more concerned about the problem of inflation. Inflation is a rise in the general price level, and leads, in effect, to a decline in the value of money: the same amount of money buys fewer goods. The market is based upon a process of buying and selling, made possible by the existence of money, which acts as a convenient means of exchange. The alternative to money, a barter system, makes exchange very cumbersome because it is difficult to establish the relative values of different goods. The health of a market economy therefore requires that money has a sound and stable value. If people lose faith in a means of exchange because its value fluctuates unpredictably, they will be discouraged from undertaking commercial or economic activity. In its most extreme case – hyperinflation – money falls so dramatically in value that it becomes worthless and the economy reverts to a barter system, as occurred during the German economic crisis of 1923.

Both Hayek and Friedman placed special emphasis upon 'sound money' and argued that the principal economic responsibility of government is to ensure the financial stability of the market economy by lowering or, as Hayek hoped, eradicating inflation altogether. They suggested that governments pursuing Keynesian policies were unknowingly fuelling inflation and generating the 'stagflation' that had characterised the 1970s. This was explained through the quantity theory of money, or monetarism as subsequent economists have called it, which is the belief that the price level is determined by the quantity of money, or money supply, in the economy. If the money supply grows more quickly than the number of goods and services in the economy, the value of money will fall and the price of goods will rise. In other words, inflation occurs when 'too much money chases too few goods'. This was precisely what monetarists claimed Keynesian policies had brought about. In allowing their spending to exceed tax revenues, governments were, in effect, 'printing money'. They expanded the money supply and simply fuelled inflation without, in the process, having any beneficial effect upon the 'natural rate' of unemployment. The economic policies of both Reagan and Thatcher administrations during the 1980s were guided by these free market and monetarist theories. Both administrations allowed unemployment to rise sharply in the early 1980s in the belief that there was only a 'market solution' to the problem. Similarly, they placed emphasis upon cutting inflation by reducing government expenditure. In the United States, Reagan gave support to the idea of a Balanced Budget Amendment, advocated by Milton Friedman.

Free market economists also believe that high spending, Keynesian-welfarist policies had damaged economic performance by pushing up tax levels. Instead of giving attention to the 'demand side' of the economy, free market economists preached supply side economics. This meant that governments should foster conditions which encourage producers to produce, rather than consumers to consume. Keynesian policies had burdened producers with heavy levels of taxation and complex regulations. Taxes discouraged enterprise and, in the view of libertarian New Right theorists like Robert Nozick, infringed property rights. 'Supply-side' economics was the central feature of what was called 'Reaganomics' in America. In 1981, Reagan successfully steered a Tax Bill through Congress which introduced the most dramatic cuts in personal and corporate taxation ever achieved in the United States. Under the Thatcher government in Britain, levels of direct taxation were progressively reduced to near American levels. For example, the highest level of Income Tax was reduced from 83 pence in the pound in 1979, to 40 pence in the pound by 1988.

The New Right was also critical of the mixed economy. After 1945, many Western countries nationalised basic industries in order to facilitate the management of their economies. This created economies that were a mixture of state owned 'public sector', and individually owned 'private sector', industries. The New Right wished to reverse this trend. Under Thatcher in Britain and, to an extent, the Chirac government in France, a policy of privatisation was pursued which transferred industries like telecommunications, water, gas and electricity from public to private ownership. Nationalised industries were criticised as being inherently inefficient because, unlike private firms and industries, they were not disciplined by the profit motive. Waste and inefficiency in the public sector could be tolerated, the New Right argued, because the tax payer would always pick up bills. In the United States, where a mixed economy had never developed, New Right pressure focused upon the attempt to de-regulate the private sector. Independent Regulatory Agencies had developed since the late nineteenth century and had proliferated since the 1960s. These agencies were set up by Congress with the intention of regulating private enterprise in accordance with the public interest. The Reagan administration believed such agencies merely disrupted the efficiency of the private economy and argued that the public interest was more likely to be guaranteed by the market mechanism itself rather than any government agency, however ably staffed and hardworking. Consequently, the funding of these agencies was dramatically reduced during the Reagan years, the Environmental Protection Agency (EPA) suffering, for example, a 50 per cent reduction in its budget. Furthermore, personnel were appointed to these agencies, for instance Ann Burford to head the EPA, who had greater sympathy for the free market than they had for government regulation.

The liberal New Right is not only anti-statist on grounds of economic efficiency and responsiveness, but also in terms of political principle, notably in its commitment to individual liberty. Freedom is a theme which recurs throughout neo-liberal writing. Friedrich Hayek's critique of the growing power of the state in 1944 was called *Road to Serfdom*, while Milton Friedman's expositions of liberal economics have been entitled *Capitalism and Freedom* and *Free to Choose*. Both Thatcher and Reagan administrations claim to have defended freedom against 'creeping collectivism'. At the extreme, these ideas lead in the direction of anarcho-capitalism, discussed in Chapter 7, which believes that all goods and services, including the courts and public order, should be delivered by the market. Government is deprived not only of its economic role, but of those 'minimal' functions which were thought to be necessary by classical liberals.

The freedom defended by the liberal, libertarian and even anarchist elements in the New Right is negative freedom, the removal of external restrictions upon the individual. As the collective power of government is seen as the principle threat to the individual, freedom can only be ensured by 'rolling back the state'. In the twentieth century, however, the state has expanded surreptitiously, by developing into a welfare state, claiming to protect its citizens from the threat of poverty, unemployment and other social ills. For the New Right, welfarism saps independence, initiative and enterprise, it creates a 'new serfdom' of dependency. It robs individuals of the dignity and self-respect which can be gained only by being responsible for one's own life and wellbeing. Welfare, therefore, is a matter of individual responsibility, it is not a social responsibility invested in the state. Margaret Thatcher expressed this idea most graphically by suggesting that 'there is no such thing as society'. The liberal New Right is critical of the 'dependency culture' which welfarism generates but also claims that growing welfare expenditure merely retards economic growth by adding to the 'tax burden', and is delivered through unresponsive and inefficient public sector bodies. In contrast to the values of New Deal liberalism, Ronald Reagan tried to foster in the States a 'frontier ideology', which emphasised self-reliance and hard work. During the 1980s his administration attempted to control welfare expenditure by the policy of 'New Federalism', in which welfare responsibilities were devolved from Federal Government in Washington to the less prosperous State Governments. In Britain, the Thatcher government proclaimed its objective as the creation of an 'enterprise culture' in place of the dependency which years of welfarism had built up. It attempted to encourage individual responsibility by a radical reform of the social security system in 1988, and to promote responsiveness and efficiency in the National Health Service by the creation of an 'internal market'.

b The conservative New Right

Consistent libertarians like Nozick and the anarcho-capitalists have no sympathy for conservative social theory. However, many supporters of New Right economics also hold profoundly conservative social views. Although they support freedom, they understand freedom in essentially economic terms. It is market freedom: 'freedom of choice'. They believe that the claims of economic liberty must be balanced against the need for social order. It is therefore possible for the New Right to defend the expansion of liberty in economic affairs and simultaneously call for the restoration of authority in social life. The dual character of Thatcherism was summed up by Andrew Gamble as 'free economy and strong state'.

Neo-conservatism is in some ways a reaction against the 'permissive Sixties'. Rising affluence in the post-war period had led, by the 1960s, to a growing willingness, especially amongst the young, to question and criticise conventional moral and social standards. Manifestations of this post-materialism were evident in the flowering of a youth 'counter-culture', which emphasised a personal choice of morality and life styles, and in the growth of a diverse range of political movements, including student radicalism, anti-Vietnam War protest, civil rights demonstrations, feminism and environmental activism. The New Right regarded these developments as evidence of the collapse of traditional moral principles. In the face of permissiveness, Thatcher in Britain proclaimed her support for 'Victorian values' and in the United States organisations like Moral Majority campaigned for a return to 'family values'.

David Edgar has argued that the conservative New Right has been prepared to place 'the Good' before 'the Free'. In its view there are two dangers in the permissiveness which allows people to choose for themselves what is 'good'. In the first place, the freedom to choose one's own morals or life style could lead to the choice of immoral or 'evil' views. There is a significant religious character to the conservative New Right, especially in the United States. During the 1970s, various groups sprang up in the United States which expressed concern about the decline in 'traditional values'. Many of these were associated with the 'Born Again' Christian movement and, in effect, constituted a 'Christian New Right'. Moral Majority, founded by Reverend Jerry Falwell in 1979 and supported by Ronald Reagan and powerful Southern Senators like Jessie Helms, acted as an umbrella organisation for this movement. During the 1980s, its principal energies were devoted to the campaign against abortion and, in particular, the attempt to overturn the 1973 Supreme Court judgement, Roe v. Wade, which legalised abortion in the United States. Similar so-called 'Pro-life' groups have sprung up in Britain and in other Western countries. They argue that women should not have the right to an abortion because the act is, quite simply, morally wrong. They equate abortion with any other kind of murder. Homosexuality, pornography, pre-marital sex and, in the States at least, the teaching of Darwinian theories of evolution rather than 'Creationism', have also been castigated as morally 'bad'.

The second danger of permissiveness is not so much that people may adopt the wrong morals or life styles, but may simply choose *different* moral positions. For a liberal, moral pluralism is healthy because it promotes diversity and rational debate, but for a neo-conservative it is deeply threatening, because it undermines the cohesion of society. A permissive society is a society which lacks any unifying moral standards. It is a 'pathless desert', which provides neither guidance nor support for individuals and their families. If individuals merely do as they please, civilised standards of behaviour will be impossible to maintain.

Neo-conservatives argue that this has been evident in rising delinquency and crime since the 1960s and a collapse of authority in society. People need and want to know where they stand, and what is expected of them. This security is provided by the exercise of authority, in the family by the father, at school by the teacher, at work by the employer, and in society at large by a system of 'law and order'. Permissiveness undermines the roots of authority in permit-ting, even encouraging, the questioning of authority. As respect for authority breaks down, disorder and instability escalate. The con-servative New Right stands, therefore, for the restoration of auth-ority. This can be seen in its call for the strengthening of 'family values'. The 'family', however, is understood in strictly traditional terms. It is thought to be naturally hierarchical: children should listen to, respect and obey their parents; and naturally patriarchal: the husband is the provider and the wife the home-maker. If these authority relationships are weakened, children will be brought up without a set of decent moral values and with little respect for their elders. A permissive society is therefore a breeding ground for anti-social behaviour, delinquency and crime.

Social order can also be strengthened by making punishment more severe both to express the revulsion of society towards crime, and to serve as a deterrent, discouraging criminal behaviour in others. In the States, neo-conservatives have campaigned for the restoration of the death penalty, regarded as a 'cruel and unusual punishment' by the Supreme Court in the 1960s, but re-adopted by a majority of States by the late 1980s. Similarly, the American New Right has campaigned to maintain the right to own firearms, enshrined in the Second Amendment of the American Constitution. In Britain, the campaign to restore hanging was unsuccessful, despite the support given it by Margaret Thatcher. Nevertheless, during the 1980s, the conditions of youth custody in Britain's Detention Centres were reformed to give young offenders a 'short, sharp shock' in the words of the then Home Secretary, William Whitelaw. The powers of the police were more clearly defined and in some respects strengthened, including their power to seize evidence, to stop, search, arrest and to detain suspects.

Such views about the need for order and discipline in society contrast strongly with the call for initiative and enterprise in the economy. Outside the economic sphere, the New Right calls for a strong state. Stuart Hall has interpreted Thatcherism as a form of 'authoritarian populism', reflecting and responding to widespread popular anxiety about the relaxation of moral standards and the weakening of authority in society. The New Right's case for a stronger state comes from its belief that order and social stability have increasingly been under threat. During the Miners' strike, 1984–5, Thatcher referred to trade union militants as an 'enemy within', against which the nation needed to be protected. Neo-conservatives fear that the growth of crime, vandalism, demonstrations and strikes all constitute a challenge to public order, against which only government can safeguard us.

At the same time, the New Right has perceived a growing threat from an 'enemy without'. This principally came from the Soviet Union, seen by Ronald Reagan and many in the American New Right as 'an evil Empire'. By the late 1970s, the Soviet Union was thought to be militarily superior to the United States, and also bent upon an ideological quest for world supremacy and the establishment of an international communist order. The New Right has been distinguished by its fierce anti-communism. In both Britain and the States there were campaigns for greater defence expenditure. In the United States, the early years of the Reagan administration saw a substantial increase in the Pentagon budget and the development of new nuclear missiles, such as the MX, as well as the launch of the Strategic Defence Initiative or 'Star Wars' project. In Britain, the Thatcher government supported the deployment of American Cruise missiles and undertook the purchase of Trident II nuclear missiles.

The conservative New Right has, finally, campaigned against what it believed to be a weakening of national ties and identities. Reagan sought to re-kindle American national pride, badly damaged by the ignominy of her withdrawal from Vietnam in 1975, and the humiliation of the seizure of American hostages in Iran in 1979. The military build-up of the 1980s was designed to re-establish America's predominance on the world stage, and it was hoped that the invasion of Granada and bombing of Libya would underline her willingness to use this power. The invasion of Panama, and the Gulf War of 1991, confirmed that this more interventionist and self-confident mood had persisted under the Bush Presidency. In Britain, the Thatcher government was also associated with resurgent national-ism, in particular in its truimphalist reaction to the Falklands War in 1982, and in its attempts to defend national sovereignty in the face of moves towards monetary and political union within the European Community.

7 The future of conservatism

The continued importance of conservatism in the late twentieth century is remarkable for an ideology which draws upon pre-industrial values and often claims to possess no coherent system of thought. Indeed the 1980s were characterised by conservative pre-dominance in a large number of Western countries. An electoral 'shift' to the Right was evident in the election of the Thatcher government in Britain in 1979 and its subsequent re-election in 1983 and 1987, and the election of Ronald Reagan as US President in 1980, his re-election in 1984, and the success of his former Vice President, George Bush, in 1988. Conservative parties also regained power in various parts of Europe, notably the CDU in West Germany in 1983, and in 1984 the Progressive Conservatives were returned to power in Canada under Brian Mulroney. Perhaps more signif-icantly, it has been claimed that these conservative governments have left an enduring mark by reshaping the public philosophy of their countries. The 1980s supposedly witnessed a 'Reagan revolution' in the States, in which both major parties, Republican and Democrat, agreed that government should 'get off the back of business'. New Deal liberalism had come to be widely associated with high taxes and unnecessary government interference, so much so that, during the 1988 Presidential campaign, Bush chided his Democratic op-ponent, Michael Dukakis, for his refusal to use 'the L word'. In Britain, the Thatcher government's stated objective was to 'roll back the frontiers of the state' and overturn the social democratic consensus, which had supported growing state intervention in social and economic life. It has been argued that a 'Thatcherite consensus' was forged during the 1980s by the establishment of an 'enterprise culture' and the conversion of other parties, notably the Labour Party, to market economics.

Such views suggest that conservatism has been successful in overthrowing a 'pro-state' tendency, which had characterised government in the twentieth century, especially since 1945, and in establishing an alternative 'pro-market' tendency. Despite this evidence of resurgence, it is difficult to accept conservatism as the dominant ideology of the late twentieth century. In the first place, its influence is still largely confined to the Western industrialised world. Conservatism developed essentially as a reaction against the growing pace of both political and economic change in the West. It defended the values of hierarchy, tradition and order against pressures generated by industrialisation and represented by the political challenge of liberalism and socialism. In developing countries, in contrast, pre-industrial values often stress the importance of community and equality, and provide a political culture more sympathetic to the growth of socialism or nationalism than the development of either liberal individualism or traditional conservatism. As a result, conservatism has not succeeded in developing into an ideology of worldwide significance. The success of the major non-Western conservative party – the Liberal-Democratic Party in Japan – can be explained by the unusually hierarchic values of traditional Japanese life.

Secondly, conservatism, as practised in the late twentieth century, is by no means uniform. The shift to the political Right in the 1970s and 1980s was, in many respects, a response to the onset of economic recession, as the interventionist policies of the earlier post-war period had been a consequence of the sustained growth of the 1950s and 1960s. The character of conservatism has varied according to how particular countries were affected by economic recession. The radical and ideological solutions presented by the New Right have had greatest impact in those countries which had experienced relative economic decline, notably Britain and the United States. In countries with stronger economies, conservatism retained its paternalistic character and its commitment to economic management. Conservatives in West Germany and Japan, for example, have shown little appetite for the free market economic philosophy which characterises Thatcherism and Reaganism.

Finally, it is questionable if the Thatcher and Reagan 'revolutions' will prove to be permanent. In the United States, the Republican

Party won five out of six of the presidential elections held between 1968 and 1988, but failed to gain similar influence within Congress. Except for the period between 1981 and 1987, the Democratic Party held majorities in both Houses of Congress. Moreover, once George Bush had won the 1988 presidential election, there was evidence of a return to the more moderate and less ideological brand of conservatism associated with Gerald Ford rather than Ronald Reagan. Bush referred in his inaugural address to his desire to create 'a kinder and gentler America', which contrasted strongly with the more rugged 'frontier ideology' language employed by his predecessor. In Britain, there is evidence that a Thatcherite consensus has not succeeded in replacing the old post-war social democratic consensus. Ivor Crewe has argued that after ten years of Thatcherism there was little evidence of the growth of the 'Thatcherite values' of self-reliance and enterprise in public opinion surveys. Rather, in cultural terms, he concluded that Thatcherism was 'a revolution that failed'. Furthermore, it is premature to conclude that the state has been permanently 'rolled back' in Britain. The Thatcher revolution was very closely tied up with the ideological enthusiasm and political will of Margaret Thatcher herself. Thatcher's pre-eminence in the party was largely based upon her ability to deliver electoral success and when that waned in 1990 she was abruptly removed. At no time did her views enjoy majority support amongst Conservative MPs, nor perhaps within her own Cabinet. Although her successor, John Major, espoused free market economic beliefs and enjoyed the support of the right-wing of the party during the leadership election, he also described himself as a 'social liberal', suggesting sympathy for One Nation values. The Major government moved very rapidly to distance itself from the conviction politics of the 1980s and returned to a more traditional and above-all pragmatic brand of conservatism. Under Major the party may not openly have renounced Thatcherism, but it certainly attempted to consolidate its success rather than turn it into a permanent revolution.

4
Socialism

Introduction

Socialism is the broadest of political ideologies, encompassing a bewildering range of theories and traditions. It is tempting to refer to 'socialisms', rather than simply 'socialism', when a common ideological heritage is claimed by communist revolutionaries, African nationalists, Western social democrats and even some fascists, notably National Socialists. Not uncommonly, these traditions have been more hostile towards one another, in their attempt to establish 'true' socialism, than they have been towards other ideologies.

Such confusion, however, largely arises from the success of socialism in establishing itself as a major political force in virtually every part of the globe, with the exception of North America. As socialist ideas have spread they have been moulded and sometimes transformed by the very different social, cultural and historical forces encountered in Western and Eastern Europe, Asia, Africa and Latin America. Although socialists have sometimes claimed an intellectual heritage that goes back to Plato's *Republic* or Thomas More's *Utopia* (1516), like liberalism and conservatism the origins of socialism lie in the nineteenth century. Socialism arose as a reaction against the social and economic conditions generated in Europe by the growth of industrial capitalism. The birth of socialist ideas was closely linked to the development of a new but growing class of industrial workers, who suffered the poverty and degradation so often a feature of early industrialisation. The earliest known use of the term 'socialist' was in 1827 in Britain, in an issue of the *Co-operative Magazine*, and by the 1840s the term was familiar in other industrialised countries, notably France, Belgium and the German states.

The character of early socialism was influenced by the harsh and often inhuman conditions in which the industrial working class lived and worked. The *laissez-faire* policies of the early nineteenth century gave factory owners a free hand in setting wage levels and factory conditions. Wages were typically low, child and female labour were commonplace, the working day often lasted up to twelve hours, and the threat of unemployment was ever-present. In addition, the new working class was disorientated, being composed very largely of first generation urban dwellers, unfamiliar with the conditions of industrial life and work, and possessing few of the social institutions that could give their lives stability or meaning. As a result, early socialists often sought a radical, even revolutionary, alternative to industrial capitalism. For instance, Charles Fourier in France and Robert Owen in Britain advocated the establishment of utopian communities based upon co-operation and love, rather than competition and greed. The Germans, Karl Marx and Friedrich Engels, developed more complex and systematic theories, which claimed to uncover the 'laws of history' and proclaimed that the revolutionary overthrow of capitalism was inevitable.

In the late nineteenth century, the character of socialism was transformed by a gradual improvement in working class living conditions. The growth of trade unions, working class political parties and sports and social clubs, served to provide greater economic security and to integrate the working class into industrial society. In the advanced industrial societies of Western Europe, it became increasingly difficult to see the working class as any longer a revolutionary force. Socialist political parties progressively adopted legal and constitutional tactics, encouraged by the gradual extension of the vote to working class men. By the First World War, the socialist world was clearly divided between those socialist parties which had come to seek power through the ballot box and preached reform, and those, usually in more backward countries like Russia, which proclaimed a continuing need for revolution. The Russian Revolution of 1917 entrenched this split: revolutionary socialists, following the example of Lenin and the Bolshevik Party, usually adopted the title 'communist', while reformist socialists retained the name 'socialist' or 'social democratic'.

The twentieth century has witnessed the spread of socialist ideas into Africa, Asia and Latin America, countries with little or no experience of industrial capitalism. Socialism often developed out of the anti-colonial struggle, rather than a class struggle. The idea of class exploitation has been replaced by that of colonial oppression, creating a potent fusion of socialism and nationalism, which is examined more fully in Chapter 4. The Bolshevik model of communism was adopted in China after the revolution of 1949 and subsequently spread to North Korea, Vietnam, Cambodia and Laos. More moderate forms of socialism have been practised elsewhere, for example, by the Congress Party which has ruled India for much of the period since independence in 1947. Distinctive forms of African and Arab socialism have also developed, being influenced respectively by the communal values of traditional tribal life and the moral principles of Islam. In South and Central America, socialist revolutionaries have waged war against military dictatorships, often seen to be operating in the interests of US imperialism. The Castro regime, which came to power after the Cuban revolution of 1959, developed close links with the Soviet Union, while the Sandinista guerrillas who seized power in Nicaragua in 1979 remained non-aligned. In Chile, Salvador Allende became the world's first democratically elected Marxist head of state in 1970, but was overthrown and killed in a CIA-backed coup in 1973.

In the late twentieth century, socialism has confronted a number of challenges. During the 'long boom' following the Second World War, social democratic parties often carried through major pro-grammes of social reform, establishing mixed economies and expanding welfare provision. In many ways, Sweden became the model Western social democracy, the Social Democratic Labour Party holding power through much of the post-war period. In Britain, similar reforms were undertaken by the Attlee Labour government, 1945–51. However, the onset of recession in the 1970s has, in many cases, eroded electoral support for socialist parties. This was most spectacular in Britain where Labour Party support fell in 1983 to its lowest since 1918, encouraging critics on the Right, like Margaret Thatcher, to proclaim the 'death of socialism'. Gorbachev's reforms in the Soviet Union and the dramatic events of 1989, which witnessed the collapse of Communist rule throughout Eastern Europe, have also been seen as a defeat for socialism itself, or at least as the end of Marxism as a world force. Nevertheless, the breadth and flexibility of socialist ideology has also been its strength. It is difficult, for example, to predict the end of an ideology that has demonstrated such a remarkable capacity to redefine itself and its goals in the light of changing historical circumstances. Moreover, underlying socialist ideology is a vision of human beings living together in harmony and peace, a vision that has existed as long as human history itself and which is unlikely ever to become irrelevant to political thought.

2 Collectivism

a Community

Despite the confusion of theories and ideas which have claimed an association with socialist ideology, there are a collection of basic principles which a large proportion of socialists would subscribe to. At its heart, socialism possesses a unifying vision of human beings as social creatures, capable of overcoming social and economic problems by drawing upon the power of the community rather than simply individual effort. This is a collectivist vision because it stresses the capacity of human beings for collective action, their willingness and ability to pursue goals by working together, as opposed to striving for personal self-interest. Socialists echo John Donne's belief that 'No man is an Island entire of itself; every man is a piece of the Continent, a part of the main'. Human beings are therefore 'comrades', 'brothers' or 'sisters', tied to each other by the bonds of a common humanity.

Socialists are far less willing than either liberals or conservatives to believe that human nature is unchanging and fixed at birth. They believe, rather, human nature to be 'plastic', moulded by the experiences and circumstances of social life. In the long-standing philosophical debate about whether 'nurture' or 'nature' determines human behaviour, socialists resolutely side with nurture. From birth – perhaps even while in the womb – each individual is subjected to experiences which shape and condition his or her personality. All human skills and attributes are learnt from society, from the fact that we stand upright, to the language we speak. Whereas liberals draw a clear distinction between the 'individual' and 'society', socialists believe that the individual is inseparable from society. Human beings are neither self-sufficient nor self-contained; to think of them as separate or atomised 'individuals' is absurd. Individuals can only be understood, and understand themselves, through the social groups to which they belong. Therefore, the behaviour of human beings tells us more about the society in which they live and have been brought up, than it does about any abiding or immutable human nature.

Liberals and conservatives often argue that, at heart, human beings are essentially self-seeking and egoistical. Socialists, on the other hand, regard selfish, acquisitive, materialistic or aggressive behaviour as socially conditioned rather than natural. Such characteristics are the product of a society which encourages and rewards selfish and acquisitive behaviour. This is precisely the allegation which socialists make against capitalism. Human beings are not 'utility maximisers' but are encouraged to act as such by the mechanism of the capitalist market, geared as it is to the pursuit of profit.

Industrial capitalism has distorted and restricted human nature; Karl Marx argued that it had alienated human beings from their true selves. Marx thought of human beings as workers, 'homo faber', who developed skills, talents and understanding through the experience of productive labour. However, in a capitalist society human beings are alienated from the product of their labour; they work to produce not what they need or what is useful, but 'commodities' to be sold for profit. They are also alienated from the process of labour itself, because most are forced to work under the supervision of foremen or managers. In addition, work is not social: individuals are encouraged to be self-interested and are therefore alienated from fellow human beings. Finally, workers are alienated from themselves because their talents and skills are stunted and their true potential is left unrealised.

The radical edge of socialism derives not from its concern with what people are like, but with what they have the capacity to become. This has led socialists to develop utopian visions of a better society in which human beings can achieve genuine emancipation and fulfilment as members of a community. African and Asian socialists have often stressed that their traditional, pre-industrial societies already emphasise the importance of social life and the value of community. In these circumstances, socialism has sought to preserve traditional social values in the face of the challenge from Western individualism. As Julius Nyerere, President of Tanzania, 1964–85, pointed out, 'We, in Africa, have no more real need to be "converted" to socialism, than we have of being "taught" democracy'. He therefore described his own views as 'tribal socialism'.

In the West, however, the social dimension of life has had to be 're-claimed' after several generations of industrial capitalism. This was the goal of nineteenth century utopian socialists, such as Fourier and Owen, who organised experiments in communal living. Charles Fourier encouraged the founding of model communities, each containing about 1800 members, which he called 'Phalansteries'. Robert Owen also set up a number of experimental communities, the best known being New Harmony in Indiana, 1824–9. The most enduringly successful communitarian experiment has, however, been the 'kibbutz' system in Israel, which consists of a system of co-operative, usually rural, settlements which are collectively owned and run by their members. The first kibbutz was founded in 1909 and now about 3 per cent of Israeli citizens live on kibbutzim, while a further 5 per cent live in rather less strict 'Moshav' settlements.

b Co-operation

If human beings are social animals, socialists believe that the natural relationship amongst them is one of co-operation, rather than competition. Liberals and conservatives regard competition amongst human beings as natural and, in some respects, healthy. It is natural because human beings are thought to be self-interested, and healthy in so far as it encourages each individual to work hard and develop whatever skills or abilities they may possess. Individuals should be rewarded for their personal achievements, whether it is running faster than anyone else, gaining higher marks in an exam, or working harder than their colleagues.

Socialists, on the other hand, believe that competition pits one individual against another, encouraging each of them to deny or ignore their social nature rather than embrace it. As a result, competition fosters only a limited range of social attributes and instead promotes selfishness and aggression. Co-operation, how-ever, makes moral and economic sense. Individuals who work together rather than against each other will develop the bonds of sympathy, caring and affection. Furthermore, the energies of the community rather than those of the single individual can be harnessed. The Russian anarchist, Peter Kropotkin, suggested, for example, that the principal reason why the human species had survived and prospered was because of its capacity for 'mutual aid'. Socialists believe that human beings can be motivated by moral incentives and not merely by material incentives. In theory, capitalism rewards individuals for the work they do: the harder they work, or the more abundant their skills, the greater their reward will be. The moral incentive to work hard, however, is the desire to contribute to the common good, which develops out of a sympathy or sense of responsibility for fellow human beings. In its extreme form, this was expressed by Marx in the formula, 'from each according to his abilities, to each according to his needs', implying that in full communism people would dedicate their labour to the betterment of society, without any thought of personal reward. Few modern social democrats would contemplate the outright abolition of material incentives to work, but most accept the need for a balance between material and moral incentives. For example, socialists would argue that an important incentive for achieving economic growth is that it helps to finance the provision of welfare support for the poorest and most vulnerable elements in society.

The socialist commitment to co-operation has stimulated the growth of co-operative enterprises, designed to replace the competitive and hierarchic businesses which have proliferated under capitalism. Both producers' and consumers' co-operatives have attempted to harness the energies of groups of people working for mutual benefit. In Britain, Co-operative Societies sprang up in the early nineteenth century which bought goods in bulk and sold them cheaply to their working class members. The 'Rochdale Pioneers' set up a grocery shop in 1844 and their example was soon taken up throughout industrial England and Scotland. Producer co-operatives, owned and run by their workforce, are common in parts of Northern Spain and in Yugoslavia, where industry is organised according to the principle of workers' self-management. Collective farms in the Soviet Union were also designed to be co-operative and self-managing, though in practice they operated within a rigid planning system and were usually controlled by local party bosses. As part of the reform process, however, Gorbachev legalised the formation of Yugoslav-style co-operatives in 1987 and encouraged their spread within the Soviet Union.

c Social class

Although socialists believe in the existence of a common humanity, they nevertheless stress the importance of social class and have traditionally linked their views to the interests of the working class.

Class designates a group of people who hold a common economic position and therefore share similar working and social experiences. Social class is important because capitalism is based upon social inequality, an unequal distribution of income or wealth. Capitalist society is characterised by deep social divisions, between the rich and the poor, employers and workers, or 'capital' and 'labour'. The working class is therefore exploited and oppressed. As a result, it provides a natural constituency for socialist ideas. However, the working class also offers the prospect of realising socialism. Socialists have traditionally looked upon the working class as an agent of social change and even social revolution.

Socialists have traditionally believed social class to be the deepest and most politically significant division in society, cutting across religious, ethnic, racial and national boundaries. Socialists have, for example, dreamed of fostering international working class solidarity. The First International Workingmen's Association was established by Marx in 1864, a Second or 'Socialist' International was set up in 1889, and revived in 1951. A Third International or 'Comintern' was formed by Lenin in 1919, while a rival 'Trotskyite' Fourth International came into existence in 1936. However, because the class system is founded upon exploitation and injustice, socialists also believe that class divisions can be and should be removed. Some socialists, like Marx, look forward to the creation of a 'classless society' in which all social and economic conflicts will be resolved because wealth will be owned in common.

Although all socialists believe class divisions to be important, they have not always agreed about the precise meaning of social class. Marxists define class in terms of economic power, the ownership of the 'means of production' or productive wealth. Marx believed that capitalist society was increasingly being divided into 'two great classes facing one another: Bourgeoisie and Proletariat'. The bourgeoisie was a small class of capitalists or property owners, while the proletariat constituted the propertyless masses who had been reduced to the status of 'wage slaves'. The bourgeoisie was a 'ruling class' because it controlled massive economic power and systematically exploited the proletariat by extracting what Marx called 'surplus value' in order to make profits. The conflict between bourgeoisie and proletariat was both fundamental and irreconcilable; it could only result in the overthrow of capitalism itself in a 'proletarian revolution'.

Class conflict was, for Marx, the key to understanding human history and society. 'The history of all hitherto existing societies', he declared, 'is the history of class struggles.' In Marx's view, each society was characterised by its 'mode of production', its economic system. History had progressed through a series of stages as each 'mode of production' collapsed because of its own internal contradictions, reflected in class conflict. Capitalism was merely the last in a series of class societies which had included slavery and feudalism. Like all previous societies, capitalism was unstable, doomed because of conflict between bourgeoisie and proletariat. This 'dialectical' process Marx believed to be the motor of history. What made capitalism different was that it was destined to be the last class society. The proletariat was the 'gravedigger' of capitalism and, being the vast majority in society, Marx believed that the 'proletarian revolution' would bring exploitation itself to an end, and thus create a classless, communist society.

Modern social democrats do not share this Marxist conception of class. In particular, capitalism has not appeared to develop as Marx had predicted. Far from becoming more intense, class conflict has gradually been diluted by growing affluence, at least in the industrialised West. The traditional division between property owners and workers has been replaced by a far more complicated social structure of differential rewards for particular occupations or jobs. As a result, social democrats have ceased to define class in terms of the ownership of wealth and have accepted instead the idea of occupational class. Class therefore reflects not an unequal distribution of economic power, but an unequal distribution of income. The working class is no longer thought of as the propertyless proletariat, but, more narrowly, as a class of manual or 'blue collar' workers, those whose jobs have traditionally been the lowest paid and enjoyed the least social status. Social democrats have therefore abandoned the goal of abolishing class divisions altogether, in favour of the desire to simply reduce them.

The link between socialism and the working class, however it is defined, has weakened during the twentieth century. In backward countries, such as Russia, the industrial working class was small and the Bolsheviks forged an alliance between workers and peasants, reflected in what was to become the symbol of communism: the hammer and the sickle. In China in 1949 and in other parts of the Third World, the peasantry rather than the working class has been regarded as the 'revolutionary class'. In the industrialised West, material prosperity has made the working class progressively less radical, encouraging some socialists, like Andres Gorz, to predict 'the death of the working class'. During the 1960s, the New Left increasingly abandoned any faith in the working class or proletariat and looked instead to the revolutionary potential of groups like students, women, ethnic minorities and the Third World.

d Equality

A commitment to equality is in many respects the defining feature of socialist ideology and the political value which distinguishes socialism from its rivals, notably liberalism and conservatism. Conservatives believe society to be naturally hierarchic and therefore that the idea of social equality is quite absurd. Liberals, however, are committed to equality, but on the grounds that all individuals enjoy an equal moral worth and are therefore entitled to equal rights and respect. They are nevertheless born with very different talents and skills and entitled to be rewarded accordingly: those who work hard and possess abilities deserve to be wealthier than those who do not. Liberals therefore favour equality of opportunity, but see no reason why this should, or will, lead to social and economic equality.

In contrast, socialists are far more reluctant to explain the inequality of wealth in terms of innate differences of ability amongst individuals. Just as capitalism has fostered competitive and selfish behaviour, so, socialists believe, human inequality very largely reflects the unequal nature of society. Socialists do not hold the naïve belief that all people are born identical, possessing precisely the same capacities and skills. An egalitarian society would not, for instance, be one in which all students gained the same mark in their maths examinations. Nevertheless, socialists believe that the most significant forms of human inequality are a result of unequal treatment by society, rather than an unequal endowment by nature. For example, despite natural differences in academic ability, educational performance is more usually a reflection of social factors, such as access to full-time schooling, the quality of teaching, encouragement and support of family, and the availability of resources like libraries, books and the space and time in which to study. As a result, socialists are not satisfied simply to allow individuals an equal opportunity to develop their unequal skills or talents. Socialists demand social equality as an essential guarantee that all individuals, and not merely the privileged, are able to develop themselves to the fullness of their potential.

Once individual differences are understood to be socially produced, social equality is seen as being both possible and desirable. Social inequality is not only unjust, being based very largely upon the accident of birth, but also fosters rivalry, resentment and social divisions. Equality, on the other hand, enables human beings to work together co-operatively and harmoniously: equality is the essential underpinning of a genuine community. Perhaps the most extreme example of the socialist commitment to egalitarianism was in China during the so-called Cultural Revolution, 1966–9. Fearful that the Chinese Revolution was in danger of taking a 'capitalist road' and falling under the influence of the 'rightist elements', Mao Tse-tung launched a radical campaign against privilege and inequality. An army of 'Red Guards' attacked and deposed 'capitalist roaders' within the government service, in schools and universities, and in the Communist Party itself. Wage differentials were swept away and even competitive sports such as football were banned.

Although socialists agree about the virtue of social and economic equality, they disagree about the extent to which this should be brought about. Marxists believe that inequality springs from the existence of private property, which has led to an unequal distribution of economic power between the property-owning bourgeoisie and the propertyless proletariat. For Marx, equality could only be achieved by the complete abolition of private property and the achievement of a classless society. Social equality will only be established when productive wealth is owned in common by all, in other words, when absolute equality is achieved.

Social democrats, however, seek to tame capitalism rather than abolish it. They believe that inequality reflects not the unequal ownership of wealth, but the fact that wealth is unequally distributed in society in terms of wages and salaries. Private property need not therefore be abolished but, less radically, simply be distributed more equally within society. Social democrats thus advocate the principle of greater distributive equality rather than that of absolute equality. In their view, equality can be brought about by the redistribution of wealth from rich to poor by, for example, expanding the welfare state or introducing a progressive system of taxation.

e Common ownership

Socialists have often traced the origins of competition and inequality to the institution of private property, by which they usually mean productive wealth or 'capital', rather than personal belongings, like clothes, furniture or houses. This attitude to property sets socialism apart from liberalism and conservatism, which both regard property ownership as natural and proper. Socialists criticise private property for a number of reasons. In the first place, property is unjust; wealth is produced by the collective effort of human labour and should therefore be owned by the community, not by private individuals. Secondly, socialists believe that property breeds acquisitiveness. Private property encourages people to be materialistic, to believe that human happiness or fulfilment can be gained through the pursuit of wealth. Those who own property wish to accumulate more, while those who have little or no wealth dream of acquiring it. Finally, property is divisive, it fosters conflict in society, for example, between owners and workers, employers and employees, or simply the rich and the poor. Socialists have therefore proposed that the institution of private property either be abolished and replaced by the common ownership of productive wealth or, more modestly, that the right to property be balanced against the interests of the community.

Karl Marx envisaged the abolition of private property and therefore proposed the creation of a classless, communist society in place of capitalism. He clearly believed that property should be owned collectively and used for the benefit of humanity. However, he said little about how this goal could be achieved in practice. When Lenin and the Bolsheviks seized power in Russia in 1917, they believed that socialism could be built through nationalisation, the extension of direct state control over the economy. This process was not completed until the 1930s when Stalin's 'second revolution' witnessed the construction of a centrally planned economy, a system of state collectivism. 'Common ownership' came to mean 'state ownership', or what the Soviet constitution described as 'socialist state property'. The Soviet Union thus developed a form of state socialism. Such an economic system was also thought to be more efficient than capitalism because it was based upon rational planning rather than the arbitrary pursuit of profit. All economic enterprises in the Soviet Union were directed by a sprawling network of government ministries and planning committees which set output targets, fixed prices and controlled all exchange.

Social democrats have also been attracted to the state as an instrument through which wealth can be collectively owned and the economy rationally planned. However, in the West nationalisation has been applied more selectively, its objective not being full state collectivism, but the construction of a mixed economy, in which some industries would remain in private hands, while others would be 'publicly owned'. In Britain, for example, the Attlee Labour government, 1945–51, nationalised what it called the 'commanding heights' of the economy, major industries like coal, steel, electricity and gas. Through these industries the government hoped to regulate the entire economy without the need for comprehensive collectivisation.

Other socialists have remained faithful to the goal of common ownership, but believe that it could be achieved without expanding the powers of the state. Although socialism has often been associated with state ownership, nationalisation and planning, it also possesses strong libertarian tradition. Marx, for instance, predicted that in a communist society the state would 'wither away', and certainly did not envisage the highly bureaucratic system of central planning which developed in Communist states during the twentieth century. Small, self-managing communities have often been thought to be more appropriate units of common ownership than the state. Anarcho-communists, like Peter Kropotkin, envisaged a stateless society made up of largely self-sufficient communes, in which people would work co-operatively and harmoniously. Other socialists have advocated the idea of 'workers' self-management', which became a central feature of the Yugoslav model of socialism after 1948.

3 Roads to socialism

Competing traditions and tendencies within socialism have been divided by two major issues. First, the goals or ends for which socialists strive. Socialists have held very different conceptions of what a socialist society would look like; in effect, there have been competing definitions of 'socialism'. These disagreements are discussed in the final two sections of this chapter. Secondly, socialists have disagreed about the appropriate means to achieve their ends, the various 'roads' that may lead to socialism. This concern with means follows from the fact that socialism developed as a radical or revolutionary ideology, critical of its host society, industrial capitalism in the West, or colonialism in the Third World. Socialists have consequently been concerned with change: the reform or overthrow of existing society. The choice of a particular 'road to socialism' is, however, of crucial significance because it both determines the character of the socialist movement and influences the form of socialism eventually achieved. In other words, 'means' and 'ends' are often very difficult to distinguish. The nature of socialism in the contemporary world has been deeply affected by choice between revolutionary and evolutionary roads to its achievement.

a Revolutionary socialism

Many early socialists believed that socialism could only be introduced by the revolutionary overthrow of the existing political system and accepted that violence would be an inevitable feature of such a revolution. One of the earliest advocates of revolution was the French socialist, August Blanqui, who proposed the formation of a small band of dedicated conspirators to plan and carry through a revolutionary seizure of power. Marx and Engels, on the other hand, envisaged a 'proletarian revolution', in which the class-conscious working masses would rise up to overthrow capitalism. The first successful socialist revolution did not, however, take place until 1917, when a dedicated and disciplined group of revolutionaries, led by Lenin and the Bolsheviks, seized power in Russia, in what was more a *coup d'état* than a popular insurrection. In many ways the Bolshevik Revolution has served as a model for subsequent generations of socialist revolutionaries.

During the nineteenth century, revolutionary tactics were attractive to socialists for two reasons. First, the early stages of industrialisation produced stark injustice as the working masses were afflicted by grinding poverty and widespread unemployment. Capitalism was seen to be a system of naked oppression and exploitation, and the working class was thought to be on the brink of revolution. When Marx wrote in 1848 that, 'A spectre is haunting Europe – the spectre of Communism' he was writing against a background of revolt and revolution in many parts of the continent. Secondly, the working classes had few alternative means of political influence, indeed almost everywhere they were excluded from political life. Where autocratic monarchies persisted throughout the nineteenth century, as in Russia, these were dominated by the landed aristocracy. Where constitutional and representative government had developed, the right to vote was usually restricted by a property qualification to the middle classes. In the exceptional cases where universal manhood suffrage was introduced much earlier, as in France in 1848, it was in predominantly agricultural and still deeply religious countries where the majority of the electorate, the small-holding peasantry, were politically conservative. In such cases the French anarchist, Proudhon, warned that 'universal suffrage is counter-revolution'. For the unenfranchised working masses the only realistic prospect of introducing socialism lay with political revolution.

Revolution was, however, not merely a tactical consideration for socialists, it also reflected their analysis of the state and its function. Whereas liberals believed the state to be a neutral body, responding to the interests of all citizens and acting in the common good, revolutionary socialists have believed the state to be an agent of class oppression, acting in the interests of 'capital' and against those of 'labour'. Marx, for example, argued that political power was, 'merely the organised power of one class for oppressing another' (p.58) and described the executive of the modern state as 'but a committee for managing the common affairs of the whole bourgeoisie'(p.37). Marxists therefore believe that political power reflects class interests, that the state is a 'bourgeois state', inevitably biased in favour of capital. Political reform and gradual change are clearly pointless. The proletariat has no alternative: in order to build socialism it has first to overthrow the bourgeois state through a political revolution. Marx believed that this revolution would be followed by a temporary period called the 'dictatorship of the proletariat', during which the revolution would need to be protected against the danger of counter-revolution carried out by the dispossessed bourgeoisie. Eventually, as socialism was established, the state would 'wither away' because there would be no call for class oppression in a classless society.

The class bias of the modern state was undeniable in a period when the working class was excluded from voting and political influence. However, revolutionary socialists believe that the 'bourgeois state' has not been reformed by the advent of political democracy. Lenin was the fiercest advocate of this view and of the continuing need for revolution. 'The real essence of bourgeois parliamentarianism', Lenin proclaimed in *The State and Revolution* (1917), was 'deciding every few years which member of the ruling class is to repress and crush the people through Parliament'(p.54). Parliamentary democracy is thus a mere facade concealing the reality of class rule, it is 'bourgeois democracy'. Modern Marxists have tended to revise this simplistic theory of the state and to acknowledge that at times the state can enjoy 'relative autonomy' from the class system. Nevertheless, a class bias continues to operate. In the first place, the personnel of the state, civil servants, judges, police chiefs and so on, are drawn predominantly from privileged social backgrounds and will thus seek to defend capitalism, as Ralph Miliband argued in *The State in Capitalist Society* (1969). Secondly, governments are usually judged by how far they can maintain growth and prosperity in the economy, which forces them to serve the interests of businessmen and industrialists. Finally, Marxists like Nicos Poulantzas have argued that it is the role of the state to support the social system within which it operates, which means, whatever party is in power, upholding the capitalist system.

In the second half of the twentieth century, faith in revolution has been most evident amongst socialists in the Third World. Since 1945, many national liberation movements have embraced the 'armed struggle' in the belief that colonial rule can neither be negotiated nor voted out of existence. In Asia, the Chinese Revolution of 1949 was the culmination of a long military campaign against both Japan and Chinese Nationalists, the Kuomintang. Vietnamese national unity was achieved in 1975 after a prolonged war fought first against France and subsequently the United States. Until his death in 1967, Che Guevara, the Argentine revolutionary, led guerrilla forces in various parts of South America and commanded troops during the Cuban revolution of 1959, which overthrew the US-backed Batista regime and brought Fidel Castro to power. Similar revolutionary struggles have taken place in Africa: for example, the bitter war through which Algeria eventually gained independence from France in 1962. In the light of the Algerian experience, Frantz Fanon argued in *The Wretched of the Earth* (1961) that violent insurrection was not merely a political necessity but also a psychologically desirable feature of the anti-colonial struggle. Fanon believed that years of colonial rule had engendered a paralysing sense of inferiority and impotence amongst the black peoples of Africa, which could only be purged by the experience of revolt and the shedding of blood.

b *Evolutionary socialism*

Although early socialists had supported the idea of revolution, as the nineteenth century progressed enthusiasm for popular revolt waned, at least in the advanced capitalist countries of Western and Central Europe. Capitalism itself had matured and by the late nineteenth century the urban working class had lost its revolutionary character and been integrated into society. Wages and living standards had started to rise, in part as a result of colonial expansion into Africa and Asia after 1875. The working class also began to develop a range of institutions – working men's clubs, trade unions, political parties – which both protected their interests and developed a sense of security and belonging within industrial society. Furthermore, the gradual advance of political democracy lead to the extension of the franchise, the right to vote, to the working classes. For example, a limited number of working class men were enfranchised in Britain in 1867, their number was expanded in 1884, and universal manhood suffrage was achieved in 1918. The combined effect of these factors was to shift the attention of socialists away from violent insurrection and to persuade them that there was an alternative evolutionary, or 'democratic', road to socialism. It is notable, for example, that towards the end of his life Marx was prepared to speculate about the possibility of a peaceful transition to socialism in the advanced capitalist countries of Western Europe, and Engels openly approved of the electoral tactics increasingly employed by the German Social Democratic Party (SPD). Where revolutionary doctrines continued to dominate it was usually in countries like Russia which were economically and politically backward.

In Britain, for instance, Marxist ideas had little impact and socialists were more influenced by the Fabian Society, formed in 1884. The Society, led by Sidney and Beatrice Webb and attracting noted intellectuals such as George Bernard Shaw and H.G. Wells, took its name from the Roman General, Fabius Maximus, who had been noted for the patient and defensive tactics he employed to defeat Hannibal's invading armies. The Fabians believed that socialism would develop naturally and peacefully out of liberal capitalism. They believed that this would be achieved by a combination of political action and education. Political action required the formation of a socialist party which would compete for power against established parliamentary parties, rather than prepare for violent revolution. They therefore accepted the liberal theory of the state as a neutral arbiter, rather than the Marxist belief that it was an agent of class oppression. The Webbs were actively involved in the formation of the British Labour Party, helping to write its 1918 constitution. The Fabians also believed that elite groups, such as politicians of all parties, civil servants, scientists and academics, could be converted to socialism through education. These elite groups would be 'permeated' by socialist ideas as they recognised that socialism was morally superior to capitalism, being based upon Biblical principles, as well as more rational and efficient. A socialist economy, for instance, could avoid the debilitating effects of class conflict and poverty.

Fabian ideas also had an impact upon the SPD, formed in 1875. The SPD quickly became the largest socialist party in Europe and, in 1912, the largest party in the German Reichstag. Although committed in theory to a Marxist strategy, in practice it adopted a reformist approach, influenced by the ideas of Ferdinand Lassalle. Lassalle had also argued that the extension of political democracy could enable the state to respond to working class interests, and envisaged socialism being established through a gradual process of social reform, introduced by a benign state. Such ideas were developed more thoroughly by Eduard Bernstein, whose *Evolutionary Socialism* (1898) carried out the first comprehensive revision of Marxist thought. Bernstein was particularly impressed by the development of the democratic state, which, he believed, made the Marxist call for revolution redundant. The working class could use the ballot box to introduce socialism, which would therefore develop as an evolutionary outgrowth of capitalism. Bernstein's own concerns were therefore largely pragmatic, his favourite maxim being that 'the movement is everything and the goal is nothing'.

The evolutionary principles of parliamentary socialism dominated the working class political parties which sprang up around the turn of the century: the Australian Labour Party, founded in 1891, the British Labour Party in 1900, the Italian Socialist Party, established in 1892, its French counterpart in 1905, and so on. In the early years of the twentieth century, the Second International was split by

disagreements between revolutionary socialists like Lenin and socialist leaders, such as Karl Kautsky in Germany, who pursued reformist
tactics. By the end of the First World War, a deep rift had developed
between the socialist and communist movements. Socialist parties,
embracing a parliamentary road to socialism, employed legal and
electoral methods and proclaimed their commitment to 'democratic
socialism'. Communist parties, on the other hand, formed in the
aftermath of the Russian Revolution, remained faithful to the
insurrectionary tactics which Lenin and the Bolsheviks had employed successfully in 1917.

In the late twentieth century, however, the distinction between
evolutionary socialism and revolutionary communism has become
increasingly blurred. In the 1970s Western Communist parties, led
by the Spanish, Italian and French Communist parties, formally
abandoned violent revolution and recast themselves as parliamentary parties. The resulting Eurocommunism is committed to
pursuing a democratic road to communism and the maintenance of
an open, competitive political system. The momentous events of
1989 witnessed the collapse of single party Communist rule throughout Eastern Europe and the establishment of political pluralism.
With the introduction of competitive party systems, the Communist
parties of the Soviet Union and Eastern Europe acknowledged the
underlying principle of evolutionary socialism, that political power
should only be gained, and retained, through success in a competitive struggle for the popular vote.

c The inevitability of gradualism?

The advent of political democracy in the late nineteenth and early
twentieth centuries caused a wave of optimism to spread throughout
the socialist movement, reflected, for example, in the Fabian
prophecy of 'the inevitability of gradualism'. The idea that the
victory of socialism was inevitable was not new. Marx, for instance,
had predicted the inevitable overthrow of capitalist society in a
proletarian revolution. However, whereas Marx believed that history
was driven by the irresistible forces of class conflict, evolutionary
socialists highlighted the logic of the democratic process itself.

Their optimism was founded on a number of assumptions. First,
the progressive extension of the franchise would eventually lead to
the establishment of universal adult suffrage and therefore of

political equality. Secondly, political equality worked in the interests of the majority, who decided the outcome of elections. Socialists therefore believed that political democracy invested power in the hands of the working class, easily the most numerous class in any industrial society. Thirdly, socialism was thought to be the natural 'home' of the working class. Capitalism was a system of class exploitation and the oppressed workers would therefore be drawn to support the socialist parties which offered them social justice and emancipation. The electoral success of socialist parties was therefore guaranteed by the numerical strength of the working class. Fourthly, once in power, socialist parties would be able to carry out a fundamental transformation of society through a process of social reform. Political democracy therefore did not only open up the possibility of achieving socialism peacefully, it made this process inevitable. The achievement of political equality had to be speedily followed by the establishment of social equality.

Such optimistic expectations have however not been borne out in reality. Some have even argued that democratic socialism is founded upon a contradiction: in order to respond successfully to electoral pressures, socialists have been forced to revise or 'water down' their ideological beliefs. Socialist parties have enjoyed periods of power in virtually all liberal democracies, outside North America. However, they have certainly not been guaranteed power. The Swedish Social Democratic Labour Party (SAP) has been the most successful in this respect, having been in power alone or as the senior partner in a coalition since 1951, except for the 1976–82 period. However, even the SAP has only achieved 50 per cent of the popular vote once, in 1968. The British Labour Party gained its greatest support, 49 per cent, in 1951, equalled by the Spanish Socialist Workers' Party in 1982. The SPD in Germany got 46 per cent of the vote in 1972 and the combined Socialist and Communist vote in Italy in 1976 amounted to 44 per cent. Moreover, although these parties have undoubtedly introduced significant social reforms when in power, usually involving the expansion of welfare provision, they have certainly not presided over any fundamental social transformation. At best, capitalism has been reformed, not abolished.

Democratic socialism has in fact encountered a number of problems not envisaged by its founding fathers. In the first place, does the working class any longer constitute the majority of the electorate in advanced industrial societies? Socialist parties have traditionally focused their electoral appeal upon urban manual workers, the 'factory fodder' of capitalist societies. Modern capitalism, however, has become increasingly technological, demanding a skilled workforce, engaged in technical rather than simply manual tasks. In Britain, Ivor Crewe has distinguished between the shrinking ranks of the 'traditional working class', engaged in established heavy industries, and the growing 'new working class', often skilled workers, usually better paid, and working in the expanding light industries, service industries, or 'sunrise' industries. In *How Britain Votes* (1984) Heath, Jowell and Curtice, define 'working class' as manual workers who have no supervisory responsibilities. They calculated that in 1983 the working class constituted a mere 34 per cent of the British electorate. If working class support no longer gives socialist parties the prospect of an electoral majority, they are either forced to appeal more broadly for support to other social classes, or to share power as a coalition partner with middle-class parties. Both options require socialist parties to modify their ideological commitments, either to appeal to electors who have little or no interest in socialism, or to work with parties which seek to uphold capitalism.

Furthermore, is the working class socialist at heart, is socialism in the interests of the working class? Socialist parties have been forced to take stock of the ability of capitalism to 'deliver the goods', especially during the 'long boom' of the post-war period which brought growing affluence to all classes in Western societies. During the 1950s, socialist parties once committed to fundamental change revised their policies in an attempt to appeal to an increasingly affluent working class. For example, at the Bad Godesberg Congress of 1959 the German SPD formally abandoned the goal of common ownership in favour of a market-based approach to the economy. In Britain, the leadership of the Labour Party under Hugh Gaitskell tried, without success, to abolish Clause IV of Labour's constitution, which committed the party to wholesale nationalisation. In 1987, after three successive election defeats, the Labour Party carried out a comprehensive policy review which placed its emphasis upon the market rather than 'social ownership'.

Left-wing socialists, however, have been reluctant to accept that the working class has abandoned fundamentalist socialism. They believe rather that the working class has been deprived of the ability to make independent political judgements which reflect their own interests. Marxists, for example, believe that capitalism is supported by a process of ideological manipulation. 'The ruling ideas in each age', Marx argued, 'have ever been the ideas of its ruling class' (p.51). 'Bourgeois ideology' pervades society, preventing the working class perceiving the reality of its own exploitation. Lenin argued that without the leadership of a revolutionary party the working class would only be able to gain 'trade union consciousness', a desire for material improvement within the capitalist system, but not full revolutionary 'class consciousness'. The Italian Marxist, Gramsci, emphasised that the bourgeoisie dominated capitalism not only through its economic power but also by a process of 'ideological hegemony'. Criticism has also focused upon the role of the mass media in forming the views and values of the electorate. Although the media in capitalist countries usually enjoys independence from government, socialists would strongly deny that it is politically impartial. In *Arguments for Democracy* (1981), for instance, Tony Benn suggested that the mass media in Britain and other capitalist countries possess an anti-socialist bias, largely because newspaper ownership lies in the hands of a small number of powerful individuals or major multi-national companies.

Finally, can socialist parties, even if elected to power, carry through socialist reforms? Socialist parties have formed single party governments in a number of Western countries: Britain, France, Sweden, Australia, New Zealand and so on. Once elected, however, they confront entrenched interests within both the state and society. In 1902, Karl Kautsky argued that 'the capitalist class rules but it does not govern, it contents itself with ruling the government'. Elected governments operate within what Miliband has called a 'state system' – the administration, courts, police and military – whose personnel are not elected and come from similar social backgrounds to businessmen. These groups reflect a class bias and are capable of blocking, or at least diluting, radical socialist policies. Furthermore, elected governments, of whatever ideological inclination, must respect the power of big business, which is the major employer and investor in the economy, as well as the wealthiest contributor to party funds. In other words, although democratic socialist parties have succeeded in forming elected governments, there is the danger that they have merely won office without necessarily acquiring power.

4 Communism

The term 'communism' has caused particular confusion in political debate because it has been used in a number of ways. First, it refers to a utopian vision of a future society envisaged and described by Marx and Engels. Secondly, it stands for the ideas and policies of Communist parties, supposedly inspired by Marxist principles but formed many years after Marx's death. Thirdly, it is used to describe the regimes which such parties established when they gained power, for example, in the Soviet Union, Eastern Europe, China, Cuba and so on. In the *Manifesto of the Communist Party* (1848), Marx summed up the theory of communism in a single sentence: 'Abolition of private property'. A communist society is therefore a classless society in which productive wealth is owned collectively. Although Marx was reluctant to describe such a future society in any detail, he clearly envisaged that it would provide conditions in which human beings could achieve full emancipation: wealth would be used for the benefit of all rather than the profit of a few, and individuals would be able to realise their talents and skills through unalienated labour. Furthermore, in the absence of class conflict, the state would lose its central function, that of class oppression, and would, Marx predicted, 'wither away', allowing human beings to manage their own affairs rationally and co-operatively.

Marx developed these ideas on the basis of what Engels called 'the materialist conception of history'. Marx's writings were materialist in the sense that he believed that human society could only be understood in the light of the dialectical relationship between humankind and the material world: as productive creatures, human beings fashioned their world but were, in the process, themselves transformed, developing talents, skills and sensibilities. Marx therefore believed that history and society could only be explained in terms of what he called the economic 'base' which conditioned the legal and political 'superstructure'. In his view, history progressed through a series of stages, each characterised by its 'mode of production' or economic system, from slavery and feudalism to capitalism and, finally, communism. At each point, historical change resulted from the internal contradictions which characterised all class societies. This occurred when the class system itself, the 'relations of production', became a constraint upon the further development of productive techniques and innovation, the 'forces of production', and was reflected in a social revolution through which a new mode of production emerged.

Marx acknowledged that capitalism had witnessed a remarkable growth in productive capacities compared with feudalism, but predicted that it, like all other class societies, was ultimately doomed, and would eventually be overthrown in a proletarian revolution. It was only with the establishment of a classless, communist society that material wealth could be exploited rationally and for the benefit of all humankind, thus bringing what Marx referred to as the 'pre-history of man' to an end. After Marx's death, these ideas were popularised in the more accessible writings of his lifelong collaborator, Engels, and spread throughout the fast-growing social democratic movement. Some have argued, however, that Engels simplified and perhaps distorted Marxism, turing it into a mechanistic, even deterministic, philosophy that claimed to uncover the universal 'laws' of nature, history and human thought. Termed 'dialectical materialism' by the Russian Marxist Plekhanov, this philosophy later became the basis of Soviet science and social theory, and thus the cornerstone of orthodox Marxism.

The Communist parties which developed in the twentieth century were undoubtedly founded upon the theories and beliefs of Marx and Engels; however, they were also forced to adapt these ideas to the task of winning and retaining political power. In the process, classical Marxism was significantly revised and extended. Moreover, when Communist parties achieved power it was not as Marx had anticipated in the developed capitalist countries of Western Europe, but in backward, largely rural countries like Russia and China. The resulting Communist regimes have therefore been shaped as much by historical circumstances and practical factors as by any ideological model. As a result, Communist rule in the twentieth century has often diverged markedly from the utopian vision which Marx developed in the nineteenth century.

a The Bolshevik model

The image of communism in the twentieth century has been dominated by the Russian Revolution and its consequences. The Bolshevik party, led by V.I. Lenin, seized power in a *coup d'état* in October 1917, and the following year adopted the name 'Communist Party'. As the first successful communist revolutionaries, the Bolshevik leaders enjoyed unquestionable authority within the communist world, at least until the 1950s. Communist parties set up elsewhere accepted the ideological leadership of Moscow and joined the Communist International or 'Comintern', founded in 1919. When communist regimes were established elsewhere, as in Eastern Europe after 1945, in China in 1949, and in Cuba in 1959, they were consciously modelled upon the structure of the Soviet Union. Soviet communism thus became the dominant model of communist rule, and the ideas of Marxism–Leninism became the ruling ideology of the communist world.

However, the Bolshevik model of communism owed much to the particular historical conditions of Russia in 1917. In the first place, Russia was economically backward, the overwhelming majority of Russians still lived on the land and the urban proletariat was small and unsophisticated. Indeed, orthodox Marxists, such as members of the Menshevik party, believed Russia to be at the feudal stage of development and to be ripe for a bourgeois revolution but to be many years away from a socialist one. It was not until Trotsky formulated his theory of permanent revolution in 1906 that anyone conceived of the immediate prospect of achieving socialism in Russia. In Trotsky's view Russian development had been 'uneven' and her bourgeoisie was not strong enough to establish a stable capitalist society. The bourgeois stage of development could therefore be collapsed and Russia could move immediately from a capitalist to a socialist revolution, led by her small but powerful proletariat. Secondly, political life had been stunted by repressive and autocratic Tsarist rule, which had forced opponents of the regime either to live in exile abroad or organise themselves into tightly disciplined, conspiratorial groups in the hope of escaping arrest and imprisonment. Finally, once in power the Bolsheviks confronted hostility from both within and without. 'White' armies, loyal to the Tsar, waged a Civil War until 1921 and were supported by foreign troops from Britain, France, USA and Japan. As a result, the emerging Communist regime became accustomed to employing coercive means in order to maintain political stability and defend itself against 'class enemies'. Far from 'withering away', as Marx had predicted, the combination of economic backwardness and political instability forced the newly-established 'proletarian state' to become increasingly centralised and powerful.

Soviet communism was also shaped by the decisive personal

contribution of the first two Bolshevik leaders, Lenin and Stalin. Lenin was both a political leader and a major political thinker. The ideas of Leninism reflect Lenin's overriding concern with the problems of winning power and establishing communist rule. Lenin remained faithful to the idea of revolution, believing that parliamentary politics were merely a bourgeois sham, aimed at deceiving the proletariat into believing that political power was exercised through the ballot box. Power had to be seized through an armed insurrection, in accordance with Lenin's exhortation to 'smash the state!'. Lenin also emphasised the need for a transitional period between the proletarian revolution and the achievement of 'full communism', called the dictatorship of the proletariat. The revolution had to be protected against the possibility of counter-revolution, mounted by 'class enemies' – the dispossessed bourgeoisie who wished to restore capitalism. The state would not therefore 'wither away' immediately after a revolution; a 'proletarian state' or 'workers' state' should be established to replace the bourgeois state, and must continue to exist until the class system was completely eradicated.

The most significant and novel of Lenin's ideas was his belief in the need for a new kind of political party, a revolutionary party or vanguard party. Unlike Marx, Lenin did not believe that the proletariat would spontaneously develop revolutionary class consciousness. The working class was deluded by bourgeois ideas and beliefs. Lacking any grasp of the Marxist analysis, workers failed to recognise that their real enemy was the capitalist system itself, and instead sought to improve its conditions within capitalism by achieving better pay, shorter hours, and safer working conditions. Lenin suggested that only a 'revolutionary party' could lead the working class from 'trade union consciousness' to revolutionary class consciousness. Such a party should be composed of professional and dedicated revolutionaries. Its claim to leadership lay in its ideological wisdom, an understanding of Marxist theory, which was thought to provide a scientific explanation of social and historical development. The party could therefore act as the 'vanguard of the proletariat' because, armed with Marxism, it would be able to perceive the genuine interests of the proletariat and was dedicated to awakening the proletarian class to its revolutionary potential.

Finally, Lenin proposed that the vanguard party should be organised according to the principles of democratic centralism. The party should be composed of a hierarchy of institutions, linking grass root cells to the party's highest organs, its Central Committee and Politburo. 'Democracy' within the party required that each level of the party could debate freely, make recommendations to higher organs and elect their delegates; however, 'centralisation' meant that minorities must accept the views of the majority, and that lower organs of the party obey decisions made by higher ones. The revolutionary party had to be tightly disciplined and centrally organised in order to provide the ideological leadership the proletariat needed. Lenin was confident that democratic centralism could achieve both 'freedom of discussion and unity of action'.

When the Bolsheviks seized power in 1917 they did so as a vanguard party and therefore in the name of the proletariat. If the Bolshevik party acted in the interests of the working class, it followed that opposition parties must represent the interests of classes hostile to the proletariat, in particular the bourgeoisie. The dictatorship of the proletariat required that the revolution be protected against its class enemies, which effectively meant the suppression of all parties other than the Communist Party. By 1920, Russia had become a one party state. Leninist theory therefore implies the existence of a monopolistic party, which enjoys sole claim to articulate the interests of the proletariat and guide the revolution toward its ultimate goal, that of 'building communism'. Moreover, the party must also be a ruling party. As the source of political authority within a communist state, the Communist Party must be the 'leading and guiding force' within government and all other institutions. Orthodox Communist states, modelled on the principles of Marxism–Leninism, have therefore invested their ruling Communist parties with entrenched political power and a monopoly of ideological wisdom.

Soviet communism was no less deeply influenced by the rule of Joseph Stalin, who won the struggle for power within the Communist Party after Lenin's death in 1924. Indeed, the Soviet Union was more profoundly affected by Stalin's 'second revolution', in the 1930s, than it had been by the October Revolution. Unlike Lenin, Stalin was not a major political thinker. His most important ideological innovation was the doctrine of 'Socialism in One Country', announced in 1924, which proclaimed that the Soviet Union could succeed in 'building socialism' without the need for international revolution and clearly distinguished him from Trotsky who maintained an unswerving commitment to internationalism. After consolidating himself in power, however, Stalin embarked upon a dramatic economic and political upheaval, commencing with the announcement of the first Five Year Plan in 1928. Under Lenin's New Economic Policy, introduced in 1921, the Soviet Union had developed a mixed economy in which agriculture and small scale industry remained in private hands, while the state controlled only what Lenin called the 'commanding heights of the economy'. Stalin's Five Year Plans, however, brought about rapid industrialisation as well as the swift and total eradication of private enterprise. From 1929 agriculture was also collectivised, the Soviet peasantry being forced at the cost of literally millions of lives to give up its land and join state or collective farms. Economic Stalinism therefore took the form of state collectivism or 'state socialism'. The capitalist market was entirely removed and replaced by a system of central planning, dominated by the State Planning Committee, 'Gosplan', and administered by a collection of powerful economic ministries based in Moscow.

Major political changes accompanied this 'second revolution'. In order to achieve power, Stalin had exploited his position as Secretary of the Communist Party by ensuring that his supporters were appointed to influential posts within the party apparatus. Party officials were appointed from above by a system known as the nomenklatura, rather than being elected from below. Democratic centralism became less democratic and more centralised, leading to a 'circular flow of power' in which the party leader acquired unrivalled authority by virtue of his control over patronage and promotion. During the 1930s, Stalin used this power to brutal effect, removing anyone suspected of disloyalty or criticism in an increasingly violent series of purges carried out by the secret police, the NKVD. The membership of the Communist Party was almost halved, over a million people lost their lives, including all surviving members of Lenin's Politburo, and many millions were imprisoned in labour camps or *gulags*. Political Stalinism was therefore a form of totalitarian dictatorship, operating through a monolithic ruling party, in which all forms of debate or criticism were eradicated by terror, in what amounted to a civil war conducted against the party itself. The nature of this regime will be discussed in more depth in Chapter 6, in connection with totalitarianism.

b The monolith cracks

Until the death of Stalin in 1953, Soviet communism retained almost unquestionable authority in the communist world. The Soviet Union had succeeded in becoming a major industrial power, it had helped to defeat fascism in the Second World War, and its influence had expanded with the establishment of Communist rule in Eastern Europe and in China. During this period, the principal critic of Soviet communism was Leon Trotsky. Although Trotsky had led the Bolshevik coup in 1917 and commanded the Red Army, he had been defeated by Stalin in the power struggle in the 1920s, was exiled from the Soviet Union in 1929, and was finally murdered by Stalin's assassins in 1940. In the 1930s, Trotsky had argued that the Soviet Union suffered from a 'bureaucratic degeneration', and proposed that a political revolution was necessary to overthrow the privileged strata of state bureaucrats and return the Soviet Union to the road to socialism. Although Trotsky formed a Fourth International to challenge the Soviet-dominated Communist International, he remained an outcast in the communist world and his ideas had little impact until long after his death.

The death of Joseph Stalin allowed a gradual process of questioning and criticism to take place within the Soviet Union and elsewhere. In 1956 Stalin's successor, Khrushchev, presented a 'secret speech' to the Twentieth Congress of the Soviet Communist Party, which catalogued the 'crimes of Stalin', alleging that he had built up a 'cult of personality' and was personally responsible for the brutality and suffering of the 1930s. Khrushchev's allegations shocked a communist world which held Stalin to be the legitimate heir of Lenin and Marx. A period of de-Stalinisation dawned in the Soviet Union, reflected in a 'cultural thaw' and a limited attempt to decentralise economic power. The Soviet invasion of Hungary, also in 1956, caused the first ripples of criticism of Moscow to spread within Western Communist parties. In 1958, Mao Tse-tung introduced the so-called 'Great Leap Forward' in China and established greater independence from Moscow, which led in 1960 to a formal break in relations with the Soviet Union. As the communist world became less monolithic, the Bolshevik model was challenged by rival conceptions of socialism in both the West and the East.

In the 1970s, Western Communist parties, which had previously accepted the ideological leadership of Moscow, began to establish greater independence and pursue a distinctive brand of Eurocommunism. The break with Moscow was provoked by two factors. First, after the overthrow of Khrushchev in 1964 there was growing distaste for both Soviet foreign and domestic policies, which under Brezhnev entered a period of neo-Stalinism. The Soviet invasion of Czechoslovakia in 1968 seriously strained the loyalty of Western parties, as did the crackdown on dissidents and the restriction of human rights which was reflected in the arrest and expulsion of Alexander Solzhenitsyn and the suppression of intellectuals like Andrei Sakharov. Secondly, in a period of economic growth and political stability in the West, the electoral appeal of Communist parties was damaged by the fact that they continued to regard themselves as revolutionary parties and by their acknowledged subordination to Moscow.

The Italian, French and Spanish Communist parties were the first to exercise greater independence and in 1977 agreed a broadly worded declaration of Eurocommunist principles. In the first place, they accepted that communism had to conform to existing national traditions and culture: Russian experience was not always relevant to conditions in Western Europe. The Italian Communist Party, for example, wished to abandon any formal link with atheism. The central principle of Eurocommunism, however, was the rejection of the Leninist idea of revolution in favour of a gradual and peaceful transition towards socialism. Western Communist parties have therefore become parliamentary parties, committed to constitutional and electoral politics. In accepting that power can be won through the ballot box, the Eurocommunists have revised the Leninist idea that the state is merely an instrument of class rule and argued that the state can enjoy at least 'relative autonomy' from the class system and be influenced by all social classes, including the proletariat. Furthermore, Eurocommunist parties have re-assessed the idea of the vanguard party. They no longer consider themselves to be the sole representatives of the working class and have therefore been prepared to enter into alliances with other parties. For example, the Italian Communist Party briefly shared power with the Christian Democrats, 1977–8, in what was called the 'historic compromise', and French Communists served in the Socialist-dominated government of 1981–4.

Finally, Eurocommunists have abandoned the idea of a dictatorship of the proletariat. If political power can be won through competitive elections, it must be retained in the same way. Eurocommunist parties therefore accept the principles of political pluralism and have no ambition to establish one-party Communist rule. Eurocommunist principles have therefore departed fundamentally from orthodox Marxism–Leninism and in many ways the political practice of European Communist parties has become indistinguishable from that of social democratic parties. This process of revision was significantly accelerated by the events of 1989. In 1989, for example, the Italian Communist Party formally adopted a social democratic programme and in 1990 it dropped the title 'Communist' from the party's name, in a trend soon followed by other Communist parties.

Some Communist states also took up the idea of reform. For example, during the 'Prague Spring' of 1968 the Czechoslovak Communist leader, Alexander Dubcek, attempted an experiment in what he called 'Socialism with a human face'. Civil liberties and political freedoms were restored, restrictions imposed upon the secret police, and the first elements of a competitive party system introduced. However, the experiment was abruptly terminated in August 1968 by a Warsaw Pact invasion, which led to Dubcek's removal and the re-imposition of Marxist–Leninist orthodoxy. A further example is Yugoslavia, which has never fully conformed to the Stalinist system of central planning. Over 85 per cent of Yugoslav agricultural land is privately owned and its industry operates according to the principle of workers' self-management. Economic decentralisation was also introduced in Hungary in 1968 as part of what was called the 'New Economic Mechanism'. Yugoslav and Hungarian reforms have created an alternative model of economic development to rival Soviet-style central planning, commonly called market socialism. The essence of this model is the attempt to gain the benefits of the market: efficiency, competition and responsiveness, without the re-introduction of private property or a capitalist class system. Such an economy remains 'socialist' because there is no market for labour and the economy is dominated by workers' co-operatives; these, however, operate within a competitive market environment.

c The death of communism?

1989 marked a dramatic watershed in the history of communism. A wave of popular demonstrations, commencing in April with the emergence of a student-led 'democracy movement' in China, challenged Communist rule in many parts of the world. Although the Tiananmen Square demonstrations were brutally suppressed in June, Communist regimes collapsed throughout Eastern Europe in the autumn and winter of 1989. The Berlin Wall was breached on 10 November and by the end of the year the 'Iron Curtain', which had divided Europe since 1945 into a capitalist West and a communist East, had ceased to exist. Where Communist rule survived, the process of internal reform was immediately accelerated.

These dramatic events were made possible by a change in political leadership in the Soviet Union: the appointment of Mikhail Gorbachev as General Secretary of the Communist Party in 1985. Alarmed by the stagnation and inefficiency of the Soviet economy, Gorbachev inaugurated a process of radical reform in the Russian tradition of a 'revolution from above'. He established three goals: the first and most important was *perestroika*, the 'restructuring' of the economy; secondly, *glasnost*, or greater 'openness', freedom of political debate; and thirdly, democratisation, broader popular participation in public life. Initially, Gorbachev's reforms continued a process of de-Stalinisation, begun under Khrushchev in the 1950s. Economic reform meant a gradual transition from central planning to a 'market socialist' economy, by encouraging Soviet enterprises to become self-managing and allowing co-operatives and single proprietor businesses to develop. Political reforms permitted greater freedom of discussion within the Communist Party and allowed more open criticism within Soviet society, in a return to what Gorbachev called 'Leninist democracy'. Gorbachev also accepted that reform required a new approach to foreign policy, in particular a reduction in military spending and a new relationship with the West. This was reflected in the INF treaty, signed in 1987, which for the first time reduced the size of nuclear arsenals. When unrest broke out in Eastern Europe in 1989, Gorbachev refused to intervene as the Soviet Union had done in 1956 and 1968, and accepted the collapse of Communist rule.

Under pressure from growing opposition within the Soviet Union, and fuelled by continued economic decline and developments in Eastern Europe, the reform process entered a more radical and more clearly liberal phase in 1989–90. The second phase of reform witnessed a process of de-Leninisation. The Communist Party gave up its monopoly of power in March 1990, accepting full political pluralism and a competitive party system. The introduction of a new Soviet Parliament and an Executive Presidency created the possibility of a peaceful and democratic overthrow of Communist rule. The Soviet Union also abandoned the goal of market socialism and chose to construct a Western-style capitalist economy. However, Gorbachev's attempts to balance the demands of radical reformers against the fears of hardline conservatives collapsed spectacularly in August 1991 when a military coup briefly removed him from power. The coup marked the point at which Soviet reforms ceased to be a 'revolution from above' and came instead to resemble the popular revolutions which had transformed Eastern Europe two years earlier. The defeat of the coup was swiftly followed by the disintegration of the centralised Soviet state as a succession of republics declared independence from Moscow or, led by the Baltic states, formally seceded from the Union. The machinery of Communist rule was dismantled and steps were taken to disband the Communist Party, at least in its traditional form. Considerable tasks of economic reform nevertheless remained to be undertaken; *perestroika* had uprooted an existing, if inefficient, economic system more quickly than it had constructed an alternative.

Some, like Francis Fukuyama, have interpreted these developments as the 'death of Marxism–Leninism as a living ideology' and the triumph of Western liberalism. Even the Marxist historian, Eric Hobsbawm, has accepted that the 'era of the October Revolution' has ended. Others, however, have interpreted these developments as an opportunity for socialism rather than its defeat. In the Soviet Union, Mikhail Gorbachev has argued that Marxist socialism is of enduring significance and is capable of retaining its popular appeal; indeed, Gorbachev had claimed that communism was experiencing a period of transition and 'democratic renewal'. Such a view is based upon the belief that it is not communism itself which has collapsed, but rather a particular Bolshevik conception of communist rule. As an ideology, communism may be flexible and resilient, capable of surviving the rejection of both Stalinist and Leninist forms of Marxism. Some socialists in Eastern Europe have argued that 1989 marked an opportunity rather than a defeat because it broke the link between socialism and authoritarianism. They have tried to develop a 'Third Way' between central planning and the free market, usually based upon the model of Swedish social democracy. However, the experience of Soviet-style state socialism has provoked a backlash against the idea of socialism itself. When free elections were held in East Germany, Hungary, Poland, Czechoslovakia and also in some of the Soviet republics, socialist as well as communist candidates were rejected. Although it is still too early to predict what form of social development the former Communist states will adopt, it seems unlikely, in the short term at least, that it will conform to any model of socialism.

5 Social democracy

The term 'social democracy' has been accorded a number of very different definitions. Its original meaning was associated with orthodox Marxism and was designed to highlight the distinction between the narrow goal of political democracy and the more fundamental objectives of socialism. Political democracy aimed to give all citizens an equal voice at election time by the achievement of universal adult suffrage. Social democracy, however, applied the principle of equality to social life and therefore to the possession of wealth. In its original sense therefore social democracy implied a commitment to the collective ownership of productive wealth and the achievement of a classless society. When parties adopted the title 'Social Democratic' – for example, the German Social Democratic Party, SPD, founded in 1875, or the Russian Social Democratic Labour Party in 1898 – they were acknowledging a formal commitment to Marxist doctrines.

However, the term soon acquired a rather different meaning as a result of the parliamentary tactics adopted by most Social Democratic parties and in particular by the largest of them, the SPD, under the leadership of Karl Kautsky. Marx himself criticised the SPD's Gotha Programme, adopted in 1875, because it proposed a peaceful transition to socialism. By the beginning of the twentieth century, social democracy was increasingly taken to refer to democratic socialism, in contrast to revolutionary socialism. After the Russian Revolution, those socialists who remained faithful to the principle of revolution followed the example of the Russian Bolsheviks and adopted the title 'Communist' to distance themselves from reformist Social Democratic parties.

The final change in the meaning of the term 'social democracy' occurred as a result of the tendency among Social Democratic parties not only to adopt parliamentary strategies, but also to revise their socialist goals. In particular, Western social democrats no longer seek to abolish capitalism but rather to reform or 'humanise' it. The social democratic tradition has come to stand broadly for a balance between the market economy on one hand, and state intervention on the other. In the process, socialists have re-examined their fundamental principles and, in effect, redefined socialism.

a Moralism

The theoretical basis for social democracy in the twentieth century has been provided by moral or religious beliefs, rather than scientific analysis. Marx and Engels had described their own theories as 'scientific socialism', and rejected the 'utopian socialism' of earlier years. Marxism's claim to being scientific rests upon the belief that it uncovered the laws of social and historical development: the victory of socialism was inevitable, not because it embodied a higher moral vision, but because the class struggle drove history on through a succession of stages until the eventual achievement of a classless society. Marx's scientific method was based upon 'historical material-ism', the belief that human thought and behaviour was conditioned by the economic circumstances of life. Social democrats have not accepted the materialist and highly systematic ideas of Marx and Engels, but rather advanced a moral critique of capitalism. In short, socialism is morally superior to capitalism because human beings are ethical creatures, bound to one another by the ties of love, sympathy and compassion. Such ideas have often given socialism a markedly utopian character.

The moral vision that underlies ethical socialism has been based upon both humanistic and religious principles. Socialism in France, Britain and other Commonwealth countries has been more strongly influenced by the utopian ideas of Fourier, Owen and William Morris than by the scientific creed of Karl Marx. Socialism has also drawn heavily upon Christianity. For example, there is a long-established tradition of Christian socialism in Britain, reflected in the twentieth century in the work of R.H. Tawney. The Christian ethic which has inspired British socialism is that of universal brotherhood, the respect that should be accorded all individuals as creations of God, a principle embodied in the commandment, 'Thou shalt love thy neighbour as thyself'. In *The Acquisitive Society* (1921), Tawney condemned unregulated capitalism because it was driven by the 'sin of avarice' rather than faith in a 'common humanity'. In *Equality* (1931) Tawney condemned the British class system as 'particularly detestable to Christians' and therefore called for a substantial reduction of social inequality.

Such religious inspiration has also been evident in the ideas of Liberation Theology, which has influenced many Catholic Third World countries, especially in Latin America. After years of providing support for repressive regimes in Latin America, Roman Catholic bishops meeting at Medellin, Colombia in 1968 declared a 'preferential option for the poor'. The religious responsibilities of the clergy were seen to extend beyond the narrowly spiritual and to embrace the social and political struggles of ordinary people. Despite the condemnation of Pope John Paul II and the Vatican, radical priests in many parts of Latin America have joined campaigns against poverty and political oppression and at times have even backed socialist revolutionary movements. For example, the Sandinista Revolution in Nicaragua in 1979 was supported, sometimes actively, by revolutionary priests. Similarly, socialist movements in the predominantly Muslim countries of North Africa, the Middle East and Asia have been inspired by religion. Islam exhorts the principles of social justice, charity and co-operation, and specifically prohibits usury or profiteering.

In abandoning scientific analysis in favour of moral or religious principles, however, social democracy has weakened the theoretical basis of socialism. Social democracy has been primarily concerned with the notion of a just or fair distribution of wealth in society. This is embodied in the overriding principle of social democracy, social justice, implying a commitment to greater equality and reflected in values such as caring and compassion. However, what this goal means in practice is very difficult to establish with any precision. For instance, just how much equality is required to 'humanise' capitalism and what is an acceptable balance between welfare and wealth creation? Social democracy has consequently come to stand for a broad range of views, extending from a Left-wing commitment to extending equality and expanding the collective ownership of wealth, to a Right-wing belief in market efficiency that may become indistinguishable from modern liberalism and can even overlap with paternalistic conservatism. Attempts have nevertheless been made to give social democracy a theoretical basis, usually involving a re-examination of capitalism itself and a re-definition of the goal of socialism.

b Revisionism

The fundamental goal of socialism was that productive wealth should be owned in common by all and therefore used for the common benefit. This required the abolition of private property and what Marx referred to as a 'social revolution', the transition from a capitalist 'mode of production' to a socialist one. Fundamentalist socialism is based upon the belief that capitalism is unredeemable, it is a system of class exploitation and oppression that deserves to be abolished altogether, not merely reformed.

By the turn of the century, some socialists had come to the belief that Marx's analysis was defective. The clearest theoretical expression of this belief was found in Eduard Bernstein's *Evolutionary Socialism*, which undertook a comprehensive criticism of Marx and the first major revision of Marxist analysis. Bernstein's analysis was largely empirical, he rejected Marx's method of analysis, historical materialism, because the predictions Marx had made had proved to be incorrect. Capitalism had shown itself to be both stable and flexible; indeed by the end of the century there was little evidence that the 'spectre of communism', referred to by Marx in the *Communist Manifesto* (1848), was still haunting Europe. Rather than class conflict intensifying, dividing capitalist society into 'two great classes', the bourgeoisie and the proletariat, Bernstein suggested that capitalism was becoming increasingly complex and differentiated. In particular, the ownership of wealth had widened as a result of the introduction of joint stock companies, owned by a number of shareholders, instead of a single powerful industrialist. The ranks of the middle class had also swollen, the growing number of salaried employees, technicians, government officials and professional workers being neither capitalists nor proletarians. In Bernstein's view, capitalism was no longer a system of naked class oppression. Capitalism could be reformed by the nationalisation of major industries and the extension of legal protection and welfare benefits to the working class, a process which Bernstein was confident could be achieved peacefully and democratically.

Western socialist parties have been revisionist in practice, if not always in theory, intent upon 'taming' capitalism rather than abolishing it. In some cases they have retained a formal commitment to fundamentalist goals, as in the case of the British Labour Party's belief in 'the common ownership of the means of production, distribution and exchange', expressed in Clause IV of its constitution. 'Common ownership' has been understood to mean the nationalisation of productive wealth and ultimately the replacement of the capitalist market by a system of central planning. During the twentieth century, social democrats have dropped their commitment to planning as they have recognised the efficiency and vigour of the capitalist market. The Swedish Social Democratic Labour Party formally abandoned planning in the 1930s, as did the West German Social Democrats at the Bad Godesberg Congress of 1959, which accepted the principle 'competition when possible; planning when necessary'. In Britain, a similar attempt formally to embrace revisionism in the late 1950s ended in failure when the Labour Party Conference rejected Hugh Gaitskell's attempts to abolish Clause IV. Nevertheless, when in power the Labour Party has shown no appetite for wholesale nationalisation.

The abandonment of planning has left social democracy with three more modest objectives. First, the mixed economy, a blend of public and private ownership which stands between free market capitalism and state collectivism. Nationalisation, when advocated by social democrats, is invariably selective and reserved for the 'commanding heights' of the economy, or industries that are thought to be 'natural monopolies'. The Attlee Labour government, 1945–51, for example, nationalised the major utilities, electricity, gas, coal, steel, railways and so on, but left most of British industry in private hands. Secondly, social democrats have sought to regulate or manage capitalist economies in order to maintain economic growth and keep unemployment low. Since 1945, most social democratic parties have been converted to Keynesian economics as a means of achieving managed capitalism. Finally, socialists have been attracted to the welfare state as the principal means of reforming or humanising capitalism. The welfare state is seen as a redistributive mechanism, which helps to promote social equality and to eradicate poverty. Capitalism no longer needs to be abolished, only modified by the establishment of welfare capitalism.

An attempt to give theoretical substance to these developments, and, in effect, update Bernstein, was made by Anthony Crosland in *The Future of Socialism* (1956). Crosland argued that modern capitalism bore little resemblance to the nineteenth century model in which Marx believed. Crosland was influenced by the ideas of James Burnham, whose *Managerial Revolution* (1941) had suggested that a new class of managers, experts and technocrats had supplanted the old capitalist class and come to dominate all advanced industrial societies, both capitalist and communist. Crosland believed that the ownership of wealth had become divorced from its control. Whereas shareholders, who owned businesses, were principally concerned with profit, salaried managers, who made day to day business decisions, had a broader range of goals, including the maintenance of industrial harmony as well as the public image of their company. Marxism had therefore become irrelevant; if capitalism could no longer be viewed as a system of class exploitation, then the fundamentalist goals of nationalisation and planning were simply outdated. However, as a socialist, Crosland remained faithful to the goal of social justice, which he understood to mean a more equal distribution of wealth. Wealth need not be owned in common, it could be redistributed through a welfare state, financed by progressive taxation. The welfare state would raise the living standards of the poor and the most vulnerable sections in society, while progressive taxation would ensure that the prosperous and strong bore the burden of expanded welfare support. Finally, Crosland recognised that economic growth played a crucial role in the achievement of socialism. A growing economy was essential to generate the tax revenue which would finance more generous social expenditure and, in addition, the prosperous would only be prepared to finance the needy if their own living standards were underwritten by economic growth.

The process of revisionism continued in the 1980s. In Britain, socialist thought tried to come to terms with three successive Thatcher victories by endorsing the value of individual freedom and distancing itself from its statist image of nationalisation, bureaucracy and planning. In *Socialism and Freedom* (1984), Bryan Gould redefined the goal of socialism as an equality of power, rather than an equality of wealth. This relieved socialism of the need further to extend public ownership and replaced it with the desire to broaden individual participation in both economic and political life. Roy Hattersley's *Choose Freedom* (1987) attacked the idea of negative freedom, which simply leaves the individual to the mercy of the market, and advocated a socialist commitment to positive freedom,

freedom from poverty and ignorance made possible by an efficiently managed and adequately funded welfare state. However, as the process of revisionism continues it has become increasingly difficult to distinguish between socialism and modern liberalism, from which social democrats increasingly draw their ideas.

c The crisis of social democracy

Whereas fundamentalist socialism has a clear and well-defined goal, the abolition of capitalism, the revisionist goal of reforming capitalism is far more vague. All social democrats accept that capitalism should be modified in accordance with the principle of social justice, but they have very different views about how this can be achieved, and even about how 'social justice' can be defined. What, for example, should be the balance between public and private ownership within a mixed economy – which industries should be nationalised and which left in private hands? How far should the welfare state be expanded before the growing tax burden becomes an impediment to economic growth? Should socialist governments accede to wage demands from low-paid workers when there is a danger of stimulating inflation?

At the heart of social democracy lies a conflict between its commitment to both economic efficiency and egalitarianism. During the 'long boom' of the post-war period, social democrats were not forced to confront this conflict because sustained growth, low unemployment and low inflation improved the living standards of all social groups and helped to finance more generous welfare provision. However, as Crosland had anticipated, recession in the 1970s and 1980s created strains within social democracy, polarising socialist thought into more clearly defined Left-wing and Right-wing positions. Recession precipitated a 'fiscal crisis of the welfare state', simultaneously increasing demand for welfare support as unemployment re-emerged, and squeezing the tax revenues which finance welfare spending, because fewer people were at work and businesses were less profitable. Difficult questions had to be answered: should social democrats attempt to restore efficiency to the market economy, which might mean cutting inflation and possible taxes, or should they defend the poor and the lower paid by maintaining or even expanding welfare spending?

Such polarisation has caused deep divisions. Nowhere has this been more evident than in Britain where the Labour Party was split in 1981 by the formation of a rival Social Democratic Party (SDP). Labour had gained power in 1974 with a manifesto committing it to a 'fundamental and irreversible shift in the balance of power and wealth in favour of working people', but by 1976, confronted with high inflation and rising unemployment, the Callaghan government carried out a U-turn, cutting public spending, particularly on health and education. After Labour's defeat in 1979, the Left made significant gains in the party, committing Labour to withdrawal from the European Community and to introduce unilateral nuclear disarmament. The party's structure was also reformed in an attempt to make both Labour leaders and MPs more accountable to party activists, in the hope of preventing any future Labour government 'selling out' socialism. This precipitated the formation of the SDP, led by the so-called 'Gang of Four', Roy Jenkins, David Owen, Shirley Williams and Bill Rodgers. The SDP regarded itself as the heir to the revisionist tradition, following in the footsteps of Tawney and Crosland, while they believed the Labour party had been 'hijacked' by Left-wingers like Tony Benn, who still harboured fundamentalist convictions.

Right-wing social democracy can become indistinguishable from modern liberalism, a fact reflected in the speedy formation of an electoral alliance between the SDP and the Liberal Party, and the merger of the two parties in 1988 to form the Liberal Democrats. Indeed, in acknowledging the virtues of the market, social democracy became vulnerable to the attractions of economic liberalism. David Owen, for instance, ceased to describe himself as a socialist after 1981, and as leader of the SDP between 1983 and 1987 developed an increasingly market-based economic strategy, at times approving of the neo-liberal policies pursued by the Thatcher government. After its third successive election defeat in 1987, the Labour Party commenced a comprehensive policy review which saw the adoption of many of the policies which the SDP had been advocating since 1981. In its 1990 policy document, *Looking to the Future*, Labour acknowledged the central role played by the market economy in producing and distributing wealth. In contrast, public ownership has been progressively relegated in Labour's priorities and few commitments have been made to re-nationalise industries privatised under the Thatcher government. Moreover, Labour embraced the idea of a low tax economy, promising to put up taxes only for the rich, and then from 40 per cent to just 50 per cent. Left-wingers like Tony Benn and Ken Livingstone argued that the policy review had abandoned socialist principles and adopted many of the policies of Thatcherism. However, Labour's continuing support for the welfare state, balanced as it now is against an open endorsement of the market, places the party firmly in the tradition of European social democracy.

Similar tensions have been evident elsewhere, notably in France. In 1981 the Socialist leader, François Mitterrand, was elected President and a Socialist-dominated government, under Pierre Mauroy, assumed office. The government embarked upon a radical and ambitious policy of reform, public spending was boosted to curb unemployment, nationalisation was extended and the economic growth was planned through a system of state investment. However, the deepening world recession forced the Mauroy Government to cut public spending in 1983, and in 1984 the U-turn was completed with the appointement of Laurent Fabius as Prime Minister to replace Mauroy. When the socialists were returned to power in 1988, President Mitterand gave up his attempts fundamentally to transform French society, looking instead to construct a Centre-Left coalition, under the Right-wing social democrat, Michel Rocard. Rocard proclaimed that the basic values of his government were 'tolerance, justice, progress and solidarity', specifically avoiding the egalitarian principles which had distinguished the earlier Mauroy government.

The socialist parties which have developed in Commonwealth countries have tended to adopt moderate and relatively non-ideological strategies, similar to those of the British Labour Party. The Australian Labour Party won power in 1983 under the leadership of Bob Hawke, but adopted a pragmatic approach to economic policy founded upon a willingness to consult major business interests as well as Australian trade unions. Hawke's ability to retain power in 1984, 1987 and 1990 owed more to the confidence the business community had in his economic policies than it did to any desire to restructure society. The New Zealand Labour Party gained power in 1984 under the leadership of David Lange, but its radicalism was reserved for foreign policy, specifically its opposition to nuclear weapons and a ban upon vessels carrying nuclear weapons, or powered by nuclear energy, from visiting New Zealand. In economic affairs, however, the Lange government was moderate, being guided more by market principles than by the goal of redistribution.

Nevertheless, Lange himself resigned in 1989, partly as a consequence of the re-admission of the former Finance Minister and Right-wing social democrat, Roger Douglas, to the cabinet. This drift to the Right led more radical elements to split from the New Zealand Labour Party in 1989 and form the New Labour Party.

5
Nationalism

1 Introduction

Nationalism is different from the political ideologies so far discussed, liberalism, conservatism and socialism. Strictly speaking, nationalism is not an ideology at all in that it does not contain a developed set of interrelated ideas and values. It is better thought of as a doctrine, a teaching or body of teachings. At heart, nationalism is the doctrine that a nation, or all nations, should be self-governing. However, the doctrine of nationalism has a schizophrenic political character, cutting across, as it does, all major ideologies. At different times, nationalism has been progressive and reactionary, democratic and authoritarian, and both Left-wing and Right-wing. Nevertheless, the uncertain political complexion of nationalism has done little to undermine its impact and may possibly be the key to its success. In many ways, nationalism has been perhaps the most successful of political creeds, helping to shape and re-shape history in all parts of the world for over two hundred years. It has often dwarfed more precise and systematic political ideologies and as continuing tension between Arabs and Jews in the Middle East, friction between Russians and non-Russians in the Soviet Union, and independence movements in countries as different as Britain, Spain and Canada demonstrate, its energy and impact is far from exhausted.

The word 'nation' has been in use since the thirteenth century, originally referring to a breed or racial group, but at that time it possessed no political significance. It was not until the eighteenth century that individuals and groups were described as 'nationalists', and only in 1789 that the term 'nationalism' was first used in print, by the anti-Jacobin French priest, Augustin Barruel. By the mid nineteenth century, nationalism was widely recognised as a political doctrine or movement, for example, as a significant ingredient of the revolutions which swept across Europe in 1848.

The doctrine itself was born during the French Revolution. Previously, countries had been thought of as 'realms', 'principalities' or 'kingdoms'. The inhabitants of a country were 'subjects', their political identity being formed by allegiance to a ruler or ruling dynasty, rather than any sense of national identity or patriotism. However, the revolutionaries in France who rose up against Louis XVI in 1789 did so in the name of the people, and understood the people to be the 'French nation'. Their ideas were influenced by the writings of Jean Jacques Rousseau, often thought of as the 'founder of modern nationalism', who had advocated that government should be based upon popular sovereignty or, in Rousseau's words, a 'general will'. Nationalism was therefore a revolutionary and democratic creed, reflecting the idea that 'subjects of the Crown' should become 'citizens of France'. The nation should be its own master. However, such ideas were not the exclusive property of the French. During the Revolutionary and Napoleonic Wars, 1792–1815, much of continental Europe was invaded by France, giving rise to both resentment against France and a desire for independence. In Italy and Germany, long divided into a collection of states, the experience of conquest helped to forge for the first time a consciousness of national unity, expressed in a new language of nationalism, inherited from France. Nationalist ideas also spread to Latin America in the early nineteenth century, where Simon Bolivar, 'the Liberator', led revolutions against Spanish rule in what was then New Grenada, now the countries of Colombia, Venezuela and Ecuador, as well as in Peru and Bolivia.

The rising tide of nationalism re-drew the map of Europe in the nineteenth century as the autocratic and multi-national empires of Turkey, Austria and Russia started to crumble in the face of liberal and nationalist pressure. In 1848, nationalist uprisings broke out in the Italian states, amongst the Czechs and the Hungarians, and in Germany, where the desire for national unity was expressed in the creation of the short-lived Frankfurt Parliament. The nineteenth century was a period of nation-building. Italy, once dismissed by Metternich as a 'mere geographical expression', became a united state in 1861, the process of unification being completed with the acquisition of Rome in 1870. Germany, formerly a collection of 39 states, was unified in 1871, following the Franco–Prussian War.

Nevertheless, it would be a mistake to assume that nationalism was either an irresistible or a genuinely popular movement during this period. Enthusiasm for nationalism was largely restricted to the rising middle classes, who were attracted to the ideas of national unity and constitutional government. Although middle-class nationalist movements kept the dream of national unity or independence alive, they were nowhere strong enough to accomplish the process of nation-building on their own. Where nationalist goals were realised, as in Italy and Germany, it was because nationalism coincided with the ambition of rising states like Piedmont and Prussia. For example, German unification owed more to the Prussian army, which defeated Austria in 1866 and France, 1870–1, than it did to the liberal nationalist movement.

However, by the end of the nineteenth century, nationalism had become a truly popular movement, with the spread of flags, national anthems, patriotic poetry and literature, public ceremonies and national holidays. Nationalism became the language of mass politics, made possible by the growth of primary education, mass literacy and the spread of popular newspapers. The character of nationalism also changed. Nationalism had previously been associated with liberal and progressive movements, but was increasingly taken up by conservative and reactionary politicians. Nationalism came to stand for social cohesion, order and stability, particularly in the face of the growing challenge of socialism, which embodied the ideas of social revolution and international working class solidarity. Nationalism sought to integrate the increasingly powerful working class into the 'nation' and so preserve the established social structure. Patriotic fervour was no longer raised by the prospect of political liberty or democracy, but by the commemoration of past national glories and military victories. Such nationalism became increasingly chauvinistic and xenophobic. Each nation claimed its own unique or superior qualities, while other nations were regarded as alien, untrustworthy, and even menacing. This new climate of popular nationalism helped to fuel policies of colonial expansion which intensified dramatically in the 1870s and 1880s and which, by the end of the century, brought most of the world's population under European control. It also contributed to a mood of international suspicion and rivalry which led to world war in 1914.

The end of the First World War saw the completion of the process of nation-building in Central and Eastern Europe. At the Paris Peace

Conference, the American President, Woodrow Wilson, advocated the principle of 'national self-determination'. The German, Austro–Hungarian and Russian empires were broken up and eight new states created, including Finland, Hungary, Czechoslovakia, Poland and Yugoslavia. These new countries were designed to be nation-states, which conformed to the geography of existing national or ethnic groups. However, the First World War failed to resolve the serious national tensions which had precipitated conflict in the first place. Indeed, the experience of defeat and disappointment with the terms of the Peace Treaties left an inheritance of frustrated ambition and bitterness. This was most evident in Germany, Italy and Japan, where fascist or authoritarian movements came to power in the inter-war period by promising to restore national pride through policies of expansion and empire. Nationalism was therefore a powerful factor leading to war in both 1914 and 1939.

During the twentieth century, the doctrine of nationalism, which had been born in Europe, spread throughout the globe, as the peoples of Asia and Africa rose in opposition to colonial rule. The process of colonisation involved not only the establishment of political control and economic dominance, but also the export of Western ideas, including nationalism, which were later to be used against the colonial masters themselves. Nationalist uprisings took place in Egypt in 1919 and quickly spread throughout the Middle East. The Anglo–Afghan war also broke out in 1919 and rebellions took place in India, the Dutch East Indies and Indo-China. Since 1945, the map of Africa and Asia has been re-drawn as the British, French, Dutch and Portuguese empires have all disintegrated in the face of nationalist movements which have either succeeded in negotiating independence or winning wars of national liberation. However, anti-colonialism has not only witnessed the spread of Western-style nationalism to the Third World, but also generated new forms of nationalism. Third World nationalism has embraced a wide range of movements. In China, Vietnam and parts of Africa, nationalism has been fused with Marxism, and 'national liberation' has been regarded not simply as a political goal but as part of a social revolution. Elsewhere, Third World nationalism has been anti-Western, rejecting both liberal democratic and revolutionary socialist conceptions of nationhood. The most important vehicle for expressing such ideas has been religious belief, and in particular Islam. The rise of Islam as a distinctive political creed has transformed political life in the

Middle East and North Africa, especially since the Iranian Revolution of 1979. In some respects, Islam currently represents the most significant challenge to the worldwide predominance of Western liberal democracy.

It is, however, often argued that nationalism has had its day and is now an anachronism, relevant only to European nation-building in the nineteenth century, or the anti-colonial struggle in the years following 1945. On the surface, the goal of nationalism has been largely achieved: all contemporary states are officially 'nations'. The modern world is increasingly shaped, in contrast, by internationalism, the growing importance of international summits and supra-national institutions. Without doubt, the importance of national sovereignty has declined since 1945, with the emergence of bodies such as the United Nations, the European Community, NATO, OPEC and so forth. This is perhaps nowhere more apparent than in economic life, where national economies have been integrated into a 'world economy', meaning that individual countries are no longer masters of their own economic destiny.

On the other hand, there is evidence not only of the persistence of nationalism, but even of its revival. For example, during the 1960s apparently stable nation-states were increasingly disrupted by nationalist tensions. In Britain, Scottish, Welsh and rival Irish nationalisms have become an established feature of political life. Separatist movements have developed in areas such as the Basque region of Northern Spain and the Canadian province of Quebec. Moreover, many of the world's most enduring political crises involve nationalism, for instance, the Arab–Israeli conflict, the Eritrean Civil War, and communal conflict in both Sri Lanka and India. Finally, the transformation of Eastern Europe in 1989–90 has also led to a resurgence of nationalism throughout the area. The Soviet Union has been seriously weakened by rising nationalism amongst its non-Russian peoples and the collapse of Communist rule has allowed ancient national rivalries to surface throughout Eastern Europe. Yugoslavia in particular has been destabilised by inter-ethnic rivalry and conflict amongst its six republics. The re-unification of Germany also awoke long-suppressed nationalist aspirations within Germany itself, and provoked nationalist fears within neighbouring states.

2 National self-determination

At first sight, nationalism may appear to be a simple doctrine, the belief that the nation is the natural and proper unit of government; however, such a formula conceals many complexities. What is a nation, and by what characteristics can it be known? What is the relationship between nationalism as a political doctrine and a consciousness of nationhood, or what is often called patriotism? Finally, why should the nation be the proper unit of government, and what are the political implications of such a belief?

a The nation

In everyday language, words like 'nation', 'state', 'country' and even 'race' are often confused and used as if they were interchangeable. For example, until 1991 the Soviet Union was a single state, but contained 15 republics, some of which actively sought independence, and 128 officially recognised ethnic and linguistic groups. Was the Soviet Union then a single nation, did it comprise 15 separate nations, or was it a collection of over 100 nations? Is Britain a single nation or a United Kingdom containing four nations, the English, the Scots, the Welsh and the Northern Irish? Similar confusions apply in the case of the Arab peoples of North Africa and the Middle East. Are all Arabs part of a single and united Arab nation, based upon a common language, Arabic, a common religion, Islam, and descent from a common Bedouin tribal past? Precisely this question was raised by the Iraqi invasion of Kuwait in 1990 and the Gulf War of 1991. Was Kuwait a separate nation, entitled to political independence, was it historically a province of Iraq, or was it merely a part of a much larger Arab nation? In the same way, the displaced Palestinians have refused to accept permanent resettlement in other Arab countries like Lebanon or Jordan, but have campaigned consistently for the creation of a Palestinian state and their own national homeland.

The doctrine of nationalism cannot be understood until the concepts of 'nation' and 'state' are clearly defined and distinguished. A 'nation' is a cultural entity, a collection of people bound together by shared values and traditions, for example, a common language, religion and history, and usually occupying the same geographical area. A 'state' is a political association, which enjoys sovereignty, supreme or unrestricted power, within defined territorial borders.

The goal of nationalism is that the nation and state should as far as possible coincide; each nation should possess a political voice and exercise the right of self-determination. In practice, not all states are nations, and a number of nations do not possess their own state. For example, until the creation of the state of Israel in 1948, the Jewish 'nation' possessed neither land nor statehood, a position the Palestinians find themselves in today. Other nations are spread over a number of states, for example, the German 'nation' lived for much of the post-War period in three states, West Germany, East Germany and Austria. Other states, like the Soviet Union and Britain, contain several nations.

However, to define a 'nation' as a group of people bound together by a common culture and traditions raises some very difficult questions. Although certain cultural features are commonly associated with nationhood, for instance, history, traditions, language, religion and ethnicity, there is no blueprint nor any objective criteria which can establish where and when a nation exists. This is crucial because the proclamation of nationhood is also a claim to the right of self-determination, the right of statehood. Does a group of people posses the right to political independence simply by virtue of calling itself a 'nation', or must some external and more reliable standard be applied? The definition of nationhood lies at the heart of many contemporary political conflicts. Are the Tamils in Sri Lanka a 'nation', separate from the majority Sinhalese, and therefore entitled to their own homeland and state? Are the Basques in Spain, or the Quebecois in Canada, 'nations' or simply ethnic or linguistic groups? Do the people of Northern Ireland belong to the 'British nation', the 'Irish nation' or indeed do they constitute a separate 'Ulster nation'?

Nations are bound together by a shared culture. However, the elements which generate a sense of nationhood are highly diverse: language, religion, history and so forth. Language is often taken to be the clearest symbol of nationhood. A language embodies distinctive attitudes, values and forms of expression, which produce a sense of familiarity and belonging. For example, German nationalism has traditionally been founded upon a sense of cultural unity, reflected in the purity and survival of the German language. Nations have also been highly sensitive to any dilution of or threat to their languages. For example, it is essentially language which divides the French-speaking peoples of Quebec from the rest of English-speaking Canada, and Welsh nationalism largely constitutes an attempt to preserve or revive the Welsh language. At the same time, there are peoples who share the same language without having any conception of a common national identity: the Americans, Australians and New Zealanders may speak English as a first language, but would be shocked at the thought that they belonged as a result to an 'English nation'. Other nations have enjoyed a substantial measure of national unity without possessing a single or even national language, as is clearly demonstrated in the case of Switzerland where, in the absence of a Swiss language, three languages are spoken, French, German and Italian.

Religion is another major component of nationhood. Religion expresses common moral values and spiritual beliefs. In Northern Ireland, people who speak the same language are divided along religious lines; most Protestants regard themselves as Unionists and wish to preserve links with Britain, while many in the Catholic community seek to establish a united Ireland. Islam has been a major factor in forming the national consciousness in much of North Africa and the Middle East. The Iranian Revolution was largely inspired by the fundamentalist beliefs of Shiite Moslems, who sought to purge Iran of Western, and particularly American, influence. Islamic fundamentalism has also strengthened nationalist sentiments in the predominantly Moslem republics of the Soviet Union. There is also a sense in which Islam creates a higher unity than that of the nation-state, and Moslems in many parts of the world refer to themselves as members of an 'Islamic nation'. Nevertheless, religious beliefs do not always coincide with a sense of nationhood. Divisions between Catholics and Protestants within mainland Britain do not inspire rival nationalisms, nor has the remarkable religious diversity found in the United States threatened to divide America into a collection of distinct nations. At the same time, countries like Poland, Italy, Brazil and the Philippines share a common Catholic faith but have not felt as a result that they belong to a common 'Catholic nation'.

Nations have also been based upon a sense of racial unity. This was particularly evident in Germany during the Nazi period. The German word for 'people', *volk*, implies both cultural unity and ties of blood. The significance of race has also been highlighted by far-Right groups such as the National Fronts of both Britain and France, which have campaigned against 'non-white' immigration or even favoured repatriation on the grounds that multi-racialism undermines national unity. However, nationalism usually has a cultural rather than a biological basis; it reflects an ethnic unity, which may be based upon race, but more usually refers to a shared culture. The nationalism of American blacks, for example, is based less upon colour than it is upon their distinctive history and culture. Black consciousness in America and the West Indies has therefore focused upon the rediscovery of black cultural roots in the experience of slavery and in African society. Such cultural nationalism can also be found in many parts of Asia and Africa, where attempts have been made to reclaim a cultural inheritance threatened by growing Western influence. However, ethnicity does not always provide a basis for national identity. The United States prides itself upon cultural diversity, the result of centuries of immigration from Europe, Asia, Central and South America. US citizens regard themselves as 'Polish Americans', 'Japanese Americans', 'Hispanic Americans' and so on, happily retaining their own religions, traditions, food and even languages, without damaging their sense of national pride in being American. On the contrary, the United States has succeeded in forging an unusually heightened sense of national patriotism.

Nations usually share a common history and traditions. National identity is often preserved by recalling the glories of past history, national independence, birthdays of national leaders or important military victories. In the United States, this is achieved by celebrating Independence Day, while in the Soviet Union the Bolshevik Revolution and the sacrifices of the Second War, the 'Great Patriotic War', have traditionally been commemorated. On the other hand, nationalist feelings may be based upon future expectations just as easily as upon shared memories of a common past. This applies in the case of immigrants into a country who have been 'naturalised', and is most evident in the United States, a 'land of immigrants'. The journey of the 'Mayflower' and the War of Independence fought against Britain have little or no relevance for most Americans whose families arrived centuries after these events occurred. American nationalism therefore has little to do with a common history or traditions, but has been forged out of a common commitment to the Constitution and the values of liberal capitalism for which the United States stands.

The cultural unity which expresses itself in nationhood is therefore very difficult to tie down. It reflects a varying combination of cultural factors, rather than any precise formula. Ultimately, nations are defined subjectively, by their members, rather than objectively, by any set of external factors. A nation exists when a group of people exhibit some form of national consciousness or patriotic loyalty, and seek to express this politically, by the demand for self-government. Objective difficulties, like the absence of land, a small population or lack of economic resources, are of little significance if a group of people insists on demanding what it sees as 'national rights'. The landless Palestinians have not given up their quest for a Palestinian state. Similarly, the people of the Soviet Union's three Baltic Republics, Estonia, Latvia and Lithuania, did not abandon their desire for independence, despite their small size and economic insecurity. Latvia, for example, has a population of only 2.6 million inhabitants, barely half of whom are ethnic Lats, no source of fuel and very few natural resources. The Kurdish peoples of the Middle East also have nationalist aspirations, even though the Kurds have never enjoyed formal political unity and are presently spread over parts of Turkey, Iraq, Iran and Syria.

b Patriotism

The terms 'nationalism' and 'patriotism' are often confused, but in fact have different meanings. In the broadest sense, patriotism is a psychological attachment or sense of belonging to a social group, which once focused upon the tribe, local area or region, but now more commonly takes the form of 'national patriotism'. Patriotism is therefore a sentiment, a feeling of loyalty to one's country or its way of life, literally a love of one's 'fatherland'. In contrast, nationalism is a political doctrine, the belief that nations should be self-governing. Patriotism, or a sense of national consciousness, can be regarded as an essential precondition for nationalism. It is unlikely, for instance, that a people will demand the right of national self-determination if they do not already possess a high degree of national loyalty or pride. Patriotism can therefore be regarded as a weak form of nationalism. However, the sentiment of loyalty to, or respect for, one's nation does not in itself generate nationalism. North American Indians, for example, have campaigned to preserve their cultural identity, traditions and land, but not sought full political independence from the United States. Linguistic, religious or ethnic groups can therefore exhibit what can be called cultural nationalism without demanding the right to govern themselves, which is the defining feature of political nationalism.

The importance of a distinctive national consciousness was first emphasised in Germany in the late eighteenth century. Writers such as Fichte and Herder highlighted what they believed to be the uniqueness and superiority of Germanic culture, in contrast to the ideas of the French Revolution. Herder believed that each nation possessed a 'national spirit', or *Volksgeist*, which provided its peoples with their creative impulse. The role of nationalism was therefore to develop an awareness and appreciation of a nation's culture and traditions. During the nineteenth century, such cultural nationalism was particularly marked in Germany in a revival of folk traditions and the rediscovery of German myths and legends. The Brothers Grimm, for example, collected and published German folk tales, and the composer Wagner based many of his operas upon ancient legends and myths.

In the twentieth century, cultural nationalism, or ethnonationalism, has become a powerful force, expressing the desire to preserve a threatened national culture, rather than demand national self-government. This has been particularly evident in countries which contain several nationalities or ethnic groups, especially when minority traditions or ways of life are in danger of being swamped by a dominant culture. Welsh nationalism in Britain, for example, has been essentially cultural rather than political. There has been a revival of interest in the Welsh language and Welsh culture in general. However, in a referendum in 1979 the Welsh voted by a clear majority against the establishment of a devolved Welsh Assembly. In France, strong regional traditions persist in many parts of the country; for example, in areas like Brittany growing attention has been paid to Breton culture and its distinctive Celtic traditions. Once again, however, such patriotism usually stops well short of political nationalism, as is demonstrated by the marked contrast between the cultural pride of the French Basques and the separatist and political ambitions of Basques living in Spain.

Black nationalism in many parts of the West also has a strong cultural character. Blacks in America and the West Indies are the descendants of slaves, who were brought up in a culture that emphasised their inferiority and demanded subservience. The development of black consciousness and national pride therefore required blacks to look beyond white culture and rediscover their cultural roots in Africa. The Jamaican political thinker and activist, Marcus Garvey, was one of the first to argue that blacks in America and the Caribbean should look upon Africa as their homeland. Garvey founded the African Orthodox Church in the hope of inculcating a distinctive black consciousness, and advocated segregation between blacks and whites. Eventually, he hoped, blacks throughout the world would be able to return to Africa, once it was liberated from colonial rule. Garvey's ideas have also inspired the founding of new religions, such as Rastafarianism. Rastafarians regard white society as a corrupt 'Babylon' and identify themselves with the Israelites of the Bible, regarding Ethiopia as their promised land. Originating in Jamaica, but spreading to West Indian communities in America and Europe, a distinctive Rastafarian culture and language has developed, involving the wearing of hair in dreadlocks, observing strict laws about what to eat, and the use of the drug marijuana, or 'ganja'.

The subjective sense of attachment or belonging to a nation, the sentiment of patriotism, is without doubt a potent force, which has the capacity to generate social cohesion and stability. However, it is sometimes unclear whether national patriotism is a natural sentiment or one that has been artificially produced by political leaders or movements. Some argue that nations are organic communities, developing out of a natural tendency for people to gravitate towards others with similar views, behaviour and appearance to themselves. If this is true, successful communities need to be culturally homogeneous, bound together by a common way of life, traditions and beliefs. In other words, nations emerge out of a widespread human desire for security and cohesion. Others regard patriotism as an artificial or false sentiment, inculcated by governments and political leaders to manipulate the masses and maintain political control. National patriotism does not develop on its own, independent from political, social or economic conditions. To some extent, all states try to invent patriotism in order to promote social cohesion and loyalty, by the use of the educational system, national anthems and flags, festivals and national ceremonies. Traditionally, conservative and authoritarian governments have often been the most open and willing to base their support upon an appeal to patriotism, but liberal, socialist and communist governments have also been prepared to follow suit.

c Political nationalism

Patriotism only becomes nationalism in the stronger sense when a consciousness of nationhood is accompanied by the desire for self-government. Political nationalism is therefore the belief that the nation is the only rightful and proper unit of government, that 'the boundaries of government should coincide in the main with those of nationality' as John Stuart Mill suggested. Nationalism is therefore both a political principle and a form of political organisation. The principle is the right of national self-determination, which is realised in the ideal form of political organisation, the nation-state. Each sovereign state should encompass a single nation.

The traditional goal of nationalism has therefore been 'nation-building', the founding of a 'nation-state'. This has usually been achieved in one of two ways. First, it may involve a process of unification. German history, for instance, has witnessed a repetitive process of unification. The German states were united under Charlemagne in medieval times, in the Holy Roman Empire, referred to by later German nationalists as the 'First Reich'. Germany was not re-united until Bismarck founded his 'Second Reich' in 1871. It was not, however, until the 'Third Reich' that Hitler completed the process of unification by incorporating Austria into 'Greater Germany'. Following her defeat in the Second World War, Germany was divided, with the founding of two Germanies in 1949, East Germany and West Germany, and the permanent independence of a separate Austria. The two Germanies were finally re-united in 1990.

Secondly, nation-states can be created through the achievement of independence, in which a nation is liberated from foreign rule and gains control over its own destiny. For example, much of Polish history has witnessed successive attempts to achieve independence from the control of various foreign powers. Poland ceased to exist in 1793 when the Poles were partitioned by Austria, Russia and Prussia. Thanks to the Treaty of Versailles, Poland was revived in 1918 and became an independent republic. However, in accordance with the Nazi-Soviet Pact of 1939 Poland was invaded by Germany and re-partitioned, this time between Germany and the Soviet Union. Although Poland achieved formal independence in 1945, for much of the post-war period it remained firmly under Soviet control. The election of a non-Communist government in 1989 therefore marked a further liberation of the country from foreign control.

Nationalists believe the nation-state to be the highest and most desirable form of political organisation. Such a belief is based upon a number of assumptions. Nationalists regard the nation as a genuine or organic community; it is certainly not an artificial creation of political leaders or ruling classes. Humanity is therefore thought to be naturally divided into a collection of nations, each possessing a separate identity. Moreover, the nation-state is thought to be the only legitimate form of government. This implies that ties of nationality are stronger and politically more significant than any rival social cleavage, such as social class, race or religion, which may cut across national borders. The nation-state is therefore the only stable and cohesive form of political organisation because citizens are bound together by a sense of both political and cultural unity. Finally, nationalism legitimises the authority of government. Political sovereignty in a nation-state resides with the people or nation itself. Consequently, nationalism represents the idea of popular self-government, the idea that government is either carried out by the people or for the people, in accordance with the 'national interest'.

However, political nationalism is a complex phenomenon. On one hand, it appears to be a progressive or liberating force, which offers the prospect of national unity or independence. On the other hand, it can be irrational and reactionary, allowing political leaders to conduct policies of military expansion and war in the name of the nation. In that sense, nationalism is schizophrenic, its political character is formed by a variety of cultural and historical factors. For instance, a country's concept of nationhood is deeply influenced by its cultural heritage: French nationalism was not only born out of the French Revolution but also bears its lasting imprint, an attachment to the revolutionary values of 'liberty, equality and fraternity'. American nationalism has similarly been affected by the heritage of colonial rule and independence. The United States has therefore traditionally regarded itself as an ally of oppressed peoples, a position represented by Woodrow Wilson at the Paris Peace Conference and, since the Second World War, in her role as leader of what she believed to be the 'Free World'. On the other hand, Japanese nationalism has been deeply affected by the traditions and values of her Imperial past. In Japan, nationalism is closely linked to respect for the Emperor, the ancient Shinto religion and the traditional values of obedience and discipline.

The character of nationalism is also moulded by the circumstances in which nationalist aspirations arise, and the political causes which nationalism articulates. When nationalism is a reaction against the experience of foreign domination or colonial rule, it tends to become a liberating force, linked to the goals of liberty, justice and democracy. Nationalism takes the form of a quest for 'national liberation' and popular self-government. However, nationalist sentiments can also be generated by international rivalry and conflict. In such circumstances, other nations may be regarded with distrust, fear or hatred, and nationalism can assume a chauvinistic and expansionist character. Nationalism has also been a product of social dislocation and demographic change. A nationalist backlash can be provoked, for example, when the cultural identity of a people is weakened or threatened by the creeping influence of a foreign culture. Nationalism has therefore sometimes been a reaction against immigration or even the pace of social and economic change. In such cases, nationalism can become a vehicle for racial prejudice or xenophobia, a hatred of foreigners.

Finally, nationalism has been shaped by the political philosophies of those who espouse it. Nationalism has proved to be the most compelling political force in the modern world and has therefore attracted the attention of liberals, conservatives, socialists, communists and fascists. It is also a political doctrine which is sufficiently broad to be incorporated into diametrically opposed ideologies. As a result, it is perhaps more helpful to study a range of 'nationalisms' than it is to pretend that nationalism is a single or coherent political phenomenon.

3 Nationalism and politics

a Liberal nationalism

Liberal nationalism is the oldest form of nationalism, dating back to the French Revolution itself and embodying many of its values. Its ideas spread quickly through much of Europe and were expressed most clearly by Guiseppe Mazzini, often thought of as the 'prophet' of Italian unification. They influenced the remarkable exploits of Simon Bolivar, who led the Latin American independence movement in the early nineteenth century and expelled the Spanish from much of Hispanic America. Woodrow Wilson's 'Fourteen Points', proposed as the basis for the reconstruction of Europe after the First World War, were also based upon liberal nationalist principles. Moreover, anti-colonial leaders in the twentieth century have been inspired by liberal ideas, as in the case of Sun Yat-sen, one of the leaders of China's 1911 Revolution, and Jawaharlal Nehru, the first Prime Minister of India.

The ideas of liberal nationalism were born out of J.J. Rousseau's defence of popular sovereignty, developed in his *Social Contract* (1762). Rousseau argued that government should be based not upon the absolute power of a monarch, but upon the authority of the people, expressed in the 'general will', or collective interest of the community. As such, Rousseau's 'general will' came close to the modern notion of a public interest or 'national interest'. In the late eighteenth century such an idea was revolutionary. During the French Revolution itself, these beliefs were reflected in the assertion that French people were 'citizens', no longer merely 'subjects' of the throne. Citizens enjoyed rights and liberties as members of the 'French nation'. The nationalism which emerged from the French Revolution therefore embodied a vision of a people or nation governing itself, and of an end to privilege, hierarchy and deference.

As the nineteenth century progressed, such aspirations were easily fused with liberal principles. This fusion was brought about by the fact that the multi-national empires against which nationalists fought were also autocratic and oppressive. Mazzini, for example, wished the Italian states to unite, but also to throw off the influence of autocratic Austria. For many European revolutionaries in the mid nineteenth century, liberalism and nationalism were virtually indistinguishable. Indeed, their nationalist creed was largely forged by applying liberal ideas, initially developed in relation to the individual, to the nation and the international order.

Liberalism was founded upon a defence of individual freedom, traditionally expressed in the language of 'rights'. Nationalists believed nations to be sovereign entities, entitled to liberty, and also possessing rights, most importantly, the right of 'self-determination'. Liberal nationalism is therefore a liberating force in two senses. First, it opposes all forms of foreign domination and oppression, whether by multi-national empires or colonial powers. Secondly, it stands for the ideal of self-government: the nation should govern itself – in other words, government should be both constitutional and representative. Woodrow Wilson, for example, argued in favour of a Europe composed not only of nation-states, but one in which political democracy rather than autocracy ruled. For him, only a democratic republic, on the American model, could be a genuine nation-state.

Moreover, liberal nationalists believed that nations, like individuals, are equal, at least in the sense that they are equally entitled to the right of self-determination. The ultimate goal of a liberal nationalist is therefore to construct a world of independent nation-states, not merely to unify or gain independence for a particular nation. Mazzini formed the clandestine organisation 'Young Italy' to promote the idea of a united Italy, but also founded 'Young Europe' in the hope of spreading nationalist ideas throughout the continent. At the Paris Peace Conference, Woodrow Wilson advanced the principle of self-determination not simply because the break-up of the European empire served American national interests, but because he believed that the Poles, the Czechs and the Hungarians all had the same right to political independence that the Americans already enjoyed.

Liberals also believe that the principle of balance or natural harmony applies to the nations of the world as it does to individuals within society. The achievement of national self-determination is a means of establishing a peaceful and stable international order. Wilson believed that the First World War had been caused by an 'old order', dominated by autocratic and militaristic empires. Democratic nation-states, on the other hand, would respect the national sovereignty of their neighbours and have no incentive to wage war or subjugate others. For a liberal, nationalism does not divide nations from one another, promoting distrust, rivalry and possibly war. Rather, nationalism is a force capable of both promoting unity within each nation and brotherhood amongst all nations on the basis of mutual respect for national rights and characteristics. At heart, liberals believe in internationalism. Although they respect the claims of nationality, their ultimate concern is for the individual and therefore for humanity. Humanity may be divided into nations, but these nations should not be exclusive or isolated from one another, rather they should be interdependent, tied together by mutual understanding and co-operation. This is why liberals have traditionally supported the policy of free trade which promotes economic independence and also the growing influence of supra-national bodies like the United Nations and the European Community. The

Liberal Party in Britain, for instance, was the earliest and most wholehearted advocate of Community membership. In no sense do liberals wish such international institutions to replace the nation-state, nor erode distinctive cultures. However, they recognise the need for such bodies to mediate amongst nation-states in order to foster peace and prosperity.

Critics of liberal nationalism have sometimes suggested that its ideas are naïve and romantic. Liberal nationalists see the progressive and liberating face of nationalism; their nationalism is rational and tolerant. However, they perhaps ignore the darker face of nationalism, the irrational bonds or tribalism, which distinguish 'us' from a foreign and threatening 'them'. Liberals see nationalism as a universal principle, but have less understanding of the emotional power of nationalism, which has, in times of war, persuaded individuals to kill or die for 'their country', regardless of the justice of their nation's cause. Liberal nationalism is also misguided in its belief that the nation-state is the key to political and international harmony. The mistake of Wilsonian nationalism was the belief that nations live in convenient and discrete geographical areas, and that states could be constructed which coincided with these areas. In practice, all so-called 'nation-states' comprise a range of linguistic, religious, ethnic or regional groups, some of which may also consider themselves to be 'nations'. For example, in 1918 the newly created nation-states of Czechoslovakia and Poland both contained a significant number of German speakers, and Czechoslovakia itself was a fusion of two major ethnic groups, the Czechs and the Slovaks. Yugoslavia, also created by Versailles, contains a bewildering variety of ethnic groups, Serbs, Croats, Slovenes, Bosnians, Albanians and so on, many of whom now have aspirations to nationhood. The ideal of a politically unified and culturally homogeneous nation-state could, in fact, only be achieved by a policy of forcible deportation and an outright ban upon immigration.

b Conservative nationalism

In the early nineteenth century, conservatives regarded nationalism as a radical and dangerous force, a threat to order and political stability. However, as the century progressed, conservative statesmen like Disraeli, Bismarck and even Tsar Alexander III, became increasingly sympathetic towards nationalism, seeing it as a natural ally in maintaining social order and defending traditional institutions. In the modern period, nationalism has become an article of faith for most conservatives. In Britain, Margaret Thatcher attempted to appeal to nationalist sentiments by resisting what she saw as the erosion of national sovereignty by an emerging 'Federal Europe', and by her triumphalist reaction to the Falklands War of 1982. Ronald Reagan also tried to rekindle United States nationalism by pursuing a more assertive foreign policy, which led to the invasion of Grenada and the bombing of Libya. George Bush continued such a policy by invading Panama and being prepared to fight the Gulf War of 1991.

Conservative nationalism tends to develop in established nation-states, rather than ones that are in the process of nation-building. Conservatives care less for the principled nationalism of universal self-determination and more about the promise of social cohesion and public order embodied in the sentiment of national patriotism. For conservatives, society is organic; they believe that nations emerge naturally from the desire of human beings to live with others who possess the same views, habits and appearance as themselves. Human beings are thought to be limited and imperfect creatures, who seek meaning and security within the 'national community'. Therefore, the principle goal of a conservative nationalist is to maintain national unity by fostering patriotic loyalty and 'pride in one's country', especially in the face of the divisive idea of class solidarity preached by socialists. Charles de Gaulle, French President 1958–69, harnessed nationalism to the conservative cause in France with particular skill. De Gaulle appealed to national pride by pursuing an independent, even anti-American, defence and foreign policy, which included withdrawing French troops from NATO control. He also attempted to restore order and authority in social life and build up a powerful state, based upon the enhanced powers of the Presidency. Such policies helped to maintain conservative control in France from the founding of the Fifth Republic in 1958 until the election of President Mitterand in 1981. In some respects, the Thatcher government practised a British form of Gaullism, by fusing an appeal based upon nationalism, or at least national independence within Europe, with the promise of strong government and firm leadership.

The conservative character of nationalism is maintained by an appeal to tradition and history; nationalism becomes thereby a defence for traditional institutions and a traditional way of life. Conservative nationalism is essentially nostalgic, backward-looking, reflecting upon a past age of national glory or triumph. This is evident in the case of British or, more accurately, English nationalism, whose symbols are based very closely around the institutions of monarchy. Britain is the United Kingdom, its national anthem is 'God Save the Queen', and the Royal Family plays a prominent role in national celebrations, such as Armistice Day, and on state occasions like the opening of Parliament. Margaret Thatcher also attempted to link Britain to her past by reference to 'Victorian values', which portrayed mid nineteenth century Britain as a 'golden age'.

Conservative nationalism is particularly prominent when a sense of national identity is felt to be threatened or in danger of being lost. The issue of immigration has kept this form of nationalism alive in many modern states, for example, in Britain, France and the United States. Hispanic immigration into the United States from Mexico, has led some American conservatives to suggest the need for a constitutional guarantee that English remains America's first language. In Britain, Enoch Powell was forced to resign from the Conservative shadow cabinet in 1968 after suggesting that further immigration into the country from the New Commonwealth would lead to racial conflict and violence. Similar views were expressed in 1990 by the former Conservative Party Chairman, Norman Tebbitt, who proposed that immigrants into Britain should pass what he called a 'cricket test' to establish whether or not they support Britain, or England, in sporting events, or remain loyal to their country of origin. In principle, conservatives doubt if multi-cultural or multi-national states can be stable because they lack the cultural and social cohesion which only a strong national identity can generate. However, in practice, this involves re-inventing or at least re-defining national identity in such a way that immigration is either deterred or immigrants are forced to assimilate to the host culture. Such nationalism is exclusive in that it attempts to preserve a sense of nationhood by narrowing the concept of nationality itself, and drawing a very firm line between those who are members of the nation and those who are alien to it.

Although conservative politicians and parties have derived considerable political benefit from their appeal to nationalism, opponents have sometimes pointed out that their ideas are based upon misguided assumptions. In the first place, conservative nationalism can be seen as a form of elite manipulation. The 'nation' is invented and certainly defined by political leaders who may use it for their own purposes. This is most evident in times of war or international crisis when the nation is mobilised to fight for the 'fatherland' by emotional appeals to patriotic duty. Furthermore, conservative nationalism may also serve to promote intolerance and bigotry. By insisting on the maintenance of cultural purity and traditions, conservatives may portray immigrants, or foreigners in general, as a threat, and in the process promote, or at least legitimise, racialist and xenophobic fears.

c National chauvinism

In many countries the dominant image of nationalism is one of aggression and militarism, quite the opposite of a principled belief in national self-determination. The aggressive face of nationalism became apparent in the late nineteenth century as European powers indulged in a 'scramble for Africa' in the name of national glory and their 'place in the sun'. The imperialism of the late nineteenth century differed from earlier periods of colonial expansion in that it was supported by a climate of popular nationalism: national prestige was increasingly linked to the possession of an empire and each colonial victory was greeted by demonstrations of public approval. In Britain, a new word, jingoism, was coined to describe this mood of public enthusiasm for aggressive nationalism or imperial expansion. In the early twentieth century, the growing rivalry of the European powers divided the continent into two armed camps, the Triple Entente, comprising Britain, France and Russia, and the Triple Alliance, containing Germany, Austria and Italy. When world war eventually broke out in August 1914, after a prolonged arms race and a succession of international crises, it provoked public rejoicing in all major cities of Europe. Aggressive and expansionist nationalism reached its high point in the inter-war period when the authoritarian or fascist regimes of Japan, Italy and Germany embarked upon policies of imperial expansion and world domination, eventually leading to war in 1939.

What distinguished this form of nationalism from earlier liberal nationalism was its chauvinism, a belief in superiority or dominance, a term derived from the name of Nicolas Chauvin, a French soldier who had been fanatically devoted to Napoleon. Nations were not thought to be equal in their right to self-determination; rather some nations were thought to possess characteristics or qualities which made them superior to others. Such ideas were clearly evident in European imperialism, which was justified by an ideology of racial and cultural superiority. In nineteenth century Europe, it was widely believed that the 'white' peoples of Europe and America were intellectually and morally superior to the 'black', 'brown' and 'yellow' peoples of Africa and Asia. Indeed, Europeans portrayed imperialism as a moral duty; colonial peoples were the 'white man's burden'. Imperialism supposedly brought the benefits of civilisation and in particular Christianity to the less fortunate and less sophisticated peoples of the world.

More particular forms of national chauvinism have developed in Russia and Germany. In Russia, this took the form of pan-Slavism, sometimes called Slavophile nationalism, particularly strong in the late nineteenth and early twentieth centuries. The Russians are Slavs, enjoying linguistic and cultural links with other Slav peoples in Eastern and South-Eastern Europe. The prefix 'pan' means 'all' or 'every', and therefore pan-Slavism reflects the goal of Slavic unity, which the Russians have believed to be their historic mission. In the years before 1914, such ideas brought Russia into deepening conflict with Austro-Hungary for control of the Balkans. The chauvinistic character of pan-Slavism was derived from the belief that the Russians were the natural leaders of the Slavic people, and that Slavs were culturally and spiritually superior to the peoples of Central or Western Europe. Pan-Slavism was therefore both anti-Western and anti-liberal. Some have feared that the revival of Russian nationalism in the 1990s could keep such aggressive and expansionist ideas alive.

Traditional German nationalism also exhibited a marked chauvinism, which was born out of the experience of defeat in the Napoleonic Wars. Writers like Fichte and Jahn reacted strongly against France and the ideals of its Revolution, emphasising instead the uniqueness of German culture and its language, and the racial purity of its people. After unification in 1871, German nationalism developed a pronounced chauvinistic character with the emergence of pressure groups like the Pan-German League and the Navy League, which campaigned for closer ties with German-speaking Austria, and for a German empire, her 'place in the sun'. Pan-

Germanism was an expansionist and aggressive form of nationalism, which ultimately envisaged the creation of a German-dominated Europe. German chauvinism found its highest expression in the racialist doctrines developed by the Nazis. The Nazis adopted the expansionist goals of pan-Germanism with enthusiasm, but justified them in the language of biology rather than politics, which are examined more fully in connection with racialism in Chapter 6. The Germans were a 'master race', naturally suited to a role of world domination, while other races were thought to be inferior and subordinate. After 1945, West Germany espoused a very different national tradition, which openly broke with the expansionist ideals of the past. However, re-unification in 1990 was accompanied by the growth of far-Right activism and anti-semitic attacks, encouraging some to suggest that contemporary German nationalism had not entirely buried its past.

National chauvinism breeds from a sentiment of intense, even hysterical, nationalist enthusiasm. The individual as a separate, rational being is swept away on a tide of patriotic emotion, expressed in the desire for aggression, expansion and war. Such intense patriotism is sometimes called integral nationalism: individuals and independent groups lose their identity within an all-powerful 'nation', which has an existence and meaning beyond the life of any single individual. Such militant nationalism is often accompanied by militarism. Military glory and conquest are the ultimate evidence of national greatness and have been capable of generating intense feelings of nationalist commitment. The civilian population is, in effect, militarised; it is infected by the martial values of absolute loyalty, complete dedication and willing self-sacrifice. When the honour or integrity of the nation is in question, the lives of ordinary citizens become unimportant. Such emotional intensity was amply demonstrated in August 1914, and perhaps also underlies the emotional power of the Jihad, or Holy War, in Moslem nations.

National chauvinism has a particularly strong appeal for the isolated and powerless, for whom nationalism offers the prospect of security, self-respect and pride. Militant or integral nationalism requires a heightened sense of belonging to a distinct national group. Such intense nationalist feeling is often stimulated by 'negative integration', the portrayal of another nation or race as a threat or an enemy. In the face of the enemy, the nation draws together and gains an intensified sense of its own identity and importance. National chauvinism therefore breeds off a clear distinction between 'them' and 'us'. There has to be a 'them' to deride or hate, in order to forge a sense of 'us'. In politics, national chauvinism has commonly been reflected in racialist ideologies, which divide the world into an 'in group' and an 'out group', in which the 'out group' becomes a scapegoat for all the misfortunes and frustrations suffered by the 'in group'. It is no coincidence therefore that chauvinistic political creeds are a breeding ground for racialist ideas. Both pan-Slavism and pan-Germanism, for example, have been characterised by virulent anti-semitism.

d Anti-colonialism

Nationalism may have been born in Europe, but became a worldwide phenomenon thanks to imperialism. The experience of colonial rule helped to forge a sense of nationhood and desire for 'national liberation' amongst the peoples of Asia and Africa, and gave rise to a specifically anti-colonial form of nationalism. In the twentieth century, the political geography of much of the world has been transformed by anti-colonialism. Although Versailles applied the principle of self-determination to Europe, it was conveniently ignored in other parts of the world, where German colonies were simply transferred to British and French control. However, during the inter-war period independence movements increasingly threatened the overstretched empires of Britain and France. The final collapse of the European empires came after the Second World War. India had been promised independence during the war and this was eventually granted in 1947. China only achieved genuine unity and independence in the Revolution of 1949, after fighting an eight year war against the occupying Japanese. The Indonesian Republic was proclaimed in 1949, after a three year war against Holland. Military resistance by the Viet Minh, led by Ho Chi Minh, eventually led the French to withdraw from Vietnam in 1954. However, their departure was followed in 1961 by the arrival of the Americans, and final liberation, together with the unification of North and South Vietnam, was only achieved in 1975, after fourteen further years of war.

Nationalist struggles in South-East Asia inspired similar movements in Africa, with liberation movements springing up under leaders like Nkrumah in Ghana, Doctor Azikiwe in Nigeria, Julius Nyerere in what was then Tanganyika, and Hastings Banda in

Nyasaland, later to become Malawi. The new-found assertiveness of African and Asian countries was expressed at the Bandung Conference of 1955, which attracted representatives from 29 countries, who jointly condemned colonialism and supported a policy of Third World non-alignment. De-colonisation in Africa accelerated from the late 1950s onwards. Nigeria gained independence from Britain in 1960 and, after a prolonged war fought against the French, Algeria achieved independence in 1962. Kenya became independent in 1963, as did Tanzania and Malawi the next year. Africa's last remaining colony, South-West Africa, finally became independent Namibia in 1990.

In a sense, the colonising Europeans had taken with them the seed of their own destruction, the doctrine of nationalism. It is notable, for example, that many leaders of independence or liberation movements were Western educated. It is not surprising therefore that anti-colonial movements sometimes articulated their goals in the language of liberal nationalism, reminiscent of Mazzini or Woodrow Wilson. However, emergent African and Asian nations were in a very different position from the newly-created European states of the nineteenth and early twentieth centuries. For these African and Asia nations the quest for political independence has been closely related to an awareness of economic underdevelopment and of their subordination to the industrialised states of Europe and North America. Anti-colonialism therefore expresses the desire for 'national liberation' in both political and economic terms, and this has left its mark upon the form of nationalism practised in the Third World.

Most of the leaders of Asian and African anti-colonial movements have been attracted to some form of socialism, ranging from the moderate and peaceful ideas represented by Gandhi and Nehru, to the revolutionary Marxism espoused by Ho Chi Minh, Che Guevara and Robert Mugabe. On the surface, nationalism and socialism appear to be incompatible political creeds. Socialists have traditionally preached internationalism, regarding humanity as a single entity and arguing that the division of humankind into separate nations was the work of 'bourgeois ideology'. Socialists have usually appealed to class solidarity rather than national unity, believing that working people in all countries are united by a common economic interest. Nevertheless, socialism has exerted a powerful appeal for Third World nationalists. In the first place, socialism embodies the values of community and co-operation which were already well-established in traditional, pre-industrial societies. More importantly, socialism, and in particular Marxism, provided an analysis of inequality and exploitation through which the colonial experience could be understood and colonial rule challenged. Marxism highlighted a class struggle between a 'ruling class' of property owners and the oppressed and exploited working class. It also preached the revolutionary overthrow of the class system in a 'proletarian revolution'. Such ideas had already been applied to the relationship amongst countries by Lenin in *Imperialism, The Highest Stage of Capitalism* (1916). Lenin argued that imperialism was essentially an economic phenomenon, a quest for profit by capitalist countries seeking investment opportunities, cheap labour and raw materials, and secure markets. Third World nationalists have applied Marxist analysis to the relationship between colonial rulers and subject peoples. The class struggle became a colonial struggle against exploitation and oppression. The overthrow of colonial rule therefore implied not only political independence but also a social revolution offering the prospect of both political and economic emancipation.

In some cases, Third World regimes have openly embraced Marxist–Leninist principles, often adapting them to their particular needs. On achieving independence, countries like China, North Korea, Vietnam and Cambodia moved swiftly to seize foreign assets and to nationalise economic resources. They founded one-party states and centrally planned economies, closely following the Soviet model. In Zimbabwe, Robert Mugabe was more pragmatic in his application of Marxism–Leninism. Zimbabwe established a mixed economy after independence in 1980, in an attempt to retain white expertise and capital, and accepted a constitution based upon Western-style parliamentary democracy for the first ten years after independence. In other cases, states in Africa and the Middle East have developed a less ideological form of nationalistic socialism. This has been evident in countries like Algeria, Libya, Zambia, Iraq and South Yemen, where one-party states have been founded, usually led by powerful, 'charismatic' leaders such as Gadhafi in Libya and Saddam Hussein in Iraq. The 'socialism' proclaimed in such countries usually takes the form of an appeal to a unifying national cause or interest, in most cases economic or social development.

Anti-colonialism has been a revolt against Western power and influence, and has therefore not always been satisfied to express itself in a language of liberalism and socialism borrowed from the West. In some cases, Western ideas have been adapted and changed beyond all recognition, as in the case of so-called 'African socialism', practised in Tanzania, Zimbabwe and Angola. African socialism takes neither the form of Soviet-style state socialism nor Western social democracy, but is rather founded upon traditional communitarian values and the desire to subordinate divisive tribal rivalries to the overriding need for economic progress. Third World countries have also expressed their nationalism by cultivating links with other former colonies in an attempt to articulate a distinctive Third World voice, independent from that of either the capitalist 'First World' or the communist 'Second World'. This was attempted by the Bandung Conference and has been kept alive by the non-aligned movement of Third World states. Third Worldism reflects a fierce rejection of imperialism and a common desire for economic progress amongst countries which usually share a colonial past. However, such ties have weakened as memories of colonial rule have receded, allowing the cultural and political differences amongst developing countries to become more apparent.

More radical forms of Third World nationalism have been shaped by a rejection of Western ideas and culture, rather than simply the attempt to remain independent from them. If the West is regarded as the source of oppression and exploitation, anti-colonialism must seek an anti-Western voice and not merely a non-Western one. In part, this is a reaction against the dominance of Western, and increasingly US, culture and economic power in much of the developing world. The United States has not favoured political colonisation, but its influence reflects the worldwide dominance of the US economy, controlling investment, creating jobs and making available a wide range of Western consumer goods. Such neo-colonialism has been far more difficult to combat because it does not take an openly political form, but it has also bred fierce resentment. During the Iranian Revolution, Ayatollah Khomeini dubbed the United States the 'Great Satan'. Anti-Americanism has been a prominent feature of Iranian politics since the Revolution of 1979, and it has been significant in Libya under Gadhafi and also in Saddam Hussein's Iraq, especially after the invasion of Kuwait in 1990. In rejecting the West in general, or the States in particular, such forms of nationalism have increasingly looked to non-Western philosophies and ideas. The growing importance of religion, and especially Islam, has given Third World nationalism a distinctive character and a renewed potency.

4 Islam and politics

Religion has traditionally been one of the major components of national identity and sometimes its most prominent feature. The population of Northern Ireland is divided by rival nationalisms, one Protestant, the other Catholic. In Sri Lanka, Christian Tamils are in conflict with the majority Buddhist population. Similarly, the Indian sub-continent was divided in 1947 into a predominantly Hindu India and a Moslem Pakistan. Although religion has provided communities with a sense of national identity, its influence in the modern world had appeared to be declining. The spread of Western influence brought with it a process of secularisation, in which the goals of material prosperity and political liberty tended to displace more traditional religious values. However, in the late twentieth century there has been evidence of a revival of religious belief and its re-emergence as a powerful political force.

The resurgence of religion may be a reaction against what is thought to be the soulless materialism of secular culture. In many cases, this has led to a growth of religious fundamentalism, a return to basic or original religious principles, commonly supported by a belief in the literal truth of religious texts. Fundamentalist religion is characterised by a certainty and intensity of belief, which typically does not confine itself to a private sphere of morality and worship. If religion is thought to constitute 'revealed truth' then its moral principles should be applied to economic and political life, just as they are to personal conduct. In the United States, this has been evident in the development of a Christian New Right, which has promoted a return to traditional family values and campaigned against abortion and in favour of the restoration of prayers in American schools. The Christian New Right was closely associated with Ronald Reagan and proposed its own candidate, Pat Robinson, for the Republican nomination in 1988. In Israel, fundamentalism has long been represented by a collection of small religious parties, whose conception of a Jewish homeland is based firmly upon Old Testament references. However, it is Islam which has emerged as the most politically significant of the world's religions, and the one which has generated both a powerful political movement and new forms of political organisation.

a Political Islam

Islam is the world's second largest religion, and its fastest growing. There are over 750 million Moslems in the world today, spread over more than 70 countries. The strength of Islam is concentrated geographically in Asia and Africa; it is estimated, for example, that over half the population of Africa will soon be Moslem. However, it has also spread into Europe and elsewhere. For instance, over 20 per cent of the Soviet Union's 285 million inhabitants are Moslems, and Islam has become the second largest religion in Britain, with over one and a half million adherents.

However, Islam is not, and never has been, simply a 'religion' It is, rather, a complete way of life, containing instruction on moral, political and economic behaviour for individuals and nations alike. The 'way of Islam' is based upon the teachings of the Prophet Muhammad, as revealed in the Koran, regarded by all Moslems as the revealed word of God, and the Sunna, or 'beaten path', the traditional customs observed by a devout Moslem, said to be based upon the Prophet's own life. There are two principal sects within Islam which developed within fifty years of Muhammad's death in 632 AD. The Sunni sect represents the majority of Moslems, while the Shiite or Shia sect contains just over one tenth of the Moslem world.

Throughout the history of Islam there has been a conflict between religion and politics, between Islamic leaders who were often secular-minded and flexible in their application of Islamic principles to political life, and fundamentalists who believed in strict adherence to the principles and life style of the Prophet. Fundamentalism in Islam does not mean a belief in the literal truth of the Koran, for this is accepted by all Moslems, and in that sense all Moslems are fundamentalists. Rather, it means an intense and militant faith in Islamic beliefs as the overriding principles of social life and politics, as well as of personal morality. Islamic fundamentalists wish to establish the primacy of religion over politics. In practice, this means the founding of an 'Islamic state', a theocracy ruled by spiritual rather than temporal authority and applying the Sharia, divine Islamic law, based upon principles expressed in the Koran. The Sharia lays down a code for legal and righteous behaviour which includes a system of punishment appropriate to most crimes as well as rules of personal conduct for both men and women. However, in common with other religions, Islam contains doctrines and beliefs which can justify a wide range of political causes. This is particularly true of Islamic economic ideas. The Koran, for example, upholds the institution of private property, which some have claimed endorses capitalism. However, it also prohibits usury or profiteering, which others have argued indicates sympathy for socialism.

The revival of Islamic fundamentalism in the twentieth century commenced with the founding of the Moslem Brotherhood in Eygpt in 1928. Although Eygpt had gained nominal independence from Britain in 1922 and full independence was recognised in 1936, Britain retained a powerful economic and military presence in the country. The Brotherhood was founded by Hassan al Banna with a view to revitalising what he believed to be a corrupted Islamic faith and providing the faithful with a political voice, a party of Islam. The Brotherhood sought to found an Islamic government that would provide an alternative to both capitalist and socialist forms of development. Such a government would transform the social system by applying Islamic principles to economic and political life as well as personal morality. This process of spiritual purification would also involve the final liberation of Eygpt from foreign control and he ultimately envisaged the liberation and unity of all Islamic peoples. The Brotherhood spread into Jordan, Sudan and Syria, where it set up branches containing mosques, schools, youth clubs and even business enterprises. It trained young people physically and militarily to prepare them for the coming Jihad, or Holy War, through which they would achieve their objectives.

The political appeal of Islam was that, unlike liberalism, socialism and conventional forms of nationalism, it had not been inherited or borrowed from the West. The desire for independence was understood to involve a process of spiritual purification because colonial peoples needed to regain self-respect and purge themselves of Western ideas and influences. In preaching a return to traditional institutions and principles, therefore, Islamic fundamentalists expressed a powerful desire for political and cultural independence from the West, achieved on their own terms. This was evident in the fact that the Moslem Brotherhood was founded in Ismailiya, at the time the headquarters of the Suez Canal Company and an important base for British troops. The other Arab countries to which fundamentalist ideas spread were also under either British or French control.

Nevertheless, fundamentalism remained on the fringe of Arab politics while Arab leaders either looked to the West or, after the rise of Gamal Nasser in Eygpt, supported some form of Arab socialism. Nasser nationalised the Suez Canal in 1956 and, after surviving military intervention from Britain, France and Israel, became the undisputed leader of the Arab world. Nasser's socialism encouraged him to forge a close diplomatic relationship with the Soviet Union, and to suppress the Moslem Brotherhood. However, Eygpt's defeat in the Arab–Israeli war of 1967 greatly discredited the ideas of Arab socialism and provided an opportunity for the growth of the fundamentalist movement. Despite the ending of colonial rule, the countries of the Middle East and North Africa were acutely aware of their continued economic dependence on the West or the Soviet Union, and of their political impotence, symbolised by the survival of the state of Israel. In such circumstances, resurgent nationalism once again took the form of a revival of Islamic fundamentalism. During the 1970s, fundamentalist groups sprang up in most Islamic countries and attracted growing support amongst the young and the politically committed.

The focal point of this process was Iran, where in 1979 a popular revolution brought the Ayatollah Khomeini to power and led to Iran being the first country to declare itself an 'Islamic Republic'. The Iranian example has inspired fundamentalist groups in many parts of the world. In 1981, the Moslem Brotherhood assassinated President Sadat of Eygpt, and leaders of several Islamic countries, under growing pressure from fundamentalists, introduced Sharia law: for example, General Zia in Pakistan and General Nimeri in Sudan. Fundamentalism has been particularly prominent in the Lebanon, divided as it is by a civil war between Christians and Moslems, and partly occupied by Israel in the south and Syria in the north. Parts of Beirut have also fallen under the control of fundamentalist groups such as the Iranian-backed *Shia Hezbollah* or 'Children of God', which have carried out a number of well-publicised kidnappings of Western hostages. Islam also became a significant component of the Gulf War of 1991. In many ways, Saddam Hussein was slow to grasp the political potential of Islamic fundamentalism. The Ba'athist movement which he led espoused an ideology based upon a fusion of socialism and pan-Arab nationalism, inspired by the example of Nasser. By initiating war against Iran in 1980, Saddam attempted to destroy radical Islamic fundamentalism and enjoyed the support from both the West and conservative states of the Gulf. However, on the eve of the Gulf War, Saddam openly embraced Islamic principles, declaring the coming war to be a Jihad between the 'true believers' and 'the infidel'. The words 'God is Great' were added to the Iraqi flag and the motto of the Ba'athist party was changed to 'The Believers stride forward'. Saddam's attempt to portray himself as the military, political and spiritual Imam of the Moslem world was greeted by many as little more than pragmatic opportunism. Nevertheless, the war itself stimulated anti-Western demonstrations in countries like Jordan, Algeria and Sudan, and strengthened fundamentalist movements throughout the region.

Political Islam has also had growing influence within Western countries. This was evident as long ago as 1929 with the formation of the Black Muslims in America, which developed under the leadership of Malcolm X into a radical Black Power movement during the 1960s. More recently, the impact of Islam has been demonstrated by conflict over the publication of Salman Rushdie's *The Satanic Verses*. Moslems in Britain and elsewhere campaigned to ban a book they believed to insult the Prophet and offend against Islamic principles. In 1988 Khomeini issued a *fatwa*, or religious order, condemning Rushdie to death. The Rushdie affair indicates the potential for the growth of fundamentalist ideas within cultures, such as the British one, which are perceived to be intolerant and insensitive to racial minorities. At the same time, it underlines the gulf which has developed between the values of Islamic fundamentalism and those of Western liberal democracy.

b Shiite fundamentalism

Iran has come to symbolise the revival of political Islam, and fundamentalist groups in countries like the Lebanon, Pakistan and Britain look to Iran for spiritual and political leadership. Iran's population is overwhelmingly from the smaller Shiite sect. The division of Islam into two sects is politically significant because the temper and political aspirations of the two sects have traditionally diverged. The split itself was provoked by the question of the succession to the Prophet Muhammad. Sunnis believe that only the first four caliphs or deputies who had succeeded Muhammad, the 'Rightly Guided Caliphs', transmitted divine wisdom. The last of these was the Prophet's cousin, Ali, and the Sunnis suggested that the succession to Ali should be determined by a consensus amongst the Ulama, or notable clerics. However, a leader so chosen could no longer be regarded as divine or infallible. In contrast, Shiites believe that divine wisdom continued to be transmitted by the descendants of Ali and Fatima, one of the Prophet's daughters. As a result, Shiites have held that each succeeding Imam, or religious leader, was immaculate and infallible, and therefore commanded absolute religious and political authority.

Sunnis have tended to see Islamic history as a gradual movement away from the ideal community, which existed during the life of Muhammad and his four immediate successors. Shiites, though, believe that divine guidance is always available in the teachings of the infallible Imam, or that divine wisdom is about to re-emerge into the world with the return of the 'Hidden Imam', or the arrival of the Mahdi, a leader directly guided by God. Shiites see history moving towards the goal of an ideal community, not away from it. Such ideas of revival or imminent salvation have given the Shiite sect a messianic and emotional quality, not enjoyed by the traditionally more sober Sunnis. The religious temper of the Shiite sect is also different from that of the Sunnis. Shiites believe that it is possible for an individual to remove the stains of sin through the experience of suffering and by leading a devout and simple life. The prospect of spiritual salvation has given the Shiite sect its characteristic intensity and emotional strength. When such religious zeal has been harnessed to a political goal it has generated fierce commitment and devotion. The Shiite sect has traditionally been more political than the Sunni sect. It has proved to be especially attractive to the poor and the down-trodden, for whom the re-emergence of divine wisdom into the world has represented the purification of society, the overthrow of injustice, and also liberation from oppression.

Although Iran, known before 1935 as Persia, has been a sovereign state since the fifteenth century, during the twentieth century it came under growing influence from foreign countries keen to exploit its oil reserves. First Britain, and then the United States, manipulated Iranian politics in order to safeguard their business investments. Under Shah Rezakhan and, after 1941, his son, Shah Rezapahlavi, the country embarked upon a programme of modernisation, in close collaboration with Western oil companies. In the 1970s, Iran experienced a dramatic resurgence of fundamentalism, stimulated by reaction against the materialism and secular culture promoted by the Shah, and the continuing domination of Iran by Western, and particularly US, interests. The movement focused around the leadership of the exiled religious leader, Ayatollah Khomeini, who co-ordinated resistance to the Shah from his Paris home. In 1979, a growing wave of popular demonstrations forced the Shah to flee the country and prepared the way for Khomeini's return. Iran was declared an Islamic Republic and power fell into the hands of the Islamic Revolutionary Council, comprising fifteen senior clerics, dominated by Khomeini himself. All legislation passed by the popularly-elected Islamic Consultative Assembly has to be ratified by the Council for the Protection of the Constitution, on which sit six religious and six secular lawyers, to ensure that it conforms to Islamic principles.

In effect, Iran became an absolutist theocracy, under the unquestioned leadership of Khomeini. Iran exhibited a fierce religious nationalism, reflected in popular antipathy to the 'Great Satan', the United States, and the application of strict Islamic principles to social and political life. For example, in 1981 the wearing of a headscarf and a hejad, loose-fitting clothes, became obligatory for all women in Iran, Moslems and non-Moslems alike. Restrictions on polygamy were removed, contraception was banned, adultery punished by public flogging or execution, and the death penalty was introduced for homosexuality. Both Iranian politics and society were thoroughly 'Islamised' and Friday prayers in Tehran became an expression of official government policy and a focal point of political life. The religious nationalism generated by the 'Islamic Revolution' reached new heights when Iran was invaded by Iraq in 1980. Popular resistance to Iraq was organised by the Islamic Revolutionary Guards, who enlisted volunteers, many of them young boys, inspired to fight by a potent combination of patriotism and religious devotion. Iraq had not only invaded Iran, but had offended against the 'Government of God' and therefore against Islam itself.

The abrupt end of the Iran–Iraq War in 1988 and the death of Ayatollah Khomeini the next year paved the way for more moderate forces to surface within Iran. The Iranian economy had been devastated by the massive cost of the eight year war and a lack of foreign trade and investment. Economic revival was impossible without ending Iran's diplomatic isolation from the industrialised West. The gradual emergence of Hashemi Rafsanjani, speaker of the Iranian parliament (the Islamic Consultative Assembly) and his election as President in 1989, marked a more pragmatic and less ideological turn in Iranian politics. Rafsanjani had himself been a prisoner of the Shah and did not wish to renounce the principles of the Islamic Republic, but he has gradually moved to restore diplomatic and economic links with the West.

The Iranian Revolution demonstrates the remarkable political power of Islam in general and of Shiite fundamentalism in particular. It has dramatically altered the political balance in North Africa and throughout the Middle East. Indeed, political Islam now constitutes a major alternative, and a significant threat, to the dominance of Western ideologies in many parts of the world. However, the survival of revolutionary zeal in Iran itself was closely tied up with the patriotic war fought against invading Iraq and the continuing messianic influence of Khomeini himself. Once these factors were removed, Iran gradually recognised that exclusive and militant nationalism was unworkable in an increasingly interdependent world.

6
Fascism

1 Introduction

In political debate, the words 'fascism' and 'fascist' are often employed with little precision. They are usually used pejoratively and are sometimes simply little more than all-purpose terms of political abuse. For instance, 'fascist' and 'dictator' are commonly used as if they were interchangeable, to mean anyone who possesses or expresses intolerant or illiberal views. However, fascism is not mere repression; fascist thinkers were inspired by a specific range of theories and values and the fascist regimes which emerged in the 1920s and 1930s developed historically new forms of political rule. The word 'fascism' derives originally from 'fasces', a bundle of rods carried before Consuls in Ancient Rome to signify their authority. By the 1890s, the word 'fascio' was used in Italy to refer to a political group or band, usually of revolutionary socialists. It was not, however, until Mussolini employed the term to describe the para-military armed squads he formed during and after the First World War that 'fascismo' acquired a clearly ideological meaning.

Whereas liberalism, conservatism and socialism are nineteenth century ideologies, fascism is a child of the twentieth century, some would say specifically of the period between the two world wars. Although all fascist ideas date back to the nineteenth century, they were fused together and shaped by the First World War and its aftermath, in particular by a potent mixture of war and revolution. Fascism emerged most dramatically in Italy and Germany. In Italy, a Fascist Party was formed in 1919, its leader, Benito Mussolini, was appointed Prime Minister in 1922, and by 1926 a one-party Fascist state had been established. The National Socialist German Workers' Party, known as the Nazis, was also formed in 1919, and, under the leadership of Adolf Hitler, consciously adopted the style of Mussolini's Fascists. Hitler was appointed German Chancellor in 1933 and in little over a year had turned Germany into a Nazi dictatorship. During the same period, democracy collapsed or was overthrown in much of Europe, often being supplanted by right-wing, authoritarian or openly fascist regimes. A nationalist coup turned the newly independent Lithuania into a dictatorship in 1926, and the two other Baltic States, Estonia and Latvia, followed suit in 1934. By 1938 Czechoslovakia was the only remaining democracy in Eastern or Central Europe, with Hungary and Romania moving steadily towards fascism and collaboration with Nazi Germany. In Portugal a dictatorship was set up under Salazar in 1928, and in Spain the Nationalist victory in the Civil War, 1936–9, led to the establishment of the Franco dictatorship. Regimes which bear some relationship to fascism have also developed outside Europe, notably in the 1930s in Imperial Japan and in Argentina under Peron, 1945–55.

The origins and meaning of fascism have provoked considerable historical interest and often fierce disagreements. It seems unlikely that any single factor can account for the rise of fascism on its own, but rather that fascism emerged out of a complex range of historical forces, present during the inter-war period. In the first place, democratic government had only recently been established in many parts of Europe, and democratic political values had not replaced older, autocratic ones. Moreover, democratic governments, representing a coalition of interests or parties, often appeared weak and unstable when confronted by economic or political crises. In such circumstances, the rival attraction of strong leadership brought about by personal rule cast a strong appeal. Secondly, European society had been disrupted by the experience of industrialisation, which had, in particular, threatened a lower middle class of shopkeepers, small businessmen, farmers and craftsmen, who were squeezed between the growing might of big business on one hand, and the rising power of organised labour on the other. Fascist movements drew their membership and support largely from such lower middle class elements. In a sense, fascism was a 'revolt of the lower middle classes', a fact which helps to explain the hostility of fascism to both capitalism and communism. Thirdly, the post-First World War period was deeply affected by the Russian Revolution and a fear amongst propertied classes that social revolution was about to spread throughout Europe. Fascist groups undoubtedly drew both financial and political support from business interests. Marxist historians have, as a result, interpreted fascism as a form of counter-revolution, an attempt by the bourgeoisie to cling on to power by lending support to fascist dictators. Fourthly, the world economic crisis of the 1930s often provided a final blow to already fragile democracies. Rising unemployment and economic failure produced an atmosphere of crisis and pessimism which could be exploited by political extremists and demagogues. Finally, the First World War had failed to resolve international conflicts and rivalries, leaving a bitter inheritance of frustrated nationalism and the desire for revenge. Nationalist tensions were strongest in those 'have not' nations which had either, like Germany, been defeated in war, or in countries such as Italy and Japan which had been deeply disappointed by the terms of the Versailles peace settlement. In addition, the experience of war itself had generated a particularly militant form of nationalism and imbued it with militaristic values.

Fascist regimes were not overthrown by popular revolt or protest but by defeat in the Second World War. Since 1945, fascist movements have achieved only marginal success, encouraging some to believe that fascism was a specifically inter-war phenomenon, linked to the unique combination of historical circumstances which characterised that period. Others, however, regard fascism as an ever-present danger, seeing its roots in human psychology or as Erich Fromm called it 'the fear of freedom'. Modern civilisation has produced greater individual freedom but has also brought with it the danger of isolation and insecurity. At times of crisis, individuals may therefore flee from freedom, seeking security in submission to an all-powerful leader or totalitarian state. Political instability or an economic crisis could therefore produce conditions in which fascism could revive. Fears, for example, have been expressed about the possible growth of neo-fascism in some parts of Eastern Europe since the collapse of Communist rule, 1989–90. Economic backwardness, political instability and nationalist rivalries have provided fertile ground for fascist movements in the past and it would be dangerous to discount the possibility of a resurgence of fascism in the future.

2 Strength through unity

Fascism stands apart from other political creeds and ideologies, indeed in a sense it was a revolt against the ideas and values which had dominated politics since the French Revolution. In Germany, the Nazis proclaimed that '1789 is abolished'. The negative features of fascist ideology are often clearer than its positive ones. Fascism was anti-rational, anti-liberal, anti-capitalist, anti-bourgeois and anti-communist. However, fascism was not merely a negation of established beliefs and principles. Fascism represents the darker side of Western political thought, the central and enduring values of which were not abandoned but rather transformed or turned upside down. For example, in fascism 'freedom' came to mean complete submission, 'democracy' was equated with dictatorship, and progress implied constant struggle and war.

Unlike other ideologies, fascism lacks a rational and coherent philosophy. Fascists have commonly despised abstract ideas and instead revered action, for example, Mussolini's favourite slogans included 'Action not Talk' and 'Inactivity is Death'. Above all, fascism was a movement; its major ideologists, like Hitler and Mussolini, were essentially propagandists, interested in ideas and theories only in so far as they had the power to elicit an emotional response and awaken the masses to action. Hitler himself preferred to describe his ideas as a *Weltanschauung* or 'world view', rather than a systematic ideology. In this sense, a world view constituted a complete, almost religious, set of attitudes that demanded commitment and faith, rather than reasoned analysis and debate.

At its core, fascism was revolutionary, but the revolution it sought bore little relationship to more conventional ideas of revolution. Fascists did not believe in a social revolution; their ideas about economic life were vague and sometimes inconsistent. Rather, fascism was a revolution of the psyche, a revolution of the human consciousness, aimed at creating a new type of human being, always understood in male terms, the 'New Man' or 'Fascist Man'. He was to be a hero, motivated by duty, honour and self-sacrifice, prepared to dissolve his personality in the social whole, and if necessary die for the glory of his nation or race. As such, fascism was the antithesis of liberalism: while liberals preached the primacy of the individual, fascists wished to obliterate the individual altogether and establish the dominance of the community or social group. It was this prospect of social cohesion, or as the Nazis promised 'strength through unity', which has given fascism its popular appeal at times of crisis and disorder.

a Anti-rationalism

The emphasis in fascism upon action and movement reflects a rejection of human reason and of intellectual life in general. Conventional political ideas were based upon a belief in rationalism, for example, liberals and socialists both believed that the world could be understood and transformed through the exercise of rational analysis. In the late nineteenth century, however, thinkers had started to reflect upon the limits of human reason and draw attention to other, perhaps more powerful, drives and impulses. The German philosopher, Nietzsche, for instance, proposed that human beings were motivated by powerful emotions, their 'will' rather than the rational mind, and in particular by what he called the 'will to power'. Sigmund Freud also highlighted the extent to which human behaviour was driven by non-rational passions, in his view by *libido*, the desire for sexual gratification.

The French syndicalist, Georges Sorel, was one of the first to apply anti-rationalism to politics. In his *Reflections on Violence* (1908), Sorel highlighted the importance of 'political myths', which were not passive descriptions of political reality but 'expressions of the will', that engaged the emotions and provoked action. Sorel believed, for example, that the proletariat could be roused from its slumbers and awakened to its revolutionary potential by 'the myth of the General Strike', a force far more potent than any amount of rational analysis and debate. Fascism reflects a similar 'politics of the will'. Intellectual life is devalued, even despised; it is cold, dry and lifeless. In contrast, fascism addresses the soul, the emotions and the instincts. Its ideas possess little coherence or rigour, but seek to exert a mythic appeal. However, fascism is not mere irrationalism. What is distinctive about fascism is not its appeal to non-rational drives and emotions so much as the specific range of beliefs and values through which it attempts to generate political activism.

b Struggle

The ideas which Charles Darwin developed in *On the Origin of Species* (1859) had a profound effect not only on the natural sciences, but also, by the end of the nineteenth century, upon social and political thought. The image of species developing through a process of 'natural selection' was developed by Herbert Spencer into the idea of the 'survival of the fittest', the belief that competition amongst individuals would reward those who worked hard and possessed talents and punish the lazy or incompetent. The notion that human existence was based upon competition or struggle exerted particular attraction in a period of intensifying international rivalry, which eventually led to war in 1914. Social Darwinism had considerable impact upon fascism. In the first place, fascists regarded struggle as the natural and inevitable condition of both social and international life. Only competition and conflict guaranteed human progress and ensured that the better and stronger prospered. As Hitler told German officer cadets in 1944, 'Victory is to the strong and the weak must go to the wall'. If the testing ground of human existence is competition and struggle then the ultimate test is war, which Hitler described as 'an unalterable law of the whole of life'. Fascism is perhaps unique amongst political ideologies in regarding war as good in itself, a view reflected in Mussolini's belief that, 'War is to men what maternity is to women'.

Darwinian thought also invests fascism with a distinctive set of political values which equate 'goodness' with strength and 'evil' with weakness. When the victory of the strong is glorified, power and strength are worshipped for their own sake. Similarly, weakness is despised and the elimination of the weak and inadequate is positively welcomed: they must be sacrificed for the common good, just as the survival of a species is more important than the life of any single member. Fascism therefore stands against the moral principles traditionally preached by both humanism and the major religions, in particular, the values of caring, sympathy and compassion. These values encourage a debilitating sympathy for weakness. Weakness and disability must not be tolerated; they should be eliminated. This was most graphically illustrated by the programme of eugenics, or selective breeding, introduced by the Nazis, in which the mentally and physically handicapped were at first forcibly sterilised and then, between 1939 and 1941, killed. In contrast to traditional humanist or religious values, fascists respect a very different set of martial values: loyalty, duty, obedience and self-sacrifice.

Finally, fascism's conception of life as 'unending struggle' gave it a restless and expansionist character. National qualities could only be cultivated through conflict and demonstrated by conquest and victory. This was clearly reflected in the foreign policy goals Hitler outlined in *Mein Kampf* (1925), '*Lebensraum* (living space) in the East', and the ultimate prospect of world domination. Once in power in 1933, Hitler embarked upon a programme of re-armament which prepared for expansion in the late 1930s. Austria was annexed in the Anschluss of 1938. Czechoslovakia was dismembered in the spring of 1939 and Poland invaded in September 1939, provoking war with Britain and France. In 1941 Hitler launched Operation Barbarossa, the invasion of the Soviet Union. Even when facing imminent defeat in 1945, Hitler did not abandon social Darwinism, but declared that the German nation had failed him and gave orders, never fully carried out, for a fight to the death and, in effect, the annihilation of Germany.

c *Leadership and elitism*

Fascism also stands apart from conventional political thought in its hostility to the very idea of equality. Once again, fascists built upon nineteenth century foundations. The idea of a 'Superman' or supremely powerful individual is often associated with the work of Friedrich Nietzsche, and particularly his *Thus Spoke Zarathustra* (1884). While Nietzsche understood the 'superman' to be an individual who rose above the 'herd instinct' of conventional morality and lived according to his own will and desires, fascists were attracted to the idea of a supreme and unquestionable leader. The idea of equality was also criticised in the early twentieth century by classical elitists like Mosca, Pareto and Michels. They argued that the rule of elites was inevitable and therefore that neither democracy, which was based upon the idea of political equality, nor socialism, which promised economic equality, was possible. Fascism was both elitist and ferociously patriarchal; its ideas were founded upon the belief that elite rule was both natural and desirable. Human beings were born with radically different abilities and attributes, a fact that would emerge as those with the rare quality of leadership rose, through struggle, above those capable only of following. Fascists believed that society was composed broadly of three elements. First, a supreme and all-seeing leader who possessed unrivalled authority. Secondly, an elite, exclusively male and distinguished by its heroism, vision and capacity for self-sacrifice. In Germany this role was ascribed to the SS which originated as a bodyguard but developed during Nazi rule into a state within a state. Finally, there was the masses, who sought guidance and direction, and whose destiny was unquestioning obedience.

Fascist regimes placed enormous emphasis upon the role of the leader. Mussolini styled himself '*Il Duce*' and Hitler adopted the title '*Der Führer*', both meaning simply 'the Leader'. In Japan, a more traditional concept of leadership persisted, in the form of the absolute authority of Emperor Hirohito. Fascist leaders emancipated themselves from any constitutionally defined notion of political leadership. The Leader was the symbolic embodiment of the people. At the Nuremburg Rallies the Nazi faithful chanted, 'Adolf Hitler is Germany, Germany is Adolf Hitler'. In Italy, the principle that 'Mussolini is always right' became the core of Fascist dogma. The Leader's authority is absolute and unquestionable because he, and he alone, understands the 'real' will of the people, the 'general will'. It is through the Leader that the people become articulate; he defines their interests and needs, and awakens them to their destiny.

The 'leader principle', or *Führerprinzip*, is the guiding principle of a fascist state. The Leader possesses both unlimited constitutional power and unquestionable ideological authority. The Leader should enjoy direct, personal contact with his people, typically organised through mass meetings, popular demonstrations and plebiscites. Intermediate institutions such as elections, parliaments and parties must either be abolished or weakened to prevent them challenging or distorting the Leader's will. In fascist theory, 'true' democracy is therefore an absolute dictatorship. In this way, fascists fused the notions of absolutism and popular sovereignty into a form of 'totalitarian democracy'.

d Socialism

Both Mussolini and Hitler portrayed their ideas, at times, as being 'socialist': Mussolini had previously been an influential member of the Italian Socialist Party and editor of its newspaper *Avanti*, while the Nazi Party espoused a philosophy it called National Socialism. To some extent, this represented a cynical attempt to elicit support from urban workers. However, it also reflected a profound distaste for capitalism amongst lower middle class fascist activists, who deeply resented the power of big business and financial institutions. Socialist or 'Leftist' ideas were therefore prominent in grass roots organisations, like the SA, or Brownshirts, in Germany, which recruited from amongst the lower middle classes. In a number of ways, fascism and capitalism are ideologically incompatible. Fascism places the community above the individual; Nazi coins, for example, bore the inscription, 'Common Good before Private Good'. Capitalism, on the other hand, is based upon the pursuit of self-interest and therefore threatens to undermine the cohesion of the nation or race. Fascists also despised the materialism which capitalism fostered: the desire for wealth or profit ran counter to the idealistic vision of national regeneration or world conquest which inspired fascists. Finally, capitalism was thought to be 'plutocratic', dominated by wealth and money, while fascists believed that leadership should be based upon nobility, honour and a sense of duty.

Fascist socialism was anti-individualistic and anti-bourgeois. It sought to subordinate capitalism to the ideological objectives of the fascist state. Oswald Mosley, leader of the British Union of Fascists, argued that 'Capitalism is a system by which capital uses the nation for its own purposes. Fascism is a system by which the nation uses capital for its own purposes'. However, historians have disagreed about how this conflict between profit and ideology was resolved in practice. On one hand, both Italian and German regimes tried to bend big business to their political ends by a policy of nationalisation and state regulation. For example, after 1936 German capitalism was reorganised in an attempt to create a 'war economy'. Moreover, the war which Hitler unleashed in 1939, which resulted in the wholesale destruction of German industry, complied more easily with Hitler's ideological objectives than it did with German capitalism's quest for profit. On the other hand, fascist regimes cultivated the support of big business and were even prepared to silence Leftist elements within their own ranks, as the Nazis did with the murder of Ernst Rohm and the purge of the SA in the 'Night of the Long Knives', 1934. German capitalism also thrived in the 1930s as Germany re-armed in preparation for war.

Fascist socialism was also profoundly anti-communist. Its objective was in part to seduce the working class away from Marxism and Bolshevism, which preached the insidious, even traitorous, idea of international working class solidarity, and upheld the misguided values of co-operation and equality. Fascists were dedicated to national unity and integration, they wished the allegiances of race or nation to be stronger than those of social class. As such, they wanted to imbue the working class with nationalist and social Darwinian values.

e Militant nationalism

Fascism inherited a tradition of chauvinistic and expansionist nationalism, which had developed in the years before the First World War. Nations were regarded not as equal and interdependent, but as natural rivals in a struggle for dominance. Fascist nationalism did not preach respect for distinctive cultures or national traditions, but asserted the superiority of one nation or race over all others, most boldly expressed in the ideas of Aryanism, the belief that the German people were a 'master race'. Such militant nationalism was fuelled by a sense of bitterness and frustration. Italy, a victor in the First World War, had failed to achieve territorial gains at Versailles. Germany had been both defeated in war and, she believed, humiliated at Versailles by reparations, the loss of territory and the deeply-resented 'war guilt clause'.

Fascism sought to achieve more than mere patriotism, the love of one's country; it wished to establish an intense and militant sense of national identity, what has been called 'integral nationalism'. Fascism embodied a sense of messianic or fanatical mission: the prospect of national regeneration and the rebirth of national pride. Indeed, the popular appeal which fascism exerted was largely based upon the promise of national greatness. However, in practice, national regeneration meant the assertion of power over other nations through expansionism, war and imperialism. Nazi Germany looked to build an empire in Eastern Europe, *Lebensraum* in the East; Italy sought to found an African empire through the invasion of Abyssinia in 1934; and Japan occupied Manchuria in 1931 and looked to found a 'co-prosperity' sphere in a new Japan-led Asia. These empires were to be autarkic, based upon the idea of economic self-sufficiency. In contrast to the liberal belief that economic progress resulted from international trade and co-operation, fascists held that economic strength was based upon independence and self-sufficiency. Conquest and colonisation were therefore a means of gaining economic security; an autarkic empire would contain vital raw materials, guaranteed markets and a plentiful supply of cheap labour. National regeneration and economic progress were therefore tied up with military power. The logic of this was most clearly understood in Germany where Hitler ensured that re-armament and preparations for war were a consistent political priority throughout the lifetime of the Nazi regime.

3 Fascism and the state

Although it is possible to identify a common set of fascist values and principles, Italian Fascists and German National Socialists also held distinctive, and sometimes conflicting, beliefs. Fascist ideology embraces two traditions, one, following Italian fascism, has emphasised the role of an all-powerful state, while the other, reflected in Nazism, is built upon the doctrine of racialism.

a Statism

The importance which the state possessed for Mussolini and his supporters can be understood in the light of Italian history. Although the formal unification of Italy was completed in 1871, the country remained deeply divided. Unlike Germany, Italy did not possess a unified culture nor even a common language. Regional dialects persisted and allegiances to local towns or provinces were not easily replaced by an affection for the newly created Italy. Most obviously, there was persistent antagonism between the industrialised North and the rural and more backward South. In short, there was an Italy but no Italians. As a nationalist, Mussolini wished to create a national consciousness, to forge an Italian nation, and the instrument through which he sought to achieve this objective was the Italian state. Mussolini's goal was to politicise the Italian people. In his words, 'The nation is created by the state, which gives to the people, unconscious of its own moral unity, a will and therefore an effective existence'.

The essence of Italian Fascism was the totalitarian ideal, the total subordination of the individual to the state. The Fascist philosopher

Gentile expressed this in the formula, 'Everything for the state; nothing against the state; nothing outside the state'. The individual's political obligations should be absolute and all-encompassing. Unquestioning obedience and constant devotion were required of the citizen, and individual existence would serve the interest of the nation. This fascist theory of the state has sometimes been associated with the ideas of the German philosopher, Hegel. Although Hegel was liberal-conservative, he did not accept the social contract theory that the state was merely a means of protecting citizens from one another. Rather, it was an ethical idea, reflecting the altruism and mutual sympathy of its members. The state was capable of motivating and inspiring individuals to act in the common interest, and therefore Hegel believed that higher levels of civilisation would only be achieved as the state itself developed and expanded. Hegel's political philosophy therefore amounted to an uncritical reverence of the state, expressed in practice in firm admiration for the autocratic Prussian state of his day.

The state also exerted a powerful attraction for Mussolini and Italian fascists because they saw it as an agent of modernisation. Italy was less industrialised than many of her European neighbours, notably Britain, France and Germany, and many fascists equated national revival with economic modernisation. All forms of fascism tend to be backward-looking, highlighting the glories of a lost era of national greatness, in Mussolini's case Imperial Rome. However, Italian fascism was also forward-looking, extolling the virtues of modern technology and industrial life. For example, many fascists were attracted to Futurism, an early twentieth century movement in the arts, led by Marinetti, which glorified factories, machinery and industrial life. Mussolini hoped that an all-powerful state could help Italy break with the traditions of backwardness and become an advanced industrialised country. Despite the fact that Mussolini's dreams of industrial greatness remained largely unfulfilled, statism has continued to exert an appeal in developing Third World countries, intent upon closing the gap with the industrialised West.

b Corporatism

Although fascists revered the state, this did not extend to an attempt to collectivise economic life. Fascist economic thought was seldom systematic, reflecting the fact that fascists sought to transform human consciousness rather than social structures. Its distinguishing feature was the idea of corporatism, which Mussolini proclaimed to be a 'Third Way' between capitalism and socialism, a common theme in fascist thought, embraced by both Mosley in Britain and Peron in Argentina. Corporatism opposed both the free market and central planning: the former would lead to an unrestrained pursuit of profit by individuals, while the latter was linked to the divisive idea of class war. In contrast, corporatism was based upon the belief that business and labour were bound together in an organic and spiritually unified whole. Social classes did not conflict with one another but worked in harmony for the common good and in the national interest. Such a view was influenced by traditional Catholic social thought which, in contrast to the Protestant stress upon the value of individual hard work, emphasised that social classes were held together by duty and mutual obligations.

Social harmony between business and labour offered the prospect of both moral and economic regeneration. However, class relations had to be mediated by the state, which was responsible for ensuring that the national interest took precedence over narrow sectional interests. Twenty-two Corporations were set up in Italy in 1927, each representing employers, workers and the government. These Corporations were charged with overseeing the development of all major industries in Italy. The 'Corporate State' reached its peak in 1939 when a Chamber of Fasces and Corporations was created to replace the Italian parliament.

In practice, fascist corporatism amounted to little more than an instrument through which the Fascist state sought to control major economic interests. Working class organisations were smashed and private business was intimidated. A more modest form of corporatism, neo-corporatism or liberal corporatism, has however become commonplace in the West since 1945. Governments which sought to manage their economies did so by consulting powerful economic interests such as business and trade unions, creating a partnership between government and economic groups. Although some have argued that this drift towards corporatism has inevitable fascist implications, others believe that liberal corporatism works in the opposite direction, enabling economic interests to dominate government. Neo-liberals, for example, fear that corporatism leads to the 'overload' of government by demands from economic interests which enjoy privileged access to the corridors of power.

4 Race and fascism

Not all forms of fascism involve racialism, and not all racialists are necessarily fascists. Italian fascism, for example, was based upon the supremacy of the Fascist state over the individual and submission to the will of Mussolini. It could embrace all people regardless of their race, colour or indeed country of birth. When Mussolini passed anti-semitic laws he did so simply to placate Hitler and the Germans, rather than for any ideological purpose. Nevertheless, fascism has often coincided with, and bred from, racialist ideas. Nowhere has this link between race and fascism been so close as in Nazi Germany, where official ideology amounted at times to little more than hysterical and pseudo-scientific anti-semitism.

a Racialism

A 'nation' is a cultural entity, a collection of people sharing the same language, religion, similar traditions and so on. The term 'race', on the other hand, reflects a belief in biological or genetic differences amongst human beings. While it may be possible to drop a national identity and assume another by a process of 'naturalisation', it is clearly impossible to change one's race, determined as it is at birth, indeed before birth, by the racial identity of one's parents. The symbols of nationality: citizenship, passport, language, and perhaps religion, can all be accepted by choice, voluntarily; however, the symbols of race: skin tone, hair colour, physiognomy and blood are fixed and unchangeable.

Racialist thought is based upon two central assumptions, the first of which is that humankind can be meaningfully divided on the basis of biological or genetic characteristics into 'races'. The use of racial terms and categories became commonplace in the West during the nineteenth century as imperialism brought the predominantly 'white' European races into increasingly close contact with the 'black', 'brown', and 'yellow', races of Africa and Asia. These races were thought of as separate human communities, biologically distinct from one another. Racialist thinkers have often denied the existence of a single human species and treated races as if they were separate species.

In reality, racial categories largely reflect cultural stereotypes and enjoy little if any scientific foundation. The broadest racial classifications, for example, those based upon skin colour – white, brown, yellow and so on – are at best misleading, and at worst simply arbitrary. More detailed and ambitious racial theories, such as those of the Nazis, simply produced anomalies, the most glaring of which was perhaps that Adolf Hitler himself certainly did not fit the racial stereotype of tall, broad-shouldered, blond-haired and blue-eyed Aryan, commonly described in Nazi literature. The Nazis themselves, who gave the question of race more attention than most, were never fully agreed how the 'master race' should be defined. Some described it as 'Aryan', implying a racial similarity between the peoples of Northern Europe, possibly extending to the peoples of the Indian sub-continent, others preferred the term 'Nordic', which incorporated the Germans but also most of the fair-skinned peoples of Northern Europe, while 'Germanic' was also used, but came close to defining race in terms of either culture or citizenship.

The second assumption of racialism is that racial divisions are in some way politically significant, indeed the most significant of social cleavages, more important, for example, than social class, nationality, gender and so forth. Racialists may hold these divisions to be significant for one of two reasons. First, they may believe in racial segregation, that it is natural or desirable to live, work and breed only with members of the same race. Secondly, they may support racial supremacy and hold that one race is naturally superior to all others and so is destined to dominate and exploit other races.

Doctines of racial segregation have, however, been based upon very different arguments and theories. In some cases they are founded on conservative ideas of social order and cohesion. For example, Enoch Powell in Britain in the 1960s, and Jean-Marie Le Pen in France in the 1980s, both argued against 'non-white' immigration into their countries on the grounds that the distinctive traditions and culture of the host, 'white' community would be threatened. Such views portray racial prejudice as a natural, indeed inevitable, expression of national consciousness. Multi-racial and multi-cultural societies are thought to be unstable and prone to violence and disorder. Elsewhere, racial segregation has been based upon religious or biological beliefs. The apartheid system in South Africa and the practice of segregation in the Southern states of America were both justified by reference to the Bible. Nazi race theory, however, treated racial differences as essentially biological; races were openly referred to as if they were separate species. In

Mein Kampf, Hitler described racial purity as an 'iron law of Nature': each animal, he argued, 'mates only with its own species'. The Nazis believed biological purity to be the key to racial greatness and feared that inter-marriage between Aryans and the non-Aryans would 'pollute' the racial stock and threaten the 'vital sap'. The Nuremburg Laws, passed in 1935, therefore prohibited both marriage and sexual relations between Germans and Jews.

Although a belief in racial segregation does not necessarily imply the idea of racial superiority, the two are commonly linked. Racial superiority suggests that races possess different, biologically-determined qualities, which suit them not merely to live apart, but to fulfil very different social roles. It is thought that biology invests some races with intelligence, courage and the capacity to lead, while other races are thought to be congenitally subservient. The most graphic example of a political philosophy built upon the doctrine of racial superiority is National Socialism in Germany.

b Nazism

Nazi ideology was fashioned out of a combination of racial anti-semitism and social Darwinism. Anti-semitism had been a force in European politics, especially in Eastern Europe, since the dawn of the Christian era. Its origins were largely theological: the Jews were responsible for the death of Christ, and in refusing to convert to Christianity they were both denying the divinity of Jesus and endangering their own immortal souls. The association between the Jews and Evil was therefore not a creation of the Nazis, but dated back to the Christian Middle Ages, a period when the Jews were first confined in ghettoes and excluded from respectable society. However, anti-semitism intensified in the late nineteenth century. As nationalism and imperialism spread throughout Europe, Jews were subject to increasing persecution in many countries. In France, this led to the celebrated Dreyfus affair, 1894–1906; in Russia it was reflected in a series of pogroms carried out against the Jews by the government of Alexander III.

The character of anti-semitism also changed during the nineteenth century. The growth of a 'science of race', which applied pseudo-scientific ideas to social and political issues, led to the Jews being thought of as a race rather than a religious, economic or cultural group. Thereafter, the Jews were defined inescapably by biological factors, such as hair colour, facial characteristics and blood. Anti-semitism was therefore elaborated into a racial theory, which assigned to the Jews a pernicious and degrading racial stereotype. The first attempt to develop a scientific theory of racialism was undertaken by Count Gobineau, whose *Essay on the Inequality of the Human Races* (1854) claimed to be a 'science of history'. Gobineau argued that there was a hierarchy of races, with very different qualities and characteristics. The most developed and creative race was the 'white peoples' whose highest element Gobineau referred to as the 'Aryans'. The Jews, on the other hand, were thought to be fundamentally uncreative. Unlike the Nazis, however, Gobineau was a pessimistic racialist, believing that by his day intermarriage had progressed so far that the glorious civilisation built by the Aryans had already been corrupted beyond repair.

The doctrine of racial anti-semitism entered Germany through Gobineau's writing and took the form of Aryanism, a belief in the biological superiority of the Aryan peoples. These ideas were taken up by the composer, Richard Wagner, and his son-in-law, H.S. Chamberlain, whose *Foundations of the Nineteenth Century* (1899) had an enormous impact upon Hitler and the Nazis. Chamberlain defined the highest race more narrowly as the 'Teutons', clearly understood to mean the German peoples. All cultural development was ascribed to the German way of life, while the Jews were described as 'physically, spiritually and morally degenerate'. Chamberlain presented history as a confrontation between the Teutons and the Jews, and therefore prepared the ground for Nazi race theory which portrayed the Jews as a universal scapegoat for all of Germany's misfortunes. The Nazis blamed the Jews for Germany's defeat in 1918, they were responsible for her humiliation at Versailles, their hand also lay behind the financial power of the banks and big business which enslaved the lower middle classes, as it did behind the working class movement and the threat of social revolution. Hitler suggested that the Jews were responsible for an international conspiracy of capitalists and communists, whose objective was to weaken and overthrow the German nation.

Nazi ideology portrayed the world in pseudo-religious and pseudo-scientific terms, as a struggle for dominance between the Germans and the Jews, representing respectively the forces of Good and Evil. Hitler himself divided the races of the world into three categories. The first, the Aryans, were a 'master race', the 'founders of culture', literally responsible for all creativity, whether in art, music, literature, philosophy or political thought. Secondly, there were the 'bearers of culture', peoples who were able to utilise the ideas and inventions of the German people, but were themselves incapable of creativity. At the bottom were the Jews, who Hitler described simply as the 'destroyers of culture', pitted in an unending struggle against the noble and creative Aryans. Hitler's 'world view' was therefore dominated by the idea of conflict between Good and Evil, reflected in a racial struggle between Germans and Jews, a conflict which could end only in Aryan world domination or the final victory of the Jews.

Such an ideology led Hitler and the Nazis in appalling and tragic directions. In the first place, the conviction that the Aryans were a uniquely creative 'master race' dictated a policy of expansionism and war. If the Germans were racially superior they were entitled to dominate other races. Indeed, other races were biologically conditioned to an inferior and subservient position. The Slavs of Eastern Europe, for instance, were regarded as 'sub-humans', suited only to carrying out manual labour for the benefit of their German masters. Nazi ideology therefore dictated an aggressive foreign policy in pursuit of a racial empire and ultimately world domination. As such, it contributed to a policy of rearmament, expansionism and war. Secondly, the Nazis believed that Germany could never be secure so long as its arch-enemy, the Jews, remained abroad. The Jews had to be persecuted, indeed they deserved to be persecuted because they were Evil. The logic of *Mein Kampf* was that German greatness could never be assured until the final elimination of the Jewish race. Nazi ideology therefore drove Hitler from a policy of racial persecution to one of terror and ultimately genocide and racial extermination. In 1941, with a world war still to be won, the Nazi regime embarked upon what it called the 'Final Solution', an attempt to exterminate the Jewish population of Europe in an unparalleled process of mass murder, which led to the deaths of six million Jews.

c *Modern racialism*

Despite the Holocaust, racialist ideas and movements have survived into the post-war period. However, with the exception of South Africa, where the National Party reconstructed society after 1948 on the principle of apartheid, racialism has normally been pushed to the political fringe. It has, nevertheless, been widespread and persistent. In the United States, the Ku Klux Klan (KKK), which preached white supremacy over blacks, rose to greatest prominence in the 1920s when it attracted over four million members, but still retains an influence in the Southern states. In Europe, a large number of racialist, sometimes neo-Nazi, groups have operated on the margins of political life, exploiting anxieties about immigration, urban decay and unemployment. In Britain, such views have been represented by the National Front, formed in 1967, and by the British National Party. The French National Front, established in 1972 and led by Le Pen, has achieved greater electoral respectability, securing around 10 per cent of the vote in parliamentary elections. Le Pen himself gained 14 per cent in the 1988 presidential election. Radical right-wing groups still operate in German politics despite the fact that anti-democratic and unconstitutional parties can be banned under the Basic Law. The Republicans, for example, a right-wing, nationalist party campaigning against immigration, and the neo-Nazi National Democrats (NDP) both performed well in local elections in 1989.

Economic growth and political stability have proved to be the most effective antidotes to racialism. However, as during the inter-war period, economic crises and political insecurity can still provide fertile ground for the politics of race. On the surface, the collapse of communist rule in Eastern Europe in 1989 paved the way for the victory of liberal democracy, but it also released older and darker political forces. One of the features of the revolutions in Eastern Europe has been an upsurge of both nationalism and racialism. The Soviet Union itself is in danger of collapsing under the centrifugal pressures of rival nationalisms. Many of the Soviet republics have also been disrupted by nationalist and racialist tensions: in 1990, for instance, Soviet troops were dispatched to Azerbaijan to restore order after clashes between Azeris and Armenians over the disputed region of Nogorno-Karabakh. In Russia, organisations like Pamyat, literally meaning 'memory', have sprung up to give expression to long-suppressed Greater Russian nationalism. In many ways, Eastern Europe was the cradle of anti-semitism in the nineteenth century. Russian anti-semites, for example, forged 'The Protocols of the Elders of Zion', which purported to be a Jewish plan for world conquest and was later used by the Nazis to discredit the Jews. Pamyat itself is anti-democratic, anti-Western and virulently anti-semitic. In many ways the political climate in much of Eastern

Europe is conducive to the spread of such ideas. Communist rule brought down a political ice age which preserved, rather than displaced, long-established national rivalries and racial hatreds. The overthrow of communist rule has permitted such forces to emerge from under the ice, at a time when the potent combination of economic backwardness and political instability could fuel the growth of extremist movements.

5 Totalitarianism

Fascist regimes, such as those in Hitler's Germany, Mussolini's Italy and in some respects even Peron's Argentina, sought to establish radically new forms of political rule. Traditional dictatorships had been authoritarian, they had suppressed political opposition and concentrated government power in the hands of a supreme leader or ruling group. Mussolini, however, proclaimed his desire to construct not a traditional, authoritarian regime but a 'totalitarian state'. The essence of this vision was the conception of total power, not merely a monopoly of political power but the extension of political control into each and every aspect of social and personal life – the economy, education, youth organisations, religion, art, culture and even the family. Totalitarianism promised to abolish the distinction between the state and civil society altogether, and to expose private life to a process of all-encompassing political control. Whereas authoritarian states, such as autocratic monarchies or traditional dicatorships, had sought to repress political activity and exclude the masses from politics, totalitarian states attempted to politicise society by mobilising popular support of the regime, typically through mass meetings, marches and demonstrations, pervasive propaganda and constant political agitation. Passive acceptance of authority was no longer sufficient; totalitarianism demanded active participation and total commitment, the politicisation of the masses. As such, totalitarianism requires the complete submission of the individual to the state.

Some writers have suggested that totalitarian states exhibit a number of defining characteristics. Friedrich and Brzezinski, for example, argued that totalitarian states can be identified by a 'six point syndrome'. First, they possess an official ideology, enjoying an almost religious status of infallibility. Secondly, these regimes are typically dominated by a single party, usually led by a single man, which controls the workings of government. Thirdly, a terroristic police force eradicates political dissent by the use of coercion and intimidation. Fourthly, a monopoly of the means of mass communication ensures that only politically 'reliable' and ideologically 'pure' views can be expressed. Fifthly, the state possesses a monopoly of the weapons of armed combat, giving it alone the capacity to use force. Sixthly and finally, totalitarian states are characterised by state control of all aspects of economic life. Friedrich and Brzezinski claimed these features could be identified in Fascist Italy and Nazi Germany but were also evident in the Soviet Union, suggesting that totalitarianism highlighted the similarities between fascism and communism. Furthermore, such regimes were historically new, indeed they were a distinctively twentieth century phenomenon. The distinguishing features of totalitarianism, pervasive ideological manipulation and the use of terror, have both been made possible by harnessing modern technology to political ends. Totalitarian states typically employ the radio, television and cinema to spread propaganda, and maintain political control by the widespread surveillance of the civilian population, a task which requires a very efficient system of information gathering and processing.

The totalitarian ideal has a particular attraction for fascism because its central goal was the creation of 'Fascist Man', loyal, dedicated and obedient, and willing to place the good of the nation or race before self-interest. There is no doubt that Nazi Germany came close to realising the ideal of total state control: political repression was brutal and effective and Nazi ideology dominated the media, art and culture, education and youth organisations. However, in Italy the Fascist state fell some way short of Mussolini's totalitarian vision. For example, the Italian monarchy survived throughout the Fascist period, many local political leaders, especially in the South, continued in power, and the Catholic Church retained its privileges and independence. In some respects, Italian fascism amounted to little more than the personal dictatorship of Mussolini. Although the Fascist state was clearly authoritarian, it was a poor example of a totalitarian regime. Authoritarian-populist regimes like those in Argentina under Peron certainly resembled totalitarian states in attempting to stimulate mass political activism, but have usually embraced broad nationalist principles rather than an official ideology, and failed to develop efficient and all-encompassing mechanisms of political control.

The concept of totalitarianism was, however, linked to Cold War attitudes and beliefs, generated in the aftermath of the Second World War. To some extent, its attraction in the West in the 1950s and 1960s was that it drew attention to parallels between fascist and communist regimes, highlighting the repressive and brutal character of both. As such, it became a vehicle for expressing anti-communism and in particular hostility towards the Soviet Union. Without doubt, similarities existed between Nazi Germany and the Soviet Union, especially during the Stalinist period. However, the blanket description of both as 'totalitarian' tends to conceal significant differences. For example, the Soviet economy was entirely collectivised and subject to a system of central planning, whereas a capitalist economy survived throughout the Nazi period and big business often worked closely with the Nazi state. Moreover, fascism and communism are ideologically divergent; fascists, for instance, preach the values of struggle, elitism and nationalism, while communists advocate co-operation, equality and international solidarity. Totalitarian analysis also ignores changes which had taken place in the Soviet Union in the post-war period. Although political repression continued, mass terror and open brutality, the hallmarks of totalitarian rule, ended with the death of Stalin in 1953.

7
Anarchism

1 Introduction

In everyday language, the word 'anarchy' often has a negative or pejorative meaning. It implies chaos and disorder, a complete breakdown of civilised and predictable behaviour. Anarchy is also linked to violence, because of a long-established public image of the anarchist as a bomber or terrorist. However, most anarchists would fiercely deny these associations. Anarchists do advocate the abolition of law and government, but in the belief that a more natural and spontaneous social order will develop. As Proudhon suggested, 'society seeks order in anarchy'. The link with violence is also misleading. At times, anarchists have openly, even proudly, supported bombings and terrorism. However, most anarchists believe violence to be mistaken and counterproductive, and many follow the ideas of Tolstoy and Gandhi and regard any form of violence as morally unacceptable.

'Anarchy' literally means 'without rule'. The term has been in use since the French Revolution, and was initially employed in a critical or negative sense. It was not until Pierre-Joseph Proudhon proudly declared in *What is Property?* (1840), 'I am an anarchist', that the word was clearly associated with a positive and systematic set of political ideas. These ideas have sometimes been traced back to the Stoics and Cynics of Ancient Greece or the Diggers of the English Civil War. However, the first, and in a sense classic, statement of anarchist principles was produced by William Godwin in his *Enquiry Concerning Political Justice* (1793), even though Godwin never described himself as an anarchist.

During the nineteenth century, anarchism was a significant component of a broad but growing socialist movement. Proudhon's followers joined with Marx to set up the International Workingmen's Association, or First International, in 1864. The International collapsed in 1871 because of growing antagonism between Marxists and anarchists led by Mikhail Bakunin. In the late nineteenth century, anarchists sought mass support amongst the landless peasants of Russia and Southern Europe, and, more successfully, through anarcho-syndicalism, amongst the industrial working classes. Syndicalism was a form of revolutionary trade unionism, popular in France, Italy and Spain, which made anarchism a genuine mass movement in the early twentieth century. The powerful CGT union in France was dominated by anarchists before 1914, as was the CNT in Spain, which claimed a membership of over two million during the Civil War. Anarcho-syndicalist movements also emerged in Latin America in the early twentieth century, especially in Argentina and Uruguay, and syndicalist ideas influenced the Mexican Revolution, led by Emiliano Zapata. However, the spread of authoritarianism and political repression gradually undermined anarchism in both Europe and Latin America. The victory of General Franco in the Spanish Civil War brought an end to anarchism as a mass movement. The CNT was suppressed, and anarchists, like the Left in general, were persecuted. The influence of anarchism was also undermined by the success of Lenin and the Bolsheviks in 1917 and the growing prestige of communism within socialist and revolutionary movements.

In fact, anarchism is unusual amongst political ideologies in that it has never succeeded in winning power, at least at national level. No society or nation has therefore been modelled according to anarchist principles. It is tempting, as a result, to regard anarchism as an ideology of less significance than liberalism, socialism, conservatism or even fascism, all of which have proved themselves capable of winning power and reshaping societies. The nearest anarchists have come to achieving power was during the Spanish Civil War when they briefly controlled much of Eastern Spain and set up workers' and peasants' collectives throughout Catalonia. Consequently, anarchists have looked to historical societies that reflect their principles, such as the cities of Ancient Greece or Medieval Europe, or traditional peasant communes like the Russian *mir*. Anarchists have also stressed the non-hierarchic and egalitarian nature of many traditional societies, for instance, the Nuer in Africa, and supported experiments in small-scale, communal living within Western society.

As a political movement, anarchism has suffered from three major drawbacks. First, its goal, the overthrow of the state and all forms of political authority, is often considered to be simply unrealistic. Certainly the evidence of modern history from most parts of the world suggests that economic and social development is usually accompanied by a growth in the role of government, rather than its diminution or complete abolition. Secondly, in opposing the state and all forms of political authority, anarchists have rejected the conventional means of exercising political influence, forming political parties, standing for elections, seeking public office, and so on. Anarchists have therefore been forced to rely upon less orthodox methods, often based upon a faith in mass spontaneity rather than political organisation. Thirdly, anarchism does not constitute a single, coherent set of political ideas. Although anarchists are united in their opposition to the institutions of the state, and indeed other forms of coercive authority, they arrive at this conclusion from very different philosophical perspectives, and disagree, often fundamentally, about the nature of an anarchic society. In a sense, anarchism is a point of overlap between two very different political ideologies, liberalism and socialism. Liberals and socialists may both oppose the state, but liberals do so in the name of individual freedom, while socialists act under the banner of social solidarity. Certain anarchists therefore conceive of an anarchist society to be an extreme form of free market capitalism, while others envisage the creation of a fully collectivised or communist society.

Nevertheless, the enduring significance of anarchism is less that it has provided an ideological basis for acquiring and retaining political power, and more that it has challenged, and thereby fertilised, other political creeds. Anarchists have highlighted the coercive and destructive nature of political power, and in so doing have countered statist tendencies within other ideologies, notably liberalism, socialism and also conservatism. In fact, anarchism has had growing influence upon modern political thought. Both the New Left and the New Right, for instance, exhibit libertarian tendencies, which bear the imprint of anarchist ideas. The New Left encompassed a broad range of movements, prominent in the 1960s and early 1970s, including student activism, anti-colonialism, feminism and environmentalism. The unifying theme within the New Left was the goal of 'liberation', understood to mean personal fulfilment, and it endorsed an activist style of politics based upon popular protest and direct action, clearly influenced by anarchism. The New Right also emphasises the importance of individual freedom, but believes that this can only be guaranteed by market competition. Anarcho-capitalists have sought to highlight what they see as the evils of state intervention, and have been prominent in the rediscovery of free market economics.

2 Against the state

The defining feature of anarchism is its opposition to the state and the accompanying institutions of government and law. Anarchists have a preference for a stateless society, in which free individuals manage their affairs through voluntary agreement, without compulsion or coercion. Such a preference has been expressed by very different philosophical traditions, by liberal individualists on one hand, and by communitarian socialists on the other. Anarchism therefore has a dual character; it can be thought of as both 'ultra-liberalism' and 'ultra-socialism'. As a result, anarchism lacks the bedrock of unifying values and principles which usually distinguish one ideology from another. Nevertheless, anarchists from very different political traditions are united by what they oppose, notably the state and all forms of political authority, the church and organised religion, and, finally, the conventional organisation of economic life.

a Political authority

Sebastien Faure defined anarchism as 'the negation of the principle of Authority' (p.62). The anarchist case against authority is that it offends against the principles of liberty and equality. Human beings are free and autonomous creatures, who should treat each other with respect and sympathy. The power of one person over another enslaves, oppresses and limits human life. It gives rise to a 'psychology of power', based upon a pattern of 'dominance and submission', a society in which, according to Paul Goodman, 'many are ruthless and most live in fear'. Strictly speaking, anarchists do not object to all forms of authority; for instance, they may accept that the views of doctors or teachers deserve particular respect because of the specialist knowledge or learning such people possess.

However, even the authority of the doctor or teacher is dangerous; knowledge can be abused and exploited in order to maintain the prestige of the educated over the ignorant. Anarchists are, nevertheless, firmly opposed to any form of authority which is compulsory or coercive, such as political authority, especially when it is backed up by the machinery of the modern state.

All other political ideologies believe that the state fulfils some worthy or worthwhile purpose within society. Liberals think that the state is an essential guarantee of social stability and protector of individual rights. Conservatives traditionally hold that the state represents a focus for loyalty and respect within society, promoting cohesion and unity. Socialists have seen the state as an instrument of social reform, counterbalancing the inequalities and injustices of a market economy. Anarchists, however, believe that such views seriously misunderstand the nature of political authority and the state, and also fail to appreciate the negative and destructive forces which are embodied in the institutions of law and government.

The state is a sovereign body, which exercises supreme authority over all individuals and associations living within a defined geographical area. As such, unlike the authority of a doctor or teacher, the authority of the state is absolute and unlimited; laws can restrict public behaviour, limit political activity, regulate economic life, interfere with private morality and thinking, and so forth. The authority of the state is also compulsory. Anarchists reject the liberal notion that political authority arises from voluntary agreement, through some form of 'social contract', but argue instead that individuals become subject to state authority either by being born in a particular country or through conquest. Furthermore, the state is a coercive body whose laws must be obeyed because they are backed up by the threat of punishment. For Emma Goldman, government was symbolised by 'the club, the gun, the handcuff, or the prison'. The state can deprive individuals of their property, their liberty, and ultimately, through capital punishment, their lives. The state is also exploitative in that it robs individuals of their property through a system of taxation, once again backed up by the force of law and the possibility of punishment. Anarchists have often argued that the state acts in alliance with the wealthy and privileged and therefore serves to oppress the poor and weak. Finally, the state is destructive. 'War', as Randolph Bourne suggested, 'is the health of the State'. Individuals are required to fight, kill and die in wars that are invariably precipitated by a quest for territorial expansion, plunder or national glory by one state at the expense of others.

Anarchists not only regard the state as evil but also believe it to be unnecessary. William Godwin sought to demonstrate this by, in effect, turning the most celebrated justification for the state, the social contract theory, on its head. The social contract arguments of Hobbes and Locke had suggested that a stateless society, the 'state of nature', would amount to a civil war of each against all, making orderly and stable life impossible. The source of such strife lay in human nature, which, for Hobbes and Locke, was essentially selfish, greedy and potentially aggressive. Only a sovereign state can restrain such impulses and guarantee social order. In short, order was impossible without law. Godwin, in contrast, suggested that human beings were rational and reasonable creatures. He believed that they had a natural capacity to organise their own lives in a harmonious and peaceful fashion. Indeed, he argued that it was the corrupting influence of government and unnatural laws, rather than any 'original sin' in human beings, which created injustice, greed and aggression.

Anarchists have often sympathised with the famous words from Rousseau's *Social Contract* (1762), 'Man was born free, yet everywhere he is in chains'. At the heart of anarchism lies an unashamed utopianism, a belief in the natural goodness, or at least potential goodness, of humankind. Social order arises naturally and spontaneously; it does not require the machinery of 'law and order'. This is why anarchist conclusions have been reached by political thinkers who possess an essentially optimistic view of human nature. Liberals, for example, highlight the ability of human beings to think and act rationally, while socialists stress their capacity to act peacefully and co-operatively. On the other hand, conservatives who believe human beings to be imperfect and corrupt, possibly tainted by 'original sin', believe anarchism to be at best a utopian dream.

b *The church*

Although the state has been the principal target of anarchist hostility, the same criticisms apply to any other form of compulsory authority. Indeed, in the nineteenth century in particular, anarchists sometimes expressed as much bitterness towards the church as they did in relation to the state. This perhaps explains why anarchism prospered in countries with strong religious traditions, such as Catholic Spain, France, Italy and the countries of Latin America, where it helped to articulate anti-clerical sentiments.

Anarchist objections to organised religion serve to highlight broader criticisms of authority in general. Religion, for example, has often been seen as the source of authority itself. The idea of God represents the notion of a 'supreme being', who commands ultimate and unquestionable authority. For anarchists like Proudhon or Bakunin, an anarchist political philosophy had to be based upon the rejection of Christianity because only then could human beings be regarded as free and independent. Anarchists have, moreover, suspected that religious and political authority usually work hand in hand. Bakunin proclaimed that, 'The abolition of the Church and the State must be the first and indispensable condition of the true liberation of society' (p.82). Religion is seen by anarchists as one of the pillars of the state; it propagates an ideology of obedience and submission to both spiritual leaders and earthly rulers. As the Bible says, 'give unto Caesar that which is Caesar's'. Earthly rulers have often looked to religion to legitimise their power, most obviously in the doctrine of the Divine Right of Kings.

Finally, religion seeks to impose a set of moral principles upon the individual and to establish a code of acceptable behaviour. Religious belief requires conformity to standards of Good and Evil, which are defined and policed by figures of religious authority, such as priests, bishops or Popes. The individual is thus robbed of autonomy and the capacity to make his or her own moral judgements. Nevertheless, anarchists do not reject the religious impulse altogether. There is a clear mystical strain within anarchism. Anarchists can be said to hold an essentially spiritual conception of human nature, a utopian belief in the virtually unlimited possibilities of human self-development and in the bonds which unite humanity, and indeed all living things. Early anarchists were sometimes influenced by millenarianism, a belief in the return of Christ and the establishment of the Kingdom of God after 'a thousand years'. Modern anarchists have often been attracted to religions such as Taoism and Zen Buddhism, which offer the prospect of personal insight and also express a vision of the oneness of life.

c *The economy*

Anarchists have rarely seen the overthrow of the state as an end in itself, but have also been interested in challenging the structure of social and economic life. Bakunin argued that 'political power and wealth are inseparable'. In the nineteenth century, anarchists usually worked within the working class movement and subscribed to a broadly socialist social philosophy. Capitalism was understood in class terms: a 'ruling class' exploited and oppressed 'the masses'. However, this 'ruling class' was not understood in narrow economic terms, but encompassed all those who commanded wealth, power or privilege in society. It therefore included kings and princes, politicians and state officials, judges and police officers, bishops and priests, as well as industrialists and bankers. Bakunin, for example, argued that in every developed society three social groups could be identified: a vast majority who were exploited; a minority who were exploited but also exploited others in equal measure; and 'the supreme governing estate', a small minority of 'exploiters and oppressors pure and simple'. Anarchists identified themselves with the poor and oppressed and sought to carry out a social revolution in the name of the 'exploited masses', in which both capitalism and the state would be swept away.

However, it is the economic structure of life that most keenly exposes tensions within anarchism. Although many anarchists acknowledge a kinship with socialism, based upon a common distaste for property and inequality, others have defended property rights and even revered competitive capitalism. This highlights the distinction between two, very different, anarchist traditions, one of which is collectivist and the other individualist. Collectivist anarchists tend to advocate an economy based upon co-operation and the common ownership of wealth, while some individualist anarchists have supported private property and in some cases free market capitalism.

Despite such fundamental differences, anarchists are nevertheless agreed in their distaste for the economic systems which have dominated both capitalist West and communist East during the twentieth century. All anarchists opposed the 'managed capitalism' which has predominated in Western countries. Collectivist anarchists argue that state intervention has merely propped up a system of class exploitation and given capitalism a human face. Individualists suggest that intervention has distorted the competitive market and created economies dominated by both public and private monopolies. Anarchists have been even more united in their disapproval of Soviet-style 'state socialism'. Individualist anarchists object to the violation of property rights and individual freedom which they argue occurs in a planned economy. Collectivist anarchists argue that 'state social-ism' is a contradiction in terms. State socialism is seen as a system of exploitation in which a ruling class of capitalists has simply been replaced by a new ruling class of state and party officials. Anarchists of all kinds have a preference for an economy in which free individuals manage their own affairs without the need for state ownership or regulation, whether through a system of 'anarcho-capitalism' or one of 'anarcho-communism'.

3 Individualist anarchism

The individualist tradition of anarchism has been particularly influential in the United States, where it has been supported by a political culture which emphasises rugged and self-sufficient individualism and also a deep distrust of government. A strong libertarian tradition developed during the nineteenth century in the writings of Josiah Warren and Benjamin Tucker, editor of the periodical *Liberty*. The late twentieth century has witnessed a revival of interest in libertarian ideas and the emergence of an anarcho-capitalist wing of the American New Right, reflected in the formation of a Libertarian Party. The philosophical basis of individualist anarchism lies in the liberal idea of the sovereign individual. In many ways, anarchist conclusions are reached by pushing classical liberal thinking to its logical extreme. The heart of liberalism is a belief in the primacy of the individual and the central importance of individual freedom. Classical liberals understand freedom in a negative sense: it is the absence of constraints upon the individual. However, the state, by definition a sovereign, compulsory and coercive body, necessarily restricts that freedom. The individual and the state are therefore always in conflict. Quite simply, the individual cannot be sovereign in a society ruled by law and government.

Although these arguments are liberal in inspiration, significant differences exist between liberalism and individualist anarchism. First, while liberals accept the importance of individual liberty, they do not believe this can be guaranteed in a stateless society. Liberal thinkers like John Locke argued that law exists to protect and enlarge liberty, rather than constrain it. Such a belief is based upon the assumption that, if not restrained by government, self-seeking individuals will abuse one another by theft, intimidation, violence and even murder. Anarchists, in contrast, believe that individuals can conduct themselves peacefully and harmoniously without the need for government to 'police' society and protect them from their fellow human beings. Anarchists differ from liberals because they believe that free individuals can live and work together constructively because they are rational and moral creatures. Reason dictates that where conflict exists it should be resolved by arbitration or debate and not by violence.

Secondly, liberals believe that political power can be tamed or controlled by the development of constitutional and representative government. Constitutions seek to protect the individual by checking the power of the various institutions of government. Regular elections are designed to force a government to be accountable to the general public or at least a majority of the electorate. Anarchists dismiss the idea of a 'minimal state' or a 'democratic state'. They regard constitutionalism and democracy as simply a facade, behind which naked political oppression operates. All laws infringe individual liberty, whether the government that enacts them is constitutional or arbitrary, democratic or dictatorial. In other words, all states are an offence against individual liberty.

a Egoism

The boldest statement of anarchist convictions built upon the idea of the sovereign individual is found in Max Stirner's *The Ego and His Own* (1845). Like Marx, Stirner was deeply influenced by the philosophy of Hegel, but the two arrived at fundamentally different conclusions. Stirner's ideas represent an extreme form of individualism. The term 'egoism' can have two meanings. It can suggest that individuals are essentially concerned about their ego or 'self', that they are self-interested or self-seeking, an assumption that would be accepted by thinkers like Hobbes or Locke. Self-interestedness, however, can generate conflict amongst individuals and justify the existence of a state which would be needed to restrain each from harming or abusing others. However, for Stirner egoism was a philosophy which placed the individual self at the centre of the moral universe. The individual, in Stirner's view, should simply act as he or she chooses, without any consideration for laws, social conventions, religious or moral principles. Stirner's ideas were a form of nihilism, literally a belief in nothing, the rejection of all political, social and moral principles, a position which clearly pointed in the direction of both anarchism and atheism. Stirner's anarchism, however, contained few constructive proposals and left the individualist argument to be more fully developed by American thinkers such as Henry David Thoreau and Benjamin Tucker.

Thoreau's quest for spiritual truth and self-reliance led him to flee from civilised life and live for several years in virtual solitude, close to nature, an experience described in *Walden* (1854). In his most political work, *Civil Disobedience* (1849), Thoreau approved of Jefferson's liberal motto, 'That government is best which governs least', but proposed instead his own anarchist sentiment, 'That government is best which governs not at all'. For Thoreau, individualism led in the direction of civil disobedience: the individual had to be faithful to his or her conscience and do only what each believed to be right, regardless of the demands of society or the laws made by government. Thoreau's anarchism placed individual conscience above the demands of political obligation. In Thoreau's case this led him to disobey an American government he thought to be acting immorally in both upholding the institution of slavery and waging war against other countries.

Benjamin Tucker took the individualist argument further by considering how autonomous individuals could live and work with one another without the danger of conflict or disorder. Two possible solutions to this problem are available to the individualist. The first emphasises human rationality and suggests that when conflicts or disagreements develop they can be resolved by reasoned discussion. William Godwin, for example, was a rationalist, who believed that truth would always tend to displace falsehood. The second solution was to find some sort of mechanism through which the independent actions of free individuals could be brought into harmony with one another. Extreme individualists, like Josiah Warren and Benjamin Tucker, believed that this could be achieved through a system of market exchange. Warren thought that individuals had a sovereign right to the property they themselves produced, but were also forced by economic logic to work with others in order to gain the advantages of a division of labour. He suggested that this could be achieved by a system of 'labour for labour' exchange, and set up 'Time Stores' through which one person's labour could be exchanged for a promise to return labour in kind. Tucker argued that, 'Genuine anarchism is consistent Manchesterism', referring to the free trade and free market principles of Cobden and Bright. By the late nineteenth century in America, individualist anarchists had come to suggest that the 'invisible hand' of the market was capable of ordering all social interaction, relieving the need for political organisation altogether.

b Anarcho-capitalism

The revival of interest in free market economics in the second half of the twentieth century has led to increasingly radical political conclusions. New Right conservatives, attracted to classical economics, wished to 'get government off the back of business' and allow the economy to be disciplined by market forces, rather than be managed by an interventionist state. Right-wing libertarians, like Robert Nozick, revived the idea of a 'minimal state', whose principal function was the protection of individual rights. Other thinkers, such as Murray Rothbard and David Friedman, have pushed free market ideas to their limit and developed the notion of anarcho-capitalism. They believe that government can be abolished and be replaced by unregulated market competition. Property should be owned by sovereign individuals, who may choose to enter into voluntary contracts with one another in the pursuit of self-interest. Thus the individual remains free and all social interaction is regulated by the market, beyond the control of any single individual or group.

Anarcho-capitalists go well beyond the ideas of free market liberalism. Liberals believe that the market is an effective and efficient mechanism for delivering most goods, but argue that it also has its limits. Some services, such as the maintenance of domestic order, the enforcement of contracts and protection against external attack, are 'natural monopolies', which must be provided by the state because they cannot be supplied through market competition. Anarcho-capitalists, however, believe that all human wants can be satisfied by the market. For example, Rothbard recognises that in an anarchist society individuals will seek protection from one another, but argues that such protection can be delivered competitively by privately-owned 'protection associations' and 'private courts', without the need for a police force or state court system. He argues that profit-making protection agencies will offer a better service than the present police force because competition will provide consumers with a choice, forcing agencies to be cheap, efficient and responsive to consumer needs. Similarly, private courts will be forced to develop a reputation for fairness in order to attract custom from individuals wishing to resolve a conflict. Most importantly, unlike the authority of public bodies, the contracts thus made with private agencies will be entirely voluntary, regulated only by impersonal market forces. Radical though such proposals sound, the policy of privatisation has already made substantial advances in many Western countries. In America, several states already use private prisons and experiments with private courts and arbitration services have been set up. In Britain, private security and protection agencies have become commonplace, and schemes such as 'Neighbourhood Watch' have helped to transfer responsibility for public order from the police to the community.

4 Collectivist anarchism

The philosophical roots of collectivist anarchism lie in socialism rather than liberalism. Anarchist conclusions can be reached by pushing the ideas of socialist collectivism to their limits. Collectivism is, in essence, the belief that human beings are social animals, better suited to working together for the common good than striving for individual self-interest. Collectivist anarchism stresses the human capacity for social solidarity, that human beings are naturally sociable, gregarious and co-operative. The natural and proper relationship amongst people is therefore one of sympathy, affection and harmony. When people are linked together by a common humanity, they have no need to be regulated or controlled by government: as Bakunin proclaimed, 'Social solidarity is the first human law; freedom is the second law.'

Anarchists are sometimes criticised for holding a naïve and hopelessly optimistic view of human nature. In reality, anarchists have seldom asserted that people are 'naturally good', but rather that they have the capacity for solidarity and co-operation, If human beings are social creatures, their characters and qualities are formed by a process of social interaction and experience. Human nature is 'plastic', it is fashioned by environmental factors rather than any innate 'goodness' or 'badness'. Human beings will be greedy and aggressive if brought up in an unjust and oppressive society, but, on the other hand, they will be caring and co-operative if brought up in a society where justice and equality reign. For example, this helps to explain the enduring interest which anarchists have taken in education, and their desire to liberate education from any association with 'schooling', regimentation or discipline – what Paul Goodman called 'compulsory miseducation'. Many anarchists would sympathise with the goal of 'de-schooling society', preached by writers like Goodman and Ivan Illich.

Peter Kropotkin, the Russian anarchist, attempted to provide a biological foundation for social solidarity in *Mutual Aid* (1897). Kropotkin set out to re-examine Darwin's theory of evolution, which had been used by social thinkers such as Herbert Spencer to support the idea that humankind was naturally competitive and aggressive. Kropotkin did not accept that biology favoured competition and struggle, but argued instead that successful species were ones which had harnessed collective energies and possessed the capacity for 'mutual aid' or co-operation. The process of evolution had therefore strengthened human sociability, favouring co-operation rather than competition. Kropotkin suggested that mutual aid was best reflected in the structure of city life in Ancient Greece and Medieval Europe.

a Mutualism

The belief in social solidarity can justify various forms of co-operative behaviour. At one extreme, it has led to a belief in pure communism, but it has also generated the more modest ideas of mutualism, associated with Pierre-Joseph Proudhon. In a sense, Proudhon's libertarian socialism stands between the individualist and collectivist traditions of anarchism, Proudhon's ideas sharing much in common with those of individualists like Josiah Warren. In *What is Property?*, Proudhon came up with the famous statement that 'Property is theft', and condemned a system of economic exploitation based upon the accumulation of capital. Nevertheless, unlike Marx, Proudhon was not opposed to all forms of private property. He admired the independence and initiative of smallholding peasants, craftsmen and artisans. He therefore sought a system of property ownership which would avoid exploitation and promote social harmony.

Mutualism was a system of fair and equitable exchange, in which individuals or groups could bargain with one another, trading goods and services without profiteering or exploitation. Social interaction would therefore be voluntary, mutually beneficial and harmonious, requiring no regulation or interference by government. Proudhon's followers tried to put these ideas into practice by setting up mutual credit banks in France and Switzerland, which provided cheap loans for investors and charged a rate of interest only high enough to cover the cost of running the bank but not so high that it made a profit. Proudhon's own views were largely founded upon his admiration for small communities of peasants or craftsmen, notably the watch-makers of Switzerland, who had traditionally managed their affairs on the basis of mutual co-operation.

b Anarcho-communism

More radically, a belief in social solidarity can lead in the direction of collectivism and communism. Sociable and gregarious human beings should lead a shared and communal existence. For example, labour is a social experience, people work in common with fellow human beings and the wealth they produce should therefore be owned in common by the community, rather than by any single individual. In this sense, property *is* theft, it represents the exploita-tion of workers who create wealth, by employers who own it. Furthermore, private property encourages selfishness and, par-ticularly offensive to the anarchist, promotes conflict and social disharmony. Inequality in the ownership of wealth encourages greed, envy and resentment, and therefore breeds crime and disorder.

Proudhon believed that communism could only be brought about by an authoritarian state, but anarcho-communists, like Kropotkin and Errico Malatesta, argued that true communism required the abolition of the state. Malatesta committed much of his life to anarchist agitation and the attempt to promote a peasant insurrection in his native Italy. In contrast, Kropotkin spent most of his life as a writer and propagandist and tried to outline how an anarchic society would operate. Anarcho-communists admire small, self-managing communities, like the medieval city or the peasant commune. Kropotkin envisaged that an anarchic society would consist of a collection of largely self-sufficient communes, each owning its wealth in common. Such communes would be held together by the natural bonds of compassion and solidarity, rather than by regulations or laws. Kropotkin suggested that law did not prevent crime, but positively promoted it. Laws that protect private property and the government are both useless and harmful, and, once political oppression and economic injustice are abolished, laws to protect the person will simply become unnecessary. Kropotkin proposed that the anti-social instincts which may live on in some individuals would be most effectively restrained by 'liberty and fraternal care'. In his view, prisons and punishment merely served to corrupt and deprave human beings, thereby promoting further crime.

c Anarchism and Marxism

A number of obvious parallels exist between collectivist anarchism and Marxism. Both regard capitalism as a system of class exploitation and injustice. Both exhibit a preference for the collective ownership of wealth and the communal organisation of social life. Finally, both believe that a fully communist society would be anarchic. Marx expressed this belief in the famous prediction that the state would 'wither away' once the class system was abolished. Anarchists and Marxists both stress the capacity of human beings to order their affairs without the need for political authority.

On the other hand, there are also major differences between these two philosophies, reflected in the antagonism which led to the break up of the First International in 1872. Anarchists have been critical of Marxism for a number of reasons. In the first place, anarchists have recoiled from the scientific pretensions of Marxism, in particular the idea of 'historical materialism'. Anarchists reject the central role which Marxists accord to economic life, and prefer to appeal to the utopian hopes and ideals of the masses, rather than their material or class interests. Many anarchists fear that Marxism is a form of 'economic determinism', which portrays human beings as puppets controlled by impersonal historical forces, rather than as masters of their own destiny. Secondly, anarchists have been critical of the Marxist belief that the proletariat is the 'revolutionary class'. Anarchists have often worked within working class movements, but rarely seen the industrial working class as uniquely oppressed or as the sole agent of revolutionary change. Anarchists believe class exploitation to be merely one form of oppression and have seen revolutionary potential in a wide variety of other social groups, including the rural peasantry, ethnic minorities, the urban under-class, students and so forth. Thirdly, anarchists have disagreed with Marxists on the issue of political organisation. Following Lenin, many Marxists have been committed to the idea of a 'vanguard party', capable of leading the working class towards class conscious-ness and revolution. Anarchists, in contrast, place their faith in the spontaneous instincts of the masses and have feared that the idea of a revolutionary party is both elitist and a recipe for dictatorship.

However, the most bitter disagreement between Marxists and anarchists centres upon their rival conceptions of the transition from capitalism to communism. Marxist believe in the need for a 'dictatorship of the proletariat', a transitional period between a proletarian revolution and the achievement of full communism, during which the proletariat will have to arm and organise itself against the threat of counter-revolution. In Marxist theory the state reflects the interests of the ruling or dominant class in society. A proletarian revolution will overthrow the 'bourgeois state' and establish a temporary 'proletarian state' which will endure only so long as class antagonisms persist. Anarchists, however, do not see the state simply as an instrument of class rule: they regard it as an independent and oppressive body in itself, and draw no distinction between a bourgeois and a proletarian state. Genuine revolution, for an anarchist, requires not only the overthrow of capitalism, but also the immediate overthrow of all forms of state power. The state cannot be allowed to 'wither away', it must be abolished. Anarchists have believed that this explains the tragedy of the Russian Revolu-tion. In practice, the proletarian state has stubbornly refused to wither away, rather it became the cornerstone of the Soviet concep-tion of socialism. When anarchist sailors at the Kronstadt naval base mutinied in 1921 in protest against increasing repression, they were massacred by a Bolshevik government employing the machinery of the newly-created workers' state.

d Decentralisation

A powerful theme running throughout anarchism is a belief in relatively small, 'human scale' communities, in which people can manage their affairs through face-to-face interaction. If human beings are to organise their own affairs constructively and co-operatively they must have direct and personal contact with fellow human beings, which is only possible within relatively small communities, such as peasant communes, workers' collectives or mutual banks. Decisions in such communities can be taken by a process of direct democracy, which allows all to express their opinions or views and to participate directly in decision-making. Communes are typically run by regular meetings of all members, rather than by the more usual representative processes which permit a small minority to make decisions on behalf of the rest.

It is not surprising that anarchists have little sympathy for a world divided into large nation-states. They object to all states and regard the nation as an artificial construct, far too large to be genuinely self-managing or permit each individual a direct voice in the affairs of the community. In place of political nationalism, anarchists have often been attracted to Proudhon's idea of federalism. Proudhon believed that nations would break up into a confederation of self-managing regions or provinces, which would co-operate with one another on the basis of voluntary and mutual agreements. Such federations would be 'topless', lacking a central authority capable of imposing its will upon the various provinces or regions. The anarchist commitment to decentralisation has also made them profoundly critical of what they see as the depersonalised, even dehumanised nature of modern civilisation. Industrial societies are dominated by large-scale institutions – schools, universities, business corporations, government bodies and so on – in which informal and spontaneous interaction is replaced by hierarchy and formal organisation. The individual gets lost within the bureaucratic machine. Modern anarchists like Paul Goodman and Murray Bookchin have been important critics of such trends. Goodman, for example, was active in the field of urban planning, suggesting how the alienation of modern city life can be overcome by promoting neighbourhood and community developments, and encouraging the growth of local power. Bookchin is one of the fathers of modern environmentalism and has emphasised the need not only for human beings to live in harmony with one another, but also to live in harmony with nature.

5 Roads to anarchy

Anarchists have been more successful in describing their ideals in books and pamphlets than they have been in putting them into practice. Quite commonly, anarchists have turned away from active politics, concentrating instead upon writing or on experiments in communal or co-operative living. Anarchists have not only been apolitical, turning away from political life, but also positively anti-political, repelled by the conventional processes and machinery of politics. The problem confronting anarchism is that if the state is regarded as evil and oppressive, any attempt to win government power or even influence government must be corrupting and unhealthy. For example, electoral politics is based upon an idea of representative democracy which anarchists firmly reject. Political power is always oppressive, regardless of whether it was acquired through the ballot box or at the point of a gun. Similarly, anarchists are disenchanted by political parties, both parliamentary and revolutionary parties, because they are bureaucratic and hierarchic organisations. The idea of an anarchist government, an anarchist party or an anarchist politician is therefore a contradiction in terms. As there is no conventional 'road to anarchy', anarchists have been forced to explore less orthodox means of political activism.

a Anarcho-syndicalism

In the nineteenth century, anarchist leaders tried to raise the 'oppressed masses' to insurrection and revolt. Mikhail Bakunin, for example, led a conspiratorial brotherhood, the Alliance for Social Democracy, and took part in anarchist risings in France and Italy. Other anarchists, like Malatesta in Italy, the Russian Populists, or Zapata's revolutionaries in Mexico, worked for a peasant revolution. However, anarchist risings ultimately failed, partly because they were based upon a belief in spontaneous revolt rather than careful organisation. By the turn of the century, many anarchists had turned their attention to the revolutionary potential of the syndicalist movement.

Syndicalism is a form of revolutionary trade unionism, drawing its name from the French word 'syndicat' meaning union or group. Syndicalism emerged first in France and was expressed by the powerful CGT union in the period before 1914. Syndicalist ideas spread to Italy, Latin America, the United States and, most significantly, Spain, where they were supported by the country's largest union, the CNT. Syndicalist theory drew upon socialist ideas and advanced a crude notion of class war. Workers and peasants constituted an oppressed class, and businessmen, landlords, politicians, judges and the police were their exploiters. Workers could defend themselves by organising syndicates or unions, based upon particular crafts, industries or professions. In the short-term these syndicates could act as conventional trade unions, raising wages, shortening hours and improving working conditions. However, syndicalists were also revolutionaries, who looked forward to the overthrow of capitalism and the seizure of power by the workers. In *Reflections on Violence* (1908), Georges Sorel, the most influential syndicalist theorist, argued that such a revolution would come about through a General Strike, a 'revolution of empty hands'. Sorel believed that the General Strike was a 'myth', a symbol of working class power, capable of inspiring popular revolt.

Although syndicalist theory was at times unsystematic and confused, it nevertheless exerted a strong attraction for anarchists who wished to spread their ideas among the masses. As anarchists entered the syndicalist movement they developed the distinctive ideas of anarcho-syndicalism. Two features of syndicalism inspired particular anarchist enthusiasm. First, syndicalists rejected conventional politics as corrupting and pointless. Working class power, they believed, should be exerted through direct action, boycotts, sabotage and strikes, ultimately a general strike. Secondly, anarchists saw the syndicates as a model for a decentralised, non-hierarchic society of the future. Syndicates typically exhibited a high degree of grass roots democracy and formed federations with other syndicates, either in the same area or in the same industry.

Although anarcho-syndicalism enjoyed genuine mass support, at least until the Spanish Civil War, it failed to achieve its revolutionary objectives. Beyond the rather vague idea of the general strike, anarcho-syndicalism failed to develop any clear political strategy or theory of revolution, relying instead upon the hope of a spontaneous uprising of the exploited and oppressed. Other anarchists have criticised syndicalism for concentrating too narrowly upon short-term trade union goals and therefore for leading anarchism away from revolution and towards reformism.

b Violence

The attempt to raise the masses to revolution has led some anarchists to support the use of terrorism and violence. Anarchist violence has been prominent in two periods, the late nineteenth century, reaching its peak in the 1890s, and again in the 1970s. Anarchists have employed 'clandestine violence', often involving bombings or assassination, designed to create an atmosphere of terror or apprehension. Amongst its victims were Tsar Alexander II, King Humbert of Italy, Empress Elizabeth of Austria, and Presidents Carnot of France and MacKinley of America. The typical anarchist terrorist was either a single individual working alone, like Emile Henry, who was guillotined in 1894 after placing a bomb in the Café Terminus in Paris, or a clandestine group such as People's Will in Russia, which assassinated Alexander II. More recently, anarchist violence has been undertaken by the Baader-Meinhof group in West Germany, the Italian Red Brigades, and in Britain by the Angry Brigade. The use of violence to achieve political ends has been endorsed or accepted by a variety of political groups. However, violence is usually regarded as a tactical consideration rather than an act of principle. It is a means to an end, not an end in itself. Revolutionary socialists, for example, often accept that bloodshed is a regrettable but necessary feature of any successful revolution. Conservatives are prepared to allow the state to use force, especially when national security or public order is under threat. Anarchist violence, however, is different. Bombings and assassinations have been thought to be just and fair in themselves and not merely a way of exerting political influence.

Anarchists have seen violence as a form of revenge or retribution. Violence originates in oppression and exploitation, perpetrated by politicians, industrialists, judges and the police against the working masses. Anarchist violence merely mirrors the everyday violence of society and directs it towards those who are really guilty. It is a form of 'revolutionary justice'. For example, the Red Brigades in Italy set up 'people's courts' and held 'proletarian trials' before assassinating victims such as former Italian Prime Minister, Aldo Moro. Violence is also seen as a way of demoralising the ruling classes, encouraging them to loosen their grip upon power and privilege. Finally, violence is a way of raising political consciousness and stimulating the masses to revolt. Russian Populists believed violence to be a form of 'propaganda by the deed', a demonstration that the ruling class was weak and defenceless, which, they hoped, would stimulate popular insurrection amongst the peasants. The idea that violence could be inspiring was expressed first by Sorel and, more recently, by Frantz Fanon, who believed that acts of violence would help liberate colonial peoples from their sense of impotence and inferiority. In a preface to Fanon's *The Wretched of the Earth* (1961), the French philosopher, Jean-Paul Sartre, argued that, 'to shoot down a European is to kill two birds with one stone, to destroy an oppressor and the man he oppresses at the same time: there remains a dead man and a free man' (p.19).

In practice, anarchist violence has been, at best, counter-productive. Far from awakening the masses to the reality of their oppression, political violence has normally provoked public horror and outrage. There is little doubt that the association between anarchism and violence has damaged the popular appeal of the ideology. Furthermore, violence seems an unpromising way of persuading the ruling class to relinquish power. Violence and coercion challenge the state on territory upon which its superiority is most clearly overwhelming. Terrorist attacks in both the 1890s and the 1970s merely encouraged the state to expand and strengthen its repressive machinery, usually with the backing of public opinion.

c Pacifism

In practice, most anarchists see violence as tactically misguided, others regard it as abhorrent in principle. These latter anarchists have often been attracted to the principles of non-violence and pacifism developed by Leo Tolstoy and Mahatma Gandhi, both of whom expressed ideas sympathetic to anarchism. In his novels and political writings, Tolstoy developed the image of a corrupt and false modern civilisation. In contrast, he suggested that salvation could be achieved by living according to religious principles and returning to a simple, rural existence, based upon the traditional life style of the Russian peasantry. Communes were founded to spread Tolstoy's teachings, central to which was the principle of non-violence. For Tolstoy, Christian respect for life required that no person would 'employ violence against anyone, and under no consideration'.

Gandhi campaigned against racial discrimination and led the movement for Indian independence from Britain, eventually granted in 1947. His political method was based upon the idea of 'Satyagraha' or non-violent resistance, influenced both by the teachings of Tolstoy and Hindu religious principles. Gandhi believed that government represented 'violence in a concentrated form', because it was based upon compulsion and coercion. He worked for a life founded upon the principle of love, which he regarded as the 'law of our being'. His ideal community was the traditional Indian village, a society both self-governing and largely self-sufficient. Its symbol, the spinning wheel, which was both the source of its livelihood and a mark of its independence, has been incorporated into the Indian flag.

The principle of non-violence was crucial to Gandhi's philosophy for two reasons. First, it reflected the sanctity of all human life, indeed of all living beings. A society regulated by love must, for Gandhi, be based upon compassion and respect. Secondly, non-violence was a political strategy. To refrain from the use of force, especially when subjected to intimidation and provocation, demonstrates the strength and moral purity of one's convictions. In the campaign against British rule, non-violent resistance was a powerful weapon, mobilising popular support for independence within India itself and around the world. Such tactics were also employed by Martin Luther King and the civil rights movement in the United States in the 1960s and by the peace movement during the 1980s. Anarchists who have been attracted to the principles of pacifism have often shied away from mass political activism, preferring instead to build model communities which reflect the principles of co-operation and mutual respect. They hope that anarchist ideas will be spread not by political campaigns and demonstrations, but through the stark contrast between the peacefulness and contentment enjoyed within such communities, and the 'quiet desperation', in Thoreau's words, which typifies life in conventional society.

8
Feminism

1 Introduction

Until the 1960s, sexual divisions were rarely considered to be politically interesting or important. If the very different social, economic and political roles of men and women were considered at all, they were usually regarded as 'natural' and therefore as inevitable. For example, men, and probably most women, accepted that some kind of sexual division of labour in society was dictated by the simple facts of biology: women were suited to a domestic and household existence by the fact that they could bear and suckle children, while the greater physical strength of men suited them to the outdoor and public world of work. Conventional political theory has played its role in upholding such beliefs, usually by ignoring sexual divisions altogether. The growth of the women's movement and feminist thought since the 1960s has, however, severely tested such complacency. Feminists have drawn attention to sexual divisions which run through all societies, contemporary and historical, and highlighted the political significance of such divisions. In so doing, feminism has developed into a distinctive ideology, embracing concepts and theories which do not merely complement but challenge the assumptions of conventional political thought. Indeed, feminism has exposed a 'mobilisation of bias' which has traditionally operated within political theory, by which generations of male thinkers, unwilling to examine the privileges and power which their sex has enjoyed, have succeeded in keeping the role of women off the political agenda.

Feminists have highlighted what they see as a political relationship between the sexes, the supremacy of men and the subjection of women in most, perhaps all, societies. However, male chauvinists

216

may also accept the fact of sexual inequality, but believe it to be an unchangeable, even desirable, feature of life. Feminism is therefore defined by the belief that sexual inequality or oppression can and should be abolished. As such, feminism has always been linked to the women's movement, a movement which seeks to enhance the social role of women. At different times and in different places, this movement has assumed a variety of forms and pursued a diverse range of goals. It has sought to end barbaric practices like female circumcision and to abolish restrictive dress codes; struggled to achieve equal rights and wider access to education or career opportunities; it has tried to increase the number of women in elite positions in public life, and so forth. Some feminists argue that only women can genuinely sympathise with such goals because men have traditionally benefited from sexual inequality and are unlikely to act against their own interests. If this is true, men cannot be 'feminists', at best they can be 'pro-feminist' or 'anti-sexist'. Others, however, argue that such views foster separatism between women and men, serving to entrench sexual divisions rather than overcome them. Although feminism has always been associated with the women's movement, it is clearly not narrowly a 'woman's issue'; rather, it addresses matters of concern and significance to both sexes. In particular, feminist thought seeks to broaden political understanding by exploring the cultural, social, economic and biological factors which underlie gender divisions and which therefore condition each and every one of us, male and female.

Although the term 'feminism' belongs to the twentieth century, feminist views have been expressed in many different cultures and have been found in the ancient civilisations of Greece and China. Christine de Pisan's *Book of the City of Ladies*, published in Italy in 1405, foreshadowed many of the ideas of modern feminism in recording the deeds of famous women of the past and advocating women's right to education and political influence. Nevertheless, it was not until the nineteenth century that an organised women's movement developed. The first text of modern feminism is usually taken to be Mary Wollstonecraft's *Vindication of the Rights of Women* (1792), written against the backdrop of the French Revolution. By the mid nineteenth century, the women's movement had acquired a central focus, the campaign for female suffrage, the right to vote, which drew inspiration from the progressive extension of the franchise to men. This period is usually referred to as the 'first wave' of feminism and was characterised by the demand that women should enjoy the same legal and political rights as men. Female suffrage was its principal goal because it was believed that if women could vote all other forms of sexual discrimination or prejudice would quickly disappear.

The women's movement was strongest in those countries where political democracy was most advanced; women demanded the rights which in many cases their husbands and sons already enjoyed. In the United States, a women's movement emerged during the 1840s, inspired in part by the campaign to abolish slavery. The famous Seneca Falls convention, held in 1848, marked the birth of the American Women's Rights movement. It adopted a Declaration of Sentiments, written by Elizabeth Cady Stanton, which deliberately drew upon the language and principles of the Declaration of Independence, and called, amongst other things, for female suffrage. The National Women's Suffrage Association, led by Stanton and Susan B. Anthony, was set up in 1869 and merged with the more conservative American Women's Suffrage Association in 1890. Similar movements developed in other Western countries. In Britain, an organised movement developed during the 1850s, and in 1867 the House of Commons defeated the first proposal for female suffrage, an amendment to the Second Reform Act, proposed by John Stuart Mill. The British suffrage movement adopted increasingly militant tactics after the formation in 1903 of the Women's Social and Political Union, led by mother and daughter, Emmeline and Christabel Pankhurst. From their underground base in Paris, the Pankhursts co-ordinated a campaign of direct action in which 'suffragettes' carried out wholesale attacks upon property and mounted a series of well-publicised public demonstrations.

'First-wave' feminism ended with the achievement of female suffrage, introduced first in New Zealand in 1893. The Nineteenth Amendment of the Constitution granted the vote to women in the United States in 1920. The franchise was extended to women in Britain in 1918, but they did not achieve equal voting rights with men for a further decade. Ironically, in many ways winning the right to vote weakened and undermined the women's movement. The struggle for female suffrage had united and inspired the movement, giving it a clear goal and a coherent structure. Furthermore, many activists believed naïvely that in winning suffrage rights, women had achieved full emancipation. It was not until the 1960s that the women's movement was regenerated with the emergence of feminism's 'second wave'.

The publication in 1963 of Betty Friedan's *The Feminine Mystique* did much to re-launch feminist thought. Friedan set out to explore what she called 'the problem with no name', the frustration and unhappiness many women experienced as a result of being confined to the roles of housewife and mother. 'Second-wave' feminism has acknowledged that the achievement of political and legal rights has not solved the 'women's question'. Indeed, feminist ideas and arguments became increasingly radical, and at times revolutionary. Books like Kate Millett's *Sexual Politics* (1970) and Germaine Greer's *The Female Eunuch* (1970) pushed back the borders of what had previously been considered to be 'political' by focusing attention upon the personal, psychological and sexual aspects of female oppression. The goal of 'second-wave' feminism was not merely political emancipation but 'women's liberation', reflected in the ideas of the growing Women's Liberation Movement. Such a goal could not be achieved by political reforms or legal changes alone, but demanded, modern feminists argued, a radical and perhaps revolutionary process of social change.

The 1980s have sometimes been described as a period of 'post-feminism', suggesting either that feminist goals had been achieved or that feminist political thought had lost its radical or critical edge. The women's movement has certainly changed, but far from weakening it has continued to expand and broaden. In the 1990s feminist organisations exist in all Western countries and women's groups have developed in the Third World, gaining impetus from the Mexico Conference which launched International Women's Year in 1975 and designated the subsequent ten years the UN Decade for Women. After the first flowering of radical feminist thought in the late 1960s and early 1970s, feminism has developed into a distinctive and established ideology, whose ideas and values challenge the most basic assumptions of conventional political thought. However, like all other ideologies, feminism embraces a broad range of traditions and even conflicting tendencies. This does not make feminism incoherent or contradictory, but merely reflects the breadth and diversity of the modern women's movement.

2 Politics of the personal

a Public man, private woman

Although feminist thought cuts across traditional ideologies, notably liberalism and socialism, it is based upon a distinctive set of theories and categories. The characteristic feature of feminism is that it highlights and examines gender divisions within society, and regards such divisions as political rather than natural. Gender divisions are therefore seen to reflect a 'power relationship' between men and women. Feminists question how such divisions originate and have been sustained, as well as how they can be challenged and overthrown. In so doing, they have not only developed a novel account of political life and relationships, but also challenged the conventional notion of what is 'political'. In particular, feminists stress that private life, personal, family and sexual conduct, is highly political and is therefore an appropriate subject for political analysis.

Traditional notions of what is 'political' locate politics in the arena of public rather than private life. Politics has usually been understood to be an activity which takes place within a 'public sphere' of government institutions, political parties, pressure groups and public debate. Family life and personal relationships have normally been thought to be part of a 'private sphere', and therefore to be 'non-political'. Feminists, on the other hand, insist that politics is an activity which takes place within all social groups and is not merely confined to the affairs of government or other public bodies. Politics exists whenever and wherever social conflict is found. Millett, for example, defined politics as 'power-structured relationships, arrangements whereby one group of persons is controlled by another'. The relationship between government and its citizens is therefore clearly political, but so is the relationship between employers and workers within a firm, and also relationships in the family, between husbands and wives, and between parents and children.

The definition of what is 'political' is not merely of academic interest. Feminists argue that sexual inequality has been preserved precisely because the sexual division of labour which runs through society has been thought to be 'natural' rather than 'political'. This is highlighted in the title of Jean B. Elshtain's *Public Man, Private Woman* (1981). Traditionally, the public sphere of life, encompassing politics, work, art and literature has been the preserve of men, women have been confined to an essentially private existence, centred upon the family and domestic responsibilities. If politics takes place only within the public sphere, the role of women and the question of sexual equality are issues of little or no political importance. Women, restricted to the private roles of housewife and mother, are in effect excluded from politics.

Feminists have therefore sought to break down the divide between 'public man' and 'private woman'. However, they have not always agreed about what it means to collapse the distinction between 'the public' and 'the private', or about how this can be achieved. For some feminists, emancipation consists of being able to escape from a narrowly domestic existence of home and family. Women's liberation therefore means that women enjoy equal access with men to the public sphere, the right to an education, to pursue a career, or to enter public life. Other feminists believe that emancipation can only be achieved if some, or perhaps all, of the responsibilities of private life are transferred to the state or other public bodies. For example, the burden of child-rearing could be relieved by more generous welfare support for families or the provision of nursery schools or crèches at work. Indeed, child-rearing could become entirely the responsibility of the community, as in the kibbutz system in Israel. However, what distinguishes 'second-wave' feminists from their 'first-wave' predecessors is a refusal to accept that politics stops at the front door, summed up in the slogan that 'the personal is the political'. Female oppression is thought to operate in all walks of life and in many respects originates in the family itself. Modern feminists have therefore been concerned to analyse what can be called 'the politics of everyday life'. This includes the process of conditioning through which children are socialised into accepting 'masculine' and 'feminine' sex roles, the distribution of housework within the family, and also the politics of personal and sexual conduct.

b Patriarchy

Feminists believe that gender, like social class, race or nation, is a significant social cleavage. Indeed, some argue that gender is the deepest and most politically important social division. Feminists have therefore advanced a theory of 'sexual politics', in much the same way that socialists preach the ideas of 'class politics'. They also refer to 'sexism' as a form of oppression, drawing a conscious parallel with 'racism' or racial oppression. However, conventional political theory had traditionally ignored sexual oppression and failed to recognise gender as a politically significant category. As a result, feminists have been forced to develop new concepts and theories to convey the idea that society is based upon a system of sexual inequality and oppression.

Feminists use the concept of patriarchy to describe the power relationship between men and women. The term literally means 'rule by the father', and can refer narrowly to the supremacy of the husband-father within the family, and therefore to the subordination of both his wife and his children. Some feminists employ 'patriarchy' only in this specific and limited sense, to describe the structure of the family and the dominance of the father within it, preferring to use broader terms like 'male supremacy' or 'male dominance' to describe sexual relations in society at large. However, feminists believe that the dominance of the father within the family symbolises male supremacy in all other institutions. Many would argue moreover that the patriarchal family lies at the heart of a systematic process of male domination, in that it reproduces male dominance in all other walks of life, in education, at work and also in politics. 'Patriarchy' is therefore commonly used in a broader sense, to mean quite simply 'rule by men', both within the family and outside. Millett, for instance, describes 'patriarchal government' as an institution whereby 'that half of the populace which is female is controlled by that half which is male'. She suggests that patriarchy contains two principles: 'male shall dominate female, elder male shall dominate younger'. A patriarchy is therefore an hierarchic society, characterised by both sexual and generational oppression.

The concept of patriarchy is, nevertheless, broad. Feminists may believe that men have dominated women in all societies, but accept that the form and degree of sexual oppression has varied considerably in different cultures and at different times. At least in Western countries the social position of women has significantly improved in the twentieth century, as a result of the achievement of the vote and broader access to education, changes in marriage and divorce law, the legalisation of abortion and so on. However, in parts of the Third World patriarchy still assumes a cruel, even gruesome, form: 80 million women, mainly in Africa, are subject to the practice of circumcision, bride murders still occur in India, and the persistence of the dowry system ensures that female children are often unwanted and sometimes allowed to die.

Feminists disagree, however, about whether the institution of patriarchy has been universal. Some argue that ancient societies were matriarchal, indicated by the fact that pagan religions often believed in Goddess-worship. However, the archaeological evidence for ancient matriarchies is, at best, inconclusive, and although the practice of Goddess-worship may suggest that the female sex was respected and valued in ancient times, it does not prove that women ever dominated men, or even lived as their equals. To some extent, the attempt to find evidence of matriarchal societies reflects a desire to prove that the institution of patriarchy is not inevitable, and can therefore be overthrown. However, even if all contemporary and historical societies are patriarchal, this does not demonstrate that male domination is either natural or inevitable.

Although the goal of feminism is the overthrow of patriarchy and the ending of sexist oppression, feminists have sometimes been uncertain about what this means in practice and how it can be brought about. Traditionally, women have demanded equality with men, but equality can have very different implications. In the first place, with which men do women wish to be equal? Male society is itself hierarchical, it embodies significant class and racial divisions. Nineteenth century feminists were usually middle class women who wished to enjoy the privileges and rights enjoyed by their own husbands and sons, middle class men. Secondly, in what do women wish to be equal? Feminists are here divided. Liberal feminists argue that women should enjoy legal and political equality with men, they should possess 'equal rights', enabling them to compete on equal terms with men, regardless of sex. Socialist feminists, however, argue that equal rights may be meaningless unless women also enjoy 'social equality', which may require the abolition of both sexual and class oppression. Thirdly, some feminists regard the very notion of equality as either misguided or simply undesirable. To want to be equal to a man may imply that women are 'male identified', that they define their goals in terms of what men already have, that they want to be 'like men'. Feminists seek to overthrow patriarchy, but not by modelling themselves upon men, which might require them to adopt the competitive and aggressive behaviour which characterises male society. For many feminists, 'liberation' means the desire to develop and achieve fulfilment as women; in other words, to be 'woman identified'.

In order to challenge and eventually abolish patriarchy, feminists must understand how the institution originated and how it is maintained. The difficulty with understanding patriarchy is that male domination operates at many different levels and in all social institutions. It is evident, for instance, in the structure of the traditional family and the process of conditioning which takes place within it, in cultural stereotypes of women as mothers, housewives or sex objects, in the absence of women from senior positions in politics, business, the professions and public life, and also in the physical intimidation and violence employed by men to control women. Feminists do not have a single or simple analysis of patriarchy. Some believe that it is rooted in the family and a process of gender socialisation, others believe that better education and broader career opportunities can rectify inequality. The economic system is the source of oppression in the eyes of some feminists, while others believe that women are controlled by male violence and the fear of rape. At the heart of these questions lies the conflict between the importance of nature and nurture in conditioning human behaviour. Are human beings born with a fixed and unchangeable character, or are they moulded and shaped by social experience? If feminists seek to liberate women from patriarchy, they must be able to distinguish between the biological and unchangeable elements in human nature, and those attitudes and forms of behaviour which are conditioned by society and can therefore be altered.

c Sex and gender

The most common of all anti-feminist arguments simply asserts that gender divisions in society are 'natural', that men and women merely fulfil the social roles which nature designed them for. A woman's physical and anatomical make-up is thought to suit her to a subordinate and domestic role in society; in short, 'biology is destiny'. In practice, all such biological arguments are hollow. A woman's brain may be, as male chauvinists point out, smaller than a man's. However, in proportion to her body it is relatively larger, which is usually a more accurate indication of intelligence. Moreover, women are usually physically less powerful than men, with less developed musculatures. To some extent, this simply reflects social factors: men have been encouraged to undertake physical and outdoor work, to participate in sport and to conform to a stereotypical 'masculine' physique. However, although physical strength is important in agricultural or early industrial societies, it has little value in developed societies where tools and machinery are far more efficient than human strength; the heavily muscled male may simply be redundant in a technological world of robots and micro-chips. In any case, physical hard work, for which the male body may be better suited, has traditionally been undertaken by people with low class and status positions, not by those in authority. Nevertheless, the biological factor which is most frequently linked to women's social position is their capacity to bear children.

Without doubt, child bearing is an attribute that is unique to the female sex, together with the fact that women menstruate and have the capacity to suckle babies. However, in no way do such biological facts necessarily disadvantage women nor determine their social destiny. Women may be mothers, but they need not accept the responsibilities of 'motherhood': nurturing, educating and raising children by devoting themselves to home and family. The link between child-bearing and child-rearing is cultural rather than biological: women are expected to stay at home, bring up children and look after the house because of the structure of traditional family life. Domestic responsibilities could be undertaken by the husband, or they could be shared equally between husbands and wives in so-called 'symmetrical families'. Moreover, child-rearing could be carried out by the community or the state, or it could be undertaken by more distant relatives, as in 'extended families'. In addition, it is misleading to regard childbirth as a social disadvantage, disqualifying women from playing a role in public life or pursuing a career. In developing countries, childbirth often imposes only the briefest of interruptions in a woman's working life. More significantly, the capacity to bear children could carry with it high social status, being a symbol of creativity and a guarantee of the survival of the human species. Indeed, some feminists argue that patriarchy has its origins in male fears about women's power, represented by women's sexuality, their fertility and their power as mothers. Men have, as a result, sought to control women by confining them to domestic or household responsibilities, so depriving them of power.

Nevertheless, although biology may not be destiny, it cannot be denied that physical differences do exist between men and women.

Just how profound these natural differences are is an issue of crucial importance for feminists who seek to enhance the role of women and build a non-sexist society. In order to examine this issue, feminists have usually distinguished between sex and gender. 'Sex' refers to biological factors which distinguish 'men' from 'women', which are therefore unalterable. 'Gender', on the other hand, is a cultural term and refers to the different roles which society ascribes to men and women, and therefore distinguishes between 'masculine' and 'feminine' stereotypes. Patriarchal ideas blur the distinction between sex and gender, and assume that all social distinctions between men and women are rooted in biology or anatomy. Feminists insist that there is no necessary or logical link between sex and gender, and emphasise, in contrast, that gender differences are entirely cultural and so are imposed upon each individual by society.

Most feminists believe that sex differences between men and women are relatively minor and neither explain nor justify gender distinctions. As a result, human nature is thought to be essentially androgynous or sexless, incorporating the characteristics of both sexes. All human beings, regardless of sex, possess the genetic inheritance of a mother and a father, and therefore embody a blend of both male and female attributes or traits. Such a view accepts that sex differences are biological facts of life but insists that they have no social, political or economic significance. Women and men should not be judged by their sex, but as individuals, as 'persons'. The goal of feminism is therefore the achievement of 'personhood'. Gender differences are entirely artificial and can be obliterated. As Simone de Beauvoir pointed out, 'Women are made, they are not born'. Gender differences are manufactured by society, which conditions women to conform to a stereotype of 'feminine' behaviour, requiring them to be passive and submissive, suited to a life of domestic and family responsibilities. In precisely the same way, men are encouraged to be 'masculine', assertive, aggressive and competitive, prepared for a world of work, politics and public life. In a patriarchal society, women are moulded according to men's expectations and needs, they are encouraged to conform to one of a number of female stereotypes, all the creation of men: the mother, the housewife, the Madonna, the whore. In so doing, the personalities of both sexes are distorted. Women are encouraged to suppress their 'masculine' natures; they must not be noisy, assertive or ambitious.

Men, in turn, are forced to deny their 'feminine' side, to repress their emotional, sensitive and gentle impulses: 'big boys don't cry'.

However, not all feminists believe that gender differences can and should be abolished. Some subscribe to a 'pro-woman' position, which holds that sex differences do have political and social importance. Such a view is sometimes called essentialism: it suggests that the essential natures of women and men are fundamentally different. The aggressive and competitive nature of men and the creative and emotional character of women are thought to reflect hormonal or genetic differences, rather than simply the structure of society. To idealise androgyny or personhood and ignore sex differences is therefore a mistake. Women should recognise and celebrate the distinctive characteristics of the female sex, they should seek liberation not as sexless 'persons' but as developed and fulfilled women. This has led to the emergence of cultural feminism, which reveres women's crafts, art and literature, and highlights those experiences which are unique to women and promote a sense of 'sisterhood', such as childbirth, motherhood and menstruation. Such an analysis presents a very different picture of men. If male aggression and chauvinism is thought to be biologically determined rather than socially conditioned, men are 'the enemy', men are incorrigible, they cannot be redeemed, nor can they be adapted to live life in a non sexist society. As a result, some feminists insist upon separatism from men and male society, a decision which has profound consequences both for their political strategies and their personal and sexual behaviour.

3 Sex and politics

Feminism is a cross-cutting ideology, encompassing three principle traditions, liberal, socialist, and radical. Feminist views cannot, however, be expressed by those with conservative or Right-wing political perspectives. Conservatives believe society to be 'organic', to have developed out of natural necessity. The patriarchal structure of society and the sexual division of labour between 'public man' and 'private woman' is therefore thought to be natural and inevitable. Women are born to be housewives and mothers and rebellion against this fate is both pointless and wrong. At best, conservatives can argue that they support sexual equality on the grounds that women's family responsibilities are every bit as important as men's public duties. Men and women are therefore 'equal but different'.

A form of reactionary feminism has, nevertheless, emerged in certain circumstances. This has occurred when the traditional status and position of women has been threatened by rapid social change, as in inter-war Germany. National Socialism was virulently anti-feminist: the role of women was summed up in the Nazi slogan 'Children, Church and Kitchen'. A cult of motherhood developed during the Nazi period with medals given to mothers of large families, and national celebrations on the anniversary of Hitler's mother's birthday. Women were nevertheless drawn to the Nazi cause, and its women's organisation, National Socialist Woman-hood, gained a membership of over 2.3 million by 1939. This was because the process of industrialisation imposed a double burden upon German women. During the 1920s, women were increasingly recruited into the workforce, usually into poorly paid and low status jobs, but were at the same time expected to maintain their traditional domestic role as housewives and mothers. National Socialism was attractive because it promised to re-establish the distinction between public and private spheres of life, protecting women from the world of work and also enhancing the status of women's traditional family role. In effect, women sought emancipation and security by abandoning the public sphere and reclaiming control of family and domestic life. Moreover, the development of women's organisations gave a small group of women, such as Gurtrude Scholtz-Klink, Nazi Women's Leader, the opportunity to rise to positions of power and influence, even though the Nazi elite was supposed to be exclusively male.

Similar problems inhibit the spread of feminism in parts of the Third World. In Moslem countries, in particular, there is a firmly-established demarcation between the social status of men and women, reflected in the institution of polygamy, the use of the veil and other dress codes, and sometimes the enforced seclusion of women in the home. There is therefore strong cultural resistance to feminist ideas which challenge traditional moral and religious principles and so appear alien and intrinsically Western. Nevertheless, growing attention has been devoted to the role of women, both because of the creeping influence of Western values, especially in urban areas, and the re-assertion of strict Islamic law in countries like Iran, Pakistan and Sudan where fundamentalism has been strong. For example, the appointment of Benazir Bhutto as Prime Minister of Pakistan in 1988 provoked fierce controversy throughout the Islamic world about whether a woman could be the head of government in an Islamic state. In some cases, a form of Moslem feminism has emerged, particularly evident in Iran, in which women have supported the re-imposition of a strict dress code and the exclusion of women from public life, in the hope that such measures will re-establish respect for women and so enhance their social status.

a Liberal feminism

Early feminism, particularly the 'first wave' of the women's movement, was deeply influenced by the ideas and values of liberalism. The first major feminist text, Wollstonecraft's *Vindication of the Rights of Women* (1792), argued that women should be entitled to the same rights and privileges as men on the grounds that they were 'human beings'. She claimed that the 'distinction of sex' would become unimportant in political and social life as women were able to gain an education and be regarded as rational creatures in their own right. John Stuart Mill's *The Subjection of Women* (1869), written in collaboration with Harriet Taylor, proposed that society should be organised according to the principle of 'reason' and that 'accidents of birth', such as sex, should be irrelevant. Women were therefore entitled to the rights and liberties enjoyed by men, and in particular the right to vote. 'Second-wave' feminism also has a significant liberal component. Liberal feminism has dominated the women's movement in the United States; its major spokesperson has been Betty Friedan, whose *The Feminine Mystique* marked the resurgence of feminist thought in the 1960s. The 'feminine mystique' to which Friedan referred was the cultural myth that women sought security and fulfilment in domestic life and 'feminine' behaviour, a myth which served to discourage women from entering employment, politics and public life in general. She highlighted what she called 'the problem with no name', by which she meant the sense of despair and deep unhappiness many women experienced because they were confined to a domestic existence, unable to gain fulfilment in a career or through political life. In 1966, Friedan helped to found and became the first leader of the National Organisation of Women

(NOW), which has developed into a powerful pressure group and the largest women's organisation in the world.

The philosophical basis of liberal feminism lies in the principle of individualism, the belief that the human individual is all important and therefore that all individuals are of equal moral worth. Individuals are entitled to equal treatment, regardless of their sex, race, colour, creed or religion. If individuals are to be judged, it should be on rational grounds, on the content of their character, their talents, or their personal worth. Liberals express this belief in the demand for equal rights: all individuals should enjoy an equal opportunity to enter and participate in public life. Any form of discrimination against women in this respect should clearly be prohibited. Wollstonecraft, for example, insisted that education, in her day the province of men, should be opened up to women. J.S. Mill argued in favour of equal citizenship and political rights. Indeed, the entire suffrage movement was based upon liberal individualism and the conviction that female emancipation would be brought about once women enjoyed equal voting rights with men. Similarly, Friedan's work and the activities of groups like NOW have aimed to break down the remaining legal and social pressures which restrict women from pursuing careers and being politically active. NOW has campaigned, for instance, in favour of the Equal Rights Amendment (ERA), which would prohibit any form of discrimination on the grounds of sex, and has also campaigned in favour of abortion on the grounds that an unwanted pregnancy undermines a woman's autonomy over her own body and also damages her career and educational prospects.

However, liberal feminism is essentially reformist: it seeks to open up public life to equal competition between women and men, rather than challenge what many feminists see as the patriarchal structure of society itself. In particular, liberal feminists do not wish to abolish the distinction between the public and private spheres of life. Reform is necessary, they argue, but only to ensure the establishment of equal rights in the public sphere: the right to education, the right to vote, the right to pursue a career and so on. Significant reforms have undoubtedly been achieved in the industrialised West, notably the extension of the franchise, the 'liberalisation' of divorce law and abortion, equal pay and so forth. Nevertheless, far less attention has been given to the private sphere, the sexual division of labour and distribution of power within the family. Liberal feminists have usually assumed that men and women have different natures and inclinations, and therefore accept that, at least in part, women's leaning towards family and domestic life is influenced by natural impulses and so reflects a willing choice. This certainly applied to nineteenth century feminists, who regarded the traditional structure of family life as 'natural', but is also evident in the work of modern liberal feminists such as Friedan. In *The Second Stage* (1983), Friedan discussed the problem of reconciling the achievement of 'personhood', made possible by opening up broader opportunities for women in work and public life, and the need for love, represented by children, home and the family. Friedan's emphasis upon the continuing and central importance of the family in women's life has been criticised by more radical feminists as contributing to a 'mystique of motherhood'.

Finally, the demand for equal rights which characterises liberal feminism has principally attracted those women whose education and social background equip them to take advantage of wider educational and career opportunities. For example, nineteenth century feminists and the leaders of the suffrage movement were usually educated, middle-class women, who would have had the opportunity to benefit from the right to vote, pursue a career or enter public life. The demand for equal rights assumes that all women would have the opportunity to take advantage, for example, of better educational and economic opportunities. In reality, women are judged not only by their talents and abilities, but also by social and economic factors. If emancipation simply means the achievement of equal rights and opportunities for women and men, other forms of social disadvantage, such as social class and race, are ignored. Liberal feminism may therefore reflect the interests of white, middle-class women in developed societies, but fail to address the problems of working class women, black women, or those in the Third World.

b Socialist feminism

Although some early feminists subscribed to socialist ideas, socialist feminism has come into particular prominence in the late twentieth century. In contrast to their liberal counterparts, socialist feminists do not believe that women simply face political or legal disadvantages which can be remedied by equal legal rights or the achievement of equal opportunities. Rather, socialist feminists believe that the relationship between the sexes is rooted in the social and economic structure itself and that nothing short of profound social change, some would say social revolution, can offer women the prospect of genuine emancipation. As a United Nations' report pointed out in 1980, 'While women represent 50 per cent of the world population, they perform nearly two thirds of all working hours, receive one-tenth of world income and own less than 1 per cent of world property'.

The central theme of socialist feminism is that patriarchy can only be understood in the light of social and economic factors. The classic statement of this argument was developed in Friedrich Engels' *The Origins of the Family, Private Property and the State* (1884). Engels suggested that the position of women in society had fundamentally changed with the development of capitalism and the institution of private property. In pre-capitalist societies, family life had been communistic, and 'mother right' – the inheritance of property and social position through the female line – was widely observed. Capitalism, however, being based upon the ownership of private property by men, had overthrown 'mother right' and brought about what Engels called 'the world historical defeat of the female sex'. Like many subsequent socialist feminists, Engels believed that female oppression operated through the institution of the family. 'The first class oppression that appears in history', Engels argued, 'coincides with the development of the antagonism between men and women in monogamous marriage, the first class oppression coincides with that of the female sex by the male' (p.129). The 'bourgeois family' was patriarchal and oppressive because men wished to ensure that their property would be passed on only to their sons. Men achieved undisputed paternity by insisting upon monogamous marriage, a restriction which was rigorously applied to wives, depriving them of other sexual partners, but was, Engels noted, routinely ignored by their husbands. Women were compensated for this repression by the development of a 'cult of femininity', which extolled the attractions of romantic love, but was, in reality, an organised hypocrisy designed to protect male privileges and property. Engels did not go so far as to offer a detailed description of what family life would be like in a socialist society. However, he clearly believed that marriage should be dissolvable, and that once private property was abolished its patriarchal features, and perhaps also monogamy, would disappear. Other socialist feminists have proposed that the traditional, patriarchal family should be replaced by a system of communal living and 'free love', as advocated by utopian socialists such as Fourier and Owen.

Although Engels's ideas were based upon the dubious anthropology of L.H. Morgan, most socialist feminists agree that the confinement of women to a domestic sphere of housework and motherhood serves the economic interests of capitalism. Some have argued that women constitute a 'reserve army of labour', which can be recruited into the workforce when there is a need to increase production, but easily shed and returned to domestic life during a depression, without imposing a burden upon employers or the state. In addition, as temporary workers women are conditioned to accept poorly paid and low status jobs, which has the advantage of helping to depress wage rates without posing a threat to 'men's jobs'. At the same time, women's domestic labour is vital to the health and efficiency of the economy. In bearing and rearing children, women are producing the next generation of labour power and guaranteeing future production. Women are also responsible for socialising, conditioning and even educating children to ensure that they develop into disciplined and obedient workers.

Similarly, in their role as housewives, women relieve men of the burden of housework and child-rearing, allowing them to concentrate their time and energy upon paid and productive employment. In that sense, the sexual division of labour between men, who undertake waged labour in factories or offices, and women, who carry out unwaged domestic work, promotes economic efficiency. Furthermore, housewives are responsible for getting their husbands to work on time, properly dressed and well fed, ready for a hard day's work. The traditional family provides the worker with a powerful incentive to find and keep a job because he has a wife and children to support. In addition, the family provides the worker with a necessary cushion against the alienation and frustration of life as a 'wage slave'. Indeed, conventional family life provides the husband-father with considerable compensations: for example, he enjoys the status of being the 'breadwinner' and is granted leisure and relaxation at home, while the housewife-mother is employed in 'trivial' domestic labour.

Some feminists have argued that it is the unwaged nature of domestic work that accounts for its low social status and leaves women financially dependent upon their husbands, thereby establishing a system of social inequality. The campaign of 'Wages for Housework', associated in the 1970s with Costa and James, suggested that women would gain economic independence and enjoy enhanced social status if their labour, like that of men, was recognised as productive and worthwhile by being paid. This argument has also been used to suggest that prostitution should be accepted as a legal and waged employment. However, most feminists argue that emancipation requires that women be afforded a broader range of social and economic opportunities, rather than merely being paid for fulfilling their traditional social roles as housewives or sex objects.

Although socialist feminists agree that the 'women's question' cannot be separated from social and economic life, they are profoundly divided about the nature of that link. Gender divisions clearly cut across class cleavages, creating tension within socialist feminist analysis about the relative importance of 'gender' and 'class', and raising particularly difficult questions for Marxist feminists. Orthodox Marxists insist upon the primacy of class politics over sexual politics. Engels, for example, believed that the 'bourgeois family', which had subordinated women, arose as a consequence of private property and was therefore, in effect, a by-product of capitalism. This suggests that class exploitation is a deeper or more significant process than sex oppression. Women are oppressed not by men, but by the institution of private property, by capitalism. It also suggests that women's emancipation will be a by-product of a social revolution in which capitalism is overthrown and replaced by socialism. Women seeking liberation should therefore recognise that the 'class war' is more important than any idea of a 'sex war'. As a result, feminists should devote their energies to the labour movement rather than support a separate and divisive women's movement.

However, modern feminists have found it increasingly difficult to accept the primacy of class politics over sexual politics. For them, sexual oppression is every bit as important as class exploitation. Writers like Juliet Mitchell subscribe to modern Marxism, which accepts the interplay of economic, social, political and cultural forces in society, rather than orthodox Marxism, which insists upon the primacy of material or economic factors. This is why Mitchell refuses to analyse the position of women in simple economic terms and has increasingly given attention to the cultural and ideological roots of patriarchy. In *Woman's Estate* (1971) she suggested that women fulfil four social functions: first, they are members of the workforce and are active in production; secondly, they bear children and thus reproduce the human species; thirdly, they are responsible for socialising children; and, finally, they are sex objects. Liberation requires that women achieve emancipation in each of these areas, and not merely that the capitalist class system be replaced by socialism.

Disenchantment with orthodox Marxism is also a result of the disappointing progress feminism has made in state socialist societies. After the Russian Revolution, the notion that social equality should lead to equality between the sexes was advocated by Alexandra Kollontai, Commissar for Social Welfare, the only woman in Lenin's government. Kollontai favoured the abolition of the conventional family and its replacement by a system of open sexuality. However, her radical ideas were increasingly marginalised after the rise of Stalin, and female emancipation in the Soviet Union came to mean little more than the recruitment of women into the workforce, made possible by the provision of state facilities to look after children. Moreover, little attention has been given to the sexual division of labour. In the Soviet Union, for example, women are substantially under-represented in the upper echelons of political and professional life, and those who wish to pursue careers are still expected to fulfil their traditional household and family responsibilities. The most important exception to this is Cuba, where the Family Code requires husbands and wives to take equal responsibility for housework and childcare.

c Radical feminism

One of the distinctive features of 'second-wave' feminism is that many feminist writers moved beyond the perspectives of existing political ideologies. Gender differences in society were regarded for the first time as important in themselves, needing to be understood in their own terms. Liberal and socialist ideas had been adapted to throw light upon the position of women in society, but neither acknowledged gender to be the most fundamental of all social divisions. During the 1960s and 1970s, however, the feminist movement sought to uncover the influence of patriarchy not only in politics and public life or in the economy, but in all aspects of social, personal and sexual existence.

This trend was evident in the work of early radical feminists such as Eva Figes and Germaine Greer. Figes's *Patriarchal Attitudes* (1970) drew attention not to the more familiar legal or social disadvantages suffered by women, but to the fact that patriarchal values and beliefs pervade the culture, philosophy, morality and religion of society. In all walks of life and learning, women are portrayed as inferior and subordinate to men, by a stereotype of 'femininity' imposed upon women by men. In *The Female Eunuch*, Greer suggested that women were conditioned to a passive sexual role, which had repressed their true sexuality as well as the more active and adventurous side of their personality. Women had, in effect, been castrated and turned into sexless objects by the cultural stereotype of the 'Eternal Feminine'. Greer's work was influenced by New Left writers like Wilhelm Reich and Herbert Marcuse, who had proclaimed the need for 'sexual liberation' and criticised the repressive nature of conventional society. However, it was with the work of writers such as Kate Millett and Shulamith Firestone that radical feminism developed a systematic theory of sexual oppression which clearly stood apart from established liberal and socialist traditions.

The central feature of radical feminism is the belief that sexual oppression is the most fundamental feature of society and that other forms of injustice – class exploitation, racial hatred and so on – are merely secondary. Gender is thought to be the deepest social cleavage and the most politically significant, more important, for example, than social class, race or nation. Radical feminists have therefore insisted that society be understood and described as 'patriarchal' to highlight the central role of sex oppression, just as socialists use the term 'capitalist' to draw attention to the significance of economic exploitation. In *Sexual Politics*, Millett described patriarchy as a 'social constant' running through all political, social and economic structures and found in every historical and contemporary society, as well as in all major religions. The different roles of men and women have their origin in a process of 'conditioning': from a very early age boys and girls are encouraged to conform to very specific gender identities. This process takes place largely within the family, 'patriarchy's chief institution', but it is also evident in literature, art, public life and the economy. Millett proposed that patriarchy be challenged through a process of 'consciousness raising', an idea clearly influenced by the Black Power movement; through discussion and education women would become increasingly aware of the sexism which pervades society and better able to challenge it. Women's liberation therefore required a revolutionary change, the institution of the family would have to be destroyed and the psychological and sexual oppression of women which operates at all levels of society would have to be overthrown.

Firestone's *The Dialectic of Sex* (1970) attempted a still more ambitious explanation of social and historical processes in terms of sexual divisions. Firestone adapted Marxist theory to the analysis of the role of women by substituting the category of 'sex' for that of 'social class'. Firestone did not believe that sex differences merely arose from social conditioning, but from biology. The basic fact that women bear babies had led to a 'natural division of labour' within what she called 'the biological family'. Society could be understood not, as Marx had claimed, through the process of production, but rather through the process of reproduction. In bearing children, women were constantly at the mercy of biology, and therefore, like children, were dependent upon men for their physical survival. Nevertheless, Firestone did not accept that patriarchy is either natural or inevitable. Women, however, can only achieve emancipation if they transcend their biological nature and escape from the 'curse of Eve'. Just as Marx believed that history had developed to the point that it was possible to envisage the abolition of class conflict, so Firestone believed that modern technology opened up the prospect of genuine sexual equality by relieving women of the burden of pregnancy and childbirth. Pregnancy could be avoided by contraception or terminated by abortion, but new technology also created the possibility of avoiding pregnancy by artificial reproduction in test tubes and the transfer of child-rearing responsibilities to social institutions. In other words, the biological process of reproduction could be carried out in laboratories by cybernetics, allowing women, for the first time in history, to escape from the biological family and enter society as the true equals of men.

Although Millett sees the roots of patriarchy in social conditioning, while Firestone locates them in biology, they agree that liberation requires that sexual differences between men and women be diminished and eventually abolished. They both believe that the true nature of the sexes is equal and identical, a fact presently concealed either by the influence of patriarchal culture or the misfortune that women are born with wombs. Both accept that human nature is essentially androgynous. However, radical feminism encompasses a number of divergent elements, some of which emphasise the fundamental and unalterable difference between women and men. An example of this is the 'pro-woman' position, particularly strong in France and America. In sharp contrast to Firestone's belief that women need to be liberated from the curse of childbirth and child-rearing, this position extols the positive virtues of fertility and motherhood. Women should not try to be 'more like men'. They should rather recognise and embrace their 'sisterhood', the bonds which link them to all other women. The 'pro-woman' position therefore accepts that women's attitudes and values are different from men's, but implies that in certain respects women are superior, possessing the qualities of creativity, sensitivity and caring which men can never fully appreciate or develop.

The acceptance of unalterable differences between men and women has led some feminists towards cultural feminism, a retreat from the corrupting and aggressive male world of political activism into an apolitical woman-centred culture and life style. On the other hand, other feminists have become politically assertive and even revolutionary. If sex differences are natural, then the roots of patriarchy lie within the male sex itself. 'All men' are physically and psychologically disposed to oppress 'all women', in other words 'men are the enemy'. This clearly leads in the direction of feminist separatism. Men constitute an oppressive 'sex-class' dedicated to aggression, domination and destruction; the female 'sex-class' is therefore the 'universal victim'. For example, Susan Brownmiller's *Against Our Will* (1975) emphasises that men dominate women through a process of physical and sexual abuse. Men have created an 'ideology of rape' which amounts to a 'conscious process of intimidation by which all men keep all women in a state of fear' (p.15). Brownmiller argues that men rape because they can, because they have the 'biological capacity to rape', and that even men who do not rape nevertheless benefit from the fear and anxiety which it provokes amongst all women.

Feminists who have pursued this line of argument also believe that it has profound implications for their personal and sexual behaviour. Sexual equality and harmony is simply impossible because all relationships between men and women must involve oppression. Heterosexual women are therefore thought to be 'male identified', incapable of fully realising their true natures and becoming 'woman identified'. This has led to the development of political lesbianism, which holds that sexual preferences are an issue of crucial political importance for women. Only women who remain celebate or choose lesbianism can regard themselves as 'woman identified women', capable of finally escaping from male oppression. As Ti-Grace Atkinson has argued, 'feminism is the theory; lesbianism is the practice'. However, the issues of separatism and lesbianism have deeply divided the women's movement. The majority of feminists see such uncompromising positions as a distorted reflection of the misogyny, or woman-hating, that is evident in male society. In contrast, they remain faithful to the goal of sexual equality and the belief that it is possible to establish harmony between women and men in a non-sexist society. As a result, they believe that sexual preferences are strictly a matter of personal choice and not a question of political commitment.

4 Post-feminism?

In some respects, feminist theory reached a high point of creativity and radicalism in the late 1960s and early 1970s. Since that time, some have alleged that the women's movement is in decline and it has become fashionable to refer to the modern period as one of 'post-feminism'. Without doubt, feminism has confronted a number of difficulties. In the first place, there are clearly splits and divisions within the women's movement, between reformist and revolutionary feminists, between radical and socialist feminists, and over highly controversial issues like separatism and lesbianism. The modern women's movement is heterogeneous and therefore lacks a coherent or unified structure. United by a common desire to advance the role of women, feminists nevertheless disagree about how this can be achieved. Will women be liberated by the enactment of laws which guarantee equal rights or forbid sexual discrimination, does emancipation require equal representation amongst the ranks of the privileged or powerful, must the state provide more generous welfare support or childcare facilities, or can the position of women only be advanced by a social revolution or some kind of sexual revolution? Such a breadth of political strategies and goals is, however, no more bewildering than is found within socialist ideology. Indeed, it merely serves to highlight the fact that feminism has developed from being a political movement into a political ideology which, like other ideologies, encompasses a range of often-competing traditions.

A further problem was that in many parts of the world feminism operated within an increasingly hostile political environment during the 1980s. In Islamic countries, the advance of fundamentalism was reflected in pressure for the exclusion of women from politics and public life, the abolition of their legal rights and a return to the veil. In the industrial West, a conservative backlash against feminism was also evident. Both Thatcher and Reagan administrations were openly anti-feminist in their call for the restoration of 'family values' and in their emphasis upon women's traditional role as mothers and housewives. The New Right tried to reassert patriarchal values and ideas in the belief that they were natural as well as a guarantee of social order and stability. For example, the responsibility for controlling and disciplining children was placed firmly in the hands of mothers, who were 'neglecting their children' if they put their own education or careers before their family duties. The rise in crime and vandalism amongst young people could therefore be blamed upon working mothers, and in Britain at least, steps were taken to make parents legally and financially responsible for the actions of their children. At the same time, such anti-feminism paid the women's movement a backhanded compliment. The attempt to reassert conventional social and religious values reflects the success which feminism has enjoyed in encouraging women to question established attitudes and re-think traditional sex roles.

Finally, it has sometimes been suggested that feminist goals have largely been achieved. Just as the right to vote was won in the early years of the twentieth century, so 'second-wave' feminism has achieved the legalisation of abortion in many countries, together with equal pay and anti-discrimination legislation and more easy access to political and professional life. Some have even suggested the victory of feminism can be seen in the emergence of a new breed of man, no longer the chauvinist bigot of old, but the 'New Man', who has come to terms with the 'feminine' elements in his make-up and is prepared to share domestic and family responsibilities within the 'symmetrical family'. There is undoubted evidence of the de-radicalisation of the women's movement since the 1970s. The militant and revolutionary wing of the movement has been increasingly marginalised and feminist literature reflects evidence of revisionism. For example, Friedan's *The Second Stage* and Greer's *Sex and Destiny* (1984) both celebrate the importance of child-bearing and motherhood and have been criticised by more radical elements in the movement for lending support to traditional gender stereotypes. Nevertheless, the central myth of 'post-feminism' is that the most obvious forms of sexist oppression have been overcome and therefore that society is no longer patriarchal. Without doubt, for example, an increasing number of women go out to work, in many Western countries a clear majority of married women. Nevertheless, they are still overwhelmingly employed in poorly paid, low status and often part-time jobs. Although legal, political and sometimes social reforms have been introduced, a significant and substantial difference still persists between the roles of women and men in all contemporary societies, suggesting that the institution of patriarchy is stubborn and firmly entrenched in the social and cultural fabric of life. Feminism constitutes a political ideology in its own right and is unlikely to 'wither away' so long as the sexual imbalance in society persists.

9
Environmentalism

1 Introduction

The idea that the relationship between human beings and the natural world is politically important is of relatively recent origin. Until the 1960s, nature was regarded by most political thinkers as nothing more than an 'economic resource', available for human beings to exploit, more or less efficiently. What has changed this view has been a growing realisation that in exploiting nature human beings have placed their own future and survival in jeopardy. Rachel Carson's *The Silent Spring* (1962) is often considered to have been the first book to have drawn attention to a developing 'ecological crisis'. The earth's human population has continued to expand. 5.3 billion people are alive today and it is estimated that this will grow to 8.5 billion by the year 2025. At the same time, human beings in all parts of the world, but particularly in the industrialised West, have demanded higher standards of living and greater affluence, which can only be achieved by utilising greater quantitites of the earth's resources. The result of this has been that the natural resources available on the planet to feed, sustain and satisfy its human population are running out and in some cases are close to exhaustion. In addition, the earth itself and all its species have increasingly been blighted by pollution and waste, the by-products of human economic activity.

As concern about environmental issues has grown, a distinctive set of political ideas and values has emerged which openly challenge established ideologies of Left, Right and Centre. As yet, this new ideology lacks a single, agreed title. Various names have been employed by different groups. 'Green' has been used since the 1950s to indicate sympathy for environmental issues or projects, and since

242

1980 has been adopted by the growing number of environmental parties, the first being the German Greens. However, as a result of the development of Green parties the term has been linked to the specific ideas and policies of such parties, rather than the principles of the larger environmental movement. 'Ecology' is commonly used to indicate the interrelatedness of natural life, a fundamental principle of environmental thought. Before 1985, the British Green Party was called the Ecology Party. The term 'ecology' was coined by Ernst Haeckel in 1858 and has been used since the early years of this century to refer to a branch of biology which studies the relationship amongst living organisms and their environment. Although all environmental thinkers respect the principles of ecology, the environmental movement has moved far beyond the ideas of scientific ecology, and scientists have, in turn, sometimes been critical of the quasi-religious character of modern environmental thought.

'Environmentalism' is a broad term which has been used since the 1950s to refer to a range of ideas and theories, characterised by the central belief that human life can only be understood in the context of the natural world. As such, environmentalism covers a broad range of theories, scientific, religious, economic and political, rather than a particular set of policies, such as those endorsed by the contemporary Green movement. The term 'environmentalism' has the disadvantage that it has sometimes been used to refer to a moderate or reformist approach to the environment which responds to environmental crises without fundamentally questioning conventional assumptions about the natural world. However, if environmentalism constitutes a distinctive and coherent political ideology, it must embody a radically new conception of the relationship between humankind and nature which challenges the ideas and values of existing political creeds rather than merely supplementing them.

Although modern environmental politics did not emerge until the 1960s, environmental ideas date back much earlier. Many have suggested that the principles of contemporary environmentalism owe much to ancient pagan religions, which stressed the concept of an Earth Mother, and also to Eastern religions such as Hinduism, Buddhism and Taoism. However, to a large extent, environmentalism was, and still remains, a reaction against the process of industrialisation. This was evident in the nineteenth century when the spread of urban and industrial life created a profound nostalgia for an idealised rural existence, conveyed by novelists such as Thomas Hardy and political thinkers like William Morris and Peter Kropotkin. This reaction was often strongest in those countries which had experienced the most rapid and dramatic process of industrialisation. For example, in little more than 30 years Germany became an industrial power capable by the late nineteenth century of challenging the economic might of Britain and the United States. This experience deeply scarred German political culture, creating powerful myths about the purity and dignity of peasant life and giving rise to a strong 'back to nature' movement amongst German youth. Such pastoralism was to be exploited in the twentieth century by nationalists and fascists.

The growth of environmentalism in the late twentieth century has been provoked by the relentless progress of industrialisation and urbanisation. Environmental concern has been more acute and radical because of the fear that economic growth threatens to endanger both the survival of the human race and the very planet it lives upon. Such anxieties were expressed by a growing body of academic literature, such as Ehrlich and Harriman's *How to be a Survivor* (1971) and Goldsmith *et al*'s *Blueprint for Survival* (1972). At the same time, a new generation of activist pressure groups developed, such as Greenpeace and Friends of the Earth, which highlighted environmental issues like the dangers of nuclear power, pollution and the dwindling levels of 'fossil fuels' left on earth. Together with established and much larger groups such as the World Wildlife Fund, this led to the emergence of a well-publicised and increasingly powerful environmental movement. Since 1980, environmental questions have been kept high on the political agenda by Green parties, which now exist in most industrialised countries.

Environmental politics has clearly drawn attention to issues like pollution, conservation, 'acid rain', the 'greenhouse effect' and 'global warming', but environmentalists refuse to accept that they constitute merely another single-issue lobby group. In the first place, the environmental movement has addressed a far broader range of issues. The Greens in Germany, for instance, have campaigned on the role of women, defence and disarmament, the welfare state and unemployment, and the need for a re-examination of Germany's Nazi past, as well as on narrower environmental issues. More significantly, environmentalists have developed a radically new set of concepts and values with which to understand and explain the world. Environmentalism has developed into a distinctive ideology which stands apart from traditional political creeds because it starts from an examination of what they have tended to ignore: the relationship between humankind and nature. As a result, it is difficult or impossible to slot environmentalism into the established Left–Right political divide or to understand it in terms of established doctrines and philosophies.

2 Back to nature

Environmentalists have criticised the most basic assumption upon which conventional political thought is based. Traditional doctrines and ideologies are anthropocentric, they commit the sad, even comic, mistake of believing that human beings are the centrepiece of existence. David Ehrenfeld has called this the 'arrogance of humanism'. For example, the categories in which conventional thought analyses the world are those of human beings and their groups, for instance, the 'individual', 'social class', 'nation' or 'humanity'. Moreover, its abiding values are ones which reflect human needs and interests, 'liberty', 'equality', 'justice', 'order', and so forth. Environmentalists argue that such an exclusive concern with human beings has distorted and damaged the relationship between the human species and its natural environment. Instead of preserving and respecting the earth and the diverse species that live upon it, human beings have sought to become, in the words of John Locke, 'the masters and possessors of nature'.

All major ideologies embody an anthropocentric bias; environmentalists point out that they merely promise different ways of exploiting nature for the convenience and benefit of humankind. The conventional Left–Right divide in politics, the conflict between collectivism and individualism, reflects different views about the ownership of wealth in society: common ownership versus private ownership, socialism versus capitalism. However, both positions are dedicated to the same goal: greater material affluence, achieved by an ever-more efficient exploitation of the natural world. Political debate is therefore reduced to a discussion of how the goal of economic growth can best be achieved, and about who should benefit from it. Such views have, environmentalists warn, tragically unbalanced the relationship between humankind and nature. Nature is portrayed as separate from human life, inhospitable to it, and even hostile. Nature has to be 'conquered', 'battled against' or 'risen above'. However, in the process, the natural world has not only been despoiled but the human species itself has been brought close to destruction.

Environmentalism represents a new style of politics. It starts not from a conception of 'humanity' or human needs, but from a vision of nature as a network of precious but fragile relationships between living species, including the human race, and the natural environment. Humankind no longer occupies centre stage, but is regarded as an inseparable part of nature. Human beings are therefore required to practise humility, moderation and gentleness, and to give up the misguided dream that science and technology can solve all their problems. In order to give expression to this vision, environmentalists have been forced to search for new concepts in the realm of science or rediscover ancient ones from the realms of religion and mythology.

a Ecology

The central principle of all forms of environmentalism is ecology. Ecology is the study of plants and animals in relationship to each other and their natural environment. Ecology literally means the study of organisms 'at home' or 'in their habitats', and developed as a distinct branch of biology in the early twentieth century, out of a growing recognition that plants and animals are sustained by self-regulating natural systems, ecosystems, composed of both living and non-living elements. A simple example of an ecosystem would be a field, forest, pond or even puddle. In a pond, for instance, the sediment lying at the bottom contains nutrients which support various kinds of plant life. These plants provide oxygen and food which sustain the fish and insects living in the pond. Finally, when plants and animals die, their bodies decompose, releasing nutrients back into the sediment in what is, in effect, a continuous process of recycling. All ecosystems tend towards a state of harmony or balance through a system of self-regulation. Food and other resources are recycled and the population size of animals, insects and plants adjusts naturally to the available food supply. However, such ecosystems are not 'closed' or entirely self-sustaining; each inter-reacts with other ecosystems. A lake may itself constitute an ecosystem, but it also needs to be fed with fresh water from tributaries and receive warmth and energy from the sun. The lake, in turn, provides water and food for species living along its shores, including human communities. The natural world is therefore made up of a complex web of ecosystems, the largest of which is the global ecosystem, commonly called the 'ecosphere' or 'biosphere'.

The development of scientific ecology has radically altered our understanding of the natural world and the place of human beings within it. Ecology conflicts quite dramatically with the notion of humankind as 'the master' of nature and, in contrast, suggests that each human community, indeed the entire human species, is sustained by a delicate network of interrelationships which had hitherto been ignored. Humankind currently faces the prospect of environmental disaster precisely because in its passionate but blinkered pursuit of material wealth it has, quite simply, upset the 'balance of nature' and endangered the very ecosystems which make human life possible. For example, since the beginning of the nineteenth century the world's population has increased five-fold, with currently 220,000 babies born each day, 150 every minute. The earth has become over-burdened with an exploding human population, which has given little thought to how its new members are going to be fed, clothed or housed. Finite and irreplaceable fuel resources, such as coal, oil and natural gas, are being used up with reckless abandon. Even if the consumption of oil remains at 1985 levels it is estimated that oil resources will last only between 50 and 88 years. The tropical rain forests, which help clean the air and regulate the earth's climate, will be completely eradicated within 50 years if current rates of deforestation continue. Moreover, factories and power stations pollute the rivers, lakes and forests which provide human beings with food, fuel, water and other vital resources. Finally, an atomic technology has been developed, which has the capacity to both wipe out the human species and destroy the planet it lives upon.

Ecology provides a radically different vision of nature and the place of human beings within it. Some environmentalists regard ecology as the key to human survival and wellbeing, which is seen to require a new understanding of, and respect for, natural processes. If we conserve and cherish the natural world, it will continue to sustain human life. In practice, this means controlling population growth, cutting back on the use of finite and irreplaceable resources, and reducing pollution. Others argue, however, that such attitudes are themselves anthropocentric: the natural world is only valued because it supports and sustains the human race, the lessons of ecology are harnessed to human ends. Radical elements within the environmental movement believe that the consistent application of ecological principles should overthrow any lingering belief that the human species is in some way superior to, or more important than, any other species or indeed nature itself. Such a position is called 'deep ecology' or 'ecologism'. It suggests the challenging idea that the purpose of human life is to help sustain nature, not the other way around. This leads to a belief in biocentric equality, the idea that all forms of life are equally entitled to existence and wellbeing. Deep ecologists suggest that human beings have been guilty of speciesism, a form of irrational prejudice not unlike racism or sexism, which asserts that the rights of one species should prevail over those of all others. Deep ecologists, for example, have given support to the growing animal rights movement, campaigning against the use of animals in scientific research, the killing of animals for their skin and fur, as well as in favour of vegetarianism.

Ecology requires, in effect, a new conception of human nature. Human beings are not the masters of their own destiny, and their resources and potential are not unlimited. They are, rather, inescapably part of nature. Humankind is merely one organism within a complex biosphere, but an organism that has become so powerful that it has come to threaten the biosphere itself. However, in order to educate humanity into living within its limits and respecting the wisdom of ecology, a new creed or philosophy must be developed which is capable of portraying nature as an interrelated whole.

b Holism

Traditional political ideologies have never looked seriously at the relationship between humankind and nature. They have typically assumed human beings to be the masters of the natural world, and therefore regarded nature as little more than an economic resource. In that sense, they have been part of the problem and not part of the solution. In *The Turning Point* (1982), Fritjof Capra traced the origin of such ideas to the early scientists and philosophers of the seventeenth century, such as Rene Descartes and Isaac Newton. The world had previously been understood to be organic; however, these seventeenth-century philosophers portrayed it as a machine, whose parts could be analysed and understood through the newly-dis-covered scientific method, which involved testing hypotheses against 'the facts' by careful and repeatable experiments. Science made possible remarkable advances in human knowledge and provided the basis for the development of modern industry and technology. So impressive have the fruits of science been that intellectual inquiry in the modern world is dominated by scientism, the belief that scientific method provides the only reliable means of establishing truth. However, Capra argued that orthodox science, what he referred to as the 'Cartesian–Newtonian paradigm', amounted to the philosophical basis of the contemporary environmental crisis. Science treats nature as a machine, and like any other machine it can be tinkered with, repaired, improved upon or even replaced. If human beings are to learn that they are part of the natural world rather than its master, Capra suggested that our fixation with the 'Newtonian world-machine' must be overthrown and replaced by a new paradigm.

In searching for this new paradigm, environmental thinkers have been attracted to a variety of ideas and theories, drawn from both modern science and ancient myths and religions. However, the unifying theme amongst these ideas is the notion of holism. The term 'holism' was coined in 1926 by Jan Smuts, the Boer General and Prime Minister of South Africa. He used it to describe the idea that the natural world could only be understood as a whole and not through its individual parts. Smuts believed that science committed the sin of reductionism, it reduced everything it studied to separate parts and tried to understand each part in itself. In contrast, holism is based upon the belief that 'the whole' is more important than its individual 'parts'; indeed it suggests that each part only has a meaning in relation to other parts and, ultimately, in relation to 'the whole'.

In medical science, for example, disease has traditionally been understood and treated as a defect of a particular organ or even of specific cells within the body, not as an imbalance within the life of the patient as a whole. Attention has therefore been paid to the treatment of physical symptoms while psychological, social or environmental factors have tended to be ignored. In the case of heart disease, conventional medicine has made remarkable advances, for instance, in correcting or replacing defective heart valves, transplant-ing human hearts, and even developing artificial hearts. However, it has often neglected psychological factors like stress, or social and environmental factors such as smoking, diet and pollution, which may have caused the condition in the first place. A holistic approach to health therefore tries to treat the 'whole person', understanding injuries or disease as only a physical symptom of what may be a complex range of factors, physical, psychological, social and environmental. Such holistic principles have deeply impressed environmental thinkers intent upon discovering new approaches to social, economic and political problems. Indeed, holism implies that the traditional division of human knowledge into separate compartments – science, philosophy, history, politics and so on – is redundant. Economics, for example, can no longer be regarded simply as the study of the production and consumption of goods. A holistic approach to economics requires that the environmental cost of production, its spiritual or moral value, and its political consequences, must also be taken into account.

Although many see science as a culprit in teaching humans how to plunder the riches of nature, others have suggested that modern science may perhaps offer a new paradigm for human thought. Capra, for example, argued that the Cartesian–Newtonian view of the world has now been abandoned by many scientists, particularly by physicists like himself. During the twentieth century, physics has moved a long way beyond the mechanistic and reductionist ideas of Newton, with the development of 'New Physics'. The break through was achieved at the beginning of the century by Albert Einstein, whose theory of relativity fundamentally challenged traditional concepts of time and space. Einstein's work was taken further by quantum theory, developed by physicists like Niels Bohr and Verner Heisenberg. New Physics emerged out of advances in sub-atomic research and has come to abandon the idea of absolute or objective knowledge. In its place Heisenberg proposed the 'uncertainty principle'. The physical world is understood not as a collection of individual molecules, atoms or even particles, but as a system or, more accurately, a network of systems. A systems view of the world concentrates not upon individual building blocks, but upon the principles of organisation within the system. It therefore stresses the relationships within the system and the integration of its various elements in the whole. Such a view had very radical implications. Objective knowledge, for example, is impossible because the very act of observing alters what is being observed. The scientist is not separate from his or her experiment but is intrinsically related to it;

subject and object are therefore one. Similarly, the concepts of cause and effect have had to be revised because changes have been seen to develop within a system, out of a network of factors, rather than as a consequence of a single, linear cause. Capra has suggested that such a systems view of life has already revolutionised physics, is in the process of changing other sciences, but can equally well be applied to the study of social, political or environmental questions. In short, New Physics could provide a paradigm capable of replacing the now redundant mechanistic and reductionist world-view.

An alternative and particularly fertile source of new concepts and theories has been religion. In *The Tao of Physics* (1975), Capra drew attention to important parallels between the ideas of modern physics and those of Eastern mysticism. He argued that religions such as Hinduism, Buddhism, Taoism and Zen have long preached the unity or oneness of all things, a discovery which Western science has only made in the twentieth century. In Buddhism, for instance, the experience of awakening or enlightenment involves transcending the ego or 'self' and recognising that each person is linked to all other living things. Many in the Green movement have been attracted by Eastern mysticism, seeing in it both a philosophy that gives expression to ecological wisdom and a way of life that encourages compassion for fellow human beings, other species and the natural world. Other writers believe that ecological principles are embodied in monotheistic religions, like Christianity, Judaism and Islam, which regard both humankind and nature as products of divine creation. Jonathan Porritt, former Director of Friends of the Earth, has, for instance, described the earth as 'the most powerful embodiment of God's work that we have', suggesting that it is a religious duty to cherish and preserve the planet. He has suggested that human beings will only act in harmony with nature if they come to see themselves as 'God's stewards on Earth'.

However, perhaps the most influential concept for modern Greens has been developed by looking back to pre-Christian spiritual ideas. Primitive religions often drew no distinction between human life and other forms of life, and indeed little distinction between living and non-living objects. All things were alive, stones, rivers, mountains and even the earth itself, often conceived of as 'Mother Earth'. The idea of an Earth Mother has been particularly important for environmentalists trying to articulate a new relationship between human beings and the natural world. In *The Gaia Hypothesis* (1979), James

Lovelock developed the idea that the planet itself was alive and gave it the name 'Gaia', after the Greek Goddess of the Earth. Lovelock defined Gaia as 'Earth's biosphere, atmosphere, oceans and soil' and argued that Gaia constitutes a living organism which acted to maintain its own existence. Lovelock claimed this on the basis that the earth exhibited precisely the kind of self-regulating behaviour which is characteristic of other forms of life. Gaia has achieved homeostasis, a state of dynamic balance, despite dramatic changes which have taken place in the solar system. The most dramatic evidence for this is the fact that although the sun has warmed up by more than 25 per cent since life began, the temperature on earth and the composition of its atmosphere have remained virtually unchanged. Any quite small change in the proportion of oxygen in the atmosphere, or in the earth's average temperature, would endanger all forms of life on the planet. In his essay 'Man and Gaia', Lovelock warned that, 'To destroy such a large chunk of the living ecosystem when we do not properly understand how it all works is like pulling apart the control system of a modern aircraft while in mid-flight' (p.63).

The idea of Gaia has developed into an 'ecological ideology' which conveys the powerful message that human beings must respect the health of the planet and act to conserve her beauty and resources. For some this has taken the form of eco-feminism, which contrasts the traditionally 'masculine' desire to exploit nature with the 'feminine' values preached by ancient religions and modern environmentalism. It also contains a revolutionary vision of the relationship between the animate and inanimate world. Lovelock suggests that the earth itself is alive and sees the living and the non-living world as one. He points out, for example, that much of the soil or rock on earth is made up of reprocessed plants, insects and other forms of life, and, in turn, provides support for plants and species living today. However, the Gaia philosophy does not always correspond with the concerns of the environmental movement. Environmentalists have usually wished to change policies and attitudes in order to ensure the continued survival of the human species. Gaia, however, is non-human, and the Gaia theory suggests that the health of the planet matters more than that of any individual species presently living upon it. Lovelock has suggested that those species which have prospered have been ones that have helped Gaia regulate its own existence, while any species posing a threat to the delicate balance of Gaia, as humans currently do, is likely to be extinguished.

c Technology versus nature

The application of ecological or holistic principles to human life and conduct would require a radical, even revolutionary, change. The modern world has witnessed the triumph of technology over nature, as human beings, armed with ever-more impressive scientific knowledge, confidently believed they had the capacity to solve all problems. All parts of the world, even the countryside itself, bear a human imprint. Human beings have tamed, civilised and even replaced nature. Life is increasingly lived in a synthetic environment, one fashioned by technology and human ingenuity. For example, food production once forced the majority of people to live and work close to the land, developing an appreciation of and respect for natural processes. Agriculture now employs very few people in the industrialised West, and has become increasingly mechanised and technological. Food itself has become progressively more artificial, crop sizes have been increased by the use of insecticides and chemical fertilisers, food is processed, canned, freeze-dried and preserved well beyond its 'natural' life, the flavours and colours of many dishes have been 'enhanced' by a battery of additives, and in some cases food is created in the laboratory by a process of genetic engineering.

Environmentalists argue that science and technology have been, at best, a mixed blessing for the human race. There is no doubt that science has unlocked many of the 'secrets of nature', but its promise to make humankind the master of its own destiny has proved to be illusory. Orthodox science has sought greater and greater knowledge of the 'world-machine' by examining its component parts. At each point, science has generated impressive 'know how': how to extract energy from steam, how to produce electricity from coal, how to unleash the power of the atom itself and build nuclear power stations or nuclear weapons. However, human development has been sadly unbalanced: human beings are blessed with massive 'know how' and material wealth, but possess precious little 'know why'. Humankind has acquired the ability to fulfil its material ambitions, but not the wisdom to question if these ambitions are sensible, or even sane. As

E.F. Schumacher warned, 'Man is now too clever to survive without wisdom'.

Environmentalists are agreed that when 'progress' or 'development' is understood in material terms alone, it becomes self-defeating. The human obsession with material prosperity has allowed little or no attention to be given to the ecological principles which sustain all forms of life. Moreover, industrial life has led to alienation and isolation as human beings struggle to live in a man-made environment of concrete and bricks, without the support of caring communities or a sense of rootedness in nature. In underlining our dependence upon natural processes, environmentalism seeks to re-establish a balance between humankind and nature, and, in the process, create more rounded and fulfilled human beings. However, this goal requires a new attitude to science and technology.

For some in the environmental movement this means a fundamental and comprehensive rejection of industry and modern technology, literally going 'back to nature'. Such views are based upon the belief that technology is in itself tainted by the desire to master nature; the only alternative is to return to a pastoral world of organic farming and accept a dramatic decline in material living standards. During the Third Reich, such an agrarian philosophy was preached by Walter Darré, under the slogan 'Blood and Soil'. Darré hoped to inspire Germans to abandon corrupt city life and return to the soil, adopting a simple but more dignified peasant existence. Similar ideas have also been favoured by those in the modern Green movement whose vision of the 'post-industrial age' is one of small rural communities, relying upon craft skills rather than industrial technology.

The majority of environmentalists, however, draw back from such a radical option. They accept that unrestrained industrialisation is misguided, but seek instead a balance between technology and nature. This view accepts that technology is not desirable for its own sake, but only if it fulfils human and ecological purposes. Schumacher, for example, called for 'technology with a human face'. Technology should not therefore exhaust finite fuel resources, pollute the air, soil or water, or force people to live and work in inhuman conditions. However, technology can also improve productivity, replace dangerous or menial work, and provide a focus for social life. In *Small is Beautiful* (1973), Schumacher advocated a system of small-scale, or 'human scale' production to replace what he believed to be the dehumanising world of large cities and mass production. The Gandhian movement in India, for example, has promoted the use of spinning wheels in Indian villages, rather than the spread of modern factories, in the belief that small-scale technology can bring employment, prosperity and independence to the masses, without damaging the natural environment.

3 Politics and the environment

Although environmentalists have striven to develop new ways of understanding the world, their ideas have also, at times, overlapped with those of more conventional political creeds. Like nationalism and feminism, environmentalism can be regarded as a cross-cutting ideology. At different times, liberals, socialists, anarchists, conservatives and even fascists have claimed a special sympathy with the environment, and environmental ideas have been enlisted in support of fundamentally different political goals.

a Reformist environmentalism

The defining feature of reformist environmentalism is the belief that a concern for the environment can be added to the responsibilities of government without the need for any radical change of policies or political philosophy. For example, conventional political parties of Left, Right and Centre have increasingly formulated policies on the environment to stand alongside their established concerns: economic policy, foreign affairs, defence, law and order, and so on. Responding to electoral pressure, parties have accepted that the environment is a political issue and one which has been 'pushed up' the political agenda. For their part, pressure groups like Greenpeace and Friends of the Earth have sought to heighten public awareness of environmental issues, in the hope of forcing governments to tackle problems like nuclear waste, acid rain and the greenhouse effect.

The reformist approach to the environment is based upon a faith in rational self-interest. Although human beings may have been blind to environmental problems for too long, once they become aware of the seriousness of the issue action will be taken. In other words, the same resources of rational analysis and scientific understanding which made possible the development of modern technology, and, for example, placed a man on the moon, can be enlisted to solve the environmental crisis. Such ideas fall clearly within the modern liberal political tradition. Modern liberals wish to create conditions in which human beings can grow and achieve fulfilment, and they acknowledge this to be the responsibility of government. The environmental crisis therefore cries out for government regulation and reform. For example, the Environmental Protection Agency (EPA) was set up in the United States in 1970 and invested with wide-ranging powers to contain pollution in America. Reformists have usually seen bodies like the EPA, or the creation of other, perhaps more powerful, agencies, as the best means of tackling environmental problems.

However, environmental reformism is essentially anthropocentric, it argues that environmental policies are necessary in order to satisfy the long-term needs and interests of human beings. It is therefore typically concerned with issues that affect humans most directly, notably pollution, which damages the quality of the air we breathe, the water we drink and the food we eat, and the depletion of energy sources like coal and oil, upon which human prosperity depends. Far less attention has been paid to issues like animal rights and vegetarianism. Reformist priorities are particularly apparent in relation to the question of economic growth. Reformists are 'light Greens', they argue that environmental policies do not mean 'zero growth', a return to the Dark Ages, or turning our backs upon affluence and technology altogether. Rather, they advocate 'sustainable growth', getting richer but at a slower pace. The desire for material prosperity can be balanced against its environmental costs. One way in which this could be achieved would be through changes in the tax system either to penalise and discourage pollution or to reduce the use of finite resources.

'Dark Greens' argue that such views are simply not radical enough. Reformists, they suggest, pay lip service to environmental fears, while carrying on as if nothing was wrong. The origin of the ecological crisis lies in materialism, consumerism and a fixation with economic growth, which reformists are incapable of addressing. Individuals and governments will not be able to adjust their behaviour to the principles of ecology until they cease to place the interests of the human race before respect for nature. Moreover, reformists fail to appreciate that science and technology are incapable of solving all human problems, and may indeed be one of the root causes of environmental catastrophe.

Human self-interest is also an uncertain friend of environmentalism. In the first place, reformists assume that people will be prepared to act in the long-term interests of humankind, as they are in their own short-term or immediate interests. This is particularly important because tackling environmental problems is very likely to call for short-term material sacrifices. Can we, for example, be confident that the present generation will be willing to forgo material prosperity during its lifetime in order to ensure that coal and oil will be available for future generations? Secondly, even if private individuals believe that environmental policies are in their interests, will businesses and major corporations listen? Consumer pressure is certainly capable of encouraging businesses to provide a growing range of 'planet friendly' products, such as lead-free petrol and CFC-free aerosols. However, 'Green consumerism' has only limited value. The vigour of a capitalist economy is based upon the profit motive, which generates a powerful incentive to increase production and encourage consumption, which in turn fuel the environmental crisis. When the problem is that there are too many people consuming too many goods, the only solution is to consume less, not consume a different range of products.

b Eco-socialism

There is a distinct socialist strand within the Green movement which is particularly pronounced amongst the German Greens, many of whose leaders had previously been members of far-Left groups. Eco-socialism, as it is often called, is based upon Marxist analysis, and has usually sought to distance itself from the quasi-religious ideas influential elsewhere in the environmental movement. Rudolph Bahro, for example, a leading German eco-socialist, argues that capitalism is the root cause of environmental problems. The natural world has been despoiled by industrialisation, but this is merely a consequence of capitalism's search for profit. Capitalism is thus characterised not only by class conflict but also by the progressive destruction of the natural environment. Both human labour and the natural world are exploited because they are treated simply as economic resources. Any attempt to improve the environment must therefore involve a radical process of social change, some would say a social revolution.

The essential idea of eco-socialism is that capitalism is the enemy of the environment, while socialism is its friend. However, as with socialist feminism, such a formula embodies tension between two elements, this time between 'Red' and 'Green' priorities. If environmental catastrophe is nothing more than a by-product of capitalism, environmental problems are best tackled by abolishing capitalism, or at least taming it. Environmentalists should not therefore form separate Green parties, nor set up narrow environmental organisations, but work within the socialist movement and address the real issue: the economic system. On the other hand, socialism has also been seen as merely another 'pro-production' political creed, wishing to exploit the wealth of the planet, in its case for the good of humanity rather than a small class of capitalists. Socialist parties have been slow to adopt environmental policies because they, like other 'Grey parties', continue to base their electoral appeal upon the promise of economic growth. As a result, environmentalists have been reluctant to subordinate the Green to the Red. The Greens in Germany, for example, proclaim that they are 'neither left nor right, we are in front'. Even eco-socialists like Bahro now argue that the ecological crisis is so pressing that it must take precedence over the class struggle.

Socialists argue that socialism is naturally ecological. If wealth is owned in common by all it will be used in the interests of all, which means in the long-term interests of humanity. However, it is unlikely that ecological problems can be solved simply by a change in the ownership of wealth. This is abundantly demonstrated by the experience of state socialism in the Soviet Union and Eastern Europe, which has produced some of the world's most intractable environmental problems. Economic priorities in the communist East, like those in the capitalist West, have been based upon the pursuit of growth. However, until the arrival of *glasnost*, or 'openness', the Soviet government was largely insulated from expressions of popular concern about the environment. The system of central planning also allowed public policy to be made in Moscow, many miles from the scene of any ecological disaster. In the 1960s, the two principal rivers which fed the Aral Sea in Soviet Central Asia were re-routed in order to irrigate cotton and rice fields. The Aral Sea was once the fourth biggest lake in the world, but has now shrunk by a third in just

25 years and its shores have receded in some places by 80 kilometres, leaving a salty, polluted desert. Local industries and agriculture have been devastated, and both human communities and the wildlife of the area have been steadily poisoned by the heavy salt deposits in their food and water. The best publicised environmental disaster in Eastern Europe has been the Chernobyl nuclear explosion in the Ukraine in 1986. Most nuclear plants in the Soviet Union are, like Chernobyl, sited in non-Russian republics, many miles from Moscow. Nevertheless, the disaster forced the Soviet Union into greater openness about this and its other environmental problems. In an era of glasnost, environmental protest groups have sprung up throughout the Soviet Union. However, it is noticeable that, unlike the Green movement in the West, these groups rarely espouse eco-socialism, but are more usually linked to conservative and even reactionary political philosophies.

c Anarcho-environmentalism

Perhaps the ideology which has the best claim to being environmentally sensitive is anarchism. Some months before the publication of Rachel Carson's influential *The Silent Spring* in 1962, the American anarchist, Murray Bookchin, brought out *Our Synthetic Environment* and Bookchin has rightly been regarded as one of the 'founding fathers' of modern environmentalism. Many in the Green movement acknowledge a debt to nineteenth century anarcho-communists, particularly Peter Kropotkin. Bookchin has suggested that there is a clear correspondence between the ideas of anarchism and the principles of ecology. Anarchists believe in a stateless society, in which harmony develops out of mutual respect and social solidarity amongst human beings. The richness of such a society is founded upon its variety and diversity. Ecologists also believe that a balance or harmony spontaneously develops within nature, in the form of ecosystems, and that these, like anarchist communities, require no external authority or control. The anarchist rejection of government within human society parallels the ecologists' warnings about human 'rule' within the natural world. Bookchin has therefore likened an anarchist community to an ecosystem, and suggested that both are distinguished by respect for the principles of 'diversity, balance and harmony'.

Anarchists have also advocated the construction of decentralised societies, organised as a collection of communes or villages. Life in such communities is lived 'close to nature', each community attempting to achieve a high measure of self-sufficiency. Such communities would be economically diverse, they would produce food and a wide range of goods and services, and therefore contain agriculture, craftwork and small-scale industry. Self-sufficiency will make each community visibly dependent upon its natural environment, spontaneously generating an understanding of organic relationships and ecology. In Bookchin's view, decentralisation will lead to 'a more intelligent and more loving use of the environment'. A society regulated by spontaneous sympathy amongst human beings is therefore likely to encourage an ecological balance between human beings and the natural world.

Without doubt, the conception which many environmentalists have of a post-industrial society has been influenced by the writings of Kropotkin and William Morris. The Green movement has adopted ideas of decentralisation and grass roots democracy from anarchist thinkers. However, even when anarchism is embraced as providing a vision of an ecologically sound future, it is seldom accepted as a means of getting there. Anarchists believe that progress is only possible when the government and all forms of political authority are overthrown. In contrast, most environmentalists see government as an agency through which collective action can be organised and therefore as the most likely means through which the environmental crisis can be addressed, at least in the short term. They fear that dismantling or even weakening government may simply give free rein to those forces which have generated industrialisation and blighted the natural environment in the first place.

d Reactionary environmentalism

A concern with the environment has not always been associated with radical or progressive political creeds. In fact, during the nineteenth and early twentieth centuries environmentalism was generally considered to be a conservative, even reactionary, cause. Such tendencies have also been evident in contemporary debate, as witnessed by Margaret Thatcher's famous 'Green speech' in 1988 in which she described the Conservatives in Britain as 'the guardians and trustees of the earth'. In the Soviet Union, groups like Pamyat, or 'memory', express concern about conservation, but also support Russian nationalism and anti-semitism.

Eco-conservatism reflects a romantic and nostalgic attachment to a rural way of life threatened by the growth of towns and cities. It is clearly a reaction against industrialisation and the idea of 'progress'. It does not envisage the construction of a post-industrial society, founded upon the principles of co-operation and ecology, but a return to, or preservation of, a more familiar pre-industrial one. Such environmentalism typically focuses upon the issue of conservation and attempts to preserve what is called the 'natural heritage', woodlands, forests and so forth, as well as the architectural and social heritage. The preservation of nature is therefore linked to the maintenance of traditional values and institutions. Environmentalism stands for a return to the feudal past, with the land in the hands of a small minority and political control imposed from above. For example, Edward Goldsmith, the father of British environmentalism, has argued that an ecological society would involve the resurrection of traditional order within the family and the community – in effect, the establishment of strong authoritarian government.

The reactionary character of some environmentalist thought was dramatically represented by the career of Walter Darré, Minister of Agriculture and Peasant Leader in Nazi Germany, 1933–42. The experience of rapid industrialisation in Germany had created a strong 'back to the land' movement, especially attractive to students and young people. The German Youth Movement developed out of the 'Wandervoegel', bands of German students who took to the forests and mountains to escape from the alienation of urban life. Darré's own ideas were a mixture of Nordic racialism and an idealisation of peasant or rural life, fused into a 'Blood and Soil' ideology, which overlapped at several points with National Socialism. As Peasant Leader, Darré was responsible for introducing the hereditary farm law, which gave owners of small and medium-size farms complete security of tenure, and also for setting up the National Food Estate to market agricultural produce, which tried to keep food prices high and maintain rural prosperity.

Despite his links with the Nazis, Darré's ideas have much in common with the modern Green movement. In the first place, he was convinced that only a life lived close to nature and on the land could be truly fulfilling, and therefore wished to re-create a peasant Germany. Such ideas have been echoed by modern ecologists such as Edward Goldsmith. Moreover, Darré became a powerful advocate of organic farming, which uses only natural fertilisers like animal manure. Darré believed in an organic cycle involving animal-soil-food-humans, which he discovered in the works of Rudolph Steiner and the Anthroposophy movement. Organic farming reflects ecological principles and has become a major plank in the ideas of Green agriculture. During the Third Reich, Darré's peasant ideology helped the Nazis to secure committed support in the German countryside. However, though a scientific racialist, Darré himself was never a Nazi and publicly distanced himself from the *Führerprinzip*, or leader principle, and also from ideas of expansion and empire. In reality, the Nazi regime did little to fulfil Darré's dreams of a sturdy, peasant Germany. Despite Hitler's attachment to the ideas of 'Blood and Soil', his obsession with military expansion intensified the process of industrialisation in Germany and brought poverty to the countryside.

4 Green politics

The emergence of Green politics in the 1960s was part of a broader movement of ideas, commonly referred to as the New Left. Young people in the West, disenchanted by the 'old Left' alternatives of Western social democracy and Soviet-style state socialism, were increasingly attracted by a range of new issues, which included anti-Vietnam war protest, feminism, the Third World and also the environment. The environmental movement born in the late 1960s and early 1970s was composed of radical and activist groups which sought to educate public opinion by highly-publicised campaigns of non-violent direct action. The Green movement acquired greater coherence in the 1980s with the formation of Green political parties. The first of these to achieve national significance, and in many ways the model for later environmental parties, was the Greens in Germany, founded in 1979. The Greens made their electoral breakthrough in 1983 by winning 27 seats in the Bundestag. In 1987, they polled 8.3 per cent of the vote in West Germany and gained 42 seats. Green parties have subsequently gained representation in the parliaments of ten countries, from Iceland to Portugal. In the 1989 European Parliament elections, Green parties won 39 seats. Les Vertes in France polled 11 per cent, and the British Green Party gained the highest vote so far achieved by any environmental party, 15 per cent, but gained no representation in Strasbourg because of the nature of the British electoral system.

The modern Green movement is a broad church and draws upon a wide range of philosophies and creeds, scientific and religious as well as political. In most countries, Green parties or environmental pressure groups are coalitions of 'light Greens' and 'dark Greens', reformists and revolutionaries, conservatives and progressives. Nevertheless, their overriding concern with the environment has produced not only a distinctive environmental philosophy, but also a new style of politics, 'Green politics'. Green politics presents the electorate with a set of policies and priorities which clearly distinguish it from the so-called 'Grey politics' practised by other parties.

a Spaceship Earth

Greens argue that the ingrained assumption amongst conventional political parties is that human life has unlimited possibilities for growth and development. People in many parts of the world enjoy a standard of living which would have been unimaginable 50 years ago. Science and technology are constantly solving old problems, like poverty and disease, and opening up new possibilities through televisions and videos, computers and robots, air travel and even space travel. Conventional parties have whole-heartedly endorsed the prosperity and material comfort which progress has brought, only disagreeing about who can best be entrusted to maintain growth, and how its rewards should be distributed. Green politics paints a very different picture, and one, at first sight, far less electorally appealing. Greens believe that the promise of unlimited prosperity and material affluence, 'growth mania' as Herman Daly called it, is not only misguided but is a fundamental cause of environmental disaster. Many of the orthodox assumptions of politics and economics have to be rethought, starting with our view of the earth and the resources it contains.

The environmental movement has been drawn to the metaphor 'Spaceship Earth' because this expresses the idea of limited and exhaustible wealth. The idea that earth should be thought of as a 'spaceship' was first suggested by Kenneth Boulding in 1966. Some 'deep ecologists' have criticised the notion, arguing that it embodies the anthropocentric assumption that the planet exists to serve the needs of humankind: earth is a vessel, our vessel. Nevertheless, the concept of Spaceship Earth serves to redress the conventional belief in unlimited resources and unbounded possibilities. Boulding argued that human beings traditionally thought that they lived in a 'cowboy economy', an economy with unlimited opportunities, like the American West during the frontier period. Boulding suggested that this encouraged, as it had done in the American West, 'reckless, exploitative, and violent behaviour'. However, a spaceship is a capsule, a 'closed system' with finite resources. In the future 'spaceman economy', human beings will have to live within limits and pay closer attention to the spaceship which is propelling us through space.

Living in a spaceship requires an understanding of the ecological processes which sustain life. Most importantly, human beings must recognise that the earth is a closed system. Open systems receive energy or inputs from outside – for example, all ecosystems on earth, ponds, forests, lakes and seas, are sustained by the sun. Such open systems are self-regulating, tending to establish a natural balance or a steady state. However, closed systems, as earth itself becomes when thought of as a spaceship, exhibit evidence of entropy. Entropy is the measure of the degree of disorder or disintegration within a system. All closed systems tend to decay or disintegrate because they are not sustained by external inputs. They rely on their own resources and these become exhausted and cannot be renewed. Ultimately, however wisely and carefully human beings behave, the earth, the sun, and indeed all planets and stars, will be exhausted and die. For example, energy cannot be re-cycled indefinitely, each time it is transformed some energy is lost, until, finally, none remains. When the Entropy Law is applied to social and economic issues it produces very radical conclusions.

The Green movement has drawn particular attention to what it sees as a 'population time-bomb'. Such concerns are not new: as early as 1798 Thomas Malthus had warned that population growth would inevitably lead to mass starvation because food production was limited. However, Malthus failed to appreciate how scientific methods of farming would succeed in feeding an ever-growing population. Nevertheless, contemporary Greens believe that Malthus's ecological ideas were not false, but simply ahead of their time. Population growth is a problem in itself, but also one that makes every other environmental problem more serious. The proportion of the spaceship which each person occupies is getting smaller: in other words, human beings increasingly live in overcrowded cities, and less and less unspoilt countryside is available for recreation and leisure. More seriously, population growth accelerates the effects of entropy. With one million people being added to the world's population every five days, human beings are simply outstripping the land and other resources available on earth and increasing their output of poisonous waste. Writers like Paul and Ann Ehrlich have warned that this situation has two possible outcomes. First, policies could be introduced to slow down and even reverse population growth. These measures could include the spread of birth control and improved education, but also changes in taxes, pensions, government benefits and foreign aid to reward small families and penalise large ones. Such policies are difficult to implement because the population explosion affects areas suffering from the greatest social deprivation. Ninety per cent of growth predicted by the end of the twenty-first century will be in the Third World, particularly Africa. The stark alternative to such measures is, the Ehrlichs warn, that nature herself will solve the problem by finally making Malthus' predictions a reality.

No issue reflects the law of entropy more clearly than the 'energy crisis'. Industrialisation and mass affluence have been made possible by the exploitation of coal, gas and oil reserves which have provided fuel for power stations, factories, motor cars, aeroplanes and so on. These fuels are fossil fuels, formed by the decomposition of tiny organisms which died in prehistoric times. However, these fuels are non renewable, once used up they cannot be replaced. In *Small is Beautiful* (1973), Schumacher argued that human beings had made the mistake of regarding energy as an 'income', which was being constantly topped-up each week or each month, rather than as 'natural capital', which they are forced to live off. This mistake has allowed energy demands to soar, especially in the industrialised West, at a time when finite fuel resources are close to depletion, very unlikely to last to the end of the next century. As the spaceship draws to the close of the 'fossil fuel age' it approaches disintegration because there are, as yet, no alternative sources of energy which could compensate for the loss of coal, oil and gas. Conserving what remains of our fossil fuel stocks, however, means driving fewer cars, using less electricity and, in short, accepting a more meagre standard of living.

Human beings have not simply depleted natural resources through over-population and over-consumption, they have also polluted and poisoned the spaceship with an ever-increasing quantity of waste. Fossil fuels, for example, are 'dirty' forms of energy which, when burnt, release dangerous sulphuric and nitric acids into the atmosphere causing 'acid rain', and also carbon dioxide, which has been associated with 'global warming'. Acid rain has threatened both the natural and artificial environment. For instance, it has damaged over two-thirds of Britain's forests and left 80 per cent of the lakes in Southern Norway dead or dying. Buildings in all parts of the world have suffered corrosion, and acid rain is now officially recognised in Japan as a danger to human health. The issue of global warming has stimulated fierce academic controversy. Some scientists have linked the 0.5C rise in world temperature during the twentieth century to the increased emission of 'greenhouse gases' since the industrial revolution. Gases like carbon dioxide warm the atmosphere by trapping heat radiated back from the earth's surface, causing sea levels to rise and threatening low-lying areas, but also producing changes in climate and agricultural patterns throughout the world. The production of synthetic chemicals has also devastated both human and non-human life. The chemical accident in 1976 at Seveso in Italy released a cloud of dioxins which produced an increase of more than 40 per cent in birth defects in the local area. The escape of poisonous gases from a factory owned by the US company Union Carbide in Bhopal, central India in 1984 left an official death toll of 2352; however, some have estimated that the actual figure could have been as high as 10000.

b Sustainability

Green politics is not only about warnings and threats, but it is also about solutions. Entropy may be an inevitable process; however, its effects can be slowed down or delayed considerably if governments and also private citizens respect ecological principles. Environmentalists argue that the human species will only survive and prosper if it recognises that it is only one element within a complex biosphere, and that it is the health of the biosphere which sustains human life. Policies and actions must therefore be judged by the principle of sustainability, the capacity of a system, in this case the biosphere itself, to maintain its health and continue in existence. Sustainability sets clear limits upon human ambitions and material dreams because it requires that production does as little damage as possible to the fragile global ecosystem.

For example, the current use of fossil fuels is clearly not sustainable – coal, oil and natural gas will simply run out. Consequently, a sustainable energy policy must be based upon a dramatic reduction in the use of fossil fuels and a search for alternative sources of energy. In the 1960s there was considerable optimism that nuclear power could provide such an alternative, leading to a transition from a 'fossil fuel age' to a 'nuclear age'. However, confidence in nuclear power has been shattered by accidents such as those at Windscale in Britain in 1957, Three Mile Island in USA in 1979 and Chernobyl in the USSR in 1986, and by the problem of disposing of nuclear waste which may remain dangerous for hundreds of thousands of years. A more attractive alternative for the Green movement is renewable energy sources, such as solar energy, wind power and wave power. These are by their very nature sustainable and can be treated as 'income' rather than 'natural capital'. Greens have therefore suggested that the 'fossil fuel age' must give way to a coming 'solar age', and encouraged governments to step up the research and development of renewable energy sources. Similarly, a new attitude must be developed to human waste. Sustainability demands that resources should be recycled and re-used, rather than simply thrown away. It has been calculated that as much as 80 per cent of household waste and up to 90 per cent of industrial waste could be recycled, and yet Japan, the best performer in this respect, only recycles 10 per cent of its household waste.

The idea of 'sustainable growth' has created a radically new approach to economic policy. Greens acknowledge that however successful human beings are in developing 'renewables', economic growth must either slow down considerably or stop altogether. Greens therefore believe that the electorate has to be educated out of materialism and consumerism and into a new philosophy based upon personal fulfilment and a balance with nature. Such ideas were put forward by Erich Fromm in *To Have or To Be* (1976). Fromm suggested that 'having' is an attitude of mind, which seeks fulfilment in acquisition and control, and is clearly reflected in consumerism.

In contrast, 'being' derives satisfaction from experience and sharing, and leads to personal growth and spiritual awareness.

There are clear parallels between the environmental movement and the development of 'New Age' ideas and belief which have attempted to develop a culture appropriate to the coming 'post-materialistic age'. Schumacher suggested similar views in what he called 'Buddhist economics'. For Schumacher, Buddhist economics is based upon the principle of 'Right Livelihood' and stands in stark contrast to conventional economic ideas which assume that individuals are nothing more than 'utility maximisers'. Buddhists believe that production has at least three functions. First, it generates goods and services which make life comfortable; secondly, it facilitates personal growth by developing skills and talents; and, thirdly, it helps to overcome egocentredness by forging social bonds and encouraging people to work together. Such a view moves economics a long way from its present obsession with wealth creation, an obsession which has paid little regard to either nature or the spiritual quality of human life. The principal goal of Buddhism, spiritual liberation, is not, however, irreconcilable with material prosperity. 'It is not wealth that stands in the way of liberation', Schumacher pointed out, 'but the attachment to wealth; not the enjoyment of pleasurable things but the craving for them' (p.47). The environmental movement therefore hopes that in future economics can be used to serve humanity, rather than enslave it.

10

Democracy

1 Introduction

Strictly speaking, democracy cannot be considered as an ideology in the same sense as, for example, liberalism, socialism or fascism. It is not a set of political ideas about the means and ends of organised social action, but rather a description of a particular system of government and of the distribution of power within it. All terms ending in 'cracy', such as autocracy, bureaucracy, plutocracy and democracy, are derived from the Ancient Greek word *kratos*, meaning 'power' or 'rule'. As such, democracy, and indeed any other theory of political rule, cuts across ideological boundaries. Democracy nevertheless deserves to be dealt with in a separate chapter because it has for so long been the focus of fierce political debate. All ideologies have a particular attitude towards democracy and many of them have a distinctive conception of how democratic rule can be achieved. Questions like 'is democracy desirable?', 'what form should democratic government take?' and, in many ways the heart of the controversy, 'what does the term democracy mean?' expose deep ideological divisions.

The term 'democracy' originated in Ancient Greece to signify rule by the *demos*, usually taken to mean 'the people'. However, in its original Greek usage *demos* was not taken to mean all the people but 'the many' or 'the poor'. 'Democracy' was therefore used in a pejorative or negative sense, to imply rule by the poor at the expense of the rich, or rule by the ignorant and uneducated at the expense of the wise. Plato's *Republic*, for example, suggested that the likely outcome of democratic government would be tyranny. The classical meaning of democracy is nevertheless largely based upon what is known of the political structure of the Greek city-states or *polis*, of

269

which Athens was the most sophisticated and successful. Athenian democracy was founded upon very different principles from modern democratic government; in particular, it was based upon the direct personal participation of each citizen in the activities of government. This was achieved in two ways. First, there were regular meetings or assemblies, which all citizens were entitled to attend and at which major decisions were taken by popular vote. In this sense, citizens actually governed themselves, rather than being governed by an external or higher body. Secondly, those government or legal offices which required a permanent incumbent were filled not by a system of appointment or election, but by lot or rota. All citizens were thus eligible and qualified to hold government office, not merely a select group of professional 'politicians'. Such a classical form of direct democracy is very rare in the modern world. However, it has survived in the form of the referendum, widely used in countries like Switzerland, and in the random selection of juries by lot which still takes place in many parts of the world. A tradition of direct popular participation has been particularly strong at a local level in the United States. In New England, town government is often based upon popular meetings, and in states like California 'propositions', referendums on specific issues, have been influential in reducing local taxes.

Democratic ideas did not vanish from political life with the fall of the Greek city-states, but were certainly pushed to the margins in a world increasingly dominated by autocratic rulers. Political upheavals, like the English Civil War of the seventeenth century, threw up new democratic hopes and ideals. For example, the Levellers, a radical faction of Cromwellian soldiers and artisans, argued that individual citizens should exercise control over their leaders, which, they believed, could be achieved by giving them the right to vote. However, this 'levelling' of political power was not intended to be universal: no women, apprentices, house-servants, or, in the view of some Levellers, even wage-earners, should be entitled to vote. 'Social contract' theorists like John Locke argued that government should be based upon the consent of the governed and that its purpose was to protect the 'natural rights' of its citizens, defined by Locke as 'life, liberty and property'. For Locke, as with the Levellers, this implied the right to vote. He also believed, however, that the franchise, the right to vote, should be restricted to male property owners, those who possessed interests which could be infringed by government.

The modern conception of democracy dates back to the emergence of 'popular politics' in the political revolutions of the late eighteenth century, notably the American Revolution (1776) and the French Revolution (1789). The American Revolution was based firmly upon social contract principles, articulated by thinkers such as Thomas Jefferson. The United States Constitution, written in 1787, established the most democratic system of government then in existence, albeit one which restricted the franchise to propertied males. The French Revolution unleashed still more radical ideas, proclaiming that government should be based upon 'popular sovereignty', understood to mean some sort of collective or national interest, an idea derived from Rousseau's 'general will'. During the nineteenth century, democracy achieved increasing prominence. More and more groups, middle- and working-class men, women, ethnic minorities and so on, campaigned for a share in political power. Invariably, this took the form of a call for the right to vote, the demand that politicians be made accountable to a broader range of people through the ballot box. In some countries, these goals were achieved by popular revolution, as in France where universal manhood suffrage was granted as early as 1848. In other countries, the franchise was extended through a process of gradual reform. In Britain, for instance, the right to vote was progressively extended by a series of Acts of Parliament, starting with the Great Reform Act of 1832. Universal manhood suffrage was not achieved until 1918 and universal adult suffrage, equal voting rights for men and women, was only introduced in 1928. Until 1949 certain classes of voters, university graduates and owners of business property, were entitled to more than one vote. This modern form of democracy is, however, very different from the classical Greek model. Government is left in the hands of a class of professional politicians; the public does not govern but only participates in the process of selecting the government. The modern conception of democracy is therefore one of representative democracy.

Throughout much of the nineteenth century, the term 'democracy' retained many of its pejorative connotations. For example, liberal thinkers like James Madison and John Stuart Mill echoed the reservations which Plato and Aristotle had harboured about democracy, warning that unrestricted democracy would both threaten property and endanger individual liberty. During the twentieth century, in marked contrast, democracy has been almost universally regarded as a 'good thing', at times becoming little more than a 'hurrah! word', implying approval of a particular system of government or regime. Almost all forms of government have been described as democratic and virtually all modern political thinkers proclaim the virtues of democracy. However, this also underlines the central problem of trying to investigate the meaning and significance of democracy: if liberals, socialists, conservatives, anarchists, fascists and nationalists all claim their ideas to be 'democratic', and even to preach 'true' democracy, the term itself is so elastic it is in danger of becoming simply meaningless. To complicate matters further, the idea of democracy is no longer confined to its original political meaning, to describe a particular system of government or what can be called 'political democracy'. Democracy crops up in other guises and forms, for example, as 'industrial democracy' or 'social democracy'. Such confusion arises precisely because there is no single definition of 'democracy', nor is there unanimous agreement about the form 'democratic government' might take. There are, rather, a number of competing theories or models of democracy, each of which reflects a particular set of philosophical assumptions and ideological convictions about when, how and why people should rule themselves. At the heart of this lies the fact that democracy is a deceptively simple idea, but one which raises challenging and difficult political questions when examined closely.

2 Power to the people

At first sight, democracy is a simple concept, it brings together just two ideas, 'the people' and 'rule'. Democracy is therefore commonly thought to mean 'government by the people', without much attention being given to what these words mean and how they can be applied in practice. A more helpful starting point is provided by Abraham Lincoln's Gettysburg Address (1863), which referred to 'government of the people, by the people, and for the people'. This definition has the virtue of recognising that 'the people' may be related to 'government' in a number of different ways. Government *of* the people raises few questions because, in a sense, all government is *of* the people, the people are subject to government authority and affected by its decisions. However, the distinction between government *by* the people and government *for* the people establishes two very different conceptions of democracy. The people can be related to government in one of two ways, either they participate in government and help to rule themselves or, in contrast, government is carried out in the interests of the public or for their benefit. Government *by* the people therefore implies the idea of popular participation in government, while government *for* the people suggests that government should be conducted in the public interest.

Although either of these principles could provide the basis for a particular model of democratic rule, each raises a number of difficulties. For example, how can or should the people participate in government? Should they govern themselves directly as citizens did in Ancient Greece, or should they merely participate in selecting 'representatives' to govern on their behalf? Similarly, if democracy means government *for* the people, how is it possible to establish what is in the public interest? Is it possible to ask the public themselves, are they capable of identifying their own interests, and if not, who is? Moreover, how do we define 'the people'? In other words, who should have the right of political participation? Are all citizens equally qualified to develop and express political views, or only a select few?

a Political equality

Any analysis of democratic theory must start with some understanding of the term *demos*, or people. Who are 'the people' to whom the business of government should be entrusted, or in whose interests government should operate? Surely *the* people implies *all* people? In practice, all democratic theorists have been taxed by this question and none have been prepared to accept that all individuals should be entitled to participate in government. The most obvious example of this is the universal acceptance of some kind of age qualification effectively to exclude children and babies from political influence. In effect, 'the people' therefore means 'all adult citizens'. Having said this, there may be considerable disagreement about when a 'child' becomes an 'adult', and therefore about the age at which an individual should be entitled to political rights, twenty-one, eighteen, sixteen or perhaps younger. It is also worth noting that the classical model of democratic rule, based upon the Greek city-state, excluded the vast majority from political life because neither slaves nor women were recognised as 'citizens'. Throughout the nineteenth century it was widely accepted that political participation should be restricted to a small minority, propertied and educated male adults. The idea that political participation should embrace all adult citizens, and therefore should include the working class, women and all racial and religious groups, has only enjoyed widespread support in the twentieth century.

The grounds for excluding individuals or groups from any definition of 'the people' have been many and varied. For some, it represented a belief that only a limited number of adults had an interest in the affairs of government, notably those who possessed property and were therefore eligible to pay taxes. This was expressed in the famous slogan of the American Revolution, 'no taxation without representation', which also implied the principle 'no representation without taxation'. More commonly, it has been argued that political participation should be restricted to those individuals capable of making rational and moral judgements. John Stuart Mill, for example, argued that the illiterate and uneducated should be denied the right to vote because they were incapable of making wise decisions on their own behalf and would be better off if government were left in the hands of the educated.

Clearly such arguments have undemocratic or anti-democratic implications if pushed further. Plato, for example, argued that human beings possess fundamentally different skills and abilities; they were born with souls of gold, silver or bronze. He proposed that government should be left to a small class of 'Guardians' or 'philosopher-kings', who alone possessed the wisdom to make rational and moral judgements and would therefore rule as benign dictators. Similar ideas were expressed in the early twentieth century by 'classical' elite theorists such as Pareto and Mosca. They believed that democratic government was impossible because a ruling minority of 'natural' leaders, possessing superior talents and skills, would always dominate the masses. In Mosca's view, in all societies 'two classes of people appear – a class that rules and a class that is ruled'. Pareto divided those with leadership qualities into 'foxes', who ruled through the use of cunning and were able to manipulate popular consent, and 'lions', who were bold and courageous and typically ruled by the use of violence.

In contrast, democratic theorists have stressed the importance of political equality: all individuals possess the right of political participation and the interests of one citizen are no more important that those of any other. Democracy therefore requires that political power is divided equally amongst 'the people', just as socialism stands for the belief that wealth should be divided equally within a society. All forms of democracy must respect the principle of equality. If democracy is based upon direct participation in a mass meeting, everyone must have the opportunity to attend and speak, and decisions must be made by a show of hands in which each vote is of equal value. In the case of electoral democracy, political equality can only be achieved if a number of conditions are met. First, all adult citizens must be entitled to stand for election regardless of race, colour, sex or religion. Secondly, all citizens must possess a vote, in other words, there should be universal adult suffrage. Thirdly, no one must possess more than a single vote, each should have an equal voice at election time. Finally, all votes must be of equal value, a principle that can only be achieved if electoral constituencies are of equal size. In short, political equality means 'one person one vote, one vote one value'.

However, democratic theorists often imply that 'the people' is a single, homogeneous entity, which acts collectively and is bound together by a common interest. In reality, people in all societies possess a range of divergent opinions and interests. Unanimous agreement amongst 'the people' is therefore rare and may be impossible, except when brought about by manipulation or fear. Democratic systems have usually solved this problem by reference to numbers and applying the principle of majority rule. Majority rule means quite simply that the minority accepts the views of the majority. Political questions are therefore resolved by the strength of support for different positions, calculated in numerical terms. In effect, government by the people means government by the majority, who thereby claim the right to speak for all.

Democracy may therefore create the danger of majoritarianism, 'the majority' may substitute itself for 'the people' and exercise unfettered power. Democracy could simply become 'the rule of the 51 per cent', a 'tyranny of the majority' in which the interests of both individuals and minorities are sacrificed in the name of 'the people'. As a result, democratic thinkers have sometimes opposed the principle of majority rule. James Madison, one of the 'founding fathers' of the United States Constitution, argued that society was composed of a collection of competing minorities, each of which possessed interests which should be respected. In his view, unrestrained majority rule would simply place government in the hands of the propertyless masses and endanger property rights. To counter this danger, he advocated a political system in which government power was fragmented and dispersed amongst a number of institutions, giving every minority group or interest the opportunity to exercise a measure of political influence. This Madisonian conception of democracy was enshrined in the American system of government, which was founded upon checks and balances between the two chambers of Congress, the Senate and the House of Representatives, and also amongst the three branches of Federal government, Congress, Presidency and the Supreme Court. In this way, Madison hoped to ensure that the voice of the majority could not silence all other opinions.

b *Popular participation*

Democracy is usually understood to imply the idea of popular self-government, summed up in the demand for 'government *by* the people'. However, although this suggests that the people should participate in governing themselves, it does not indicate what form this participation should take, nor to what extent the principle should be applied. At one extreme, government in the Greek city-states was organised according to the principle of direct democracy. Citizens participated directly in government, either by making decisions themselves in mass meetings or by holding public offices on a rota basis. In effect, direct democracy obliterates the distinction between government and people, and between the state and civil society. The people become the government and govern themselves. This classical model of democracy has inspired more modern writers, notably Jean Jacques Rousseau and John Stuart Mill. Rousseau understood democracy to mean popular sovereignty: absolute political authority lay with the citizens themselves, who were expected to participate directly and continuously in the process of government. For Rousseau, freedom meant autonomy or self-rule. He ridiculed the system of electoral democracy practised in Britain by pointing out that the British citizen is 'free only during the election of Members of Parliament; as soon as the Members are elected, the people is enslaved'. Mill also defended popular participation in government and advocated both the extension of the franchise and the expansion of local government in order to broaden the opportunities available to citizens to stand for and hold public office. For Mill, political participation had an educational value; it broadened the public's understanding of the society in which it lived and enabled individuals to develop and fulfil their potential.

Such classical theories of democracy bear little relation to modern forms of democratic government. Democracy in the modern world is representative democracy; the responsibilities of governing are not undertaken by all adult citizens but are entrusted to an elite group of professional politicians. Popular participation in government is therefore at best indirect; it has been reduced to choosing a government, usually by the act of voting. As a result, modern conceptions of democracy have abandoned the classical ideal of popular self-government and instead have concentrated upon the rules which guide the electoral process. It is widely believed, for example, that democratic government means nothing more than universal adult suffrage to enable all adult citizens to vote, a secret ballot to ensure a free vote, and party competition to guarantee a measure of electoral choice. Providing these conditions are fulfilled, a system of government can claim to be 'democratic' and its politicians can describe themselves as 'representatives'.

However, beyond the fact that they are elected, it is less clear how and why professional politicians can claim to represent their electorate. The term 'representation' has a number of meanings. It can imply that representatives act as delegates or agents, conveying the views of their constituents faithfully and accurately without imposing their own opinions. This can only be achieved if politicians are subject to recall and removal if they fail to satisfy their electors. More commonly, representation means to act for, or on behalf of, a larger group of people. This allows politicians to think for themselves, allegedly in the interests of their electors. In this case, politicians constitute an elite group, wiser, more experienced or better educated than the voters themselves. Finally, representation may mean that politicians are typical or characteristic of the public in the sense of sharing similar backgrounds, social experiences, interests and so on. However, no system of free and competitive elections can ensure that government is a microcosm of society, and in all such systems certain groups are 'over-represented', invariably men, whites, the wealthy and the middle-aged or elderly.

Supporters of representative democracy have often argued that direct popular participation in government is only possible in relatively small societies, such as Greek city-states, but is quite unworkable in the modern world. Government by mass meetings is certainly difficult to envisage in countries with populations of tens or hundreds of millions. Moreover, direct participation is often thought to be undesirable. Representation is seen as a solution to the problem of popular ignorance and apathy. If government is placed directly in the hands of the people it is entrusted to ill-informed amateurs who have neither the education nor the specialist knowledge to govern efficiently. Elections allow the public to express its views and opinions, while leaving decision-making to experts, professional politicians. In that sense, representative democracy merely applies the need for specialisation and a division of labour to the organisation of political life. Furthermore, indirect and limited participation may also promote political stability and order. If citizens participate directly in government, they will perceive their interests more keenly and pursue them with greater determination. Participation may therefore raise popular expectations and generate social conflict. In contrast, representative democracy can help to moderate popular expectations, allowing people to live together harmoniously in an imperfect world which can never satisfy all their needs and wants.

On the other hand, there has been growing anxiety about the lack of popular participation in modern government and a revival of interest in the classical theories of democracy. At the heart of this lies the belief that self-determination or autonomy is desirable. Participation in government reflects the influence which the public has over the affairs of government, their ability to affect the content of government policy. Both Rousseau and Mill subscribed to a positive conception of freedom as the ability to take charge of, or control, one's own life. The widespread apathy about politics that is evident in many industrial societies may not reflect popular satisfaction or broad acquiescence so much as political stagnation and inertia, brought about by reducing political participation to a largely meaningless ritual of voting. Furthermore, the danger of representative democracy is that government is progressively distanced from the people. The task of governing is entrusted to professional politicians who may act as they think is best, or in their own interests, rather than those of the general public. The electorate may retain the power to vote a government out of office, but its capacity to do this is severely limited by ignorance and apathy, and it can, at best, only replace one government by transferring the right to govern to another self-selected group of professional politicians.

c The public interest

A rival conception of democracy is based not on the question 'who governs?' but on the question 'who benefits from government?'. Democracy may therefore be based upon the principle of 'government *for* the people'. The mere fact that people govern themselves, directly or indirectly, does not necessarily ensure that they do so in their own interest, in what can be termed the public interest. Some political thinkers, however, have criticised the very notion of a public interest. Utilitarians, following Jeremy Bentham, argue that each individual is self-interested and wishes to improve his or her own position or promote personal wellbeing. Any conception of the 'public interest' is therefore absurd because it suggests that there is a common or collective interest which unites the public, when in reality there is only a collection of competing individual interests. There are, for instance, very few policies which all members of the public would regard as being in their interests, with the possible exception of the preservation of public order and protection from external attack. Even in those cases there are profound differences about how these goals can be achieved: some argue that public order requires respect for individual liberty, while others call for strong government and stiff penalties; some believe that external attack can only be deterred by having a strong army and nuclear weapons, while others believe such policies to be unnecessary and even immoral.

Other political thinkers have taken the idea of a public interest more seriously and suggested that it is possible to identify the common good or the collective interest. Rousseau, in particular, suggested that government should be based upon popular sovereignty, which required that government be based upon the 'general will'. The 'general will' meant the general or common interest of society collectively, and Rousseau insisted therefore that 'the general will is always right'. However, this common interest could not be established simply by asking citizens what they wanted because of the danger that they may express their own narrow and selfish interest, their 'private wills' rather than the collective 'general will'. The 'general will' was thus the will of all, providing each citizen acted selflessly. Rousseau's ideas have been criticised for containing the germ of what has been called 'totalitarian democracy'. On one hand, Rousseau proclaimed that government should be based upon popular sovereignty but, on the other, he suggested that, blinded by selfishness, the people themselves may not be able to define their true interests. This could perhaps allow a dictator who claimed to articulate the 'general will' to coerce and repress the public in the name of democracy itself. Both Hitler and Mussolini claimed to practise 'true' democracy on the grounds that they, and they alone, could articulate the destiny of their people.

If ordinary people are thought to be incapable of perceiving their own 'true' interests, democratic government, government *for* the people, is only possible if government is entrusted to those who can define the public interest. Such a belief is elitist because it holds that there is a group of people with superior knowledge, wisdom or experience, better able than the public is itself to define its interests. In its extreme form, elitism leads to anti-democratic conclusions, as in the case of Plato's belief that absolute power should be entrusted to the Guardians. Others, however, have tried to find a balance between the desire for self-government with the need for wise government. J.S. Mill, for example, suggested that those with better education and broader experience possess more worthwhile political opinions. He therefore proposed a system of plural voting in which unskilled workers would have one vote and skilled labourers two votes, while graduates and members of the learned professions would be entitled to five or six votes. He also argued that the electorate would tend to vote for candidates with a higher level of education than themselves and therefore that representatives must be free to exercise their own judgement, rather than sacrifice it to the ill-informed and immature views of the electorate.

V.I. Lenin developed a similar argument, but on a very different basis. Lenin feared that the working masses would be incapable of recognising their own genuine interests because of the influence of 'bourgeois ideology'. Workers would seek higher wages, shorter hours and better conditions of work, but would not recognise that their enemy was the capitalist system itself, which could only be overthrown by revolution. This knowledge was possessed only by the most class-conscious workers, those who had studied and understood Marxist theory. Lenin therefore believed in the need for a 'vanguard party' to lead the working class to revolution and guide it towards the realisation of its ultimate destiny: a communist society. In effect, the revolutionary party defined the interests of the proletariat. The danger of all such theories is that they invest in 'the few' responsibility for defining the interests of 'the many', and so run the risk that 'the few' may rule in their own interests, and only in the name of 'the many'. In a sense, democratic theory originated with Aristotle's response to Plato, 'Who will guard the Guardians?'.

3 Models of democracy

Democracy is a difficult and sometimes unhelpful term in political debate because its meaning is so fluid that it is in danger of losing all coherence. In different parts of the world, democracy has assumed a variety of forms and conformed to a wide range of ideological and political demands. In reality, there is no single, agreed conception of democracy in modern politics, but rather a number of rival models, each claiming to be 'true' democracy. Like so many other political ideas, democracy has been shaped by the historical and social complexion of the societies in which it has been applied, as well as by the political uses to which it has been put.

a Liberal democracy

The system of government most commonly found in the industrialised 'First World', countries in Europe, North America, Australia and so on, is one of 'liberal democracy'. Liberal democracies are based upon the idea of 'government by consent'. Government exists to fulfil the needs and protect the rights of its citizens, who therefore consent or agree to be governed. This implies a system of representative democracy, in which the right to exercise government power is acquired through success in elections. In liberal democratic theory, great attention has been paid to the rules which govern the electoral process in order to ensure that it is 'democratic'. In the first place, elections must be regular to ensure that once elected politicians continue to listen to the electorate because they know they can be removed at subsequent elections. Secondly, elections should be free, enabling voters to make up their own minds and express their views without intimidation or corruption, a requirement that is usually ensured by means of a secret ballot. Thirdly, there must be political equality, which means universal adult suffrage and one person one vote. Finally, and perhaps most crucially, these elections must be competitive. A number of candidates and parties must be able to stand for election and offer the voter a choice of different programmes or policies, a principle known as political pluralism.

Such a system of government is very different from the classical model of Greek democracy which insisted upon direct self-government by all citizens. Professional politicians govern, in the sense of making policy and taking decisions; the general public is merely engaged in the task of selecting which group of politicians should be entrusted with government power. It is therefore a limited and indirect form of democratic rule. In effect, democracy in the West has come to mean a particular mechanism for creating governments and ensuring the succession of government power. This mechanism was defined by Joseph Schumpeter in *Capitalism, Socialism and Democracy* (1942) as 'that institutional arrangement for arriving at political decisions in which individuals acquire the power to decide by means of a competitive struggle for the people's vote' (p.269). Popular self-government has therefore been replaced by democratic elitism, which attempts to reconcile the fact that government is always carried out by an elite, a self-selected group of professional politicians, with the need for democracy, the ability of the electorate to decide which elite group rules.

This idea was taken further by Anthony Downs in *An Economic Theory of Democracy* (1957), which attempted to explain how and why competitive elections achieve the goal of democratic government. Downs called his model an 'economic theory' because it drew upon the ideas of market economics to help explain political behaviour in a liberal democracy. Politicians were thought to be primarily interested in acquiring power, just as businessmen seek to maximise profits. They can only realise this goal, however, by gaining votes in an election, or, in other words, selling their goods in the market place. Because the 'political market', like the economic market, is competitive, voters are able to exercise choice and select the product, or set of policies, which best satisfies their interests. The result is that the party which wins power is the one which is most successful in formulating policies which appeal to the largest number of voters, just as successful businesses produce those goods which consumers are willing to buy. Electoral choice therefore ensures that parties and politicians are firmly linked to public opinion simply because that is the only way they can win or retain government power.

The Downsian model suffers from a number of obvious defects, similar to those which apply to the economic model of 'perfect competition', upon which it is based. The 'economic theory' of democracy rests upon a number of questionable assumptions. First, it holds that competition amongst politicians or parties is genuine and effective when in practice only two or three parties may enjoy a realistic prospect of gaining power. British politics has traditionally been dominated by the Conservative and Labour parties, American politics by the Democrats and the Republicans. Competition in the political market is restricted by the existence of barriers against new parties entering the political market, such as the high cost of electioneering and the habitual nature of established political allegiances. Secondly, the electorate possesses neither full knowledge nor complete independence in deciding who to vote for and may therefore not vote rationally, nor in its own interests. Just as businesses seek to influence consumer tastes and needs by advertising, so political parties try to manipulate the views and values of the electorate by the use of propaganda. The public knows what politicians tell it. Finally, the Downsian model assumes that the principal influence upon politicians is the electorate and therefore it ignores all other forms of political pressure and influence. In reality, governments must heed the views of organised groups, especially those which possess economic power, for example, private businesses and trade unions. As a result, liberal democratic theory has been forced to give attention to the distribution of power amongst these influential groups.

A growing recognition of the importance of organised interests in exerting political pressure has led to the development of pluralism and the emergence of a further model of democracy, pluralist democracy. Pluralists believe that if individuals exert political influence in the modern world it is not as voters but as members of organised interests or pressure groups: businesses or trade associations, trade unions, professional associations, community groups and so forth. Society is therefore pluralistic, it comprises a diverse collection of groups and interests. Pluralists argue that such a society is democratic because political power is widely dispersed amongst these competing groups, in that each can enjoy some access to government and exert a measure of political influence. For example, in his study of New Haven, Connecticut, *Who Governs?* (1961), Robert Dahl claimed to identify a process of 'polyarchy' or rule by the many. Dahl suggested that a wide number of groups enjoyed the ability to influence policy-making in Newhaven and therefore concluded that group politics ensured a sufficiently high level of political equality to be regarded as democratic.

The pluralist model of democracy has, however, been criticised by 'modern' elitists, who believe that in liberal democracies some groups enjoy permanently greater influence than other groups. Certain groups of people, for example, are effectively excluded from political influence because they are not organised and therefore possess no formal political voice. This can be said of the unemployed, housewives, the homeless and the poor. Moreover, elitists emphasise that the ability of groups to exert influence depends upon professional, financial and economic resources, which are unequally distributed in any society. For instance, political organisation requires education, knowledge and experience. Pressure group politics may therefore empower the articulate middle classes, who are able to draw upon professional skills, personal contacts and so on, but not the working classes or the socially disadvantaged. Clearly, money or economic power is also a significant factor in determining political influence. In *Politics and Markets* (1977) Charles Lindblom argued that business should be regarded as an 'elite group' in all Western liberal democracies because it controls the crucial decisions which affect the health of the economy, in particular the levels of employment and investment. All governments, Lindblom suggested, whatever their ideological inclinations, must listen to the views of business before those of any other organised group. Pluralist democracy is therefore a facade.

b People's democracy

The terms 'people's democracy' and 'proletarian democracy' have been used to describe the political systems of orthodox Communist political systems, or 'Second World' regimes. The first such system was established in Russia after the 1917 Revolution and subsequently it was established in Eastern Europe and also in countries like China, North Korea, Vietnam and Cuba. This form of democracy is based upon Marxist–Leninist principles very different from the liberal ideas which underlie Western democracy. From the Marxist point of view, liberal democracy is a sham which conceals the reality of class oppression; it is a form of 'capitalist democracy'. Marxists do not believe that competitive elections make the government accountable to the general public. Rather, a capitalist society is dominated by the interests of the 'ruling class', the bourgeoisie or capitalist class, which owns and controls productive wealth.

The Marxist conception of democracy is based upon the belief that politics reflects class interests. In a capitalist society, the state embodies the interests of private property: Marx described the state as nothing more than 'a committee for managing the affairs of the whole bourgeoisie'. Political democracy, in the form of regular and competitive elections, is pointless so long as economic power remains in the hands of the few. Genuine democracy therefore requires the overthrow of the class system itself and the establishment of 'social democracy', which Marx understood to mean a classless, socialist society. However, Marx himself said little about the form of political organisation which socialist or communist societies should adopt, except to note that a 'dictatorship of the proletariat' would need to be established once the capitalist state was overthrown, but that the state itself would eventually 'wither away' as full communism was achieved. Marxist theory was elaborated in more detail by V.I. Lenin who, as leader of the Bolshevik Party, was responsible for the construction of the world's first 'proletarian state'.

Lenin accepted Marxist class analysis, but significantly revised Marx's belief in an inevitable and popular revolution by stressing the need for political organisation. In Lenin's view, the oppressed proletariat would not rise up in spontaneous revolution against capitalism, but needed the guidance and leadership of a vanguard party. The party should comprise professional and dedicated revolutionaries, the most class-conscious elements amongst the proletariat, who therefore grasped Marxist analysis of history and society. Armed with Marxism, the party would be able to perceive the genuine interests of the proletariat and guide the class towards its revolutionary destiny. Once the Bolsheviks took power in Russia, this theory became the cornerstone of 'Leninist democracy'. Following the Soviet Union, all other orthodox Communist states conformed to these Marxist–Leninist principles. In the first place, democracy requires a monopolistic party, the suppression of all parties other than the Communist party. Only the vanguard party, the Communist Party, represents the interests of the working masses, the proletariat. All other parties represent class interests hostile to those of the proletariat; in other words, they seek to promote counter-revolution and re-establish a class system. Secondly, the Communist party should be a ruling party. As the representative of the proletariat, the party should 'lead and guide' both government and society; the party should enjoy unchallenged control over the state and its influence must penetrate every walk of social life. Thirdly, the party itself should conform to the principles of democratic centralism; party members should be able to discuss policy freely and openly, but also be prepared to unite behind an agreed party line. In theory, this was achieved by a system in which each organ within the party elected members of higher organs and was able to make recommendations to them. Defeated minorities were obliged to accept the will of the majority and the decisions of higher organs within the party were binding on those below.

However, this Marxist–Leninist model of democracy failed to provide the basis for a stable and responsive political system. The weakness of the model lay in Lenin's belief that the revolutionary party would be drawn from the most committed and class-conscious sections of the proletariat and so could be entrusted with the role of 'leading and guiding' the proletarian class. Lenin failed, however, to establish any mechanism that would ensure that the party, and particularly party leaders, would remain sensitive and accountable to the working class. This became evident when Stalin assumed the leadership of the party after the death of Lenin. Stalin was able to exploit his control over party organisation to suppress democratic processes and open debate in the party, and establish a personal dictatorship. During the 1930s a series of brutal purges removed all vestiges of opposition from the party, the government and the army. Leninist democracy was therefore replaced by a Stalinist dictatorship, which continued to rule in the name of the proletariat, and later the 'whole Soviet people', while at the same time carrying out what in the 1930s amounted to a civil war against the Soviet people themselves.

Attempts were made to reform the Soviet political system by re-establishing internal democracy within the Communist Party and returning to Leninist principles. After his appointment in 1985 as General Secretary, Mikhail Gorbachev significantly broadened the limits of political debate within the Soviet Union, under the slogan of *glasnost* or 'openness', and carried through a policy of 'democratisation' which encouraged the use of competitive elections within the Communist Party itself and for the new Soviet Parliament. Gorbachev's original goals were Leninist; he sought to promote not full political pluralism but 'socialist pluralism', genuine freedom of debate but within the confines of a monopolistic party. However, political reform stimulated an upsurge in political participation in the form of public demonstrations, the growth of nationalist movements and the formation of rival political parties. Gorbachev's response was in 1990 to abolish the Communist Party's constitutionally guaranteed monopoly of power and to accept, at least in principle, multi-party politics and a Western-style competitive political system. In effect, the Soviet Communist Party abandoned the cornerstone of Leninism, the belief that its right to rule was based upon ideology, and accepted the liberal principle that government power should only be gained by success in competitive elections. The reform process occurred even more spectacularly in Eastern Europe, where a wave of popular demonstrations in 1989–90 led to the collapse of single party Communist governments and their replacement by liberal democratic political structures.

c *Third World democracy*

In a number of 'Third World' countries a form of democracy has developed which owes little to the ideas of either liberalism or Marxism–Leninism. Like orthodox communist states, Third World governments are often dominated by a single party, typically headed by a charismatic leader. The philosophical basis for calling such political systems 'democratic' lies in the ideas of Rousseau and a belief in an overriding common purpose or 'general will'. Where competitive party systems have been set up, modelled upon liberal democratic principles, they have sometimes failed because they encouraged discussion and debate rather than action, they promoted conflict rather than unity. Civilised debate and an interplay of conflicting interests is a luxury which the affluent West can afford, but which can paralyse and weaken the political systems of developing countries.

During the colonial period, the unifying common goal for many Third World peoples was the struggle for independence. Since independence, however, it has been the desire for modernisation and economic progress. In many cases, the ruling party in Third World countries developed out of the anti-colonial movement. In Zimbabwe, for example, Robert Mugabe's ZANU-PF has dominated political life since independence in 1980, after having led the armed struggle against the white-dominated Rhodesian regime since 1963. Single party governments can be regarded as legitimate only if there is widespread acceptance that the ruling party is dedicated to realising a set of overriding common goals. In many poor or backward countries, the overriding goal may simply be feeding the entire population, or providing basic medical care and rudimentary education. Thereafter, there is the desire for economic security and material prosperity.

Single party government may also correspond to the culture and traditions of Third World societies, which are often collectivist rather than individualist. Unlike the West, where a liberal capitalist revolution has fostered the idea of self-seeking individuals and groups, in Africa and Asia there is typically a stronger emphasis upon co-operation and social harmony, expressed in the desire for unity rather than conflict. Moreover, Third World countries have often inherited a geography determined for them by former colonial rulers and therefore need to foster a sense of national unity and solidarity. In countries like Tanzania, Kenya and Zimbabwe, tribal resentments and rivalries, which have threatened to block the process of nation-building, have only been overcome by the creation of a single dominant party. Newly-independent Third World countries could be torn apart by the introduction of political pluralism, and perhaps only single party rule can ensure national survival and political order. This was the experience of Zimbabwe which inherited a Western-style competitive party system from Britain in 1980, but subsequently developed into a one party state when ZANU-PF absorbed its principal rival, ZAPU.

The danger of Third World democracy is that in the absence of competitive elections the charismatic leader and ruling party may become corrupt, serving their own interests rather than those of society at large. This danger is the more acute as the ruling party invariably controls the army and the police and can therefore repress and silence its political opponents. This is evident in the authoritarian and repressive regimes that developed under Saddam Hussein in Iraq and General Marcos in the Philippines. Furthermore, if the overriding goals of modernisation and nation-building are fulfilled, Third World countries will become increasingly sophisticated and diversified. As in the case of Communist regimes, industrial development diminishes any sense of an overriding common interest and generates, in contrast, an increasingly complex and diversified society. As the acceptance of an overriding 'general will' fades, pressure builds up for a more open and competitive political system. For example, the Marcos dictatorship was overthrown in the Philippines in 1986 after a growing campaign of popular demonstrations and was replaced by a liberal democratic system under the leadership of Corazon Aquino. However, the process of transition from single party rule to liberal democracy in the Third World is difficult and often erratic, especially when powerful groups like the army are unwilling to relinquish power. The Aquino regime, for instance, has been challenged by a series of military uprisings.

d Radical democracy

The spread of liberal democratic processes from the industrialised West to the former Communist Second World and also into the Third World has encouraged Francis Fukuyama to proclaim the imminent worldwide triumph of liberal democracy. However, it would be a mistake to believe that the liberal conception of democracy enjoys universal or uncritical support even in its Western heartland. The principal defect which critics have identified in liberal democracy is the gulf which exists between the government and the people, despite the existence of regular and competitive elections. This concern has been expressed in many forms. Elitists and Marxists, for example, have argued that government is more accountable to powerful economic interests than it is to the electorate. Others have suggested that when popular participation is reduced to casting a vote every few years, democracy has effectively abandoned its original goals of popular sovereignty and personal autonomy. Since the 1960s, an alternative model of democracy, participatory democracy, has attracted growing support. In many ways, this radical theory of democracy goes back to the classical Greek ideal and tries to establish how it is possible in modern industrial societies for citizens to gain a measure of direct and personal control over the decisions which affect their lives, rather than leave these in the hands of a political elite.

It has often been argued that whereas direct democracy was appropriate and workable in Greek city-states containing about ten thousand citizens, it is entirely unsuited to modern nation-states with populations of many millions. However, a higher level of popular involvement in politics can be achieved in several ways. For example, since the 1960s a new generation of activist and campaigning pressure groups has developed: environmental groups, feminist groups, peace campaigners, gay rights groups, animal rights activists, and so forth. Such groups afford individuals broader and more continuous participation in political life because they seek to mobilise popular support by protests, demonstrations and marches, and because they typically possess open and decentralised structures, which conform to the principles of 'grass roots democracy'.

The same objective has influenced those who would promote popular participation by reforming the structure of conventional political parties. Political parties have traditionally been dominated by parliamentary leaders who control policy-making and insist upon strict discipline. If, however, the principle of intra-party democracy were adopted, ordinary party members could also participate and exercise greater power. Constituency activists in the British Labour Party, for instance, attempted to promote internal democracy in the early 1980s by introducing an Electoral College for the election of the party leader and deputy leader, which placed 70 per cent of the votes in the hands of constituency parties and affiliated trade unions, and by introducing the mandatory re-selection of MPs by their constituency parties. However, to extend grass roots democracy to pressure groups and political parties has the limitation that although it may broaden participation beyond the ranks of an elite group of professional politicians, it only benefits another, if larger, self-selected group: political activists and party members. Only a minority of the population is going to join political parties or to participate actively in pressure group campaigns, therefore radical democracy requires more far-reaching changes to ensure that political participation extends throughout society.

Direct popular participation in government has long been possible through referendums, in which citizens can express opinions on specific political issues, rather than elect representatives to make decisions for them. Referendums are commonly used in Switzerland and have been used in Britain in 1975, on continued membership of the European Community, and in 1979, on establishing devolved assemblies in Scotland and Wales. It has often been objected, however, that the referendum is a cumbersome mechanism which can impose considerable burdens upon the electorate. The development of modern technology, on the other hand, opens up new prospects for direct political participation. Interactive television creates the possibility that citizens can communicate with each other, participate in debates and discussions without leaving their own living rooms. They can, moreover, express opinions about a range of issues and directly make decisions without having to go to the inconvenience of visiting the polling station. Experiments with such methods have already been undertaken in local politics in some parts of the United States, and have at least the potential to replace all forms of representative democracy. The television could replace the elected assembly as the forum of political debate, enabling ordinary citizens to exercise power directly and dispense altogether with the need for full-time professional politicians.

4 Terror and the democratic state

Democracy is both an end in itself and a means to an end. As an end in itself, democracy embodies the virtues of popular self-government, personal autonomy and the superiority of the collective interest over the sectional. As a means to an end, democracy is simply a way of settling political disputes. In effect, democracy is a means of resolving conflicts, by dispersing political power widely within society, giving major groups and interests some kind of voice in the affairs of government. As such, the attraction of democracy is that it serves to promote debate, compromise and consensus, and thus to avoid both disorder and violence. However, as the twentieth century has progressed it has become clear that democratic states are peculiarly vulnerable to a particular form of violence, political terrorism.

It is ironic that while no authoritarian state has faced a sustained campaign of terrorism this century, few democratic states have escaped its impact. At the turn of the century, a wave of terrorism was carried out by anarchists, operating either as individuals or in underground bands. During the inter-war period, assassinations and bombings were more usually associated with fascist or nationalist groups. The 1970s witnessed an upsurge in terrorism in many parts of the world, carried out by groups like the Japanese Red Army, in Europe by the Red Brigade and Baader–Meinhof, and in the United States by the Weathermen and the SLF. Other countries have experienced bitter and often violent sectarian conflicts usually based upon nationalism or religion. For example, rival Republican and Loyalist terror groups operate in Northern Ireland, and in the case of the IRA this has extended to campaigns in mainland Britain and Europe. In Spain, ETA has conducted a prolonged campaign of terrorism in favour of Basque independence, while Sikhs in India have fought for a homeland in the Punjab and were responsible for the assassination of Prime Minister Indira Gandhi in 1984. Since the Six Day War of 1967, terrorism has also become an international phenomenon, commonly associated with Palestinian groups such as Al Fatah, Black September and Abu Nidal.

It would be a mistake, however, to believe that terrorism poses a threat to the stability of democratic regimes. When terrorists have succeeded, for instance, it has usually been because their goals have been specific and limited, such as the release of political prisoners. Nevertheless, terrorism strikes at the very heart of democracy. In the first place, terrorism only breeds in a climate of tolerance and liberty which democracy helps to guarantee. Secondly, terrorism provokes a repressive reaction on the part of the state which stifles free debate and political liberty, thus threatening to strangle democracy itself. Finally, why has political violence persisted despite the achievement of democracy? Does terrorism provide evidence that the democratic system is flawed, or are only certain political conflicts capable of being resolved peacefully?

'Terrorism' is a politically loaded term. A 'terrorist' to one person may be a 'freedom fighter' to another. Nevertheless, terrorism helps to classify a very particular kind of political violence. Terrorism is a form of psychological warfare, which uses violence to create a climate of fear and apprehension, described by Paul Wilkinson as 'coercive intimidation'. Terrorist violence is typically expressed in bombings, assassinations or kidnappings; its target may be political leaders, judges, the military, industrialists or ordinary citizens. Unlike insurrections or revolutions, which openly challenge the might of the state, terrorist violence is covert. It uses violence to gain a platform for a political cause, or to engender 'terror' by demonstrating the capacity to inflict further suffering in the future. It is a form of violence not easy to contain because it is typically carried out by clandestine groups, usually small, tightly-knit and difficult to monitor or infiltrate. Terrorism is defined by its method not by its goals, which have been many and various. Modern terrorist groups may often have identified themselves as anarchists or revolutionary communists, but in other circumstances terrorists have supported fascism, nationalism and religious fundamentalism.

Terrorism breeds from a sense of oppression, injustice and inequality; its perpetrators therefore believe their violence to be morally and politically justified. Moreover, the resort to violence reflects the perception that the political system is unresponsive or insensitive, and therefore fails to offer a solution to injustice. Without doubt, certain forms of terrorism can be cured by political or social reform. For instance, the violence of groups like the Black Panthers in the United States in the 1960s sprang out of the discrimination, poverty and decay which characterised America's urban ghettos. Since then, a combination of urban renewal and civil rights legislation has neutralised the threat of organised terror campaigns, as well as the sporadic violence and rioting which broke out during the 'long hot summers' of the mid 1960s. It would, however, be naïve to believe that social and political reform can cure all forms of injustice and so eradicate political violence altogether. To some extent, justice is a zero-sum game: any improvement in the position of one group may simply threaten the interests of another. In Northern Ireland, for instance, Republican terror groups like the IRA struggle to establish a united Ireland, while Loyalist groups such as the UVA fight to ensure that Northern Ireland remains part of the United Kingdom. Since the campaign of protest and violence began in 1969 a series of political initiatives have foundered because they have failed to bridge the gap between the diametrically opposed goals of extremist groups in both communities. Any 'political solution' that appears to make concessions to one community merely serves to inflame the other and provoke a terrorist backlash. In such cases, terrorism may increasingly be thought of as a 'security problem', a threat to be contained or neutralised, rather than as a 'political problem', which is capable of being solved. Violence can therefore become an almost permanent feature of a political conflict, as has occurred in Northern Ireland.

The terrorist threat can, however, be overcome. What is at issue is the cost. Terrorism can be stamped out if governments are willing and able to undertake a systematic and comprehensive repression. Ironically, the societies with the greatest injustice and oppression have been free from terrorist violence. Neither Nazi Germany nor Fascist Italy suffered from bombings, assassination or kidnapping, nor did orthodox Communist states. Terrorism has been and remains a threat confined to democratic regimes. Democratic states guarantee a range of civil liberties, including freedom of movement, which enable terrorist groups to organise and operate. Furthermore, a free press and freedom of expression offer terrorists the 'oxygen' of publicity. If violence is employed to secure a political platform or to provoke fear and apprehension, it is doomed to failure if it is not discussed in newspapers or reported on radio or television. However, the price of tackling terrorism is that these 'democratic freedoms' may have to be curtailed or abolished.

Democratic governments have increasingly faced the dilemma of maintaining civil liberty and open political participation, while at the same time guaranteeing personal security. In some cases, state repression is merely counterproductive and plays into the hands of terrorist groups. For example, the introduction in 1971 of internment without trial in Northern Ireland simply outraged the Catholic community and boosted support for the IRA. In other cases, democratic governments have been accused of violating civil liberties and of establishing a 'national security state'. The British government has, for instance, been criticised by the European Court of Human Rights, both for its use of torture against terrorist prisoners in Northern Ireland and the powers it exercised under the Prevention of Terrorism Act (1976). This Act gave the police the power to arrest and question suspects and detain them for up to seven days without charge or appearance in court; they can also search people and places without a warrant. The problem of achieving an acceptable balance between the rights of the individual and the need to maintain domestic order is one that is peculiar to democratic regimes. In 1988 a ban was imposed on radio and television interviews with members of terrorist organisations like the IRA and the UDA in the hope of starving them of publicity. The broadcasting ban has, however, been criticised by both journalists and opposition parties for infringing freedom of discussion and so threatening the very life-blood of democracy. As T.A. Critchley argued, 'Any nation which so orders its affairs as to achieve a maximum freedom of speech and a maximum freedom from public disorder may fairly claim a prize amongst the highest achievements of the human race' (p.2).

11
Conclusion: Ideology without End?

Political ideology has been an essential component of world history for over two hundred years. Ideology sprang out of the upheavals, economic, social and political, through which the modern world took shape, and has been intimately involved in the continuing process of social transformation and political development. Although ideology emerged first in the industrialising West, it has subsequently appeared throughout the globe, creating a worldwide language of political discourse. However, opinion has been deeply divided about the role which ideology has played in human history. Has ideology served the cause of truth, progress and justice or has it presented a distorted and blinkered world view which has fostered intolerance and oppression? This debate goes back to the nineteenth century and the clear distinction which Marx drew between 'ideology' and 'science'. The notion that science provides an objective and value-free method of advancing human knowledge, so releasing humanity from enslavement to irrational ideologies, has been one of the enduring myths of modern times. Science is not the antithesis of ideology, but can perhaps be seen as an ideology in its own right. Science, for instance, has been linked to the interests of powerful social forces, in particular, those represented by industry and technology. It has therefore contributed to a profound process of social change and become, in a sense, the ruling ideology of industrial society. Ideology is simply a means through which a social group or entire society achieves a measure of self-consciousness, by establishing a common identity or a set of collective goals. As such, ideology should neither be thought of as liberating or oppressive, nor as true or false. It can be any these things. The character of ideology is shaped by the historical forces out of which it emerges and is fashioned by the social and political needs which it serves. Ideology has therefore come to be an indispensable and ineradicable feature of the human condition.

It is remarkable, nevertheless, how often political thinkers have proclaimed that ideology has been, or should be, brought to an end. One of the earliest versions of such an argument was the belief that politics itself can disappear or be abolished. In its broadest sense, politics is a social activity which occurs whenever conflict is present. Politics involves the expression of rival opinions or opposing interests; in essence it is the attempt to resolve any form of social conflict. It therefore takes place when disagreements emerge within a family, when antagonism occurs between communities or social classes, and also when conflict breaks out amongst nations. Politics can only end when conflict is replaced by harmony and agreement. Some political thinkers have believed this to be possible. For example, Marxists and anarchists have conceived of a possible 'end of politics'. Marxists believe that the major divisions in society are economic, and that they take the form of class conflict between capitalists and workers, or between the rich and the poor. However, if wealth is owned in common by all, the source of conflict will have been removed and with it the need for politics, a view which Marx expressed in his famous prediction that with the achievement of full communism the state would 'wither away'. The mere fact that this goal has never been achieved does not prove it to be impossible, but it is certainly a utopian vision. Even if all significant conflicts are agreed to be economic, the ability to satisfy material needs is restricted by the fact that economic resources are limited. Universal prosperity was probably ever a hopeless dream, but this fact is now underlined by growing awareness of environmental 'limits to growth'. Moreover, the experience of consumerism in the affluent West offers little support for the belief that material needs can ever be satisfied: the more people have, the more they seem to want. If politics is about 'who gets what', it is difficult to envisage it ever coming to an end.

In other cases thinkers have accepted that politics may persist, but predicted an 'end of ideology'. The most influential statement of such a position was made by Daniel Bell in *The End of Ideology* (1960). Bell was impressed by the fact that following the Second World War, politics in the West was characterised by broad agreement amongst major political parties and the absence of ideological division or debate. Fascism and communism had both lost their appeal, while the remaining parties disagreed only about who could be relied upon to deliver economic growth and material prosperity. In effect, economics had triumphed over politics. Politics was reduced to technical questions about 'how' to deliver affluence, and had ceased to address moral or philosophical questions about the nature of the 'Good Society'. In effect, ideology had become an irrelevance.

However, the process to which Bell drew attention was not the 'end of ideology' so much as the emergence of a broad ideological consensus amongst major parties and therefore the suspension of ideological debate. In the immediate post-war period, representatives from the three major Western ideologies, liberalism, socialism and conservatism, came to accept the common goal of 'managed capitalism'. This goal, however, was itself ideological: it reflected, for example, an enduring faith in market economics, private property and material incentives, tempered by a belief in social welfare and economic intervention. In effect, an ideology of 'welfare capitalism' or 'social democracy' had triumphed over its rivals. Furthermore, this triumph proved to be only temporary. The 1960s, for example, witnessed the rise of more radical New Left ideas, a revival of interest in Marxist thought, and the growth of more modern ideologies such as feminism and environmentalism. The onset of economic recession in the 1970s provoked renewed interest in long-neglected free market doctrines and stimulated the development of New Right theories, which also challenged the post-war consensus. Finally, the 'end of ideology' thesis focused attention exclusively upon developments in the industrialised West and ignored the fact that communism remained firmly entrenched in the Soviet Union, Eastern Europe, China and elsewhere, and that revolutionary political movements were operating at the time in Asia, Africa and parts of Latin America.

A more recent and broader perspective has been adopted by Francis Fukuyama in his essay 'The End of History' (1989). Unlike Bell, Fukuyama does not suggest that political ideas have become irrelevant, but that one particular set of ideas, Western liberalism, has triumphed over all its rivals. Fascism was defeated in 1945, and Fukuyama clearly believes that the collapse of Communist rule in Eastern Europe in 1989 marked the passing of Marxism–Leninism as an ideology of world significance. By the 'end of history', Fukuyama means that the history of ideas has ended, and with it fundamental ideological debate. Throughout the world there is broad agreement about the desirability of liberal democracy, by which he means a market or capitalist economy and an open, competitive political system. Without doubt, the collapse of Communist rule in Eastern Europe in 1989 and the reform process in the Soviet Union have altered the worldwide balance of ideological debate. However, it is far less certain that it marks an 'end of history'.

Fukuyama accepts that both nationalism and religious fundamentalism still constitute significant rivals to Western liberalism, especially in the Third World. While liberal democracy may have made progress during the twentieth century, as the century draws to a close there is undoubted evidence of the revival of very different ideologies, notably political Islam, whose influence extends from the Moslem countries of Asia and Africa into the Soviet Union and also the industrialised West. It is possible, for example, that the 'death of communism' in the Soviet Union and Eastern Europe may prepare the way for the revival of nationalism, racialism or religious fundamentalism, rather than a smooth and inevitable transition towards liberal democracy. Fukuyama, furthermore, shares the optimism of early liberals who believed that industrial capitalism would offer all members of society the prospect of social mobility and material security, encouraging every citizen to regard it as reasonable and attractive. In other words, Fukuyama believes that it is possible for a broad, possibly universal, agreement to be achieved about the nature of the 'Good Society'. However, this can only be achieved if a society can be constructed which is capable of both satisfying the interests of all social groups and fulfilling the aspirations of all its individual citizens. Despite the undoubted vigour and efficiency which the capitalist market has demonstrated, it certainly cannot be said that capitalism has ever treated all social classes or all individuals alike. Ideological conflict and debate are unlikely to end in the late twentieth century with the ultimate worldwide triumph of liberalism, any more than they did with the inevitable victory of socialism widely predicted in the late nineteenth century.

Indeed, the very assertion of an 'end of history', an 'end of ideology', or an 'end of politics' is itself ideological. Each of these theses is essentially an attempt to portray one particular set of political ideas and values as superior to all its rivals, and to do so by predicting its ultimate triumph. The mandate of history is called upon to validate a single ideology, be it Marxist socialism, welfare capitalism or liberal democracy, and so to discredit every other ideology. Rather than heralding the final demise of ideology, such assertions merely demonstrate that ideological debate is alive and well, and that ideology is a continuing and perhaps unending process.

Suggestions for Further Reading

This book attempts to provide an introduction to the major doctrines and traditions of political thought. The ideas and themes it raises can be pursued at more length and in greater depth in the books suggested below. The Bibliography that follows lists all the works refered to in the text.

General

Barry N. *An Introduction to Modern Political Theory* (London: Macmillan, 1989, second edition) (New York: St Martins, 1989, second edition)

Bracher, K.D. *The Age of Ideologies* (London: Methuen, 1985) (New York: St Martin's, 1984)

Gamble, A. *An Introduction to Modern Social and Political Thought*, (London: Macmillan, 1984) (New York: St Martin's 1981)

Goodwin, B. *Using Political Ideas* (Chichester and New York: Wiley & Sons, 1982)

Specifically on Britain:

Barker, R. *Political Ideas in Modern Britain* (London: Methuen, 1978) (New York: Routledge Chapman & Hall, 1983)

Greenleaf, W.H. *The British Political Tradition, Volume 2: The Ideological Heritage* (London: Routledge, 1983) (New York: Routledge Chapman & Hall, 1983)

Ideology

Larrain, J. *The Concept of Ideology* (London: Hutchinson, 1979) (Athens, Georgia: University of Georgia Press, 1980)

Larrain, J. *Marxism and Ideology* (London: Macmillan, 1983)

McLellan, D. *Ideology* (Milton Keynes: Open University Press, 1986) (Minneapolis: University of Minnesota Press, 1986)

Seliger, M. *The Marxist Conception of Ideology* (Cambridge: Cambridge University Press, 1977)

Liberalism

Arblaster, A. *The Rise and Decline of Western Liberalism* (Oxford and Cambridge, Mass.: Blackwell, 1984)

Gray, J. *Liberalism* (Milton Keynes: Open University Press, 1986) (Minneapolis: University of Minnesota Press, 1986)

Hall, J. *Liberalism: Politics, Ideology and the Market* (London: Paladin, 1988)

Lukes, S. *Individualism* (Oxford: Blackwell, 1974)

Manning, D.J. *Liberalism* (London: Dent, 1976) (New York: St Martin's, 1976)

Conservatism

Honderich, T. *Conservatism* (London: Hamish Hamilton, 1990)

Nisbet, R. *Conservatism* (Milton Keynes: Open University Press, 1986) (Minneapolis: University of Minnesota Press, 1986)

O'Sullivan, N. *Conservatism* (London: Dent, 1976) (New York: St Martin's, 1976)

Scruton, R. *The Meaning of Conservatism* (Harmondsworth: Penguin, 1980)

Specifically on the New Right:

Gamble, A. *The Free Economy and the Strong State* (London: Macmillan, 1988) (Durham, N.C.: Duke University Press, 1988)

King, D. *The New Right* (London: Macmillan, 1987) (Pacific Grove, Cal.: Brooks-Cole, 1988)

Levitas, R. (ed.) *The Ideology of the New Right* (Cambridge: Polity Press, 1986) (Cambridge, Mass.: Blackwell, 1985)

Socialism

Berki, R.N. *Socialism* (London: Dent, 1975) (New York: St Martin's 1975)
Crick, B. *Socialism* (Milton Keynes: Open University Press, 1987) (Minneapolis: University of Minnesota Press, 1987)
Lichtheim, G. *A Short History of Socialism* (London: Fontana, 1975)

On Marxist thought:

McLellan, D. *The Thought of Karl Marx: An Introduction* (London: Macmillan, 1971)
McLellan, D. *Marxism After Marx* (London: Macmillan, 1979) (Boston, Mass.: Houghton Mifflin, 1981)
Miliband, R. *Marxism and Politics* (Oxford and New York: Oxford University Press, 1977)

Nationalism

Alter, P. *Nationalism* (London: Edward Arnold, 1989) (New York: Routledge Chapman & Hall, 1989)
Hobsbawm, E.J. *Nations and Nationalism since 1780* (Cambridge and New York: Cambridge University Press, 1990)
Kamenka, E. (ed.) *Nationalism, The Nature and Evolution of an Idea* (London: Edward Arnold, 1976) (New York: St Martin's 1976)
Kedourie, E. *Nationalism* (London: Hutchinson, 1985, revised edition)

On political Islam:

Hiro, D. *Islamic Fundamentalism* (London: Paladin, 1988)
Jensen, G.H. *Militant Islam* (London: Pan, 1979.)

Fascism

Kitchen, M. *Fascism* (London: Macmillan, 1976)
Laqueur, W. (ed.) *Fascism: A Reader's Guide* (Harmondsworth: Penguin, 1979) (Berkeley: University of California Press, 1979)
O'Sullivan, N. *Fascism* (London: Dent, 1984)

Specifically on Nazism:

Jäckel, E. *Hitler's Worldview* (Cambridge, Mass: Harvard University Press, 1972)
Kershaw, I. *The Nazi Dictatorship* (London: Edward Arnold, 1986) (New York: Routledge Chapman & Hall, 1989)

Specifically on totalitarianism:

Schapiro, L. *Totalitarianism* (London: Macmillan, 1972)

Anarchism

Carter, A. *The Political Theory of Anarchism* (London: Routledge, Kegan Paul, 1982)
Joll, J. *The Anarchists* (London: Methuen, 1979) (Cambridge, Mass: Harvard University Press, 1979)
Miller, D. *Anarchism* (London: Dent, 1983)
Woodcock, G. *Anarchism: A History of Libertarian Ideas and Movements* (Harmondsworth: Penguin, 1986, revised edition) (New York: New American Library, 1974)
Woodcock, G. *The Anarchist Reader* (London: Fontana, 1977)

Feminism

Bryson, V. *Feminist Political Theory* (London: Macmillan, 1992)
Carter, A. *The Politics of Women's Rights* (London and White Plains N.Y.: Longman, 1988)
Elshtain, J.V. *Public Man, Private Woman* (Oxford: Martin Robertson, 1981) (Princeton: Princeton University Press, 1981)

Evans, J. *et al* (ed.) *Feminism and Political Theory* (London and Newbury Park, Cal.: Sage, 1986)

Randall, V. *Women and Politics* (London: Macmillan, 1987, second edition)

Stacey, M. & Price, M. *Women, Power and Politics* (London: Tavistock, 1981) (New York: Routledge Chapman & Hall, 1981)

Environmentalism

Most environmentalist texts focus upon environmental issues and remedies rather than on doctrines or philosophies. Amongst books which have influenced this emerging ideology are:

Capra, F. *The Turning Point* (London: Flamingo, 1983) (New York: Bantam, 1987)

Lovelock, J. *Gaia: A New Look at Life on Earth* (Oxford and New York: Oxford University Press. 1982)

Roszak, T. *The Making of a Counter Culture* (London: Faber, 1970)

Roszak, T. *Person/Planet* (London: Granada, 1981)

Schumacher, E.F. *Small is Beautiful* (London: Abacus, 1974) (New York: Harper & Row, 1989)

Democracy

Arblaster, A. *Democracy* (Milton Keynes: Open University Press, 1987) (Minneapolis: University of Minnesota Press, 1987)

Held, D. *Models of Democracy* (Cambridge: Polity Press, 1987) (Stanford, Cal., Stanford University Press, 1987)

Lively, J. *Democracy* (Oxford: Blackwell, 1975)

MacPherson, C.B. *The Real World of Democracy* (Oxford: Oxford University Press, 1972)

MacPherson, C.B. *The Life and Times of Liberal Democracy* (Oxford: Oxford University Press, 1977)

Pateman, C. *Participation and Democratic Theory* (Cambridge and New York: Cambridge University Press, 1970)

Bibliography

Aristotle, *The Politics*, trans. T. Sinclair (Harmondsworth: Penguin, 1962) (Chicago: University of Chicago Press, 1985).

Bakunin, M., 'Church and State' in *The Anarchist Reader*, ed. G. Woodcock (London: Fontana, 1977).

Beauvoir, S. de, *The Second Sex*, trans. H. M. Parshley (New York: Bantam, 1968).

Bell, D., *The End of Ideology* (Glencoe, Ill.: Free Press, 1960).

Benn, T., *Arguments for Democracy* (Harmondsworth: Penguin, 1982).

Bentham, J., *Introduction to the Principles of Morals and Legislation*, ed. J. Burns and H. L. A. Hart (London: Athlone Press, 1970) (Glencoe, Ill.: Free Press, 1970).

Berlin, I., *Four Essays on Liberty* (London: Oxford University Press, 1969).

Bernstein, E., *Evolutionary Socialism* (New York: Schocken, 1962).

Bookchin, M., 'Anarchism and Ecology' in *The Anarchist Reader*, ed. G. Woodcock (London: Fontana, 1977).

Bookchin, M., *Our Synthetic Environment* (London: Harper & Row, 1975).

Boulding, K., 'The Economics of the Coming Spaceship Earth' in *Environmental Quality in a Growing Economy* (Baltimore: Johns Hopkins Press, 1966).

Bourne, R., 'War is the Health of the State' in *The Anarchist Reader*, ed. G. Woodcock (London: Fontana, 1977).

Brownmiller, S., *Against Our Will: Men, Women and Rape* (New York: Simon & Schuster, 1975).

Burke, E., *On Government, Politics and Society*, ed. B. W. Hill (London: Fontana, 1975).

Burnham, J., *The Managerial Revolution* (Harmondsworth: Penguin, 1945) (Bloomington: Indiana University Press, 1960).

Capra, F., *The Turning Point* (London: Fontana, 1982) (Boston, Mass.: Shambhala, 1983).

Capra, F., *The Tao of Physics* (London: Fontana, 1983) (New York: Bantam, 1987).

Carson, R., *The Silent Spring* (Harmondsworth: Penguin, 1982) (Boston, Mass.: Houghton Mifflin, 1987).

Cecil, H., *Conservatism* (London and New York: Home University Library, 1912).

Chamberlain, H. S., *Foundations of the Nineteenth Century* (New York: John Lane, 1913).

Cobden, R., *Speeches on Questions of Public Policy*, ed. J. Bright and J.E.T. Rogers (London, 1878).

Constant, B., *Political Writings* (Cambridge: Cambridge University Press, 1988).

Costa, M. D. and James, S., *The Power of Women and the Subordination of the Community* (Bristol: Falling Wall Press, 1972).

Crewe, I., 'Values: The Crusade that Failed' in *The Thatcher Effect*, ed. D. Kavanagh and A. Seldon (Oxford: Oxford University Press, 1989).

Critchley, T. A., *The Conquest of Violence* (London: Constable, 1970).

Crosland, C.A.R., *The Future of Socialism* (London: Cape, 1956) (Des Plaines, Ill.: Greenwood, 1977).

Dahl, R., *Who Governs? Democracy and Power in an American City* (New Haven: Yale University Press, 1961).

Darwin, C., *On the Origin of Species* (London: Dent, 1972) (New York: New American Library, 1986).

Downs, A., *An Economic Theory of Democracy* (New York: Harper & Row, 1957).

Ehrlich, P. and Ehrlich, A., *Population, Resources and Environment: Issues in Human Ecology* (London: W. H. Freeman, 1970).

Ehrlich, P. and Harriman, R., *How to be a Survivor* (London: Pan, 1971).

Elshtain, J. B., *Public Man, Private Woman* (Oxford: Martin Robertson, 1981) (Princeton: Princeton University Press, 1981).

Engels, F., *The Origins of the Family, Private Property and the State* (London: Lawrence & Wishart, 1976) (New York: Pathfinder, 1972).

Eysenck, H., *Sense and Nonsense in Psychology* (Harmondsworth: Penguin, 1964).

Fanon, F., *The Wretched of the Earth* (Harmondsworth: Penguin, 1962) (New York: Grove – Weidenfeld, 1988).

Faure, S., 'Anarchy–Anarchist' in *The Anarchist Reader*, ed. G. Woodcock (London: Fontana, 1977).

Figes, E., *Patriarchal Attitudes* (London: Macmillan, 1986) (New York: Persea, 1987).

Firestone, S., *The Dialectic of Sex* (London: Women's Press, 1980).

Friedan, B., *The Feminine Mystique* (New York: Norton, 1963).

Friedan, B., *The Second Stage* (London: Michael Joseph, 1982) (New York: Summit, 1981).

Friedman, M., *Capitalism and Freedom* (Chicago: University of Chicago Press, 1962).

Friedman, M. & Friedman, R., *Free to Choose* (Harmondsworth: Penguin, 1980) (New York: Bantam, 1983).

Friedrich, C. J. and Brzezinski, Z., *Totalitarian Dictatorships and Autocracy* (New York: Praeger, 1963).

Fromm, E., *To Have or To Be* (London: Abacus, 1979).

Fromm, E., *The Fear of Freedom* (London: Ark, 1984).

Fromm, E., *Escape to Freedom* (New York: Avon, 1932).

Fukuyama, F., 'The End of History' in *National Interest* (Summer 1989).

Gamble, A., *The Free Economy and the Strong State* (London: Macmillan, 1988) (Durham, N. C.: Duke University Press, 1988).

Gandhi, M., *Selected Writings of Mahatma Gandhi*, ed. R. Duncan (London: Fontana, 1971).

Gilmour, I., *Inside Right: A Study of Conservatism* (London: Quartet Books, 1978).

Gobineau, J. -A., *Gobineau: Selected Political Writings*, ed. M. D. Biddiss (New York: Harper & Row, 1970).

Godwin, W., *Enquiry Concerning Political Justice*, ed. K. C. Carter (Oxford: Oxford University Press, 1971).

Goldsmith, E. *et al.*, *Blueprint for Survival* (Harmondsworth: Penguin, 1972).

Goodman, P., 'Normal Politics and the Psychology of Power' in *The Anarchist Reader*, ed. G. Woodcock (London: Fontana, 1977).

Gorz, A., *Farewell to the Working Class* (London: Pluto Press, 1985) (Boston, Mass.: South End Press, 1982).

Gould, B., *Socialism and Freedom* (London: Macmillan, 1985) (Wakefield, N. H.: Longwood, 1986).

Gramsci, A., *Selections from the Prison Notebooks*, ed. Q. Hoare and G. Nowell-Smith (London: Lawrence & Wishart, 1971) (Chicago: International Publishing Corp., 1971).

Green, T. H., *Works*, ed. R. Nettleship (London: Oxford University Press, 1988). (New York: AMS Press, 1984).

Greer, G., *The Female Eunuch* (London: Granada, 1970) (New York: McGraw-Hill, 1971).

Greer, G., *Sex and Destiny* (New York: Harper & Row, 1985) (New York: Harper & Row, 1985).

Hattersley, R., *Choose Freedom* (Harmondsworth: Penguin, 1987).

Hayek, von F. A., *The Road to Serfdom* (London: Routledge & Kegan Paul, 1944) (Chicago: University of Chicago Press, 1956).

Heath, A. Jowell, R. and Curtice, J., *How Britain Votes* (Oxford: Pergamon, 1985).

Hegel, G. W. F., *The Philosophy of Right*, trans. T. M. Knox (Oxford: Clarendon Press, 1942).

Hitler, A., *Mein Kampf* (London: Hutchinson, 1969) (Boston, Mass: Houghton Mifflin, 1973).

Hobbes, T., *Leviathan*, ed. C. B. Macpherson (Harmondsworth: Penguin, 1968). (Buffalo. N. Y.: Prometheus. Bks., 1988)

Illich, I., *Deschooling Society* (Harmondsworth: Penguin, 1973) (New York: Harper & Row, 1983).

Jefferson, T., 'The United States Declaration of Independence' in *The Human Rights Reader*, ed. W. Laqueur and B. Rubin (New York: Meridan, 1979).

Keynes, J. M., *The General Theory of Employment, Interest and Money* (London: Macmillan, 1963) (San Diego: Harecourt Brace Jovanovich, 1965).

Kropotkin, P., *Mutual Aid* (London: Heinemann, 1902) (Cheektowaga, N. Y.: Black Rose Books, 1988).

Lenin, V. I., *Imperialism, the Highest Stage of Capitalism* (Moscow: Progress Publishers, 1970).

Lenin, V. I., *The State and Revolution* (Peking: People's Publishing House, 1964).

Lenin, V. I., *What is to be Done?* (Harmondsworth and New York: Penguin, 1988).

Lindblom, C., *Politics and Markets* (New York: Basic Books, 1977).

Locke, J., *Two Treatises of Government* (Cambridge: Cambridge University Press, 1962). (New York: New American Library, 1965)

Lovelock, J., 'Man and Gaia' in *The Earth Report*, ed. E. Goldsmith and N. Hilyard (London: Mitchell Beazley, 1988) (Los Angeles: Price Stern, 1988).

Lovelock, J., *Gaia: A New Look at Life on Earth* (Oxford and New York: Oxford University Press, 1982).

Macmillan, H., *The Middle Way* (London: Macmillan, 1966).

Macpherson, C. B., *Democratic Theory: Essays in Retrieval* (Oxford: Clarendon Press, 1973).

Marx, K. and Engels, F., *Selected Works* (London: Lawrence & Wishart, 1968).

Meadows, D. *et al.*, *The Limits to Growth* (London, Pan, 1972) (New York: New American Library, 1972).

Michels, R., *Political Parties* (Glencoe: Free Press, 1958).

Miliband, R., *The State in Capitalist Society* (London: Verso, 1983) (New York: Basic, 1978).

Mill, J. S., *Utilitarianism, On Liberty and Consideration on Representative Government* (London: Dent, 1972).

Mill, J. S., *On the Subjection of Women* (London: Dent, 1970) (Allington Heights, Ill.: Harlan Davidson, 1980).

Millett, K., *Sexual Politics* (London: Virago,1977) (New York: Simon & Schuster, 1990).

Mitchell, J., *Women's Estate* (Harmondsworth: Penguin, 1971).

Montesquieu, C. de, *The Spirit of Laws* (Glencoe, Ill.: Free Press, 1969).

More, T., *Utopia* (Harmondsworth: Penguin, 1965) (New York: Norton, 1976).

Mosca, G., *The Ruling Class*, trans. and ed. A. Livingstone (New York: McGraw-Hill, 1939) (Des Plaines, Ill.: Greenwood, 1939).

Nietzsche, F., *Thus Spoke Zarathustra*, trans. R. J. Hollingdale (Harmondsworth: Penguin, 1961) (New York: Random, 1982).

Nozick, R., *Anarchy, State and Utopia* (Oxford: Blackwell, 1974) (New York: Basic, 1974).

Oakeshott, M., *Rationalism in Politics and Other Essays* (London: Methuen, 1962) (New York: Routledge Chapman & Hall, 1981).

Pareto, V., *The Mind and Society* (London: Cape, 1935) (New York: AMS Press, 1935).

Plato, *The Republic*, trans. H. D. Lee (Harmondsworth: Penguin, 1955) (New York: Random, 1983).

Poulantzas, N., *Political Power and Social Class* (London: New Left Books, 1973) (New York: Routledge Chapman & Hall, 1987).

Proudhon, P.-J., *What is Property?*, trans. B. R. Tucker (London: Dover Publications, 1971) (New York: Fertig, 1966).

Rawls, J., *A Theory of Justice* (London: Oxford University Press, 1972) (Cambridge, Mass.: Harvard University Press, 1971).

Rothbart, M., *For a New Liberty* (New York: Macmillan, 1978).

Rousseau, J.-J., *The Social Contract and Discourse*, ed. G.D.H. Cole (London: Dent, 1913) (Glencoe, Ill.: Free Press, 1969).

Schumacher, E. F., *Small is Beautiful* (London: Abacus, 1974) (New York: Harper & Row, 1989).

Schumpeter, J., *Capitalism, Socialism and Democracy* (London: Allen & Unwin, 1976) (Magnolia, Mass.: Petersmith, 1983).

Scruton, R., *The Meaning of Conservatism* (Harmondsworth: Penguin, 1980).

Seliger, M., *Politics and Ideology* (London: Allen & Unwin, 1976) (Glencloe, Ill.: Free Press, 1976).

Smiles, S., *Self-Help* (Harmondsworth: Penguin, 1986).

Smith, A., *An Enquiry into the Nature and Causes of the Wealth of Nations* (Chicago: University of Chicago Press, 1976).

Sorel, G., *Reflections on Violence*, trans. T. E. Hulme and J. Roth (New York: Macmillan, 1950).

Spencer, H., *On Social Evolution: Selected Writings* (Chicago: University of Chicago Press, 1967).

Stirner, M., *The Ego and His Own*, ed. J. Carroll (London: Cape, 1971) (New York: Revisionist Press, 1984).

Sumner, W., *War and Other Essays* (New Haven, Conn. and London, 1911).

Tawney, R. H., *The Acquisitive Society* (London: Bell, 1921) (San Diego: Harcourt Brace Jovanovich, 1955).

Tawney, R. H., *Equality* (London: Allen & Unwin, 1969).

Thoreau, D. H. D., *Walden* and *'Civil Disobedience'* (Harmondsworth: Penguin, 1983).

Tocqueville de, A., *Democracy in America* (London: Fontana, 1968) (New York: McGraw, 1981).

Wollstonecraft, M., *A Vindication of the Rights of Women*, ed. C. W. Hagelman (New York: Norton, 1967).

Glossary of Terms and Concepts

This glossary provides brief definitions of key terms or concepts used in the text. These definitions are neither exact nor comprehensive, but merely provide an indication of what these terms mean in political discourse.

Absolutism. A form of government in which political power is concentrated in the hands of a single individual or small group, in particular, an absolute monarchy.

Alienation. To be separated from one's genuine or essential nature. Used by Marxists to describe the process whereby under capitalism labour is reduced to being a mere commodity and work becomes a depersonalised activity rather than a creative and fulfilling one.

Altruism. Concern for the interests and welfare of others. Based either upon enlightened self-interest, or a belief in a common humanity: the responsibility of each for every other human being.

Androgyny. The possession of both male and female characteristics, used to imply that human beings are sexless *persons* in the sense that sex is irrelevant to their social role or political status.

Atomism. The belief that society is made up of a collection of self-interested and largely self-sufficient individuals, or atoms, rather than social groups.

Authoritarianism. The belief that strong central authority, imposed from above, is either desirable or necessary, and therefore demands unquestioning *obedience*. Very different from **authority**, a form of

310

power which operates because it is perceived to be rightful or legitimate, and is therefore based upon *consent*.

Autonomy. Literally self-government, the ability to control one's own destiny by virtue of enjoying independence from external influences. Can be applied to the individual, social group, region, political institution or state.

Capitalism. An economic system in which wealth is owned by private individuals or businesses and goods produced for exchange, according to the dictates of the market.

Chauvinism. Uncritical and unreasoned dedication to a cause or group, typically based upon a belief in its superiority, as in 'national chauvinism' or 'male chauvinism'.

Civil society. A realm of autonomous associations and groups, formed by private citizens and enjoying independence from the government; includes businesses, clubs, families and so on. A 'private' sphere of life in contrast to the 'public' sphere of government and the state.

Class, social. Social division based upon economic or social factors: wealth, income, status, living conditions and so on. A social class therefore constitues a group of people who share a similar social and economic position. Marxist use **class-consciousness** to denote an awareness of class interests and a willingness to pursue them.

Collectivism. A belief in the community, group or collective, stressing the importance of a common identity and the capacity for collective action. Can be applied to any group: social class, race, nation or humanity itself. Is sometimes linked narrowly to the state as the institution through which collective action is usually organised, as in **state collectivism**, a centrally planned economy in which productive wealth is owned by the state.

Conflict. Opposition or competition between two or more forces, arising either from the pursuit of incompatible goals or a clash of rival opinions.

Consensus. An agreement on basic issues or principles which may permit disagreement about matters of detail or emphasis.

Constitutionalism. The belief that government power should be exercised within a framework of rules, a constitution, which define the duties, powers and functions of government institutions and the rights of the individual. Constitutions are based upon a balance of power amongst the institutions of government and may be codified in a single authoritative document, a 'written constitution'. Constitutional government is therefore consistent, predictable and, above all, limited.

Contract. An agreement entered into voluntarily and on mutually acceptable terms. A **social contract** is an agreement amongst individuals through which they form a state in order to escape from disorder and chaos in the 'state of nature'.

Co-operation. Working together, collective effort intended to achieve mutual benefit.

Corporatism. The theory that the major economic interests, business and labour, should be incorporated into the processes of government. Developed in Mussolini's vision of a 'corporate state', but also evident in the industrialised West in the form of 'liberal corporatism' or 'neo-corporatism', a system of tripartite bargaining amongst government, employers associations and trade unions.

Development. A process of social, economic and political change, usually associated with the Third World, so-called 'developing nations'. Often based upon a specifically Western model of development, the emergence of industrial capitalism, and a competitive political system.

Dialectic. A process of development in which interaction between two opposing forces leads to a further or higher stage. Marx regarded history as a dialectical process in terms of the interaction between humankind and the natural world, and the fact that change results from internal contradictions within a society. **Dialectical materialism** is the philosophy of Marxism elaborated in the writings of

Engels and adopted as the basis of science and philosophy in the Soviet Union.

Ecology. The study of the relationship between living organisms and the environment. Ecology stresses the network of relationships which sustain all forms of life.

Egoism. (i) Concern for one's own interest or welfare, selfishness. (ii) The belief that each individual is the centre of his or her own moral universe, and is thus entitled to function as a morally autonomous being. Different from **egotism**, an inflated sense of self-importance,

Elitism. A belief in rule by an elite or minority. Elite rule may be thought to be *desirable*, the elite possessing superior talents or skills, or *inevitable*, egalitarian ideas like democracy and socialism being simply impractical.

Equality. The principle that human beings are of identical worth or are entitled to be treated in the same way. Can have widely differing applications: equality before the law (equal rights), equality of opportunity, political equality, social equality, even biocentric equality, (the belief that all species are of equal significance).

Freedom or **liberty.** The ability to think or act as one wishes, a capacity which can be associated with the individual, a social group or a nation. **Negative freedom** is the absence of restrictions or constraints, allowing freedom of choice. **Positive freedom** involves self-realisation, the achievement of autonomy and the development of human capacities.

Fundamentalism. A belief in the original or most basic principles of a creed, often associated with fierce commitment and sometimes reflected in fanatical zeal.

Gender. A social and cultural distinction between males and females. Different from **sex** which refers to biological and therefore ineradicable differences between men and women.

Holism. The belief that the whole is more important than its parts.

Implies that understanding is gained by studying relationships among the parts, rather than by **reductionism**, in which each component part is examined in isolation from the others.

Human nature. The essential and innate character of all human beings, what they owe to nature rather than to society. Often thought to be the key to understanding social conduct and political life.

Humanism. A philosophy that focuses upon the needs and interests of human beings and is therefore committed to the promotion of human happiness and wellbeing.

Imperialism. The extension of control by one country over another. This can take the form of **colonialism**, the attempt to establish overt political control and jurisdiction over another country; **neo-colonialism**, control exercised through economic domination; or **cultural imperialism**, the destruction or weakening of an indigenous culture and the imposition of an alien one.

Individualism. A belief in the central importance of the human individual as opposed to the social group or collective. Implies that political action should serve the needs of the individual, the promotion of individual liberty and equality of opportunity. **Economic individualism** is a belief in the unrestricted right of private property.

Justice. A moral standard of fairness and impartiality. **Social justice** is the notion of a fair or justifiable distribution of wealth and rewards in society.

Laissez-faire. The doctrine that economic activity should be entirely free from government interference, an extreme belief in the free market.

Law. Established and public rules of social conduct, backed up by the machinery of the state, the police, courts, prisons.

Legitimacy. The acceptance that political authority is *rightful* and therefore that those subject to it have a moral obligation to obey.

Government is legitimate if it is based upon the consent of the governed rather than on manipulation or coercion.

Libertarianism. The belief that the individual should enjoy the widest possible realm of freedom; implies the removal of both external and internal constraints upon the individual.

Majoritarianism. A belief in majority rule, implying either that the interests of the majority take precedence over those of the minority, or that the minority should defer to the judgement of the majority.

Managerialism. The theory that a governing class of managers, technocrats and state officials, those who possess technical and administrative skills, dominates all industrial societies, both capitalist and communist.

Market. A system of commercial exchange between buyers and sellers, controlled by impersonal economic forces, 'market forces'. Often regarded as the organising principle within a capitalist economy.

Materialism. The belief that material or economic factors are fundamental to any explanation of social or political conduct. Marxists have believed in **historical materialism**, the notion that economic factors condition social, political and cultural life. Liberals have believed individuals to be **materialistic**, to be motivated principally by the desire to acquire and consume wealth.

Meritocracy. Literally rule by those with merit. **Merit** is intelligence plus effort. A society in which social position is determined exclusively by ability and hard work.

Modernisation. The process of social and political change through which the industrialised West came about; the emergence of a capitalist economic order and a liberal democratic political system.

Myth, political. A belief that has the capacity to provoke political action by virtue of its emotional or symbolic power rather than through an appeal to reason.

Nation. A collection of people bound together by cultural factors: shared values and traditions, a common language, religion, history; and usually occupying the same geographical area.

Nihilism. A rejection of all moral and political principles, literally a belief in nothing. Sometimes, but by no means necessarily, associated with a doctrine of destruction and the use of violence.

Normative. The prescription of a moral standard of what 'should', 'ought' or 'must' be, rather than a descriptive statement of what 'is'.

Order. Settled, predictable and peaceful social circumstances in which personal security is upheld.

Organic. Exhibiting the characteristics of a natural organism. Organisms form complex wholes, whose parts are inseparable from the whole and whose development is determined by internal or natural forces, beyond human control. **Organicism** is the belief that society or social institutions behave organically rather than as mechanical artefacts.

Orthodoxy. Adherence to established or conventional views. For example, orthodox Marxism, which is based upon the interpretation of Marx found in the writings of Engels and Lenin, and in the theories of Soviet communism.

Pastoralism. A belief in the virtues of rural existence: simplicity, community and a closeness to nature, in contrast to the allegedly corrupting influence of urban and industrialised life.

Paternalism. Authority exercised from above for the guidance and support of those below, modelled on the relationship between fathers and children.

Patriarchy. Literally 'rule by the father'. Often taken more generally to describe the dominance of men and the subordination of women in society.

Permissiveness. The acceptance that all freely chosen life styles or moral positions are equally valid. Different from **tolerance**, which may *allow* a range of views or conduct, but reserves the right to judge and criticise them.

Pluralism. The theory that political power is, or should be, widely and evenly dispersed amongst the groups that comprise civil society. **Political pluralism** refers to an open and competitive political system, based upon multi-party politics and freedom of expression.

Politics. (i) Activity related to the institution of the state, or 'polis', and the machinery of government. (ii) Activity through which social conflict is expressed and attempts (not always successful) to resolve conflict are made.

Populism. The belief that popular instincts and wishes are the principal legitimate guide to political action. The attempt to mobilise or respond to the instincts of the masses, often reflecting distrust of, or hostility towards, political elites.

Pragmatism. Behaviour shaped in accordance with practical circumstances and goals rather than ideological objectives.

Progress. Moving forward, usually implying improvement. Based upon the belief that human history is marked by the advance of knowledge and the achievement of higher levels of civilisation. Progressive ideas or movement therefore support change, reform and, possibly, revolution.

Property. Ownership of physical goods or wealth. **Private property** is owned by private individuals who can therefore control how it is used or disposed of. **Collective property** is owned in common by a group of people: workers or consumers, a local community, nation or humanity itself.

Race. A collection of people who share a common genetic inheritance and are thus distinguished from others by biological factors. **Racialism**, the belief that racial divisions are politically significant, either because races should live apart or because they possess different qualities and so are suited to different social roles. **Racism**, the expression of hostility towards or discrimination against a person or group on grounds of race.

Radicalism. A belief in fundamental or far-reaching change, as opposed to moderate or incremental reforms.

Reactionary. Resistance to change or desire to return to a former system. Often based upon the belief that human history is marked by descent or decay, which can be halted and possibly reversed.

Reformism. A belief in gradual, piecemeal improvements, opposed to both revolution and reaction. A **reform** is an action or policy designed to remedy a problem or grievance. **Social reform** refers to government policies designed to promote the social welfare of its citizens.

Revisionism. The advocacy of a revision or reworking of a political theory, which departs from earlier interpretations in an attempt to present a 'corrected' view.

Revolution. A fundamental and irreversible change. Often implies a brief but dramatic period of upheaval, as in the case of a **political revolution**, the overthrow and replacement of one system of government by another. Can involve a longer and more gradual process of change, as in an **industrial revolution**. Marxists use **social revolution** to describe the transition from one economic system or 'mode of production' to another.

Rights. Moral entitlements to act or be treated in a particular way. Can take the form of **natural** or **human rights**, supposedly invested in humans by either God or nature; or **civil rights**, legal, political or welfare rights gained by virtue of citizenship.

Science. A method of acquiring knowledge through a process of careful observation and the testing of hypotheses by repeatable experiments to establish if they are true or false. **Scientism** is the belief that scientific method is the only value-free and objective means of establishing truth, applicable not only in the natural sciences but also in fields such as philosophy, history and politics.

Sovereignty. The principle of absolute or unrestricted power. Has been regarded as the defining feature of the state; it can be invested in the nation, as in national sovereignty, in government institutions, as in Parliamentary sovereignty, or in the people themselves, popular sovereignty.

State. An association which establishes sovereign power within a defined territorial area, usually possessing a monopoly of coercive power. **Government**, the machinery through which collective decisions are made on behalf of the state, usually comprising a legislature, executive and judiciary.

Third Way. The notion of an alternative form of economics to both state socialism and free market capitalism, sought, at different times, by conservatives, socialists and fascists.

'Three' Worlds. A broad classification of countries according to material wealth and ideology. The **First World** comprises the most affluent nations of the world, those of the industrialised West. The **Second World** included the orthodox communist countries of Eastern Europe. The **Third World** refers to the developing countries of Africa, Asia and Latin America. Both ideological and material distinctions have become blurred in recent years. The 'North–South' division is preferred by some.

Totalitarianism. An all-encompassing process of political rule in which the state penetrates and controls all social institutions, thus abolishing both civil society and private life.

Tradition. Practice or institution that has endured through time and has therefore been inherited from an earlier period. A **political tradition** is a recognised and established body of political ideas.

Utilitarianism. A moral and political philosophy that evaluates 'goodness' in terms of pleasure and pain, and ultimately seeks to achieve 'the greatest happiness for the greatest number'. Pleasure and pain are calculated in terms of **utility**, which in effect means use-value. In economics, 'utility' is used specifically to describe the satisfaction gained from the consumption of material goods and services.

Utopianism. A belief in the unlimited possibilities of human development, typically embodied in the vision of a perfect or ideal society, a utopia.

Violence. Destructive action undertaken against either property or persons. Can be deliberate or spontaneous, undertaken by governments or private individuals. It therefore embraces a wide range of actions, including intimidation, terrorism, repression, riots, revolutions and all forms of warfare.

Welfarism. The belief that the state or community has a responsibility to ensure the social wellbeing of its citizens, usually reflected in the emergence of a welfare state.

West, the. The countries of Europe and North America, and countries tied culturally and historically to them like Australia and New Zealand. Distinguished culturally by common Greco-Roman and Christian roots, socially by the dominance of industrial capitalism, and politically by the prevalence of liberal democracy.

Glossary of Political Thinkers

This glossary provides brief biographical details about the major political theorists discussed in the text.

Bakunin, Mikhail (1814–1876). Russian anarchist, agitator and propagandist, rather than systematic political thinker. Struggled with Marx for control of First International between 1869 and 1872.

Bentham, Jeremy (1748–1832). British philosopher, economist and legal theorist, the principal exponent of Utilitarianism.

Bernstein, Eduard (1850–1932). German socialist, proponent of reformist rather than revolutionary socialism. *Evolutionary Socialism* (1898) attempted the first major revision of Marx.

Burke, Edmund (1729–1797). Dublin-born, British statesman and political theorist. *Reflections on the Revolution in France*(1790) established him as a founding father of modern conservatism.

Burnham, James (b. 1905). American philosopher and social thinker. *The Managerial Revolution* (1941) was the seminal text of managerialism.

Chamberlain, Huston Stewart (1855–1929). British-born, German racial theorist. *The Foundations of the Nineteenth Century* (1911) advanced Aryanism and anti-semitic ideas which deeply influenced Hitler and the Nazis.

Constant, Benjamin (1767–1830). Swiss-born, French liberal, a sustained critic of Rousseau and advocate of civil liberty and constitutionalism.

Crosland, Anthony (1918–1977). British politician and socialist theorist. *The Future of Socialism* (1956) made an influential contribution to the process of socialist revisionism.

Disraeli, Benjamin (1804–1881). British statesman and Conservative Prime Minister (1868, 1874–1880). An advocate of Tory paternalism, his political philosophy was developed in his early novels, *Coningsby* (1844), *Sybil* (1845), and *Tancred* (1847).

Engels, Friedrich (1822–1895). German socialist philosopher, collaborator and lifelong friend of Karl Marx. After Marx's death, Engels' writings had a profound effect upon the growing socialist movement and did much to popularise Marxism, but have subsequently been criticised for misrepresenting Marx's ideas.

Fanon, Frantz (1925–1961). Martinique-born, Algerian revolutionary and psychiatrist, best known for his support of the Algerian liberation struggle (1954–62). *The Wretched of the Earth* (1961) was a powerful and influential critique of the political and psychological impact of colonialism.

Firestone, Shulamith (b.1945). Canadian radical feminist, author and activist, best known for *The Dialectic of Sex* (1970).

Friedan, Betty (b. 1921). American liberal feminist and a leading activist in the women's movement. *The Feminine Mystique* (1963) was one of the earliest and most influential texts of 'second wave' feminism.

Friedman, Milton (b. 1912). American economist, a leading exponent of monetarism and free market principles. *Capitalism and Freedom* (1962) and *Free to Choose* (1980) have had a powerful influence upon the New Right.

Gandhi, Mohandas (1869–1948). Indian spiritual and political leader, called Mahatma ('Great Soul'). Leader of Indian independence movement and exponent of 'non-violent non-cooperation' (*satyagraha*).

Garvey, Marcus (1887–1940). Jamaican political thinker and activist, an early advocate of black nationalism. Founder of the 'Back to Africa' movement and supporter of both racial purity and separatism.

Gobineau, Joseph-Arthur (1816–1882). French diplomat, writer and social thinker, the father of modern racialism. *Essay on the Inequality of Human Races* (1855) was the first systematic attempt to explain human history in terms of race.

Godwin, William (1756–1836). British political philosopher and novelist, best known for *An Enquiry Concerning Political Justice* (1793), which advanced anarchist and utopian principles.

Hayek, Friedrich (b.1899). Austrian-born, British economist. An exponent of free market principles and guru of the New Right. *The Road to Serfdom* (1944) was a powerful attack upon government economic management, written long before such views became fashionable.

Hegel, Georg Wilhelm Friedrich (1770–1831). German philosopher, whose complex writings inspired a generation of German intellectuals, the 'Young Hegelians', including Marx and Stirner. *The Philosophy of Right* (1821) influenced both liberal and fascist conceptions of the state.

Hobbes, Thomas (1588–1679). English philosopher and political theorist, best known for his social contract defence of monarchical absolutism, developed in *Leviathan* (1651).

Jefferson, Thomas (1743–1825). American political philosopher and statesman, third President of the United States (1801–9). A leading advocate of natural rights and social contract theories, clearly reflected in the Declaration of Independence (1776).

Keynes, John Maynard (1883–1946). British economist. *The General Theory of Employment, Interest and Money* (1936) challenged laissez-faire principles and provided the theoretical basis for the policy of government 'demand management'.

Kropotkin, Peter (1842–1921). Russian anarchist. A scientist and anarcho-communist, whose philosophy was outlined in *Mutual Aid* (1897) and whose vision of a decentralised society of the future was described in *Fields, Factories and Workshops* (1901).

Lenin, Vladimir Ilyich (1870–1924). Russian Marxist theorist and active revolutionary, leader of the Bolshevik party and first Soviet leader (1917-1924). Most influential works were the pamphlets *What is to be Done?* (1902), *Imperialism, The Highest Stage of Capitalism* (1916) and *The State and Revolution* (1917).

Locke, John (1632–1704). English philosopher and politician. A social contract theorist who placed special weight upon natural rights, his views had considerable impact upon early liberalism, especially his *Two Treatises of Government* (1690).

Lovelock, James (b.1919). British scientist and environmentalist thinker, best known for his highly influential *Gaia* (1979).

Madison, James (1751–1836). American political philosopher and statesman, fourth President of the United States (1809–17). In *The Federalist* (1787-8) he highlighted the danger of majoritarian tyranny and advocated the fragmentation of government power through bicameralism and the separation of powers.

Maistre, Joseph de (1753–1821). Savoy-born, French writer and political theorist. A reactionary conservative, defender of monarchical absolutism and advocate of the supreme power of the Pope.

Mao Tse-Tung (Mao Zedong) (1893–1976). Chinese Marxist theoretician and communist revolutionary, Chinese leader (1949–76). He stressed the need for a rural rather than urban-based revolution in Asia, helped to precipitate the split with Moscow in 1960, and during the Cultural Revolution supported a radical egalitarian campaign against bureaucracy and hierarchy in China.

Marx, Karl (1818–1883). German philosopher, economist and political thinker. An active revolutionary and founder of the First International. His work provided the basis of much of nineteenth century socialist thought and greatly influenced communism in the twentieth century. His classic work was the three volume *Capital* (1867, 1885 and 1894), his best known and most accessible work is the *Communist Manifesto* (1848).

Mill, John Stuart (1806–1873). English philosopher, economist and politician. A major exponent of liberalism, his most influential work includes *On Liberty* (1859), *Considerations on Representative Government* (1861), and *The Subjection of Women* (1869).

Millett, Kate (b.1934). American feminist writer and sculptor. A leading radical feminist theorist and activist, best known for *Sexual Politics* (1970).

Mitchell, Juliet (b.1940). British socialist feminist and psycho-analyst. Her best known work is *Woman's Estate* (1971). In *Psychoanalysis and Feminism* (1974) she showed a sympathy for Freudian analysis, unusual within feminism.

Montesquieu, Charles-Louis de Secondat (1689–1755). French political philosopher. An admirer of British constitutionalism, who in his great work *The Spirit of Laws* (1748) developed the doctrine of the separation of powers.

Mosca, Gaetano (1857–1941). Italian political sociologist, best known as the founder of elitism, most clearly developed in *The Ruling Class* (1896).

Nietzsche, Friedrich (1844–1900). German philosopher and cultural critic. His complex and ambitious work, including *Thus Spake Zarathustra* (1883–4), *Beyond Good and Evil* (1886) and *On the Genealogy of Morals* (1887), has influenced fascism, in part because his books were edited and his views misrepresented by his sister Elizabeth after his death.

Nozick, Robert (b. 1938) American political philosopher, best known for *Anarchy, State and Utopia* (1974), which restated the classical liberal case for a minimal state and rejected both economic management and social welfare.

Oakeshott, Michael (1901–1991). British political philosopher. An influential conservative theorist, his political ideas were most systematically developed in *Rationalism In Politics and Other Essays* (1962) and *On Human Conduct* (1975).

Owen, Robert (1771–1858). British socialist. Established a model village in New Lanark, a communitarian project in America, at New Harmony, and supported the emergent co-operative and trade union movements. His best known work, *A New View of Society* (1812–3), emphasised that personal character is wholly determined by environment.

Pareto, Vilfredo (1848–1923). Paris-born, Italian economist and political philosopher. A vigorous opponent of socialism and democracy and, with Mosca, the originator of elitism. His major work was *The Mind and Society* (1916).

Proudhon, Pierre-Joseph (1809–1865). French anarchist and founder of mutualism, best known for *What is Property?* (1841).

Rawls, John (b.1921). American philosopher. *A Theory of Justice* (1971) did much to re-establish the status of political philosophy and has influenced both modern liberalism and social democracy.

Rousseau, Jean-Jacques (1712–1778). French moral and political philosopher. An advocate of popular sovereignty and direct democracy, his ideas, particularly those developed in *Social Contract* (1762), have influenced liberalism, socialism, anarchism and, some argue, totalitarianism.

Schumacher, Ernst (1911–1977). German-born economist, journalist and philosopher. *Small is Beautiful* (1973) advocated small-scale economic organisation and was a seminal text of environmentalism.

Schumpeter, Joseph (1883–1950). Vienna-born, American economist and sociologist. *Capitalism, Socialism and Democracy* (1942) suggested that capitalism was developing into a form of socialism, and proposed the influential notion that democracy is a mechanism through which politicians acquire power by means of a competitive struggle for the people's vote.

Smith, Adam (1723–1790). Scottish economist and philosopher. The founder of modern political economy, his *The Wealth of Nations* (1776) was the first systematic attempt to explain the workings of the economy in market terms.

Sorel, Georges (1847–1922). French philosopher and theorist of syndicalism. His major work, *Reflections on Violence* (1908), proposed that socialism could be brought about by the 'myth of the general strike', a notion that subsequently influenced fascism.

Spencer, Herbert (1820–1903). British philosopher and sociologist. Best known as an exponent of social Darwinism, most clearly expressed in *The Man Versus The State* (1884).

Stirner, Max (1806–1856). German philosopher, best known for the radical egoism developed in *The Ego and His Own* (1845), which influenced both Marx and the individualist school of anarchism.

Tawney, Richard Henry (1880–1962). British historian and social philosopher. An influential exponent of ethical socialism, developed in books like *The Acquisitive Society* (1921) and *Equality* (1931).

Thoreau, David Henry (1817–1862). American author and radical. *Walden* (1854) has influenced environmentalism and the back-to-nature movement, while the more political 1849 essay 'Civil Disobedience' developed radical individualist principles.

Tocqueville, Alexis de (1805–1859). French politician, political theorist and historian. Best known for *Democracy in America* (1836), which explored the relationship between individual liberty and emergent political democracy.

Tolstoy, Leo (1828–1910). Russian novelist, best known for *War and Peace* and *Anna Karenina*. In later life, a religious mystic and advocate of moral purity, whose opposition to urban civilisation and rejection of violence and authority have influenced anarchism, but also reflect a nostalgic pastoralism.

Trotsky, Leon (1879–1940). Russian Marxist, political theorist and revolutionary. Developed the concept of 'permanent revolution' to suggest that proletarian revolution was possible in backward Russia. *The Revolution Betrayed* (1937) presented an influential critique of Stalinism as a form of 'bureaucratic degeneration'. A consistent advocate of international revolution, he founded the Fourth International in 1937.

Tucker, Benjamin (1854–1939). American anarchist and publisher. A leading exponent of individualist anarchism, developed between 1881 and 1908 in his magazine *Liberty* and in *Instead of a Book* (1893).

Wollstonecraft, Mary (1759–1797). British social theorist and feminist. Best known for *A Vindication of the Rights of Women* (1792), a seminal work of liberal feminism, which demanded equal educational opportunities for women.

Index